The Encyclopaedia of Celtic Wisdom

Caitlín and John Matthews are internationally respected
for their research into the Celtic Tradition.

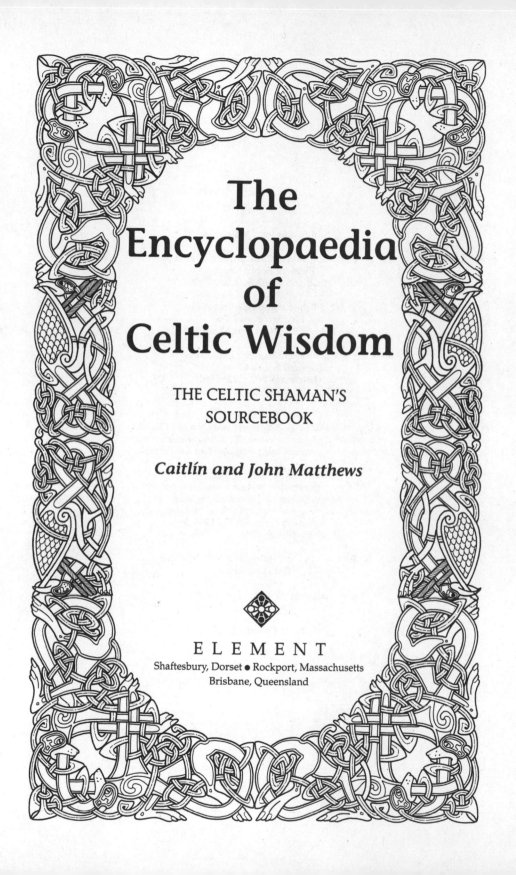

The Encyclopaedia of Celtic Wisdom

THE CELTIC SHAMAN'S SOURCEBOOK

Caitlín and John Matthews

ELEMENT
Shaftesbury, Dorset ● Rockport, Massachusetts
Brisbane, Queensland

© Caitlín and John Matthews 1994

First published in Great Britain in 1994 by
Element Books Limited
Shaftesbury, Dorset SP7 8BP

Published in the USA in 1994 by
Element Books, Inc
PO Box 830, Rockport MA 01966

Published in Australia in 1994 by
Element Books Limited for
Jacaranda Wiley Limited
33 Park Road, Milton, Brisbane 4064

Illustrated by Christopher Down
Cover illustration by Lorraine Harrison
Cover design by Peter Bridgewater
Typeset and designed by Linda Reed and Joss Nizan
Printed and bound in the USA by
Book-of-the-Month Club, Inc., New York

British Library Cataloguing in Publication
Data available

Library of Congress Cataloging in Publication
Data available

ISBN 1–85230–561–4

Contents

To Ceridwen, Mistress of the Cauldron,
and Brighid, Lady of the Hearth:
guardians of inspiration

Acknowledgements

Our primary debt of gratitude goes to our spirit teachers and shamanic helpers: without their otherworldly support and encouragement, this book would not have been completed. Secondly, we would like to thank all those who have memorized, transcribed and translated this material – the *aes dana* and Celtic scholars who have made a path through the unexplored territory of our tradition; it has made our travels easier.

Our deep gratitude to the members of the Three Clans knows no bounds: their support, enthusiasm and practice have helped us harvest this material and process it in ways that can be practised. The *fferyllt* and the dragons have also done their part.

The essay 'Incubation and the Dream Quest' by John Matthews first appeared in a slightly different form in R.J. Stewart's *Psychology and the Spiritual Traditions* (Element Books, 1990) and is reprinted with permission.

Introduction

Over the years many people have asked us about the sources for our books and teachings. Since the publication of our joint book, *Taliesin: Shamanism and the Bardic Mysteries in Britain and Ireland* (Thorsons, 1991) and John's *The Celtic Shaman* (Element, 1992) and *The Celtic Shaman's Pack* (Element, 1994), it had become increasingly evident that there was a need for a book which made accessible as many as possible of the works which form the backbone of our written and practical explorations into Celtic wisdom and shamanism.

The present book is the result. It contains a generous selection of the texts, myths and commentaries which we have made use of over the past twenty years, edited and augmented by our own commentaries. In addition there are essays by us on specific aspects of Celtic tradition and shamanism, for example John's article on precognitive dreams, and Caitlín's on the circuits of the Celtic soul.

Both 'shaman' and 'shamanism' have become current buzz-words, often applied inaccurately and without warrant to disparate esoteric practices. The word 'shaman' was not applied by the Celts to their spiritual practitioners, but it is a term which people understand today, which is why we have used it. Those who seek an indigenous name can choose from the many Celtic titles which have been applied to this role, chief of which are: *file* (pron. fee'lyee, pl. *filidh*) – Irish Gaelic for 'vision poet'; *taibhsear* (pron. tah'shar) – Scots Gaelic for 'vision-seer'; and *awenydd* (pron. ah-wen'-ith, pl. *awenyddion*) – Welsh for 'inspired one'.

Shamanism is a worldwide practice in which the spiritual interrelationship of the earth with the otherworlds forms an interwoven fabric of physical and psychic being, affecting all forms of life, both seen and unseen. Within shamanism certain individuals are chosen, by the spirits or by virtue of their unusual skills, to act as walkers between the worlds, interpreters of the spirit realms. Their task is to explore these unseen realms by means of the spirit-journey (which occurs in shamanic trance), to interact with the beings they encounter there and to retrieve knowledge, healing and advice which may benefit the people.

Shamanism exists among peoples who have an animistic worldview; in many cultures it functions as a spirituality, although it often exists separately from formal religion as a healing, divinatory and spiritual practice. Shamanism is identifiable the world over by its practices, chief of which are the spirit-journeys to gain information, healing, divinatory and prophetic insight, and to enter into ancestral intercourse. All these are part of the Celtic tradition; some are still operative today, while others are fragmented or dormant.

The core beliefs of Celtic tradition are based upon animistic understandings. The otherworlds interpenetrate mortal realms in all departments of life: spirits, creatures, faeries, ancestors and deities associate regularly with humans; omens of the elements, of plants, animals and people predetermine outcomes. There is little doubt that early Celtic peoples had a predominantly shamanic culture. Their shamans were the inspired ones, the gifted people or *aes dana*, who could walk between the worlds with ease – the druids, poets and seers. The *aes dana* enjoyed the kind of professional spiritual indemnity which was later assumed by clerics after the adoption of Christianity. The shamanic skills of the professional *filidh* became gradually more formalized and less identifiably shamanic as time wore on, although the ancient shamanic skills were often passed down outside the professional classes by blood and ability. A few individuals and families retain this knowledge as their direct heritage. What of those who are not so privileged?

When John recently visited Wallace Black Elk, a revered Lakota elder, he told him about the work in which we are engaged and asked him if he had anything to say to our people, working with a fragmented and in some instances forgotten tradition. Wallace Black Elk's answer was forthrightly direct: 'There is,' he said, 'no such thing as a forgotten tradition. It is possible to neglect such traditions, but these can *always* be recovered. No tradition ever dies until the last person who honours it dies.'

There are now few places in the world with an unbroken shamanic tradition; even among Native American, Australian Aboriginal, circumpolar and Asian cultures – the very bastions of existing shamanic practice – Western urban 'civilization' and other factors have begun the erosion of belief and practice. In an urban society such as ours in the West, the appeal of shamanism may be thought to be romantic and impractical, an atavistic yearning after a primitive and uncomplicated lifestyle which cannot be ours. However, there are aspects of core shamanic traditions which are open to all under the right circumstances, which can reactivate pathways between the worlds and a regular converse with the spirits, and which can in time reshape our attitudes to living, without sending us off on a trek back into the past. Many people possess a latent ability to work in the shamanic way; with training and humility this work can change our lives.

It is with this view that we have brought together the knowledge in this book, that those who still wish to honour the Celtic tradition and find its practical applications for today may be nourished and inspired by it.

The texts and extracts given here need some explanation. We have drawn upon good academic editions and reproduced them here with commentary and background, sparing the general reader the complexities of philological annotation. Readers may find the texts occasionally bare, and should remember that the cradle of introduction and descriptive narrative was a feature of the oral, not the written tradition; paper, vellum and parchment were rare commodities. Often the transcriber was closely familiar with the story and omitted well-known details which would have clarified subjects which are now obscure.

The texts come from a wide range of Celtic eras, with different transmission points from the Dark Ages into the medieval era. It is important to note that all were transcribed in the Christian era and that Christianity is referenced in different ways – both supportively and combatively. It is not our place to expunge these references from the texts or pretend they do not exist, since they must be read and understood in context. Throughout, we have referenced instances of modern Celtic seership and healing, to demonstrate that genuine survivals of ancient practices still exist, independent of written testimony. Where such shamanic healing abilities survive, as in Ireland, they are most often applied to the sick with invocations which appeal to Christian, not Pagan spirits. The names may change, but the intention and the spiritual effect are changeless; for, in shamanism, intention is the key to everything. Spirits appear in the forms most acceptable to those who need their help.

We have made every effort to keep the texts in their entirety: some have had to be abridged or edited by us to make their contents more accessible, or for reasons of space. Copious commentaries in foreign languages have been deleted or briefly translated. Repetitious passages and wilful diversion from the subject in hand have been similarly deleted. Inevitably within the space provided, we have had to leave out much that we would have liked to include. Such omissions will be rectified in future books. However, it is hoped that this selection will help to inspire readers to work practically with the material presented here, and to seek out the texts from which we have quoted. We also urge those Celtic scholars who deign to read our book to continue to make available fresh and accessible translations of texts still in their original manuscript forms. There are many readers frustrated by their lack of even modern Irish and Welsh, let alone their ancient counterparts. Our own translations in this book are accurate, informed by a practitioner's experience as well as by a scholar's observance.

Part 1 of the book concentrates on the contribution of memory to the Celtic shamanic tradition. Part 2 deals with the subjects of shamanic initiation, shapeshifting and the visionary skills of poets and druids. Part 3 looks in depth at prophecy, healing and divination, and includes not only some important texts that are hard to find, but also some original essays dealing with the subjects of healing and dream incubation, two areas which, for reasons of space, were not dealt with fully in either of the previous books. Part 4 leads to the subject of otherworld journeys, and a selection of texts which detail encounters with the Celtic otherworld.

The collection ends with an extended bibliography for the benefit of those who wish to pursue their studies even further. Most of the books included are in print, and the remainder can be found or requested through the inter-library loan service offered by most libraries. A thematic index has been included to help readers find their way amid this intricate material.

We ourselves have written throughout as practitioners of the shamanic tradition. While we have provided a background to the texts commentated on or translated here, there can be no footnotes to the actual practice of these skills: only experience can validate the information or make its intricacies clearer. Our training courses in Celtic shamanism have drawn extensively upon this material, and continue to teach us by revealing the practical handholds and applications which no text alone could have shown us.

Fragmentary maps and third-hand commentaries are useless to the shamanic explorer, which is why our work continues to be dedicated to revealing the prime sources of the Celtic tradition. We hope that *The Encyclopaedia of Celtic Wisdom* will provide a sustaining stew that may be shared by all people who honour their ancestral wisdom.

The words of a traditional Scots Gaelic saying exhort us to *lean-sa dlùth ri cliù do shinnsear*, follow closely the renown of our ancestors, the ones who have quested for the cup, grail or cauldron which gives without stint and which brings healing and knowledge to the people. May you follow them, sharing what they impart to you with generous hospitality to all who come to your hearth!

Caitlín and John Matthews
Oxford
Imbolc 1994

PART ONE

Shamanic Memory

CHAPTER ONE

The Memory of the Earth

The earth remembers everything and is a witness to history in a way we cannot fully appreciate. In Celtic tradition, the land is characterized by spiritual manifestations of its power: by the Goddess of the Land, by the appearance of warring dragons, by the flowing of rivers of mystical properties. It is the shaman's task to read and know the land, to be so part of it that any imbalance within it registers in a conscious manner. In the first extract, we see how Amairgin has this skill along with the necessary ability to bring healing and alignment. In the second, we see how the land remembers whatever has been done upon it. It is from stories such as these that we derive our earliest oral histories and understand the Celtic shamanic task of the seanachie, the chronicler and storyteller, as guardian of memory.

The Milesian Taking of Ireland
(translated by Caitlín Matthews)

Irish mythology tells of successive invasions from the east. Later literary Christian tradition gave the chief protagonists of these accounts a biblical ancestry, thus honouring the ancestral memory and connecting it with the new spiritual tradition. In the following passage from the *Lebor Gabala Erenn*, (*The Book of the Taking of Ireland*) we read of the Milesian attempt to take Ireland from the incumbent Tuatha de Danann, (The Race of Danu, their primal ancestress). The Dananns are skilled in druidry and enchantment, but the Milesians themselves have no mean exponent among their fleet – Amairgin White-knee.

The text has suffered various interpolations by puzzled scribes who have confused the clear narrative, so that Erannan and Donn seem to die twice in the various recensions! However, we have done our best to rationalize the text so that the narrative runs more consistently. The following notes will help clarify the text.

1. The Milesians attempt to invade Ireland and are beaten back by the combined spiritual forces of the Tuatha de Danann. After circling the island three times, the Milesians are able to approach the shore. They hold a rowing contest during which Ir dies, for Eber Donn, the eldest brother has the power to ill-wish his brother. This contest to reach shore first is a feature of many Celtic invasion stories. Amairgin's wife, Scéne dies, giving her name to Inber Sláine, now modern Inverskena (Kenmare River in Kerry). Although Inber Slaíne and Inber Scéne are referred to variously through this text, they are in fact the same place.

We hear of the seven chief wives of the Milesians, all of whom give their names in some way to parts of Ireland, or in the case of Scota to Scotland. Scota is the daughter of the Pharaoh Nectanebus, married to Milesius on his travels. This piece of information reads implausibly, perhaps, yet there were two pharaohs of this name, in the Thirtieth Dynasty (fourth century BCE,) so the Celtic memory may not be so faulty after all! Tea gives her name to Tea-mhair or Tara.

The poem about the seven wives may seem irrelevant, but significant clues lie in the invasion dates of this and previous invasions to Ireland. They are dated by the days of the moon; the Fir Bolg arrived on the nineteenth and waning day of the moon, while the Dananns landed on the ninth and waxing day; the Milesians arrive just after the full moon on the seventeenth day. We speculate that juxtaposition of the seven wives with these landing dates may indicate that they themselves are associated with the phases of the moon.

2. As Amairgin White-knee, chief poet and shaman of the Milesian invaders, greets the land of Ireland from his ship, he remembers all existences of which he has partaken in flesh and in vision. He makes this rhapsodic song of self-introduction to the land, speaking of his creative powers by way of strange kennings: of the cattle of Tethra as the stars arising from the sea, greeting the ox of the moon. In Amairgin's mystical identification with all things, he becomes one of the physicians of the soul, reweaving the scattered elements of life into a new wholeness. This is the task of Celtic poets, whose skill is to bring the soul to the point of vision, rest and stillness. He also per-

forms that ancient shamanic, propitiatory task of singing fruitfulness into the seas, so that the Milesians shall not want for fish.

3. After landing, the Milesians have to fight the Tuatha de Danann on land. Here we find a selection of *dindsencha* or 'place-name stories'. The proscription of seeing nakedness in certain circumstances reads, at first glance, like a Christian interpolation. Nudity was not contrary to Celtic custom. Classical accounts speak of Gaulish matrons processing naked, stained with woad, in ritual practices, and Celtic warriors frequently go into battle with no or few clothes. The fact that Lugaid and Fíal are both cleaning themselves may be a clue to a ritual prohibition being breached. As we see further in this chapter, the uncovering or bursting forth of waters often occurs when certain ritual procedures are ignored.

Eremon loses his horse in the battle, and it gives its name to the River Liffey, Gabar Life. The Irish for horse – *gabar* – is significantly related to the Irish word for invasion – *gabaltar*. The Indo-European method of invasion from India to Ireland seems to have been to turn loose one's horses upon the land and to claim the territory over which their hooves travelled. It is in a more salutary way that the Milesians claim Ireland, leaving their dead littered about its shores like propitiatory sacrifices.

4. Amairgin White-knee, is instrumental in this invasion, since he petitions the three major Goddesses of Ireland and makes a deal with them. He promises Banba and Fotla that their names shall be *a* name for Ireland; but to Eire (Eriu) he grants that her name shall be used forever. Banba's name signifies 'Woman of the Cows' – the cow was the common unit of Celtic currency, along with the female slave. Fotla's name has connotations of loam or soil. Both Banba and Fotla may therefore be associated with an earlier race of people, and with the lower-caste task of farming. Eire's name may signify 'one who is elevated', and it is she who is rewarded for her generous endorsement of the Milesians.

5. Having made their deal, the Milesians go onward to consolidate their invasion by arriving at Tara, seat of the high kings. However, they discover that its three kings have different terms to offer them. Under the guise of setting a truce for three days, the high kings demand that the Milesians retire to their ships. They have every intention of making it magically impossible for the invaders to return. Amairgin keeps his professional head and, exercising his abil-

ity as a true judge and witness of the truce, agrees to retire: he has his own plans.

The full significance of the Milesians' meeting with the three Goddesses and the three kings of Tara may be seen at a glance from this family tree:

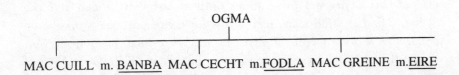

Fig. 1. Family tree of Ogma

Ogma is the God of Eloquence among the Irish Tuatha de Danann. His three sons are married to the ancient goddesses of the land. The deal that Amairgin has made behind the kings' backs gives him sufficient power to overcome their magic.

6. Retiring beyond the ninth wave – the traditional distance of exile from the land – Amairgin reacts calmly to the magical storm which the Dananns send against them. In checking that this is a druidic wind and not a natural one, Erannán falls from the mast. His mother's lamentation over him merely reinforces the plight of the Milesians, who are still a landless race of no affiliation until they can win Ireland.

Amairgin's response is a measured and keenly triumphant incantation. Its construction repays careful examination, since it is a totally circular poem, repeating the image of the previous line in order to build the next line. Lines 2–10 are the first ninefold, one line for each wave from the ship to Ireland; they conjure up the power of the land itself. The remaining lines include the second ninefold, conjuring up the strength of the Milesians as established at Tara, and ending with an acclamation of Eire herself. 'The wives of Bres', line 16, is a kenning for the triple Goddess, Brighid, the patroness of poets, of whose wisdom Amairgin himself partakes. After the death of Eber Donn, who resorts to military rather than shamanic tactics, the Milesians are established as the rulers of Ireland. The story of the subsequent retreat and retirement of the Tuatha de Danann can be read in Chapter 12.

1. Forty-eight married couples, four servants and Scota, daughter of Pharaoh, accompanied the Sons of Míl across the sea when they went to seek for Ireland. They proposed to take Ireland at Inber Sláine because of a prophecy that said a famous company would take Ireland at that place. But every time they approached land, the spirits would raise the land in a boar's back at the harbour, and it is because of this that Ireland is called Muc-Inis, or the Pig's Island. They skirted the entire coast of Ireland three times until at last they landed at Inber Sláine. Then the Milesians had a rowing contest to see who should reach the shore of Ireland first. It was here that Ir, son of Míl, bequeathed his right to sea-plunder to the others. Eber Donn, son of Míl, the eldest son, envied Ir and said, 'It is unlucky for Ir to be ahead of Lugaid mac Ith.' And as he spoke, Ir's oar broke under his hand and he fell backwards and died the following night. His body was taken to Sceilig, west of the southern eminence of Corco Duibne. [This was how Sceilig was named 'the story under the flagstone – literally *sceil* (story) *leac* (stone).]

Eber Finn, Erimón and Amairgin were sorrowful at Ir's death, and judged that Eber Donn should have no share of the land because of his envy. It was the day after that that Scéne died and was buried there; her gravemound (and that of Erannan) may still be seen.

One Thursday, on May Eve, the Milesians came to Ireland at Inber Sláine. They had sent out their fleet on the seventeenth day of the moon. There died Scéne the Shapely, wife of Amairgin White-knee, son of Míl. They dug her grave on one side of the estuary and (later) Erannán's on the other, and called the harbour after her. She was one of the seven wives of the Milesians, as it is sung:

> The seven wives of Míl's sons, a bright honour!
> I know the names of them all:
> Tea, Fíal, Fás – it is good to tell of them –
> Líben, Odba, Scota and Scéne.

> Tea – wife of Erimón of the horses,
> Fíal – woman-warrior, wife of Lugaid;
> Fás – wife of Un mac Uicce,
> Scéne – wife of Amairgin.

> Líben – wife of Fuad, sweet her memory;
> Scota – the virginal, and Odba –
> these were the wives, do not wonder,
> who accompanied the sons of Míl.

On the nineteenth day of the moon — no faint memory —
Did the Fir Bolg take the palace of Ireland;
after them, on the ninth day,
the Tuatha de Danann took the outer seas.

But on the seventeenth day of the moon, without fail,
the Milesians landed in Ireland;
at Inber Scéne of the sails
they took the shore on the seventeenth.

Amairgin said to his brothers, 'This harbour of our landing shall be named after Scéne.'

2. And Amairgin White-knee, son of Míl set his right foot upon Ireland and sang:

I am a wind on the sea,
I am a wave of the ocean,
I am the roar of the sea,
I am an ox of seven exiles,
I am a hawk on a cliff,
I am a tear of the sun,
I am a turning in a maze,
I am a boar in valour,
I am a salmon in a pool,
I am a lake on a plain,
I am a dispensing power,
I am a spirit of skilful gift,
I am a grass-blade giving decay to the earth,
I am a creative god giving inspiration.

Who else clears the stones of the mountain?
Who is it who declaims the sun's arising?
Who is it who tells where the sun sets?
Who brings cattle from the house of Tethra?
Upon whom do the cattle of Tethra smile?
Who is this ox?
Who is the weaving god who mends the thatch of wounds?
The incantation of a spear,
The incantation of the wind.

And he also uttered this spell, to bespell fish into the inlets:

Fishful the sea!
Fruitful the land!
A fountain of fish!
Fish under wave
Like a torrent of birds,
A crowded sea!

A white hail
Of countless salmon,
Of broad-mouthed whales!
A harbour spell –
A fountain of fish,
A fishful sea!

3. After three days and nights after that, the Milesians broke the enchantment of the spirits and undersea beings at the Battle of Slieve Mis, against the Tuatha de Danann. Fás, wife of Un mac Uicce, fell there, after whom is named Feart Fais and Gleand Fais – the grave and valley of Fás. In that battle also died Scota, daughter of the Pharaoh of Egypt, wife of Erimón. For previously Míl mac Bíle had gone sailing into Egypt with his seven ships and had taken Scota for his wife. After his death, Erimón was her husband.

The night the Milesians landed in Ireland, Loch Luigdech in West Munster burst forth. [The reason was thuswise:] Lugaid mac Ith was bathing in Loch Luigdech and Fíal, his wife, in the river that flows in and out of the loch. Her husband came to her naked, so that she saw his nakedness, and so died of shame. Or maybe it was because her husband saw her and her chastity got the upper hand?

Slieve Mis, for the Milesians, was literally the worst (*meas*) mountain (*sliabh*); it was there they fought their first battle in Ireland.

The Milesians also fought the Battle of Liffey. There were monsters in gigantic form, wrought of druidry, sent against them by the Tuatha de Danann. Eber and Eremón fought valiantly in that battle. Eremón's horse fell there, hence that place is called Gabar Life, or just Liffey.

4. After that they came until they were upon the mountain beside Loch Dergderc. Here the Milesians and Banba spoke together. Banba said, 'If you have come with the intention of taking Ireland, you are not justified in this agreement.'

'It is for this we have come,' said Amairgin White-knee.

'I ask a gift of you for myself,' she said.

'What is it?' they asked.

'That my name shall be upon this land,' she said.

'What is your name,' they asked.

'Banba,' she replied.

'Then Banba shall be a name of this island,' said Amairgin White-knee . . .

Then they sang incantations against her, and Banba left them. They also spoke with Fotla in Eibliu. She spoke with them in the same way, and also begged that her name be upon Ireland, to which Amairgin replied that Fotla would be a name for Ireland.

Then they spoke with Eire (Eriu) in Uisnech. She said this to them, 'Welcome be upon you, warriors. Long have prophets known of your coming to us. You shall be in this island forever, and no comparable island in the eastern world shall be better than this and no race more perfect than yours.'

'That is a good prophecy,' said Amairgin.

'No thanks is due to her,' said Donn, eldest of Míl's sons.

'Rather thank our spirits and our powers.'

'Sorrowful shall that saying be to you,' said Eire. 'You will neither profit from the island nor will your descendants live within it. A gift for myself,' she said, 'you sons of Míl, you race of Breogain; let my name be upon this island.'

'It shall be its name forever,' replied Amairgin.

In the Book of Druim Snechta, it says that it was upon Slieve Mis that Eire spoke to them, that she shaped a mighty host against them, so that the Milesians were embattled. But their druids and vision poets sang incantations, so that they saw that their opponents were only the sods of the mountain bogland. The same book says that it was Fotla who spoke to them upon Uisnech.

5. Afterwards the sons of Míl and of Breogain travelled to Druim Cáin, at Temair (Tara). Three kings of Ireland were there, Mac Cuill, Mac Cecht and Mac Greine. They demanded that the island should be theirs for three days' length, to be free of plunder, submission or the hosting of battle. They demanded this in order to ensure that the invaders would not return, since they would make incantations behind them, and so be unable to come back again.

'We promise this,' said Mac Cuill mac Cermait, 'just as Amairgin, your judge, shall promise on your behalf; if he utters a false judgement, he will die at our hands.'

'I shall give it,' said Amairgin, 'Let the island be left to them.'

'How far should we go?' asked Eber Donn.

'Beyond the ninth wave,' said Amairgin. That was the first judgement that was given in Ireland by the Milesians. And Amairgin sang:

> Men who seek possession,
> Beyond nine green-shouldered waves
> You shall not go, save with powerful spirits!
> Let this be quickly settled! Let battle be waged!
>
> I reapportion the sharing
> Of the land you have journeyed to;
> If it pleases you, judge the rights of it;
> If it pleases you not, do not bother –
> I speak only with your goodwill.

Said Donn mac Míl, 'If it were my advice that was being followed here, we should give battle.'

Said the druids of Tuatha de Danann, 'Though you squandered your powers, you should never return to Ireland.'

6. And so they came southward from Temair and reached Inber Féle and Inber Scéne, where their ships were moored. [According to their promise] they sailed over nine waves. The druids and vision poets sang spells against them, so that whatever was upon the sea floor was raised to the surface, so great was the storm raised against them. Then they arrived at the far west of Ireland and were sick of the sea.

'This is a druidic wind that blows,' said Donn mac Míl.

'It is indeed,' said Amairgin, 'unless it is blowing higher than our sail.'

The youngest of the family, Erannán, then ascended the mast and fell upon the rocks and was shattered. But as he fell, he said, 'the wind is not higher than our sail.' It was he who was the pilot of Donn's ship, and a fosterling of Amairgin's. His head was placed in his mother's breast and she heaved a deep sigh at his death. 'It is fitting,' she said, [speaking of their journey]. 'The way between two emperors was his course: he had to separate from the emperor he attended, but he has not reached the emperor he sought to attend.'

'It is disgraceful that the gifted ones [aes dana] can do nothing to stop this druidry,' said Donn when they had reassembled in one place.

'It is no disgrace,' said Amairgin, and he rose up and sang:

I seek the land of Ireland.
Forceful is the fruitful sea,
Fruitful the serried mountains,
Serried the showery woods,
Showery the cascade of rivers,
Cascaded the tributaries of lakes,
Tributaried the well of hills,
Welling the people of gatherings,
Gathering of Tara's king,
Tara, hill of tribes,
Tribes of Míl's people,
Míl's ships and galleys,
Galleys of mighty Eire,
Eire, mighty and green.
A crafty incantation,
Craftiness of Bres's wives,
Bres, of Buaigne's wives,
Great Lady Eire:
Eremón harried her,
Ir and Eber sought for her —
I seek the land of Ireland.

And the wind calmed itself immediately.

But Donn said, 'I shall now go forth and put under the edge of my spear and sword all that are alive in Ireland.'

A great wind arose against his ship, separating Donn mac Míl from the others. In that ship were twenty-four men, four servants and twelve women. They were all drowned at Dumachaib on the western seaboard, and so it is called Tech Duinn, the House of Donn.

Selections from the Dindsenchas

Every place on the earth's surface is remembered in some way or holds the memory of events which happened there. This memory is preserved in many ways in our own culture. Visitors from America to Britain, many of whom do not have such continuity of memory and place, are often astounded at the richness of lore surrounding even seemingly mundane sites, and wonder at the memory of the local inhabitants. Such stories, songs and anecdotes about places are still mythically central to the memory of Aboriginal Australians. Bruce Chatwin's remarkable book, *The Songlines*, gives some insight into the manner in which they regard even tracks and dried-up river-beds as the numinous locus for extraordinary spiritual activity. Some echo of this deep memory is preserved in the *Dindsenchas*, stories of place from Ireland. We give a short selection from this gazetteer.

The style of the *Dindsenchas*, like most Irish texts, veers between baldly terse and over-descriptive. Many of the stories turn on wildly onomastic explanations, suggesting that the scribe made the description to fit the name! But the allusive and sometimes too plausible stories associated with each place are continually referenced in the Irish literary tradition, keeping their remembrance lively. The *Dindsenchas* are found in *The Book of Leinster* and in a manuscript preserved at Rennes, Brittany.

Mide

This story tells of the hill of Uisnech between Mullingar and Athlone, which marked the sacred centre of Ireland. It is named after Mide, the druid and historian of the Nemedians, the invaders who overcame the Fomorians. He gives his name to the county of Meath. Fire was jealously guarded in Celtic times; the domestic fire was never allowed to go out except at the ritual rekindling of the fire at Beltane, when everyone brought a brand to the hill of Uisnech to relight their homes from the royal fire kindled by the king's druid. We have here a memory of the bloody silencing of the Fomorian druids.

Mide son of Brath, son of Deoth, was the first to light a fire in Erin for the clans of Nemed, and it was six years a-blaze, and from that fire was kindled every chief fire in Erin. Wherefore Mide's successor is entitled to a sack [of corn] with a pig from every house-top in Ireland. And the wizards of Ireland said: ''Tis an evil smoke [mi-dé] for us, this fire that hath been lit in the land.' So the wizards of Ireland were collected into one house, and, by Mide's advice, their tongues were cut out of their heads, and he buried them in the ground of Uisnech, and Mide, chief wizard and chief historian of Ireland, sat above them. Then said Gairech Gumor's daughter, Mide's fostermother: 'Sublime (*uais*) is one (*nech*) who is here tonight.' Whence *Uisnech* and *Mide*.

Boand

This story tells of the source of the river Boyne, County Meath. Its eponymous Goddess, Boand, is reported to have walked around it three times widdershins; walking, 'against the sun', rather than deosil, 'towards the sun' (clockwise) is a foolhardy or malicious act in Celtic lore, contradicting the natural order and courting misfortune. The well of Nechtan, her husband, is a secret place, the source of all knowledge. Boand's act releases the waters for all people – a fact which is acknowledged in most poetic texts, since it is Boand, not Nechtan, who is remembered as the source and patroness of the fertile imagination of poets.

Bóand wife of Nechtán son of Labraid went to the secret well which was in the green of Síd Nechtáin. Whoever went to it would not come from it without his two eyes bursting, unless it were Nechtán himself and his three cupbearers, whose names were Flesc and Lám and Luam.

Once upon a time Bóand went through pride to test the well's power, and declared that it had no secret force which could shatter her form, and thrice she walked withershins round the well. [Whereupon] three waves from the well break over her and deprive her of a thigh and one of her hands and one of her eyes. Then she, fleeing her shame, turns seaward, with the water behind her as far as Boyne-mouth, [where she was drowned]. Now she was the mother of Oengus son of the Dagda.

Or thus: *Bó* the name of the stream [of Síd Nechtáin] and *Find* the river of Sliab Guairi, and from their confluence is the name *Bóand* [Bó + Find].

Dabilla was the name of her lapdog, whence *Cnoc Dabilla* ('D.'s Hill'), today called *Sliab in Colaig* 'the Mountain of the Covenant'.

Ceilbe

This place has not been identified and retains the hiding place implied by its name, but we include this story to show the devastating power and knowledge of the shaman poet. In the first explanation of the place-name, Be Gelchnes (Whiteskin Maiden) fails to give due honour and attention to her uncle, Find mac Ross, who is both a king and a poet. He smites her with a tumour. The second explanation tells of Cairpre mac Ross who buries hostages alive. The third explanation tells of Dallan, who visits the King of Leinster's granddaughter, Gel-be. She attempts to test Dallan's prophetic skills by hiding a twig of sloes under her skirt and asking him to guess what she has. The poet's answer is two-edged: the sloe-bush is a 'peasant' or lowly tree, and the implication is that her descendants shall be likewise lowly. Dallan also demands his poet's fee: her lands for her rash demand. In each of the stories, the name Ceilbe is given, since it means 'the Hidden Maiden'.

Find the Poet son of Ross the Red went to the house of Bé Whiteskin daughter of Coirpre Niafer. Now there was an ale-feast ready for her father and she shewed it not to her father's brother, though there were in his single person a poet and a king. And nought was found by him save milk and corn. Whereupon Find the Poet said 'Have thou no worth of thy goods, O strong Bé, without brotherhood! may thy honours ebb utterly!: noble lords are not upraised before thy womb-family.'

Then a tumor seized the damsel, so that she was swollen, and it closed her door, and choked her breath so that she died thereof, and she was buried in that place [Ceilbe], and her gravedigger said: 'Here under concealment (*ceil*) is Bé.'

Otherwise: Cairpre son of Ross had the by names Cairpre *Colbi* and *Nia fer*. 'Tis he that there buried alive (*beo*) the free hostage of Tara, wherefore he is called *Col-beo*, or *Ceil-beo*, and hence is *Cel-be*.

Or thus: Dallán son of Macachán son of Echtigern, a sage was he in wisdom and in poetry. He went to the house of Gel-be daughter of Cerball son of Muirecan King of Leinster. 'Tis he that used to divine everything concealed. The damsel went to welcome him, and she had under her garment a branch of thorn with its sloes. She said: 'What is under my garment, O Dallán?' Dallán replied: 'I apply a miracle of prophecy, with a cry of knowledge of white wisdom that near may be what a prophecy that is silent [?] manifests. A brown bush of spiky thorn bearing ignoble [?] black sloes there is under thy garment, thou dear damsel. I will make thee wail[?].'

Thereat Gel-be was silent, and the poet said: 'Thy . . . for I will blemish thee.' 'Nay,' says the damsel: 'thou shalt have the place where we met, only let it bear my name, to wit, Ráith Gelbe.' And hence is *Ceilbe*.

Slaney

This story tells of the River Slaney in County Wexford and the vision of Cathair Mor, first-century AD High King of Ireland. Slaine was a son of Partholon, and the first physician. In modern Irish, the name signifies 'health'. The 'hundreded hospitaller' is one who, because he possesses over a hundred slaves and animals, is legally bound to entertain travellers: the earliest five-star hotel manager! Whitley Stokes has chosen here to translate the original Irish *druid* as 'wizard'. Here we see the interpretive role of the poet-shaman fully exercised.

From Slainge son of Dela, from the king of the Fir Bolg, the river Slaney is named, and also Inver Slaney. In Catháir's time was the naming of the lake, as he said in *Catháir's Vision*.

Once in the early part of Catháir's life, as he was asleep, he saw a hundreded hospitaller's daughter with a beautiful form, and every colour in her raiment, and she was pregnant. Eight hundred years she was thus, until she brought forth a manchild, and on the day he was born he was stronger than his mother. They begin to fight, and his mother found no place to avoid him save by going through the midst of the son. A lovely hill was over the heads of them both: higher than every hill, with hosts thereon. A shining tree like gold stood on the hill: because of its height it would reach to the clouds. In its leaves was every melody; and its fruits, when the wind touched it, specked the ground. The choicest of fruit was each of them.

Thereat Catháir awakes and summoned his wizard, Brí son of Baircid, and tells him his tales. 'I will rede that,' says Brí, ['if I have a guerdon therefor.' 'Thou shalt have,' says the king, 'every thing that thou mayest demand.'] 'This,' [says the wizard,] 'is the damsel, the river which hath the name of Slaney. These are the colours in her raiment, artists of every kind without sameness of distinction or peculiarity. This is the hundreded hospitaller who was her father, the Earth through the which come a hundred of every kind. This is the son who was in her womb for eight hundred years, the lake which will be born of the stream of the Slaney, and in thy time it will come forth. Stronger the son than his mother, the day that the lake will be born it will drown the whole river. Many hosts there, every one a-drinking from the river and the lake. This is the great hill above their heads, thy power over all. This is the tree with the colour of gold and with its fruits, thou over Banba (Ireland) in its sovranty. This is the music that was in the tops of the tree, thy eloquence in guarding and correcting the judgments of the Gaels. This is the wind that would tumble the fruit, thy liberality in dispensing jewels and treasures. And now,' says Brí, 'thou hast partaken of the rede of this vision.'

Sinann

This is the origin story of the longest river in Britain or Ireland, the Shannon. The eponymous Goddess of the river, Sinann, has a story which is comparable to that of Boand's above. Her visit to the well of Connla in the undersea world of Tir Tairngire releases the waters to the middleworld of Ireland.

Sinend daughter of Lodan Lucharglan son of Ler, out of Tir Tairngire ('Land of Promise, Fairyland') went to Connla's Well which is under sea, to behold it. That is a well at which are the hazels and inspirations [?] of wisdom, that is, the hazels of the science of poetry, and in the same hour their fruit, and their blossom and their foliage break forth, and these fall on the well in the same shower, which raises on the water a royal surge of purple. Then the salmon chew the fruit, and the juice of the nuts is apparent on their purple bellies. And seven streams of wisdom spring forth and turn there again.

Now Sinend went to seek the inspiration, for she wanted nothing save only wisdom. She went with the stream till she reached *Linn Mnú Féile* 'the Pool of the Modest Woman', that is Brí Ele — and she went ahead on her journey, but the well left its place, and she followed it to the banks of the river *Tarr-cáin* 'Fair-back'. After this it overwhelmed her, so that her back (*tarr*) went upwards, and when she had come to the land on this side [of the Shannon] she tasted death. Whence *Sinann* and *Linn Mná Féile* and *Tarr-cain*.

Mag Mucraime

Mag Mucraime is a plain west of Athenry in County Galway. Its origin story is one of the countless Celtic tales of magical pigs which periodically break out of the underworld to spread confusion and destruction or to bring an end to hunger, depending on the tradition. Here Ailill and Medb (Maeve), sovereigns of Connacht, set up a pig-chase to apprehend, count and assess the magical swine which have blighted their corn and milk. Pigs usually originate in the underworld and are associated with earlier races than the Celts, to whom pig-keeping was the lowest occupation. The polluting influence of pigs did not stop Celts of all ranks from enjoying pork, needless to say! The juxtaposition of royalty and pigs in this story is then significant in overcoming their destructive propensities. These pig legends are also numerous in Wales where the story of the reiving of Pwyll's pigs by Gwydion has resulted in many places being named Muc Tref or pig-chase. The natural boundary between northern and southern Ireland is to this day called the Black Pig's Dyke and has its own tradition of a ravaging boar which ploughs up the land in its present configuration.

A herd of magical swine came to Ailill and Medb out of the Cave of Cruachu, and they used to blight corn and milk wheresoever they were, nor could the men of Erin in any place count them or look them over. So to set their hunt afoot Ailill and Medb came to Fraechmag 'Heatherfield', and chased the swine as far as *Belach na Fert* 'the Pass of the Graves', and there Medb caught one of them by the leg; but it left its skin in her hand, and thereupon they were counted in that plain. Whence *Mag Muc-ríme* 'Plain of Pignumbering'.

CHAPTER TWO

The Memory of Trees

Among the Celts, trees were always considered to be sacred and were recognized as repositories of memory, lore and the presence of spirit-beings. Some of the ways in which this manifests itself within Celtic shamanic tradition are illustrated in the following selection of writings grouped around this area of knowledge.

In the first instance we look at the subject of Ogam, an ancient alphabet consisting of twenty or twenty-five letters inscribed in stone in the form of straight lines bisecting a long line or stave, as follows:

B L F S N H D T C Q M G NG STR R   A O U E I EA OI UI IO AE

Fig. 2. *Ogam alphabet*

It was used primarily by the ancient bards of Britain and Ireland as a means of passing coded messages, and as a storehouse of accumulated knowledge. Not only were the individual letters associated with various trees (the best-known type of Ogam) but also with objects, people and places. Thus by referring to any of these groupings, or by making signals to their brethren, the shaman-poets could pass on a whole array of information and knowledge. Tree Ogam was always the key to this and for this reason alone it is an essential part of the memory of trees.

To begin with we have an essay by Charles Graves, who was Bishop of Limerick towards the middle of the nineteenth century. A learned man, his account of the origins and development of Ogam is still one of the best, despite its age and some occasional wrong guesses. It has been slightly edited for smoother reading.

We then move on to *The Ogam Tract*, one of the best, and certainly the clearest, of the several medieval tracts on Ogam published under the title *Auricept na n-eces* (*The Scholar's Primer*) by George Calder in 1917. Most of the tracts are intricate and are really only of interest to those making a detailed study of Ogam. However, as Ogam is one of the chief tools of the bardic shamans of Britain and Ireland, some knowledge of it is essential. The tract published here includes not only the essential Ogam alphabet, with original glosses, but also an account of some of the many other kinds of Ogam – including Sow Ogam, Fortress Ogam, and River-Pool Ogam. Its author liberally sprinkled Latin words in his text, and these have been edited out, making for a much smoother and more sensible reading.

Other accounts of Ogam exist, and some of these will be seen to be contradictory, both in the glossing of the letters and in their order. This is due to the long period of time in which this information was carried only orally. When it did come to be written down, hundreds of years after the origins of Ogam, it had split into several different versions. This accounts for the problems which still beset those who work with Ogam today, and for the conflicting views of several writers on the subject, such as Robert Graves, Kaledon Naddair and Sean O'Boyle, details of whose works will be found in the bibliography at the end of the book. A diagram of Ogam also appears on p. 22.

This is followed by three poems from *The Dindsenchas* from which we have already quoted in Chapter 1. Here the subject is part of the once extensive lore of the great trees, of which only fragmentary accounts are now extant. From this we learn that there were at least five great trees in Ireland: The Tree of Ross, the Tree of Mugna, the Tree of Dathi, the Tree of Uisnech and the Tree of Tortu. Each of these was guarded by one of the Irish shaman-poets, who seem to have cut their trees down when they were threatened by Christian incursions. For a more detailed discussion of the traditions relating to this and other aspects of tree lore see *Taliesin* by John Matthews, especially Chapter 8.

On the Ogam Beithluisnin
by Charles Graves[1]

In an article printed in the preceding volume of Hermathena, I endeavoured to show, by an analysis of the Beithluisin, that the Ogam is a cipher, a series of symbols, each of which represents, not a sound, but a letter in an alphabet of the ordinary kind, used at the same time for ordinary purposes. Now, if this conclusion be correct – and to me it seems all but self-evident — we are immediately led to ask, first, What was the real alphabet represented by the Ogam cipher? and next, Is there any evidence of the Ogam having been used for cryptic purposes? To the first of these questions we reply by saying that the Roman letters must have formed the alphabet whose elements were represented by the *feadha* (rod) of the Beithluisnin. Of no other alphabet could we assert this with any grounds of probability. Roman letters made their way into Ireland before the coming of St Patrick. There were Christians there to whom his predecessor, Palladius, was sent by Pope Celestine; and we have very ancient testimony to the effect that St Patrick, in the course of his missionary labours, met with Bishops who had been in Ireland before his arrival. These Christians cannot have been left without the books which were 'written in order that they might know the certainty of those things wherein they had been instructed.' Still less can we suppose that their Bishops were illiterate. The parents of Celestius received, and no doubt were able to read, the letters addressed to them by their son at an early period of his career, towards the end of the fourth century. Nay more, I would not hastily reject the testimony of the Irish writers who claim for Cormac Mac Art, King of Ireland in the third century, the credit of having been himself an author, and superintended the collection of a body of written Laws and Chronicles. In fact, it seems wholly unreasonable to imagine that Ireland, with its Kings and its Druids, with all its national institutions, civil and religious — for it was not a barbarous country — could have remained unaffected, for hundreds of years, by the social and intellectual influences developed in the neighbouring island during the period of its occupation by the Romans.

Supposing, therefore, that it could be shown from the testimony of the monuments themselves, or in any other way, that the Beithluisnin was in use in Ireland even as early as the first century, nothing would be done to disprove the connexion which I endeavoured to establish in my former paper between it and the Roman alphabet.

And next, if the Beithluisnin be a cipher, it must have been intended to be a secret character. What other purpose could it serve? Hence we are led to seek for evidence to prove that it was cryptic. I propose in this Paper to notice allusions to the use of Ogam occurring in ancient Irish documents of various kinds. A review of them will show, amongst other things, that ancient Irish writers, going back for about a thousand years, believed that the Ogam was not generally written or read, but understood and used only by the initiated: in fact, that it was a cryptic character.

The ancient Irish laws, commonly called The Brehon Laws, contain many allusions to the use of the Ogam character. They speak of Ogam cut on stones, or indestructible rocks, as evidence of the purchase or ownership of land. The stones thus inscribed are said to have been sought in mounds. The inscribed stone is called a monument or memorial of the *Seanchaidhe*, who was a professional antiquary or historian, charged with duties such as are attached to the office of a notary or registrar. It is also called the memorial or monument of the tribe. The inscription itself is called fair writing, and is distinguished from the kind of writing found in books. Such monuments were set up between two territories or estates as boundary stones; and seem to have contained the name of the owner of the land, of which the pillar-stone (*Gallan*) marked the limit. *Gallan*, or *Dallan*, is still a living word in the counties of Kerry and Cork, and is applied at the present day to pillar-stones which exhibit Ogam characters; and Mason, in his 'Parochial Survey of Ireland,' vol. iii. p. 611, note, observes that 'The stones inscribed with the Ogam character, and occasionally met with through the country, are generally supposed to have been landmarks.' Cormac, in his Glossary, gives the word *Gall*, and explains it as a pillar-stone. His etymology, however, is questionable:

'GALL, *i.e.* a pillar-stone, *e.g. nis comathig combatar selba co cobrandaib gall* 'they are not neighbours till their properties are [provided] with boundaries [?] of pillar-stones.' *Gall*, then, means four things, *i.e.* first *gall*, a pillar-stone: it is so called because it was the Gaill that first fixed them in Ireland, etc. (*Cormac's Glossary*, Edited by W. Stokes, LLD, p. 84)

The ancient *d* so often passed into *g*, that the word might be more naturally referred to *dal*, a division.

The following passages, which may be taken as representing many others of similar import, substantiate the greater part of what has been stated above:

How many ever-burning candles are there by which perpetual ownership of land is secured? *i.e.* How many conditions like an ever-burning candle secure the ownership of the territory in perpetuity to the occupant? Memorials (*cuimne*) of the Historians, of ancient writings, in ancient mounds, *i.e.* if it is secured in the memorial of the tribe (*tuath*), or in the memorial of that fair writing; and that is to be sought for in the old mound. (MS in Trinity College, Dublin, H. 3, 18, p. 230, b)

In other passages, in the same tract, where proofs of ownership are enumerated, we read:

> And when poems record it; *i.e.* when it has been chanted in the long poem, or when it has been recited in the language of the historians. When it has been written in writings; *i.e.* in the books. When it has reached security of stones; *i.e.* when it has been determined to have indefeasible securities for the restoration [of the land after the term of tenancy has expired].

> The joint memorial of two territories; *i.e.* the common memorial that stands between the two territories; *i.e.* the Ogam in the *Gallan* (pillar-stone), or, it might be the evidence of two neighbours in the two adjoining territories that will prove the man's possession.

> To decide by the recital of a rock; *i.e.* that the name of the man who bought [the land] be in the bond of Ogam; *i.e.* that the Ogam of the purchase be in the flag of a mound [or grave]. That it be written; *i.e.* that it be in old writing. In the presence of credible witnesses; *i.e.* that it be recorded [or kept] by credible persons. Darkness; *i.e.* to be without recital [of the name], without poem, without Ogam.

In a law on taking lawful possession, the following passage occurs: 'Land which the chief divides after the death of the tenant, where a hole is made, where a stone is put'. It is thus explained by the commentator:

> Where a hole is made; *i.e.* a mound wherein a hole is sunk in the division of the land. Where a stone is put; *i.e.* a pillar-stone, *i.e.* after its being enclosed, *i.e.* the boundary stone; there is a hole and a stone, and the chief's standing stone there, in order that his share there may be known.

The mention of the Ogam in the second of these passages, in conjunction with poems, as a proof of title, points certainly to an early period. But we must not insist too much upon this fact, seeing that in the same list of proofs reference is made to writings such as were found in books. The reader will also notice that the use of Ogam as an evidence of proprietorship falls in with the notion that this was a cryptic character. It seems natural to suppose that when a bargain was made, the *Seanchaidhe* recorded it in a character which was not commonly known – neither written nor read by ordinary persons. If a dispute arose afterwards about the ownership, the *Seanchaidhe* of that time would have been able to read the inscription. It would have been a part of his official business. But the forgery of an Ogam would not have been an easy matter in those days. This can hardly be regarded as a conjecture. In the tract on the names, qualifications, and privileges of the seven degrees of Poets, we find that men belonging to the literary hierarchy were bound to study the Ogam character. When we come to treat of the Ogam monuments themselves, the reader will see that many of them have been found in caves in the interior of raths. These were perhaps the mounds (*ferta*) spoken of in the ancient laws. The meaning of the word *fert* is not fixed. It commonly means a tomb or grave; sometimes an earthen fence or dike thrown up by the spade . . .

When the poet attached to a tribe or family failed to receive the remuneration due to him for one of his compositions, the Irish law directed him to seek his remedy by the following curious procedure:

> Let an Ogam alphabet be cut [on a four-square wand], and an *Ua* alphabet; *i.e.* let the writing begin in the name of God. And the efficacy of this is to inscribe a Cross in the first edge for a notice; the name of the offence in the second edge; the name of the offender in the third edge; and encomium in the fourth edge. And let the wand be set up at the end of ten days by the poet of the *trefocul*. Or, [it is necessary] that the notice should be at the end of ten days. If he [the poet] has neglected [to set up] his wand, and has made a satire, he is liable for the *Eraic* for a satire. If he has made a seizure, he must pay the fine of an illegal seizure. (H. 3, 18, p. 424)

The *trefocul* here spoken of was a kind of poem, each measure of which consisted of three words — two words of praise, followed by one word of satire; and this was considered the highest praise.

The weight of the testimony borne by the Brehon Laws to the use of the Ogam character is unquestionable. These laws, as they have come down to us, are genuine documents, which were employed by judges in the discharge of their duties, and by jurists in giving instruction in their law-schools.

But the question as to the time at which they assumed their present form, how much is the substance of the Ancient Law, and how much has been added by comparatively recent Brehons and commentators, has not yet been decided; neither can it be, until the language and substance of the laws has been subjected to a careful analysis by competent philologists and jurists. Meanwhile, with all readiness to acknowledge their genuineness and antiquity, I see no reason to admit that the notices of Ogam contained in them refer to a period anterior to the introduction of Roman letters and Christian civilization; and point, in confirmation of this view, to the fact that no mention of Ogam occurs in the text of the Book of Aicil, or in that of the Senchus Mor, supposed to be the oldest codes of Irish law. For the present, I venture to avow my belief that the commentaries are for the most part as recent as the tenth or eleventh century; and that even in the texts, however ancient may be the substance of the laws, we do not meet with such a prevalence of the ancient grammatical forms as, according to Zeuss's view, would characterize the language as Old Gaedhelic.

Let us now turn to the ancient Irish tales and poems, to gather from them what information they supply with respect to the use of Ogam. They speak frequently of Ogam as employed to record the names of deceased persons on sepulchral monuments. The following is the formula commonly used in such cases: 'The grave was dug, the funeral games were held, and *the Ogam name* was inscribed on a stone erected over his grave.' In other passages, mention is made of Ogam used to convey information, in such a way that the communication was understood by the initiated, whilst it was unintelligible to ordinary persons. Ogams of this kind were generally cut in wood. We also meet with instances in which Ogam is said to have been used for purposes of divination or incantation. Whilst the occult nature of the Ogam is thus frequently and plainly brought under our notice, I have not met with a single passage which is inconsistent with this view. The ancient Irish writers, whatever be the value of their testimony, believed, one and all, that the Ogam was a cryptic mode of writing.

The following passage is taken from an account of the death of Fiachra, the son of Eochaidh Muighmhedhoin, and brother of Niall of the Nine Hostages. The whole story has a very pagan aspect:

Then the men of Munster gave him battle in Caenraighe. And Maidhi Meascorach wounded Fiachra mortally in the battle. Nevertheless, the men of Munster and the Erneans were defeated by dint of fighting, and suffered a great slaughter. Then Fiachra carried away fifty hostages out of Munster, together with his tribute in full, and set forth on his march to Temar. Now when he had reached Forraidh in Uibh Maccuais in West Meath, Fiachra died there of his wound. His grave was made, and his mound was raised, and his *cluiche cainte* (funeral rites, including games and dirges) were ignited, and his Ogam name was written, and the hostages which had been brought from the south were buried alive round Fiachra's grave. (*Book of Ballymote*)

Dr Petrie has drawn attention to the following very ancient story preserved in the Leabhar na h-Uidhre, which details the circumstances connected with the death of Fothadh Airgthech, who was for a short time monarch of Ireland, and was killed by the warrior Cailte, the foster-son of Finn Mac Cumhaill, in the battle of Ollarba, fought, according to the 'Annals of the Four Masters', in the year 285. In this tract, Cailte is introduced as identifying the grave of Fothadh Airgthech, at Ollarba, in the following words:

. . . The ulaidh (carn) of Fothadh Airgthech will be found at a short distance to the east of it [the iron head of a spear buried in the earth]. There is a chest of stone about him in the earth. There are his two rings of silver, and his two *bunne doat* [bracelets?], and his torque of silver on his chest; and there is a pillar stone at his carn; and an Ogam is [inscribed] on the end of the pillar stone which is in the earth. And what is in it is, Eochaid Airgthech here. (*Leabhar na h-Uidhre*)

But Dr Petrie does not seem to have noticed some circumstances mentioned here which claim our attention. First, the fact that the Ogam was inscribed on the end of the pillar-stone which was in the earth, and therefore intentionally concealed from view. Why should this be, unless there were something disgraceful connected with the birth, life, or death of the person who was buried there? Next, the epithet *Airgthech* appears to declare the nature of the stigma thus secretly recorded. *Airgthech* means a robber or plunderer. Again, is it not perplexing to find that the person called Fothadh Airgthech in the story is named Eochaid Airgthech in the Ogam inscription? It is not impossible that   may have been substituted for   a name very like it, by the error of the transcriber. But it is also possible that the Ogam name inscribed on the pillar-stone was not the name by which the monarch was commonly known. He and his brother, Fothadh Cairptheach, are mentioned in the 'Annals of Clonmacnoise' as joint monarchs of Ireland. But it is added that they 'were none of the Blood Royal'. Tighernach does not mention either of them as kings of Ireland, evidently because he regarded them as usurpers. Fothadh Airgthech slew his brother Fothadh Cairptheach, and reigned, if he ever

was king, only for a single year (see 'Annals of the Four Masters', at
the year 285 AD). There is yet another circumstance which throws a
shade of doubt or discredit on this story. Antiquaries do not believe
that silver ornaments were in use in Ireland in the third century. The
torques and armlets of that time are believed to have been of gold.

In the ancient tract entitled the Dialogue of the Sages (*Agallam na
Seanonae*), this same Cailte, who is said to have lived till the coming
of St Patrick, and to have communicated to him much of the ancient
history of Ireland, gives an account of Finn's marriage with Aine, the
daughter of Modhurn, king of Scotland, and of her subsequent death.
It ends thus:

> And Finn had her for six years after that, and she bore him two
> sons – Iollan Faebarderg and Aedh Beg. She died in giving birth
> to Aedh, and she was buried in this mound near us. Her tomb-
> stone was raised over her grave, and her Ogam name was writ-
> ten, and her *cluiche cainte* were held. (*Book of Lismore*)

We have a similar notice of a monumental inscription placed by Finn
and his followers over Art and Eoghan, two sons of the king of
Connaught, who served in Finn's host, and were killed by foreigners
at the strand of Rory, in Ulster.

> We, the Fiann, said Cailte, both high and low, great and small,
> king and knight, raised a loud shout in lamentation for the brave
> and valiant champions. And a mound was dug for each of them;
> and they were put into them; and his own arms along with each.
> Their tombstones were raised over their graves, and their Ogam
> names were written then. (*Book of Lismore*)

It is not stated that their names were written in Ogam (*tri Ogam*), but
that their *Ogam names* were written.

A like account is given of the burial at Benn Edair of Edain, the
wife of Oscar, son of Oisin. She died of grief at seeing the dreadful
wounds of her husband after the battle of Benn Edair.

> She shed floods of tears, and raised a loud and piteous cry of
> lamentation. Then she went to her own bed, and her heart
> broke, and she died straightway of grief for him who was her
> husband and her first love, though a spark of life still remained
> in him. Finn was filled with sorrow for this, and so were the
> Fiann of Erin, said Cailte; and we carried her to the fairy man-
> sion of Ben Edair for burial, and we spent that night around

Edain, dejected and weeping. Finn bade his followers dig a
mound for the woman on the morrow. They did so. They dug
a mound, and they buried her, and they put her tombstone over
her grave, and her Ogam name was written, and her *Cluiche
cainte* were held by the champions; and the mound is named after
her, *Fert Edain*, at the fairy mansion of Edair. (Hodges & Smith MS,
RIA, p. 149)

So again, when Etercomol was slain by Cuchulainn, we read in the
Tain bo Cuailgne, that his Fert was dug, his *lia*, or headstone, was set
up, his Ogam name was written, and his funeral rites were celebrated (*Leabhar na h-Uidhre*, p. 69, col. 1); and the same formula occurs
at the end of the tale called the Elopement of Deirdré with the Sons
of Uisnach. (*Transactions of the Gaelic Society, Deirdré*, Dublin, 1808, p. 129).

The *Book of Leinster* preserves a poem attributed to Oisin, in which
return is made of an Ogam inscription of the same kind:

> An Ogam in a *lia, a lia* over a *leacht*,
> In a place whither men went to battle,
> The Son of the King of Erin fell there,
> Slain by a sharp spear on his white steed.
>
> That Ogam which is in the stone
> Around which the heavy hosts have fallen,
> If the heroic Finn had lived,
> Long would the Ogam be remembered.

In the valuable work on Christian Inscriptions in the Irish language,
just completed by Miss Stokes, we are presented with a poem by
Enoch O'Gillan, of which the following are the first two stanzas:

> Ciaran's city is Cluain-mic-Nois,
> A place dew-bright, red-rosed.
> Of a race of Chiefs whose fame is lasting,
> [Are] hosts under the peaceful clear-streamed place.
>
> Nobles of the Children of Conn
> Are under the flaggy brown-sloped cemetery;
> A knot (*snaidm*) or branch (*craobh*) over each body,
> And a seemly, correct Ogam name.
>
> (*Christian Inscriptions in the Irish Language*, chiefly collected and
> drawn by George Petrie, LLD, and edited by M. Stokes, p. 8)

It appears, then, that Christian chieftains were buried at Clonmacnoise with Ogam names inscribed on their monuments. Only one Ogam inscription has been found there, so far as I know. It bears the name of COLMAN in letters of the ordinary kind, followed by the epithet *bocht*, written in Ogam characters, from right to left. This single word, meaning poor or needy, and written in a form which was doubly cryptic, seems to have been intended to express disparagement.

An instance in which Ogam is said to have been used for the purpose of conveying information occurs in a poem by Oisin, in which he relates a tale of his father Finn. Finn happening to be with a party of his Fiann on Slieve Crot, in Munster, a noble youth, accompanied by a beautiful lady, came into his presence, and announced that he had travelled from Norway and Lochlann, but had met no man able to beat him at chess. Finn accepted his challenge, and the stranger staked his wife against fifteen of the Fenian women who were present. The stranger won the game, and immediately disappeared, enveloping himself and the sixteen women in a magical mist. Finn resolved to follow him to Norway, but desiring to let his followers know whither he had gone, he cuts an Ogam

> A pillar stone there was on the rugged hill,
> Whither the hosts were wont to come –
> Finn knotted an Ogam in its edge,
> That no man should be ignorant.
>
> A year were they (the Fiann) without tidings of their king,
> All that time they were distressed,
> Until they came to Dun Crot,
> When they had left Finn of the keen blade.
>
> Mac Lugach found in the pillar stone
> An Ogam which he understood,
> That Finn had gone in search of his women
> Unto Eoghan, the King of Lochlann.

> (Hodges & Smith MSS, RIA, p. 444)

If the writing had been intelligible to everyone, there would have been no reason to mention that it had been found *and understood* by Mac Lugach.

In *Cormac's Glossary*, under the heading ORC TRÉITH, a strange story is told of Finn and his fool Lomna. The fool having discovered that his master had been dishonoured during his absence from home, and not choosing to be concerned either in betraying him, or in directly accusing the guilty person, cut an Ogam on a four-square rod, so as to communicate his discovery to Finn as soon as he returned. Finn, understanding the Ogam, manifested his displeasure in such a way that the woman who had wronged him became aware that Lomna had divulged her secret. She quickly avenged herself by procuring the murder of the fool; and the story goes on to record a conversation between the woman's paramour and the decapitated head of the fool, whom he had slain (*Cormac's Glossary*, edited by Whitley Stokes, LLD, p. 130).

The secret nature of the Ogam character could not be more plainly indicated than it is in this passage.

Corc, son of Lugaidh, King of Munster, was banished by his father, and fled to Scotland about the year 600. There his person and rank were recognized by Gruibne, the Druid and Poet of Feradach, King of Scotland. The Druid, observing an Ogam in the shield of the prince, by whom his life had formerly been saved in Ireland, asks him, 'Who hath supplied thee with the Ogam which is in thy shield? It is not luck he hath brought thee.' 'What is in it?' said Corc. 'This is what is in it,' answered the Druid: 'If thou come to Feradach by day, that thy head be off before evening; if by night, that it be off before morning.' (*Book of Leinster*.)

Observe that the prince cannot read the Ogam on his own shield. But the Druid is able to decipher it. This story reminds us of the οηματα λυγρα, (sealed letter) which Bellerophontes carried with him to Lycia, unconscious of their fatal import. Note, too, that in the *Edda*, mention is made of Runes on shields (*Edda Rythmica*, Brynhildar-Quida, I, Stroph. xv). Corc's shield was probably made of alder wood.

The following is the only passage in which I have read of an Ogam cut upon iron:

They went forward to the Dun; and the youth (Cuchulainn) alighted from the chariot in the green. The green of the Dun was on this wise. There was a pillar-stone upon it, and an iron ring round the pillar; and this was a ring of championship; and there was an Ogam name in the *menuc*[?], and this was the name that was in it: 'Whoever comes on the green, if he be a champion, he is enjoined not to depart from the green without giving challenge to single combat.' The little boy (*an Mac Beg*) read the name, and he put his two hands to the pillar-stone as it stood with its ring, and cast it into the pool, and the water closed over it. (*Book of Leinster*)

Cuchulainn, instructed in all military exercises and accomplishments, is able to read the Ogam. It was only addressed to persons of his class – to knights.

Keating says that one of the conditions which each warrior was obliged to fulfil previous to his admission into the ranks of the Fiann was as follows: No man could be admitted into the Fiann until he had become a bard, and had mastered the twelve books of Poetry.

In the Táin Bo Cuailgne we meet with curious instances of the use of Ogam, which I give at length, in order that the reader may see the reasonableness of the inference which I draw from them:

> Cuchulainn, the great hero of this war, coming to a certain pil-lar-stone, at a place called Irard Cuillenn, makes a ring out of a rod, writes an Ogam in it, and then throws it over the pillar, so as to encircle it. The invading army, led by Fergus Mac Roich, coming up to the place, the ring is found by their scouts, Err and Inell, with Foich and Fochlam, their two charioteers. These were the four sons of Irard mac Anchinne, who always went in advance of the host to save their brooches and garments from the splashing of the mire and the dust raised by the troops in their march. Finding the ring which Cuchulainn had cast, they gave it into the hand of Fergus, who read the Ogam which was in it. 'For what wait you here?' said Queen Maeve, coming up. 'We halt,' said Fergus, 'because of this ring. There is an Ogam in its *menuc*, and this is what it signifies: Go no further till a man is found who with one hand will cast a ring like this, made of a single rod; and let my master Fergus answer.' 'It is true,' said Fergus, 'it was Cuchulainn who cast the ring; and it was by his horses the plain was so closely grazed. Then he gave the ring into the hand of the Druid, and spake the following poem . . .'
>
> (*Leabhar na h-Uidhre*, p. 57)

In this passage the occult nature of the Ogam is plainly indicated. The scouts could not read it. They were obliged to bring it to Fergus, who possessed all the attainments of an accomplished knight, in order that he might decipher it. This is made more evident in the later and more developed version of the story, as we find it in the *Book of Leinster*, pp. 59 and 60:

> And Ailell (the king) took the ring into his hand, and put it into the hand of Fergus, and Fergus read the Ogam name that was in

the *menuc* of the wood; and declared to the men of Erinn what was signified by the Ogam name which was in the *menuc*. So he began to tell it; and he spake this poem:

A ring here, what doth it declare unto us?
A ring: what doth its *mystery* conceal?
And what number of persons placed it here?
Were they few or were they many?

If ye should march past this to-night,
And not remain here in encampment,
The Hound of all terrors will surely visit
On you your contempt and dishonour of him.

It will bring evil on the hosts
If they pursue their march beyond this.
Discover now, O Druids!
Why this ring was made.

[*Answer of the Druids.*]

He disables champions, the champion who placed it.
Utter discomfiture he brings on heroes.
To check [the advance of] the chiefs of men assembled,
One man placed it with his one hand.

'Tis the work of a man whose anger was roused,
The hound of the South in the Creeve Roe.
'Tis the knot (*snaidm*) of a champion, not the tie of a fool;
'Tis his name that is in the ring.

To inflict the calamity of hundreds of combats
Upon the four provinces of Erin,
Unless it be for this, I know not
Why this ring was made.

After the delivery of that poem, 'By my word,' said Fergus, 'if ye disregard that ring, and the royal champion who made it, without making a night's enclosure and encampment here, unless a man amongst you shall make a ring like this, [standing?] on one foot, and with one hand and one eye, like as he has done, whether ye be laid under the earth or in a fortress, he will inflict wounds and death on you before it is time to rise to-morrow.'

The following passage is taken from the *Book of Leinster*. The corresponding portion of the text is found in the *Leabhar na h-Uidhre*, page 58:

And he came to the lake of a great wood by Cnoghba-of-the-Kings, on the north, which is now called Ath n-Gabhla. Then Cuchulainn went into the wood, and alighted from his chariot, and cut down a fork with four prongs, root and branch, at a single stroke. He shaped and fashioned [?squared] it, and put an Ogam name upon its *menuc*, and he threw it with an unerring cast, from the hinder part of his chariot, from the tips of his fingers, so that two-thirds of it went into the ground, and only one-third remained above. It was then that the two [four] guides above-mentioned, viz., the two [four] sons of Tocan came up to him whilst thus employed; and they strove which should be the first to wound and behead him. But Cuchulainn turned upon them, and cut off their four heads on the instant, and he fixed the head of each man on one of the prongs of the fork. And Cuchulainn sent the horses of that party back the same way to meet the men of Erin, with their reins loose; with the gory trunks, and the bodies of the warriors dropping blood on the frames of the chariots: because he thought it not honourable or becoming him to take the horses, or clothes, or arms of the men that were slain. Then the hosts beheld the horses of the party who had been in advance of them, and the headless bodies of the warriors dropping down blood copiously on the frames of the chariots. The van of the host halted for the rere to come up; and they all raised loud cries, and clashed their arms. . . . 'What have we here?' said Maeve. 'We will tell,' said they. 'The horses of the party who always went before us are there, and their headless bodies in their chariots.' Then they held a council, and they concluded that these were the tracks of an army, and the contact of a great host; and that it was the Ultonians that had come. And the counsel they found was to send Cormac Connlonges mac Concobar to discover who it was that was in the ford. Because if it were the Ultonians that were there, they would not kill the son of their own lawful king. Then Cormac went forth; and the number of the company that he took was three thousand armed men, to find out who was in the ford. And when he came thither, he saw nothing but the fork in the middle of the ford, with four heads on it dropping their blood copiously down, the body of the fork [fixed] in the stream, the foot-prints of two steeds, the track of a single chariot, and the trace of a single champion going out of the ford eastwards. The nobles of Erin came to the ford, and they all began to view the fork. It was a matter of surprise and wonder to them who it might be that had set up the trophy. 'What was the name of this ford hitherto with you [Ultonians], Fergus?' said Ailell. '*Ath n-Grena* (Ford of the Sun),' said Fergus; 'and *Ath n-Gabhla* (Ford of the Fork) shall be its name henceforth for ever, because of this fork and this deed,' said Fergus. And he spake this poem:

> *Ath-Grena* will now change its name,
> By the deed of the hound [Cu-chulainn] red and furious;
> Here is a fork of four prongs,
> Which is a hindrance to the men of Erin.

> On two of the prongs are signs of valour,
> The head of Faech and the head of Fochnain;
> On the other two prongs are
> The head of Eire and the head of Innill.

> What Ogam is this in its *menuc*?
> Tell us, O ye Druids most learned.
> And who was it that hath marked it in it?
> What number helped to plant it?

> [*Answer of the Druids.*]

> Yonder fork of terrible import
> Which thou seest there, O Fergus,
> Was cut by one man, whom thou didst once love,
> At a single sweeping stroke of his sword.

> He fashioned and brought it on his back.
> Even this was no trifling achievement.
> And he planted it down there,
> That one of you might pluck it up from the earth.

> *Ath n-Grena* was its only name until now;
> Well is it remembered by your people;
> *Ath n-Gabhla* shall be its name evermore,
> From this fork which you see in the ford.

(*Book of Leinster*, pp. 59–60)

The Ogam seems to have intimated that it was Cuchulainn who had
killed the scouts and set up the trophy as a challenge to the enemy,
defying any single man amongst them to pluck up the stake which he
had planted with one hand. From the first stanza of the poem, it
appears that Fergus understood the Ogam, which was unintelligible to
the rest of the host. He had been Cuchulainn's friend, and master: and
possessed all knightly accomplishments. But he refers to the Druids to
confirm his interpretation.

This is not the only instance where Cuchulainn gives a notice or
challenge to his enemies by means of an Ogam. At Magh Mucceda he
cuts down an oak, and writes an Ogam on its side, and this is what
was on it when found by Ailill's host: 'Whoever passes this shall be
slain by a hero of one chariot.' (*Leabhar na h-Uidhre*, p. 63)

Cuchulainn knew that in the host of Ailill and Maeve there were
men who could read Ogam – Fergus Mac Roich and the Druids, if not
others.

If the Ogam was a cryptic mode of writing, we might expect to
find it employed in divination. I am able to give instances of this kind
from tales which are certainly as ancient as others from which I have
quoted:

Eochaidh Airem, according to the Irish Annalists, monarch of
Ireland about one hundred years BC, was visited at Temar by a
youthful stranger, who announced himself as Midir of Bri Leith.
Bri Leith was a famous fairy hill and mansion in the County of
Westmeath, in which dwelt Midir, a hero renowned for his gal-
lantry. The king inquired of him his business. Midir answered
that he came to play a game of chess with the king. The king
consented. Midir won the game, and as winner of the stakes
claimed permission to embrace the Queen Etain. The king was
compelled to consent, else he would have been branded with
falsehood, which was in those days the greatest dishonour that
could be laid to the charge of a king. Then Midir threw his arms
around the queen, and flew with her out of the palace, no one
could tell whither. After some time had gone by, Eochaidh sent
his Druid Dallan to search for Etain . . . That day he travelled
westwards until he reached the mountain which is called Slieve
Dallan; and he abode there for the night. Then the Druid was
grieved that Etain should remain concealed from him for a whole
year; and he made four wands of yew, and wrote an Ogam on
them; and it was revealed to him, through his keys of poetic

knowledge, and through his Ogam, that Etain was in the fairy mansion of Bri Leith, whither she had been carried by Midir.

This extract was made for me by Professor O'Curry, from a tale entitled 'Tocmarc Etaine' 'The Courtship of Etain' preserved in one of the MSS which formerly belonged to Mr Monck Mason, written about the year 1450. There are fragments of the beginning and end of the same tract in Leabhar na h-Uidhre; but this part has not been preserved in that MS. Copies of this tale are also to be found in the Yellow Book of Lecain, and in the MS H. 1. 13. The Courtship of Etain is named in the Book of Leinster as one of the principal tales which a duly qualified poet was bound to know, and be able to recite to kings and chiefs (O'Curry's Lectures on the MS Materials of Ancient Irish History, p. 584).'

Another example of the use of Ogam for the purposes of divination occurs in an ancient tale entitled 'The Exile of the Sons of Duil Dermait'.

In this tale we are told that three personages mentioned in it disappeared mysteriously, and that Cuchulainn was enjoined to discover them. It is stated that he accordingly went from the palace of Emania to his own town of Dun-Dealgan (or Dundalk), and that, while taking counsel with himself there, he observed a boat coming to land in the harbour. This boat, it seems, contained the son of the King of Albain (Scotland), and a party who came with presents of purple, and silks, and drinking cups for King Conor Mac Nessa. Cuchulainn, however, being at the moment in an angry mood, entered the boat, and slew all the crew, till he came to the prince himself. The tale then proceeds:

'Grant me life for life, O Cuchulainn! Thou dost not know me,' said the prince. 'Knowest thou what carried the three sons of Duil Dermait out of their country?' said Cuchulainn. 'I know not,' said the youth; 'but I have a sea-charm, and I will set it for thee, and thou shalt have the boat, and thou shalt not act in ignorance by it.' Cuchulainn then handed him his little spear, and the prince inscribed an Ogam in it.

Cuchulainn then, according to the story, went out to sea, and his talisman directed him unerringly to the island, where the objects of his search were detained.

The following passage, taken from Cormac's Glossary, is perhaps the most curious and important of all those in which allusion is made to the use of Ogam by ancient Irish writers:

Fé, then, is a wand of aspen, and gloomy the thing which served with the Gaels for measuring bodies and graves; and this wand was always in the cemeteries of the heathen, and it was a horror to every one to take it in his hand, and everything that was odious to them they marked on it in Ogam.

> Sorrowful to me to be in life
> After the King of the Gaels and Galls.
> Dim is my eye, wasted my flesh,
> Since the *fé* was measured on Flann.

Also, a rod of aspen was used by the Gaels for the measuring of the bodies, and the graves in which they were interred; and this wand was always in the cemeteries of the heathen, and it was a horror to every one taking it in his hand; and everything that was odious with the men was struck with it, as the proverb says: *fé fris* 'a fé to it'! for the wand of aspen is odious. Therefore, says Morann, in the *Briathar Ogam, aercaid fid edath, i.e.*, the reproach which attached to the rod whose name is *fé*.

The whole passage connects the use of the Fé with notions of superstition, and carries us back to times when Paganism still subsisted in Ireland. The wand was kept by the Gaels in the cemeteries of the heathen. It was in every way odious. It was made of aspen, an unlucky tree. It was used for a gloomy purpose, to measure corpses and graves. And it had symbols of what was hateful cut upon it. It seems, too, that a baleful charm was supposed to have been wrought by striking with it whatever was itself an object of detestation. What M'Curtin says of the Ogam craobh in general helps us in some degree towards the explanation of all this:

> The Irish antiquaries have preserved this Ogam in particular as a piece of the greatest value in all their antiquity, and it was penal for any but those that were sworn antiquaries either to study or use the same. For in these characters those sworn antiquaries wrote all the evil actions and other vicious practices of their monarchs and great personages, both male and female, that it should not be known to any but to themselves and their successors, being sworn antiquaries as aforesaid. *(Treatise on the Irish Grammar at the end of M'Curtin's English-Irish Dictionary. Paris, 1732.)*

The practice of striking with an Ogam-marked rod is mentioned in a medical MS of the date 1509, in the Library of the Royal Irish

Academy. As a cure for a man rendered impotent by charms, it is there recommended to write the man's name in Ogam on an elm wand, and to strike the man with it.

As regards the stanza in which reference is made to the death of Flann, it must be observed that it cannot have been introduced by Cormac Mac Cullinan himself. The Flann here mentioned can hardly have been any one else but Flann Sinna, King of Ireland, who died of the plague in the year 914, eleven years after the death of Cormac. The poem must have been interpolated by a subsequent editor of the *Glossary*, and this is not improbable. A collation of the MSS of *Cormac's Glossary* has shown that considerable additions have been made to it by later hands; and further, the interpolator could hardly have been a friend or follower of Cormac, who was killed in battle, fighting against Flann Sinna. The words which state that the wand was odious, as being made of aspen, refer to a phrase in one of the verbal Ogams contained in the *Ogam Tract*. As the Fé, said to have been kept in the cemeteries of the heathen, was used to measure the body of Flann, who was a Christian, we are left to infer that an old Pagan custom had been transmitted from ancient to modern times.

It may be worth our while to consider whether the Fé has any relation to the Scotch *Fey*, or the Icelandic *feigr*. But I abstain here from etymological speculations.

These are our testimonies. But before we draw conclusions from them we are bound to consider the circumstances which determine their weight. Many of these pieces are found in MSS dating from the eleventh and twelfth centuries, and there is reason to believe that the substance of them was more ancient, even by hundreds of years. Still there remains a question as to the credibility in matters of detail of stories professing to record events which are referred to the third century, or even to the commencement of the Christian era, when we find that these tales are full, not only of exaggeration, but of manifest fiction, and are written in a turgid style, which distinguishes them from historical narrations. Though Professor O'Curry assigned a high, perhaps the highest, place in the list of our ancient Irish historical tales to the *Tain bo Cuailgne*, from which I have made so many extracts, I confess that I find it difficult to give it the praise which it has received as a great prose Epic, or as a piece the main statements of which respecting matters of fact are substantially true. I fancy that I see in it traces of comparatively modern thought; and am rather inclined to concur in the judgment pronounced by the learned scribe who copied it into the

Book of Leinster in the twelfth century, and perhaps expended on it some editorial care. The following is the colophon which he append-ed to his transcript of the *Tain*: 'A blessing on every one who shall faithfully study the *Tain* as it is here, and who shall not add to it in any other shape . . .'

Nevertheless, even admitting that the element of fiction abounds in the tales from which our quotations have been taken, their concurrent witness sufficiently proves the existence in the minds of their authors of a belief that the Ogam was in use in times long anterior to their own; that it was a cryptic character; and that there was something peculiar in the form of the Ogam names inscribed on sepulchral mon-uments.

The first twenty characters of the Ogam craobh are peculiarly well suited for cutting on wood; whether on the edge of a square stave, or on a round rod; seeing that all the strokes are rectilinear, and admit of being cut either exactly at right angles with the grain, or obliquely across it. The same may be said of the first, second, and fourth of the *forfedha*, or diphthong symbols. Anyone who tries will find that if a stroke coincides in direction with the grain, it will not be easy to make it with a clean ending, and of the proper length. Such a stroke will require an additional cut at the end to finish it.

That the Ogam craobh was first used in this way before it was employed in inscriptions on stone is extremely probable. According to the apocryphal account given in the Ogam Tract, the first Ogam was cut upon a birch wand: and the passages which I have quoted from ancient Irish romantic tales indicate that the practice of cutting these characters on wood was common. The testimony of Martianus Capella, 'Barbarians carve runes on tablets of ashwood', proves that Runes were cut upon planed ashen tablets in the fifth century. The practice may therefore have been considerably older. And Saxo Grammaticus speaks of letters graven on wood as having been formerly recorded upon paper. Now the Ogam character is at least as well suited for this purpose as the Rune. It is simpler than the Twig-rune, and looks like an improvement upon it, after passing through the intermediate and imperfect state in which it appears in the first Beithluisnin. First came the Twig-rune, with its upright stem and side branches inclined at an acute angle to the stem; or, perhaps, the Hahel-run, described in the Alcuin MS. These, according to my view, suggested the primitive Ogam with its upright stem, and its branch-strokes meeting the stem obliquely or at right angles; and from this finally the transition was easy to the perfect Ogam craobh. All that was necessary was to sub-stitute a single stem-line, or the edge of a squared stave, for the straight line formed by placing the stem-strokes of the rune-like Ogams so as to be continuous.

Let us next consider what was actually written in Ogam upon wood. Was it only a name, or a sentence of a few words? or was it something more, as Professor O'Curry and others have asserted? He held the belief 'that the pre-Christian Gaedhils possessed and practised a system of writing and keeping records quite different from and inde-pendent of both the Greek and the Roman form and characters.' He maintained, in fact, that the Ogam character was *employed to record his-torical events and even sustained historical or romantic tales* among the Gaedhils, long before the supposed introduction of the Roman letter, about the time at which the Gospel of Christ was brought among them by lettered scholars of Continental education. And in support of this hypothesis he endeavoured to show that histories and tales were inscribed in Ogam on staves or wooden tables. If he could have adduced satisfactory proof of this, it is not likely that he would have attached much importance to the testimony of the following romance, on which he has commented at length in his lectures:

> About the commencement of the first century of our era, two lovers, Baile mac Buain, an Ulster chieftain, and Ailinn, a Leinster Princess, died suddenly of grief; each having been deceived by false tidings of the other's death. Out of the grave of Baile a yew tree presently sprang up; and from the grave of his beloved Ailinn, an apple tree. In seven years, the two trees grew large, with leafy heads bearing a resemblance to the two lovers whose graves they over-shadowed. They were then cut down by the poets, and each was made into a tablet (*tabhall filedh*). In one were written the Visions, and the Espousals, and the Loves, and the Courtships of Ulster: in the other the tales of like import relating to the kingdom of Leinster. In the time of Art, King of Ireland, that is, about a hundred and fifty years afterwards, these tablets, being brought face to face, flew towards each other of their own accord, and became joined so firmly that they could not be separated. They were thenceforth preserved amongst the precious things kept in the treasury at Tara, till the palace was burned in the year 241.

The reader will smile at finding an argument respecting the use of letters in Ireland some eighteen or nineteen hundred years ago founded in all seriousness on this romantic tale. The writer of it had probably read the story of Daphne in Ovid's *Metamorphoses*, and that of Polydorus in the *Aeneid*; and was thinking of the waxed *tabulae*, commonly used during the Middle Ages, as well as in the time of ancient Rome. The reader may see in the Museum of the Royal Irish Academy one of these tablets, still preserving some legible characters; and will be interested in reading Dr Todd's description of it, printed in the 'Transactions' of that Society. I suspect that the *taibhli filedh*, so often mentioned by Irish writers, were nothing more than tables of this kind. But there may have been something peculiar in their formation, as we find the following entry in a Catalogue of the contents of the library of St Gall: 'Six wooden staves covered with wax (once handbooks of Irish sayings) which retain full accounts.' Who could imagine all the love stories of two kingdoms scored in Ogam on the edges of staves? Cartloads of timber would not have sufficed for the purpose. Even Professor O'Curry seems to have been prepared for the incredulity of persons who, like myself, will say that the letters inscribed on these mystic tablets 'could not well have been Ogam' (O'Curry's Lectures on the MS Materials of Ancient Irish History, p. 466). The external evidence bearing on this question is as follows: The tale of Baile and Ailinn is found in a MS written about the year 1511. I am not aware that any other copy of it exists. And allusions to the yew of Baile and the apple-tree of Ailinn are contained in two poems in the *Book of Leinster* (written about AD 1130). One of these is ascribed to Ailbhe, daughter of Cormac mac Art, who must have lived in the middle of the third century. The other poem is attributed to Flann mac Lonan, chief poet of Ireland, who died AD 918. But the poems do not mention the *taibhli* (tablets): so that we have no evidence confirming that part of the story as it is told in a MS of the sixteenth century. This is not a sufficient foundation on which to rest an argument respecting the use of letters or Ogam in Ireland fifteen hundred years before. The romance of Baile and Ailinn may be an ancient one; but we cannot trust to it as supplying 'evidence of the existence in Art's time of what was then believed to have been a very ancient book, and, of course, of the existence in and before Art's time, at least, of letters among the Pagan Gaedhils.' Still less can we accept it as proving that wooden *tabulae* existed at that period filled with long tales written in Ogam. Professor O'Curry indeed believed that the *taibhli filedh* (poet's tablets) were made of long flat pieces of wood which folded up like the parts of a fan, so as to form a substantial staff, and actually served as such. Here is what he says: 'In a very ancient article in the Brehon Laws, which prescribes the sort of weapon of defence which the different classes of society were allowed to carry on ordinary occasions to defend themselves against dogs, etc., in their usual walks, a passage occurs which throws some light on this subject. The article belongs to the Christian times, I should tell you, in its present form, as it prescribes a slender lath, or a graceful crook, for a priest, while it assigns to the poet a *Tabhall-lorg*, or tablet staff, in accordance with the privileges of his order, etc.' Professor O'Curry goes on to state that *Tabhall-lorg* is only a modernised or Latin-Gaedhelic form of *tamh-lorg* (a headless staff), and quotes a passage from the *Agallamh na Seanórach* in support of his views. 'Where are the seniors and Antiquaries of Erin? Let this be written in *Tamhlorgaibh Filcadh* (headless staves of Poets), and after the manner of professors, and in the language of the *Ollamh*; so that every one may take his copy (or share) with him to his own territory and land of all the knowledge, and all the history, and all the topography, and all the deeds of bravery and valour that Caeilté and Oisín have related. *And it was done accordingly.*'

I confess I do not believe that each of the Antiquaries of Erin was able to carry away all this learning in his walking-stick. And I am equally sceptical as to Professor O'Curry's etymology. I say this although I am aware that waxed tablets such as the Romans used might have been large enough to contain a considerable amount of writing. Dr Todd has reminded us that in degenerate days, when a wholesome discipline was no longer kept up in schools, a pupil under seven years old would not hesitate to break the master's head with his writing table, if a hand was laid upon him.

It may be rash to deny that the *tabhall-lorg* was something different from the *tabhall filedh*. But we must be slow to admit that long histories were written in Ogam characters on either one or the other. We have no trustworthy evidence of it.

If we may believe the testimony of one of the ancient writers who compiled the Acts of St Patrick preserved in the *Book of Armagh*, wooden staves, bearing characters upon them, were in use in Ireland in the fifth century.

'Patrick came from the field of Arthice to Drummut Cerigi, and to Nainnu Toisciart and Ailech Esrachtai; and he saw among them eight to nine men carrying tablets, written in the manner of Moses' tablets (i.e. engraved). (*Book of Armagh*, trans. C. and J. Matthews).

Now it will be observed that the persons who bore these staves were Christian followers of St Patrick, who came to Ireland attended by men of different nations – Romans, Britons, Gauls, and Lombards. And there is nothing in the narrative to indicate that the use of such staves on this occasion was uncommon. On the other hand, the natives in whose minds they created alarm were pagans, who would have expressed neither fear nor surprise if inscribed staves of this kind were in use amongst themselves. This is a testimony of great antiquity – the very MS in which we find it was written in the year 807; and the fragmentary notices from which the passage is taken were collected by three persons of whom the latest died about the middle of the eighth century. Unless we pronounce the whole story to be a fabrication, we must accept it as an authority to prove that in the middle of the fifth century wooden staves, in form not unlike the short straight swords of the Irish, were used for writing on. And further, it indicates that the practice was brought into the country by Christian missionaries from other lands . . .

In pagan times, the Druids combined in their own persons all the functions of priests, philosophers, and poets, and therefore held in the State a place with which great power and important privileges were connected. But it seems probable that when Christianity was established in Ireland the Druids were conciliated, or at least their opposition was neutralised, by giving to their order an establishment similar to, and co-ordinate with, that which was provided for the ministers of the Christian Church. Pagan rites were suppressed; religious functions were committed to the Christian ecclesiastics; and the duties of exercising judicature, promoting letters, and keeping the public records, was entrusted to the order of poets. In process of time, the parallelism between the two hierarchies became complete. As the Medieval Church had its seven orders, so there were seven grades of poets – The Ollamh, the Anrath, the Cli, the Cana, the Dos, the Mac Fuirmidh, and the Fochlach. And the laws prescribed the course of study which they were required to master.

The learned have divided the Gaedhelic writings into four classes, and these are their names:

I. Senchus Mor, and Breatha Nemeadh, Ai Chearmna, and Ai Chana form the first: and CANOIN is the name of this division, because of the greatness of the knowledge and explanations these writings contain.

II. The thrice fifty Ogams, and the *Remenda*, i.e., *Rem nena*, and the Duile Feadha, and what appertains to them, constitute the second division. GRAMIDACH is its name, because of the greatness of its good knowledge: for correct speech is a search for knowledge.

III. The Feasts, and the Reliefs, and the Destructions, and the thrice thirty Tales, and the three score subordinate Tales, together with what appertains to them, constitute the third division, which is called STAIR, because narratives and acts are related in it.

IV. Bretha Cai (the judgments of Cai), with their supplements form the fourth division; and RIM (Enumeration) is its name. (*Book of Lecan*)

An acquaintance with the whole of this extensive course of study was required from the Ollamh; and we learn from a tract on the names, qualifications, and privileges of the seven degrees of poets that the Fochlach, a member of the seventh or lowest order, 'learned in the first year fifty Ogams, and *Uraicept na h-Eicsin*, with its preface and its *Remenda*, and ten *Dreachts*, and six *Dians*, thirty Tales, etc.

Thus we have traced the Ogam into the possession of the literary class, as a branch of the learning which they were legally bound to profess. So far then we have verified the statement quoted above from M'Curtin. And when we remember how many proofs these poets gave of their preference for what was obscure and occult, it seems quite credible that they used the Ogam for cryptic purposes. The *Disputation of the two Sages* furnishes a notable example of their desire to keep to themselves a monopoly of their learning, such as it was.

More and more obscure to the people were the words in which these two Filés discussed and decided their dispute, nor could the kings or the other Filés understand them. Conor and the other princes at that time present at Emania said that the disputation and decision could be understood only by the two parties themselves, for that they did not understand them. (*Book of Ballymote*)

The poets are said to have been deprived on that occasion of functions which they had previously possessed; and the commentator on the Senchus Mor tells us that, in the revision of the laws effected in the time of St Patrick their functions were again limited and defined.

Patrick abolished these three things among the poets when they believed, as they were profane rites, for the Teinm Laegha and

Imbus Forosna could not be performed by them without offering to idol gods. He did not leave them after this any rite in
which offering should be made to the devil, for their profession
was pure. And he left them after this extemporaneous recital,
because it was acquired through great knowledge and application; and [also the registering of] the genealogies of the men of
Erin, and the technical rules of poetry, and the Duili Sloinnte,
and Duili Fedha, and storytelling with lays.   (*Senchus Mor*, vol. i.,
p. 45)

The Fedha here mentioned were the Beithluisnin; and the Duili Fedha
seem to have been a portion of the Uraicept, or some other treatise
on Ogam.

The *Book of Leinster*, written about the year 1130, contains a short
paragraph, in which is given a complete Beithluisnin, including the
Forfedha, together with rules as to the use of the latter characters in
words containing diphthongs and triphthongs. This passage has little
interest beyond what is connected with the fact that it is the most
ancient manuscript authority which has come down to us on the subject of Ogamic orthography. The Ogam marginal notes in the *St Gall
Priscian* were written, as I think I have proved *(Proceedings of the Royal
Irish Academy*, vol. vi., p. 199), in the year 874. But there is at the end
of the Gospel of St John, in one of the Stowe MSS, a single word in
Ogam, which I read as DINOS, and which, I suspect, is the *Ogam name*
of the scribe Dimma Macc Nathi, who wrote the copy of the Gospels
in the Trin. Coll. Dublin MSS, known as the *Book of Dimma*. This signature of DINOS is by far the oldest specimen of manuscript Ogam
which is known to exist, if we are right in believing that the *Book of
Dimma* was written for St Cronan of Roscrea, who died in the year
620; and that if DINOS is not the Ogamic equivalent of Dimma, the
two MSS were written about the same time, as the handwritings seem
to prove . . .

The writer was a peccator, guilty of some crime for which he was
doing penance in a pilgrimage, and this may have been the reason why
his signature is presented under the double veil of a backward-written
Ogam. It is true that scribes delighted to show their learning by writing colophons in Greek, Runic, and other characters differing from
those used in the transcript which they made. But it must be admitted the explanation first offered is by no means an improbable one.

In what precedes I think I have succeeded in showing from ancient
Irish documents, that the Ogam was regarded by their authors as a

cryptic character, the art of reading and writing which was an acquirement confined to persons who possessed peculiar qualifications, personal or professional, such as accomplished knights or men of learning. I argue, moreover, that its alleged use for the superstitious purposes of divination and incantation is in accordance with the notion that it was something occult and mysterious. And I have adduced reasons for the belief that the *Ogam names* inscribed on monuments were different in form from the ordinary names of the persons commemorated. In executing my task I have fairly set before the reader the passages which appeared to me to contain statements or allusions tending to elucidate the subject which I had in hand. I have left a few unnoticed, which were identical in substance with others which I have quoted; but I have kept back nothing that was doubtful or at variance with my own views. In dealing with the Irish texts, I have used translations made for me five and twenty years ago by Professor O'Curry. As he knew my opinion with respect to the antiquity of the Ogam to be different from his own, he would not have failed to confront me with facts and testimonies overthrowing my theories, had he been himself possessed of any such materials. If an examination of our manuscripts or monuments should open up fresh sources of information, I shall welcome the discoveries which scholars may thus be enabled to make, whether they are consistent with or opposed to the conclusions put forward in this Paper. I do not expect to find that we have Ogam monuments belonging to the centuries BC. But I am sanguine enough to believe that the deciphering of our Ogam inscriptions will furnish results of considerable importance, confirming portions of our history which have hitherto remained without that kind of attestation which is supplied by monuments and coins.

The Ogam Tract[2]

What are the place, time, person, and cause of the invention of the Ogham (Ogam)? Not hard. Its place the island of Ireland where we Irish live. In the time of Bres son of Elatha king of Ireland it was invented. Its person Ogma son of Elatha son of Delbaeth brother to Bres, for Bres, Ogma and Delbaeth are the three sons of Elatha son of Delbaeth there. Now Ogma, a man well skilled in speech and in poetry, invented the Ogham. The cause of its invention, as a proof of his ingenuity, and that this speech should belong to the learned apart, to the exclusion of rustics and herdsmen. Whence the Ogham got its name according to sound and matter, who are the father and the mother of the Ogham, what is the first name that was written by Ogham, in what letter it was written, and why b precedes every letter.

Ogham from Ogma was first invented in respect to its sound according to matter, however, *ogum* is *og-uaim*, perfect alliteration, which the poets applied to poetry by means of it, for by letters Gaelic is measured by the poets; the father of Ogham is Ogma, the mother of Ogham is the hand or knife of Ogma.

This moreover is the first thing that was written by Ogham, ⊐‖‖‖ ‖‖ , *i.e.* (the birch) b was written, and to convey a warning to Lug son of Ethliu it was written respecting his wife lest she should be carried away from him into faeryland, to wit, seven b's in one switch of birch: Thy wife will be seven times carried away from thee into faeryland or into another country, unless birch guard her. On that account, moreover, b, birch, takes precedence, for it is in birch that Ogham was first written.

How many divisions of Ogham are there, and what are they? Not hard. Four: b five, h five, m five, a five, besides diphthongs.

How many groups of Ogham? Not hard. Three, viz., eight chieftain trees, eight peasant trees, and eight shrub trees. Eight chieftain trees first: alder, oak, hazel, vine, ivy, sloe, furze, heath. Eight peasant trees, viz., birch, quicken tree, willow, ash, whitethorn, whin, apple tree. As to their letters all other shrubs are peasant trees.

Whence is the origin of the Ogham? Not hard. I shall speak firstly of the woods of the trees whence names have been put for the Ogham letters. Query, well then, whence are the Ogham vowels and consonants named? Not hard. It is from the school of Fenius Farsaidh, to wit, the school of poetry which Fenius sent throughout the world to learn the languages. There were five and twenty that were noblest of them so that it is their names that were put for the Bethe Luis Nin of the Ogham, both vowels and consonants; and there were four who were the noblest of these again, so that it is their names that were given to the seven principal vowels:

and they added other three to them so that from these are named the other three diphthongs, wherefore are classified apart. It is from the trees of the forest that names were given to the Ogham letters metaphorically. Moreover *beithe*, b, is from the birch of the forest for the first letter on the path of the Ogham alphabet. *Luis*, l, that is, elm in the forests. *Fern*, f, that is, alder in the forest. *Sail*, s, of the Ogham, that is, willow, again, in the forest. *Nin*, n, of the Ogham, to wit, maw of spear, or nettles in the woods. *Uath*, h, of the Ogham, that is, test-tree or whitethorn, on account of its thorniness. *Dur*, d, of the *Ogham* is oak, again, in the forest. *Tinne*, t, of the Ogham, holly or elderberry in the forest. *Coll*, c, of the Ogham, hazel in the forest. *Quert*, q, of the Ogham is holly in the forest, or quicken tree, or aspen. *Muin*, vine, m, mead [from it]. *Gort*, cornfield, g, fir. *Getal*, ng, broom. *Straif*, str, willowbrake in the forest. *Onn*, o, furze or ash. *Ur*, u, thorn. *Edad*, e, yew. *Ida*, i, service tree. *Ebad*, ea, elecampane. *Oir*, oi, spindle tree. *Uilleann*, ui, ivy. *Pin*, io, of the Ogham, pine, again, in the forest. Hence are named *caera pinne*, gooseberries; *ifin*, again is the name of that letter. *Emancoll*, witch hazel, ae, again, c doubled according to fact or according to form, c across c in its form.

Word Ogham of Morann Mac Main here. *Feocus foltchain*, faded trunk and fair hair, that is for birch, b, in the Word Ogham, because names which Morann gave of himself to the Ogham letters, these are they which take the effect of letters in the Word Ogham. *Feocus foltchain* for b, for these are two aspects of the birch, and it was hence put for the Ogham letter which has taken a name from it.

Lí súla, delight of eye, that is *luis*, quicken tree, l, to wit, the flame.

Airinach Fian, i.e., shield of warrior-bands, i.e., shield for *fern*, f, with him owing to their redness in the same respect: or because the alder, the material of the shield was from *fernae* given to the Ogham letter which has taken a name from it. *Airenach Fian*, i.e., shield, that is *fern*, f, with him.

Lí n-aimbí, hue of the lifeless, i.e., hue of one dead, to wit, *am* for denial, so that he is not living but is dead. *Lí n-aimbí*, again, to wit, that is *sail*, willow, s with him, and hence it was put for the Ogham letter.

Cosdad sida, checking of peace, that is *nin*, ash, n: it is the maw of a weaver's beam as applied to wood: a sign of peace is that. A checking of peace with him is that from the ash of the weaver's beam.

Conal cuan, pack of wolves, that is *uath*, thorn h, for a terror to any one is a pack of wolves. *Conal cuan* said of the Ogham h, owing to the affinity of the name, for they are a thorn, in the same way.

Ardam dossaibh, highest of bushes, that is *dur*, oak, d, with respect to its wood in the forest.

Trian, t, another thing the meaning of that to-day.

Cainin fedaib, fairest of trees, that is hazel, c, owing to its beauty in woods.

Clithar mbaiscaill, shelter of a hind, i.e., a fold: to wit, *boscell*, lunatic, that is *bas-ceall*, death sense, it is then his sense comes to him when he goes to his death. *Clithar boiscell*, again, that is an apple tree: or *boscell*, that is, hinds, to wit, they are light. *Clithar boiscell*, again, i.e., lunatics or hinds: *quert*, an apple tree, q, with reference to its letter.

Tresim fedma, strongest of effort, that is *muin*, vine, m, with him, i.e., owing to identity of name with *muin*, back of man or ox, for it is they that are the strongest in existence as regards effort.

Millsin feraib, sweeter than grasses, that is *gort*, ivy, g, with him owing to the identity of the name with the cornfield. When it is in the blade, sweeter than any grass is that grass, to wit, the cornfield. Hence for that letter in Ogham owing to the complete identity of the name between them.

Luth legha, a physician's strength; that is broom, ng, because it is strength with the physicians, and there is an affinity between *cath*, panacea (?), and *getal*, broom.

Tresim ruamna, strongest of red, that is str with him in Ogham. *Straif*, sloe, according to fact; for in the sloe red for dyeing the things is stronger, for it is it that makes the pale silver become azure, making it genuine (?) silver. It is it which is boiled through the urine into the white gold so as to make it red. *Tresim ruamna* is the sloe according to fact. Hence it was put in the letter named str, owing to identity of name between them, i.e., *straif* is the name of each of them.

Tinnem ruccae, intensest of blushes, that is *ruis*, elderberry, r, from the reddening or shame according to fact, for by r it is written, and it is a reddening that grows in a man's face through the juice of the herb being rubbed under it. *Tindi ruccae*, an ingot of a blush, again, said of the *ruis*, elder-berry, from shame or from reddening, for it is by r that it is itself written.

Ardam iachtadh, loudest of groanings, that is wondering, that is *ailm*, fir, a, with him; for it is *ailm* or a a man says while groaning in disease, or wondering, that is, marvelling at whatever circumstance.

Congnamaid echraide, helper of horses, the *onnaid* of the chariot, i.e. the wheels, that is *onn*, furze, with him, for it is by *onn*, o, that the wheels of the chariot are written. Also, *comguinidech*, equally wounding, i.e. whin. Hence it was put for that letter which is named *onn*, o, owing to identity between them, for *onn* is a name for each of them; and it is from whin that the name *onn* was put for the Ogham letter *o*.

Etiud midach, robe of physicians, *cath*, panacea (?). Hence it was put for *getal*, broom, ng.

Uaraib adbaib, in cold dwellings, that is *ur*, fresh, with him, for from *uir*, the mould of the earth is the name *uaraib adbaib*. Hence it was put for the letter named *ur*, heath, in Ogham, owing to identity of name between them, each of them is *ur*, and it is written by u.

Ergnaid fid, distinguished wood, that is aspen with him, for *ergnaid fid* is a name for the trembling tree. Hence it was put for the Ogham letter named *edad*, aspen, for hence was *edad*, e, put for it.

Siniu fedaib, oldest of woods, that is *idad*, yew, with him; for *siniu fedaib* is a name for service-tree. Hence it was given to that letter in Ogham named *idad*, yew, i, for hence the name *idad* was put for it; for *idad*, yew, is a name for *ibur*, service-tree.

Snamchain feda, most buoyant of wood, that is *ebad*, aspen, with him, for fair swimming is wood; that is a name for the great raven. Hence it was put for the letter named the Ogham *ebad*, for é is a name for salmon, and it is written by ea like the alphabet of the fauna: i.e., by stag (deer), eo by *eonasc* (ousel).

Sruitem aicdi, most venerable of structures, i.e., *oir*, oi, spindle tree, according to fact. Hence it was put for the letter owing to the identity of the name that is between them, to wit, *oir* is the name of each of them.

Tutmur fid uilleann, juicy wood is woodbine, that is woodbine with him, for it is a name for honeysuckle. Hence it was put for the Ogham named woodbine, ui; for hence was woodbine put for it, for it is a name for honeysuckle.

Millsem feda, sweetest of wood, that is gooseberry with him, for a name for the tree called *pin* is *milsem feda*. Gooseberries are hence named. Hence it was put for the letter named *pin*, for hence *pin,* or *ifin*, io, was put for it.

Luad soethaig, expression of a weary one, i.e., *ach, ah! uch,* alas! that is *emancoll*, ae, with him, for *emancoll* is taken for *ach*, though it may be taken for something else. *Finit* Word-Ogham of Morann.

Alphabet of word-oghams of Mac ind Óic here below.

Glaisium cnis, most silvery of the skin, that is the birch of the Ogham from birch of the forest, for hence birch, b, was put for it.

Cara ceathra, friend of cattle, elm. *Cara*, dear to the cattle is the elm for its bloom and for down. Hence it was put for the Ogham *luis*, quicken tree, l, for hence was quicken tree, l, put for it.

Comet lachta, guarding of milk, that is the Ogham alder, f, from alder of the forests, for it is it that guards the milk, for of it are made the vessels containing the milk.

Luth bech, activity of bees, that is willow, s, for its bloom and for its catkin. Hence it is put for the cognate Ogham letter.

Bag ban, fight of women, ash, n, of weaver's beam, i.e., maw of weaver's beam. Hence for its cognate letter.

Banadh gnuisi, blanching of face, fear, *huath*, h, for blanched is a man's face when he is encompassed with fear or terror. Hence for the Ogham letter owing to identity of name between the same two, *uath* stands for each of them.

Gres sair, carpenter's work, oak, d. Hence it was put for its cognate Ogham letter.

Smir guaili, fires of coal, that is holly. Hence for its cognate, Ogham letter, i.e., *tinne*, t, for *tindi* is a name for holly.

Cara bloisc, friend of cracking, *coll*, hazel, c. Hence for its cognate Ogham letter.

Brigh an duine, force of the man, *queirt*, q, apple tree. Hence for its cognate letter.

Arusc n-airlig, condition of slaughter, a man's back, m. Hence for its synonymous letter.

Med nerce, ivy, g. Hence for its synonymous letter.

Morad run, increasing of secrets, sloe, str. Hence it was put for its synonymous letter.

Ruamna dreach, redness of faces, sap of the rose which causes the redness of the faces, so that blushing is in them. *Ruamna dreach*, again, said of the Ogham *ruis*, elder, r, from the blush or from the reddening, for it is by elder, r, it is itself written.

Tosach fregra, beginning of an answer, that is *ailm*, a; for the first expression of every human being after his birth is a.

Fethim saire, smoothest of work, or *fedem, onn*, stone, o.

Silad clann, growing of plants, that is *ur*, heath, u with him, for it is *uir*, the soil of the earth, that causes the growing of the plants that are put into it. Growing of plants, again, said of the soil of the earth, is said of the Ogham letter which has taken the same name with it, each of them is *ur*.

Comainm carat, synonym for a friend, aspen, e, in the forest. Hence for its synonymous Ogham letter.

Crinem feda, most withered of wood, or sword, service tree, i. Hence for the Ogham letter, which has taken a name other than it, *idad*, yew.

Cosc lobair, corrective of a sick man, woodbine for the Ogham letter, which has taken a name other than it, *ebad*, aspen, ea.

Li crotha, beauty of form, heath. Hence for its synonymous letter, the Ogham oi.

Cubat n-oll, great equal-length, woodbine, i.e., honeysuckle. Hence for the Ogham letter which it has taken from it, woodbine, ui.

Amram blais, most wonderful of taste, *pin or ifin*, gooseberry. Hence for the letter that has taken its name from it, *pin or iphin*, io.

SOW OGHAM[3]
Group B. White b, grey l, black f, amber s, blue n.
Group H. Accompanying litter of a white (i.e. milch-) sow h,
    grey d, black t, amber c, blue q.
Group M. Litter of a white sow m, grey g, black ng, amber str,
    blue r.
Group A. Pig-in-pen of a white sow a, grey o, black u, amber e,
    blue i. Diphthong group here:
Hog-in-pen of a white sow ea, grey oi, black ui, amber io, blue ae.

RIVER-POOL OGHAM
Group B. Barrow b, Lower Shannon l, Foyle f, Shannon s,
    Nith n.
Group H. h-Othain (Fahan) h, Dergderg d, Teith t, Catt c,
    Cusrat q.
Group M. Muinten m, Gaval g, Graney ng, Sruthair str, Rye r.
Group A. Aru a, Eobul, Uissen, Erbus, Indiurnn.

FORTRESS OGHAM
Group B. Bruden, Liffey, Femen, Seolae, Nephin.
Group H. h-Ocha, Dinn Ríg, Tara, Cera, Corann.
Group M. Meath, Gabur, nGarman, Streulae, Roigne.
Group A. Ae(Cualand), Odba, Usney, Navan, Islay.

BIRD OGHAM

Group B. *besan* pheasant (?), *lachu* duck, *faelinn* gull, *seg* hawk, *naescu* snipe.

Group H. *hadaig* night raven (?), *droen* wren, *truith* starling, *querc* hen.

Group M. *mintan* titmouse, *géis* swan, *ngéigh* goose, *stmólach* thrush, *rócnat* small rock (?).

Group A. *aidhircleóg* lapwing, *odoroscrach* scrat (?), *uiseóg* lark, *ela* swan, *illait* eaglet (?).

COLOUR OGHAM

Group B. *bán* white, *liath* grey, *flann* red, *sodath* fine-coloured, *necht* clear.

Group H. *huath* terrible, *dub* black, *temen* dark grey, *cron* brown, *quiar* mouse-coloured.

Group M. *mbracht* variegated, *gorm* blue, *nglas* green, *sorcha* bright, *ruadh* red.

Group A. *alad* piebald, *odhar* dun, *usgdha* resinous, *erc* red, *irfind* very white.

CHURCH OGHAM

Group B. Bangor, Laith, Ferns Saigear, Noendruim.

Group H. h-Irard (Cluain), Durrow, Terryglass, Clonmacnois, Kildare.

Group M. Mugna, Shrule, Rahen, etc.

Group A. Armagh, etc.

MAN (HUMAN BEING) OGHAM

Man or hero for group B, one man, two, three, four, five men.

Minna nobles (or women) or clerics for group H, i.e., a woman, two, three, four, five women.

Youth for group M, one youth, two, three, four, five youths.

Boy or lad for group A, one boy, two, three, four, five boys, one boy for a, two for o, three for u.

WOMAN OGHAM

Heroines for group B after the same procedure (or method), one for b, two for l, thus all down.

Nuns for group H.

Maidens for group M.

Girls for group A, one for a, two for u.

AGRICULTURAL OGHAM

Group B. *biail* axe, *loman* rope, *fidba* hedge-bill, *srathar* pack-saddle, *nasc* ring.

Group H. *huartan, dabach* cask, *tal* adze, *carr* waggon, *cual* faggot.

Group M. *machad, gat* withe, *ngend* wedge, *sust* flail, *rusc* basket.

Group A. i.e., *Arathar* plough, *ord* hammer, *usca* heather-brush, *epit* billhook, *indeoin* anvil.

KING OGHAM

Bran, Labraidh, etc., and so all, to take for the name, the name of the king that begins with the letter.

WATER OGHAM

Rivulet for group B, one rivulet for b, five for n.

Weir for group H, one weir, two, three, four, five weirs.

River for group M, one river, two, three, four, five rivers.

Well for group A, one well, two, three, four, five wells.

DOG OGHAM

Watch-dog for group B, one watch-dog, two, three, four, five watch-dogs.

Greyhound for group H, one greyhound, two, three, four, five greyhounds.

Herd's dog for group M, one herd's dog, two, three, four, five herds' dogs.

Lapdog for group A, one lapdog, two, three, four, five lapdogs.

OX OGHAM

Bull for group B, one bull, two, three, four, five bulls.

Ox for group H, one ox, two, three, four, five oxen.

Bullock for group M, one bullock, two, three, four, five bullocks.

Steer for group A, one steer, two, three, four, five steers.

COW OGHAM

Milch cow for group B, one milch cow, two, three, four, five milch cows.

Stripper for group H, one stripper, two, three, four, five strippers.

Three-year-old heifer for group M, one three-year-old, two, three, four, five three-year-old heifers.

Yearling heifer for group A, etc.

BLIND MAN OGHAM

The man's name is divided, to wit,
Group B to the right side.
Group H to the left side.
Group M to the right side.
Group A to the left side.

LAME OGHAM

They are the same, viz., a division of the name.

BOY OGHAM

Pregnant women Ogham, that is, the name of the woman
is divided there unless she bear a child previously. If, however, she
bear a child, it is the child's name that is divided there; and if there
be a letter over, it is a boy. If it be an even number, it would be a
daughter that will be born of that pregnancy.

FOOT OGHAM

The fingers of the hand about the shinbone for the letters and to put
them on the right of the shinbone for group B. To the left for group
H. Athwart the shinbone for group M. Straight across for group A,
viz., one finger for the first letter of the groups, two for the second
letter, till it would reach five for the fifth letter of whichever group it
be.

NOSE OGHAM

The fingers of the hands about the nose, viz., similiar to right and left,
athwart, across.

SAINT OGHAM

The name of the Saint with which it will commence is taken for the
    letter, viz.,
Brenainn, Laisren, Finnen, Sincheall, Neasan.
H-Adamnan, Donnan, Tighearnach, Cronan, Ciaran.
Manchan, George, nGeminus, Strannan, Ruadhan.
Aed, Oena, Ultan, Ernen, Ita.

ART OGHAM

Livelihood, pilotage, poetry, handicraft, notary work.
Trisyllabic poetry, wizardry, turning, harping, fluting.
Soldiering, smithwork, modelling, deer-stalking, dispensing.
Sovereignty, harvesting, brasswork, fowling, fishing, or yew wood
work.

FOOD OGHAM

Bread, sweet milk, etc.

Lore of the Great Trees[4]

MAG MUGNA

Mugna, my sister's son of the glorious wood,
God fashioned it long ago,
a tree blest with various virtues,
with three choice fruits.

The acorn, and the dark narrow nut,
and the apple – it was a goodly wilding –
the King sent by rule
on it thrice a year.

The Tree of Mugna, great was the trunk,
thirty cubits its girth,
conspicuous in sight of all the place where it stood,
three hundred cubits it is in height.

Then was the bright plant laid low,
when a blast broke Tortu's Bole;
He makes transient every combat,
like the long-lived Tree of ancient Mugna.

EO MUGNA

Eo Mugna, great was the fair tree,
high its top above the rest;
thirty cubits – it was no trifle –
that was the measure of its girth.

Three hundred cubits was the height of the blameless tree,
its shadow sheltered a thousand:
in secrecy it remained in the north and east
till the time of Conn of the Hundred Fights.

A hundred score of warriors – no empty tale –
along with ten hundred and forty
would that tree shelter – it was a fierce struggle –
till it was overthrown by the poets.

EO ROSSA, EO MUGNA

How fell the Bough of Dathi?
it spent the strength of many a gentle hireling:
an ash, the tree of the nimble hosts,
its top bore no lasting yield.

The Ash in Tortu – take count thereof!
the Ash of populous Usnech.
their boughs fell – it was not amiss –
in the time of the sons of Aed Slane.

The Oak of Mugna, it was a hallowed treasure;
nine hundred bushels was its bountiful yield:
it fell in Dairbre southward,
across Mag Ailbe of the cruel combats.

The Bole of Ross, a comely yew
with abundance of broad timber,
the tree without hollow or flaw,
the stately bole, how did it fall?

CHAPTER THREE

The Memory of Animals

Finding and working with an animal helper is one of the primary initiations of the shaman In worldwide folk-story the younger son or daughter who is sent out into the wide world without goods or friends invariably meets with an animal or series of animals which help and empower them. Many Celtic saints are associated with animals: St Gobhnat of Ballyvourny in County Cork is led to her monastic foundation by nine white deer and her enclosure is guarded by bees, while St Kevin of Glendalough, County Wicklow, offers his hand as nest for a blackbird and learns patience while the eggs hatch. These stories have little to do with 'kindness to animals'; rather they concern a total understanding of and attunement with the animal teachers of the natural world.

The notion that animals can teach humans is profoundly present in shamanic work. The animal helpers whom we meet in the inner-worlds are wiser in the ways of the otherworld than we, and we discover they can be trusted to help us in ways unknown to us. The animals whom we meet in the world about us teach us the simple and manifest truths about life and relationship to life-forms, which are extraordinarily therapeutic for human beings who have forgotten their place in the universe. The memory of the animals helps us remember our paradisal interconnection.

The destiny of human beings is often regulated by or connected with helping animals which may be seen as properly totemic to a person or tribe. Thus the boy Setanta gains his manhood name, Cuchulainn (the Hound of Culainn) after fighting and overcoming the Culainn, the smith's hound; in recompense for killing the dog, Cuchulainn himself becomes the smith's watchdog. Ever afterwards it is his *geas*, his binding duty, never to eat dogmeat. Similarly it is Diarmuid O'Duibhne's *geas* never to hunt the boar. In both cases, Cuchulainn and Diarmuid die because they violate their *geasa*, having severed their spiritual connection with their animal helpers. They both literally forget their obligation and connection to their totemic animals, and become bound up in human affairs.

The two examples given here are about the traditional Celtic teaching concerning the Oldest Animals. Long before Darwinian theories of evolution were proposed, indigenous peoples the world over had an innate understanding of the chain of memory to which all life-forms have access. The Oldest Animals are those whose memory is the longest of all and who can penetrate the depths of time. This is a cumulative and networking memory which shamans access by means of their own animal helpers, whether they have one or many. It is fascinating to discover from this teaching that fish and birds – both pre-mammalian species – are among the Oldest Animals.

Eleanor Hull's essay on the Hawk of Achill has not been bettered as a rounding-up of the disparate story traditions relating to the Oldest Animals. Within it she gives the text of Fintan (whom we will meet again in Chapter 4) and the Hawk of Achill. The diverse examples of this tradition which relate the lives of animals to the ages of the world demonstrate the mutually supportive and interconnected nature of the shamanic universe.

The Hawk of Achill
or the Legend of the Oldest Animals
by Eleanor Hull[1]

Lovers of Westminster Abbey will not have failed to remark the very beautiful mosaic floor of the sanctuary before the High Altar. It is the work of a noted Italian artist named Odericus, brought from Rome in the time of Abbot Ware, and it was completed in the year 1268, in the reign of King Henry III. In the centre is a great circle of plain porphyry, with circles and curling pattern round it. Outside these is a lozenge-shaped border, set in a square, which itself is in an outer square, all the available space being filled up with circular or rectangular patterns. What few people notice is that here and there are letters and fragments of an inscription which once filled up the space in the inner square and the circle round the centre. Some words and one whole line remain, with scattered letters of words of which the remainder has been obliterated by time and by renewals of the floor.

Fortunately, the original Latin inscription has been preserved in full by Camden, and runs as follows in a literal translation:

> If the reader considers prudently all that is set down
> Here, he will find the end of the *primum mobile*.
> The boundary is three-fold; you add dogs, horses and men,
> Stags and ravens, eagles and huge whales.
> Whatever follows multiplies by three the years of the passing earth.
> The spherical globe shows the archetypal microcosm.
> In the year of Christ one thousand two hundred and twelve
> With sixty minus four (1268)
> King Henry the Third, the City (London or Rome?)
> Odericus and the Abbot
> Joined together these porphyry stones.

Without going now into the Ptolemaic system which Odericus had in mind when he planned this wonderful pavement and in some-wise thought of as illustrated by it, what we have to fix our minds on is the curious calculation of dates by the lives of animals. There are no figures of animals or men in the design, but the calculation is made on a threefold system by the lives of dogs, horses, men, stags, ravens, eagles and huge whales. It is difficult to see how the actual date is got by this means, but it is the method that is interesting to us at the moment and not the result. It was clearly an understood method of calculating dates by multiplying by three the lives of a number of living creatures, sometimes including men.

The method was not invented by Odericus; it is much older than his time. There are versions in Greek, Latin, Italian, Spanish, Portuguese, Breton, and German, all very like each other, though with slight variations, according to the position of the country and the animals best known in it. The Portuguese and a Venetian parallel follow exactly the order of the Westminster pavement up to the first five numbers, i.e. a fence (which seems to be a corruption of the three-fold boundary of the Latin), next dog, horse, man, stag, but ends with elephant.

The Greek version has been translated for me by my kind friends, Professor and the Misses Gardner. It runs as follows:

> Thus the croaking cormorant (or sea-crow) lives nine generations of ageing men. The stag, four times the cormorant; the

crow outlives three stags; but the phoenix nine crows; and we, the fair-haired nymphs, daughters of Aegis-bearing Zeus, outlive ten phoenixes. Hesiod (ed. Lehrs, *Fragm.* ciii.)

A Portuguese version has:

> Uma sebe dura tres annos,
> Tres sebes um cão,
> Tres cães um cavallo,
> Tres cavallos um homem,
> Tres homens um cervo,
> Tres cervos um elephante.

A Spanish version from Estremadura is similar:

> Tres annos dura un seto,
> Tres setos un perro,
> Tres perros un cabayo,
> Tres cabayos un hombre,
> Y tres cuerbos un milano.

The Germans carry their calculations farther still. In a book of animal legends published in 1616, we get:

> A town lasts three years,
> A dog outlasts three towns,
> A horse outlasts three dogs,
> Man outlives three horses,
> An ass outlives three men,
> A wild goose outlives three asses,
> A crow outlives three wild geese,
> A stag outlives three crows,
> A raven outlives three stags
> And the bird phoenix outlives three ravens.

Another German version keeps nearer to the original form. In it we get the succession of the fence, hound, horse, man, ass, wild goose, crow, stag, raven, and the phoenix. The phoenix is adopted from Greek and Latin versions, which give the series as man, crow, deer, raven, phoenix and hamadryad. A poem by the minnesinger Reinmar von Zweter (13th century) contains a similar passage. Man's life is thus fixed at eighty-eight years; the phoenix at 83,052 years.

Let us now come nearer home. We have in these islands parallel passages in Welsh, Scottish and Irish tradition. In a legend in the Iolo manuscripts the six oldest creatures in the world are said to be the eagle of Gwernabwy, the stag of Rhedynvre, the salmon of Llyn Llivon, the ousel of Cilgwri, the toad of Cors Vochno, and the owl of Cwmcawlwyd. This calculation is treated in a more poetical manner in a poem by Ap Gwilym to his mistress, in which he complains that he has waited so long for her under the thorn that 'a thousand persons or more' liken him to these long-lived animals. The animals chosen are almost always the same. The eagle, the stag, the ousel or blackbird, the dog and horse, the salmon (which in our home stories takes the place of the great whales of Odericus), are considered to be the longest-lived animals.

In Scotland, Sheriff Alexander Nicolson, in his *Gaelic Proverbs and Familiar Phrases* (Edinburgh 1881), gives us the following, being again, as always, multiples of three:

> Thrice a dog's age, age of a horse;
> Thrice a horse's age, age of man;
> Thrice a man's age, age of the deer;
> Thrice a deer's age, age of the eagle;
> Thrice an eagle's age, age of the oak.

Human life must be precarious in Scotland. This only gives a man 27 years to live; the deer, 81 years; eagle, 243 years; the oak, 729 years.

In Ireland, fortune is more liberal, and bestows the 81 years on the human being, with one thrown in. In a passage in the Book of Lismore (fo. 151, *b* 2) we get the following:

> A year for the stake (*cuaille*),
> Three years for the field (*gort*),
> Three lifetimes of the field for the hound (*cú*),
> Three lifetimes of the hound for the horse (*ech*),
> Three lifetimes of the horse for the human being (*duine*),
> Three lifetimes of the human being, the stag (*dam allaid*),
> Three lifetimes of the stag for the ousel (*lon*),
> Three lifetimes of the ousel for the eagle (*ilar*),
> Three lifetimes of the eagle for the salmon (*bradan*),
> Three lifetimes of the salmon for the yew (*iubar*),
> Three lifetimes of the yew for the world from its beginning
>   to its end.

This is almost exactly the sequence we had in the Westminster Abbey inscription except that the ousel or blackbird takes the place of the

raven, and the salmon that of the whales. A year for a stake is added
at the beginning; otherwise the sequence is perfect. The rather difficult final lines of the Westminster inscription are here taken to mean
the age of the world from its beginning to its end. We arrive at 59,050
years, two multiples of three more than the Westminster calculation,
which made 6561 years; i.e. down to the salmon in the Irish list. But
I do not know what exact cycle this represents.

The exact calculations, however, are not of importance from our
point of view. What is remarkable is that we get almost a precise parallel between an inscription in Latin of the thirteenth century in
Westminster and a Gaelic method of calculation in a compilation of
the fifteenth century which is made from much earlier material.
Moreover, these lists remain as common sayings among the people
down to the present day. Dr Hyde says in his *Legends of Saints and
Sinners* (pp. 56–57) that he has often heard variants of the saying in the
country. The usual one varies very little from those we have mentioned. It runs:

> Three wattles (or stakes) equal a hound's life,
> Three hounds a steed;
> Three steeds a man;
> Three men an eagle;
> Three eagles a salmon;
> Three salmon a yew tree;
> Three yew-trees a ridge;
> Three ridges from the beginning to the end of the world.

Dr Hyde says that the peasants who recited the sequence to him
explained the wattles or stakes (the same Irish word that we had in the
Lismore version, i.e. *cuaille*) as those that are put into a hedge to fill
a gap; and the three ridges (*eitre*) as the old very wide ridges used in
plough-land in very ancient times, which left an almost indelible mark
in the ground. But the idea of the enclosure or boundary at the beginning is still the same as in the other instances quoted, and the idea of
the age of the universe at the end is found all through the series. It
corresponds to the ancient *primum mobile* or outer sphere or limit of
space in the Westminster inscription; but the Irish peasant would be
surprised if he were told that he was speaking in the terms of the
Ptolemaic system.

There are a number of similar lists of ancient animals in Irish literature. In the Book of Fermoy is a poem of ten stanzas beginning:

A year for the stake by right,
Three for the field in its green bearing
In fallow and in second fallow,
And the third in its third fallow.

From the Book of Ballymote we get:

Three fields to a tree,
Three trees to a hound,
Three hounds to a horse,
Three horses to a human being,
Three human beings to a deer (*ségh*),
Three deer to a chain (*nase*),
Three chains to a salmon (*iach*),
Three salmon to a yew (*éo*),
Three yew trees to an age (*bith*),
 ever-living, God.

A somewhat different and more modern form is found in Egerton 133, Art. 20, in the British Museum:

Three winters, a stake (*cuaille*),
Three stakes, a dog (*cú*),
Three dogs, a human being (*duine*),
Three human beings, a deer (*fiagh*),
Three deer, an eagle (*fiolar*),
Three eagles, a male salmon (*fiur citre*),
Three salmon to the end of the world.

Here 'winter' (*geimhre*) seems to be a mistake for 'field' (*gort*). Many of the confusions and changes in these runs are due to the fact that some of the words used have two meanings, and it is often uncertain which the writer had in his mind. Thus *éo* may mean a 'salmon' or a 'yew tree', and consequently either the salmon or the yew is said to be the longest-living. Again, *eitre* 'a furrow' and *eithre* 'a salmon'; and *séigh* 'a hawk' and *ségh* 'a deer' or 'a wild ox', can easily be mistaken. These similarities have caused confusion.

There is an early English form of the same idea in the *Demaundes Joyous* of Wynkyn de Worde (1511) which runs as follows:

Demaunde, what is the aege of a felde mous?
A yere, and a hedge may stande thre mous lyves,
and the lyfe of a dogge is the terme of thre hedges standynge,
and the lyfe of a hors is thre dogges lyves,

and the lyfe of a man is thre hors lyves,
and the lyfe of a gose is thre mennes lyves,
and the lyfe of a swanne thre gose (gooses) lyves,
and the lyfe of a swalowe is thre swannes lyves,
and the lyfe of an egle is thre swalowes lyves,
and the lyfe of a serpent is thre egles lyves,
and the lyfe of a raven is thre serpentes lyves,
and the lyfe of a harte is thre ravens lyves,
and an oke groweth fyve hondreth yere,
besyde the rote which doubleth thre tymes everyche of the
    thre aeges aforesayd.

(Wright and Halliwell, *Reliquiae Antiquae*, ii. 75)

Stories of the oldest animals are common throughout the literature of the world, ancient and modern. Such legends are to be found in Jewish, Persian, Chinese and Hindu literature; possibly in many others. In the Asiatic versions, as was to be expected, the animals are different, and as a rule they number only three. They have been fitted into no system of cosmology, as the Latins fitted theirs, but are merely answers to the puzzling question, Which animal lives the longest? One of the oldest forms is found in the Buddha Birth-stories or Jataka; and as it belongs to one of the most ancient portions, it must be at least as old as the fourth century. I take it from the translation by Mr T. W. Rhys Davids.

Long ago there were three friends living near a great banyan-tree, on the slope of the Himalaya range of mountains – a partridge, a monkey, and an elephant. They were wanting in respect and courtesy for one another, and did not live altogether on befitting terms.

But it occurred to them, 'It is not right for us to live in this manner. What if we were to cultivate respect towards whichever of us is eldest?' 'But which is the eldest?' they asked; until one day they thought, 'This will be a good way for finding out.' So the monkey and the partridge asked the elephant, as they were sitting altogether at the foot of the banyan-tree: 'Elephant, dear, how big was this banyan-tree at the time you first knew it?' 'Friends!' said he, 'when I was little I used to walk over this banyan, then a mere bush, keeping it between my thighs; and when I stood with it between my legs its highest branches touched me underneath. So I have known it since it was a shrub.'

Then they both asked the monkey in the same way. And he said: 'Friends! when I was quite a little monkey I used to sit on the ground and eat the topmost shoots of this banyan, then quite young, by merely stretching out my neck. So that I have known it from my earliest infancy.'

Then again the two others asked the partridge as before. And he said: 'Friends! there was once a lofty banyan-tree in such and such a place, whose fruits I ate and dropped the seeds here. From that this tree grew up; so that I have known it even before the time when it was born, and I am older than either of you.'

Thereupon, the elephant and monkey said to the clever partridge: 'You, friend, are the oldest of us all. Henceforth we will do all manner of service for you, and pay you reverence, and make salutations before you, and treat you with every respect and courtesy, and abide by your counsels. Do you in future give us whatever counsel and instruction we require.'

Thenceforth the partridge gave them counsel and kept them up to their duty, and himself observed his own. So they three kept the five commandments; and since they were courteous and respectful to one another, and lived on befitting terms with each other, they became destined for heaven when their lives should end.

The holy life of these three became known as 'The Holiness' or 'Beautiful Life' of the partridge. When the Teacher had thus concluded his discourse, he, as Buddha, uttered the verse:

'Tis those who reverence the old
That are the men versed in the Faith.
Worthy of praise while in this life,
And happy in the life to come.

When the Teacher had thus spoken on the virtue of paying reverence to the old, he summed up the Jataka by saying, 'The elephant of that time was Mogallana, the monkey Sariputta, but the partridge was I myself.'

A distorted version of the same tale in the Uttara-kanda of the Sanskrit Ramayana gives this Buddhist legend as follows: A vulture and an owl who had lived in a certain wood from time immemorial, quarrelled about the possession of a certain cave, each of them claiming it by ancient right. They agreed to bring the matter before Rama for his decision. The vulture said: 'The cave has been my home since this earth was filled by men newly come into being.' The owl said: 'It has been my home ever since the earth was adorned with trees.' Rama decided that the cave belonged to the owl, as trees and plants were produced before the creation of mankind from the marrow of two demons.

The Persian version introduces into the tale a spice of humour. In the Sindibad Nama it occurs as follows: An old wolf and fox, intimate friends, were once travelling together. A short distance in front of them they saw a camel, who joined them. They had no food but a pumpkin. They travelled a long time until, exhausted by the heat of the road, their eyes became black with thirst. At last they reached a pond full of water and sat down on the brink. The pumpkin was produced and it was agreed that it should be the prize of him who was oldest. The wolf began: 'Indian, Tajik and Turk know that my mother bore me one week before God had created heaven and earth, time and space. I have a right to the pumpkin.' 'Yes,' said the old crafty fox, 'that is true, for the night you were born I was standing by in attendance. It was I who lit the taper that morning and I burned beside your pillow like a morning taper.'

When the camel had heard their speeches to an end, he stalked forward, and, bending down his neck, he snapped up the pumpkin, observing, 'It is impossible to conceal anything so manifest as this, that with such a neck and haunches as mine, it was neither yesterday nor last night that my mother bore me.'

In the stories we have hitherto been considering, the only question of interest has been the comparative length of life of certain animals. But in Ireland we have a group of stories in which birds and other long-lived creatures survive for a very definite purpose. They are historians, surviving the Deluge and undergoing all sorts of hardships and miseries for the single purpose of carrying down to later days the early traditions of the race. But there were difficulties. There was, for instance, the Flood; and as Irish tradition went back long before the Flood, it became a serious question how, in view of the fact that only eight persons are said in the Pentateuch to have survived the Deluge and none of these persons were known to have settled in Ireland, these historical details were preserved. Quite a number of different stories were invented to get over the difficulty. The oldest is the story of Tuan, an Ulsterman, who, somewhere about the year 550, is heard of by Saint Finnian, who had just planted his monastery of Moville in the territory of this pagan warrior in Donegal. His curiosity is aroused by hearing that this ancient warrior knows all the history of the races who formerly inhabited the country and he promptly sends off a messenger to ask him to come and tell his stories to him and his fellow-monks. The stern old warrior 'whose faith,' we are told, 'was not good,' not only refuses but closes his door upon them. They take a time-honoured Irish method of enforcing their demands and go on hunger-strike before his gates. On this he gives way, and on the morrow early he presents himself at Finnian's monastery. He has, according to the story, become transformed into a 'venerable cleric' during the night (Tuan is accustomed to rapid changes) and in this form he presents himself to Finnian and invites him to accompany him to his hermitage. Having performed their Lord's Day duties (for it is Sunday), the saint impatiently asks his host now to begin his stories. Tuan, in his new-found piety, objects that he is more concerned to meditate on the Word of God which he has just heard from Finnian than to tell his pagan stories; but the Saint, with all the eagerness of the true folk-lorist, declares that they will not eat with him until they have heard his tales. So he begins his story of the five invasions of Ireland: that of Partholan, that of Nemedh, that of the Firbolg, that of the Tuatha De Danann, and finally that of the Milesians or sons of Mil, a story that is as firmly believed by the peasant Irishman today as it was by Tuan and Finnian. All these races were swept away – one by plague, others by warfare between each other, others by the waves of the sea, so that the country was alternately filled by inhabitants and emptied again. But as Tuan remarks: 'It is not usual for any slaughter to happen that one man does not survive to tell the tale. That man am I,' he said. But it was not as a man that he witnessed all these changes. It was in turn as a stag, a boar, a hawk, a salmon; and then, once again he was reborn as a human being. The story is most dramatically told. Each time that a change takes place in the peopling of Ireland a parallel change comes over Tuan as he passes from one form into another. Each time he resorts to his own dwelling in Ulster as he feels old age coming on. Each time he fasts three days. 'I remembered every shape in which I had been before. Old age and wretchedness fell upon me. I had no strength left. Then I changed into the shape of a hawk. My mind was glad again. I was able to do anything. I was eager and lusty; I would fly all over Ireland and everything that happened I would find out . . . For a long time was I in the shape of that hawk, so that I outlived all those races who had invaded Ireland.' Here we have the full story of those metamorphoses which are common to Welsh and Irish story and are purely pagan in origin but overlaid by Christian interpolations. Certainly the length of Tuan's life presents some difficulties even allowing for his transformations. Even Giraldus Cambrenses, though he had a receptive mind, was somewhat staggered at the longevity of a man who out-lived Methuselah by four hundred and thirty-one years. 'We read in the Irish tales,' he writes, 'that Tuan far surpassed all the patriarchs of the Bible in years. However incredible or questionable it might seem, he reached the age of fifteen hundred years.'

But Tuan is outdone as regards the length of his life by another man, who lived from before the Flood to the middle of the sixth century. His name was Fintan, and as we shall have more to say about him, I will say a few words about his legend. It is evidently inspired by Biblical memories. In this version it is a woman, Cessair, who takes refuge in Ireland to escape the Deluge. She was the grand-daughter of Noah, and daughter of Noah's son Bith, not mentioned in the Bible. They had besought Noah to give them a room in the ark, but Noah had refused; but he suggested to his grand-daughter that if she could reach the western borders of the world, where there was no sin because no one lived there, and where therefore the Flood would not come, she would surely escape. She and her companions, or such of them as survived, arrived eventually in the south-west of Ireland, after seven years of wanderings; but alas! the Deluge overtook them even there, and all of them were drowned except Fintan, who, like Tuan, was providentially preserved alive to tell the tale.

And this brings us to the poem of the Hawk of Achill, printed in Irish in 1907 from the Book of Fermoy and other manuscripts but so far as I know not hitherto printed in English. The poem details a conversation held by Fintan with an aged hawk on the lonely island of Achill, off the west coast of Mayo, in which they relate the events of their lives, and the adventures and miseries that have overtaken each of them in its course. As they discover that their ages are exactly equal, and as in each case they amount to the respectable length of 6515 years, they have had time for many sorrows and many adventures. To Fintan the greatest griefs of his life have been the death of Cessair, his companion, and of his son Illann and others who adventured forth with them to escape the Deluge, and above all the loss of his own eye, which had been plucked out by a hawk or crow. Like Tuan, he had been in many shapes since coming to Ireland. As a salmon he had been in all the rivers of Ireland in turn, and it was at the falls of Assaroe, on the coldest night he had ever experienced, with the ice like a blue wall above him, that a crow out of cold Achill came above him and plucked out his eye. On this the Hawk hastily intervenes to say that it was he who robbed him of his eye, on which an angry altercation ensues, Fintan demanding 'eric' or compensation for his blinded eye and the hawk stoutly refusing it. Then Fintan takes up his story again and relates that he had been changed from a salmon into the shape of an eagle and afterwards into that of a falcon. Five hundred years he had been a salmon, fifty years an eagle, and a hundred years a falcon; then God put him back into his own form as a man, and during many reigns of kings of Ireland he had acted, up to the coming of Patrick, as a chief judge or brehon and portioned out to them their territories.

On this the bird takes up the story and relates his own adventures in the Southern Battle of Moytura Cong, where the Firbolg were vanquished by the Tuatha De Danann but where their king Nuada lost his hand, which was picked up by the hawk and carried to his nest. He then passes to the second Battle of Moytura, in which Balor of the Mighty Blows, the leader of the Fomorian hosts, was slain, and the valorous Lugh the Long-handed, the God of Light, and the Dagda, the Great Father, kings of the Tuatha De Danann, reigned in peace. Fintan again takes up the story and relates the history of the coming of the Milesians, and the dividing of Ireland between their two princes Eber and Eremon, one of whom, on the incitement of his wife, promptly slew the other, and possessed himself of the kingdom. After this, to the great regret of the bird, who could get no pickings anywhere, there were some years of quiet.

The next scene to which we are introduced is a striking one. The great hosts of Ireland are assembled at Tara for one of the annual festivals, and the King, Coning, is seated in state in the midst of his nobles, when there enters a marvellous personage, of lofty stature and clad in a pure white robe with edges of gold. He holds in his hand a fragrant branch, on which are nuts, apples, and sloes (or acorns), the immortal food of the Gael. They ask who he is and he says he is strong Trefuilngidh Tre-eochair, and that he is travelling from the western bounds of the world, in the setting of the sun, to the port of Adam's Paradise in the east. They ask him how he has supported life during such a long journey, and he points to the branch in his hand and says he has no need of earthly food for the scent of the fair branch supports him both day and night. It would make the old man young, and put from him all sickness and evil. Before setting forth again on his majestic course, he leaves with them three fruits from the branch for their help, and they become the three ancient marvel-trees of Erinn — the Yew of Ross, the mighty Tree of Mughna and the ancient Tree of Tortan — of all of which many stories are told.

This mysterious personage is explained in a parallel prose version of this part of the story, to be 'either an angel of God or God Himself', and the cause which brought him to the setting of the sun was that on this very day in Jerusalem a Man had been tortured and crucified by the Jews; and that the sun had 'stepped past them after this deed and had not shone upon them'. Therefore he had come to find out what ailed the sun; for he knew that no land lay to the west beyond Inis Gluair in County Mayo, so that there must be the setting of the sun. 'For that is the threshold over which the sun sets, just as the Paradise of Adam is the threshold over which it rises.'

The bird again takes up the tale to relate incidents in the later history, especially the death in battle of various heroes, from which he reaped his fill of food for himself and his nestlings. He tells how he plucked the eye out of the dying Cuchulain; and how old age and feebleness came upon him, so that he who in old times could bear away in his claws a great boar or stag, now grew faint under the weight of a blackbird. But he makes a good ending as a Christian, and Fintan, forgetting his ill-deeds, promises him heaven.

(*Fintan*)
1. Relate now, O Bird of Achill,
   Tell us the substance of thy adventures;
   I am able finely
   To converse with thee in bird-language.

(*The Bird*)
2. Though there are no signs of youth upon thee
   It is long since thy body became shrunken
   In Dun Tulera washed by the sea,
   O Fintan, O wise man.

(*Fintan*)
3. The greater the wonder that I am alive.
   The sorrow of Ros Greda is distracting me;
   Darkness came over my heart,
   The death of Illann has grieved me sore.

4. O Bird of Achill of the Fian,
   Thou that I have ever been fain to see,
   Now that I do see thee, tell me
   The cause of thy cleaving to Achill.

(*The Bird*)
5. Lightsome its air, gentle are its havens,
   Warm are its thickets, they are not cold;
   Fruitful its chase, noble its streams,
   Lonesome its estuaries.

6. O Fintan, never was there
   A single night west in Achill
   When I got not my fill by my vigour
   Of fish and wild game and venison.

7. O Son of Bochra, in fair speech, [i.e. Latin]
   Since we have a favourable opportunity to converse,
   For the Love of Jesus, tell me,
   Of thy coming hither and thy life.

(*Fintan*)
8. My life before the black flood
   Was fifteen years of years;
   After the Flood God gave me
   Five thousand five hundred years.

9. Over and above that, O Bird,
   (Good reason have I to be aged);
   I was like that for a thousand years:
   That is the cause of the increase in my age.

10. O Hawk, out of cold Achill,
    Blessing and success attend thee!
    From the time thou wast hatched from the egg
    Tell the number of thy years.

(*The Bird*)
11. Equal is my life to thine
    O Fintan, son of mild Bochra:
    Exactly equal the period
    The same full age after the Deluge.

12. O Fintan, son of fair Bochra,
    Since thou art a poet and a prophet,
    Tell us now without delay
    The evils and wonders that befell you.

    (*Fintan*)
13. The loss of Illann, the death of my sons,
    The death of white-handed Cessair;
    My nights at seal-haunted Assaroe
    Tormented me even more from that out.

14. On the loss of Ladra and sweet-voiced Bith
    At the black out-pouring of the Flood,
    The Lord put me, to my misery,
    Into the shape of a salmon at every spring.

15. Short, methought, was my stay on the Boyne
    After my coming over the ocean,
    In the Bush, the Bann, the brown Bru,
    On the Suck, the Suir, and the Shannon.

16. At the Slaney, and at the Liffey in the East,
    The Maigue, and crystal Ethne,
    The Moy, the Mourne and the Muir,
    At the Solan, the Lee and the Laune.

17. At the Shannon, the Dael and the Dubh,
    In the Sligo and the river Monad,
    Until I came without trouble hither
    To the waterfall of the estuary of the Erne.

18. I passed a night in the Northern wave,
    And I at Assaroe of the seals,
    Never felt I a night like that
    From the beginning of the world to its end.

19. I could not stay under the waterfall,
    I took a leap, but it did not help me,
    The ice came like clear blue glass
    Between me and the falls of Mac Moduirn.

20. A crow came out of cold Achill,
    Above the river-mouth of Assaroe;
    I will not hide the fact, mysterious as it was,
    He carried away with him one of my eyes.

21. From that night [the name] 'The Blind One of Assaroe'
    Clung to me: it was a cruel act.[2]
    From that out I am without my eye:
    Small wonder for me to be aged.

(*The Bird*)
22. It was I who swallowed thy eye,
    O Fintan of the fresh heart;[3]
    I am the grey hawk . . .
    Alone in the middle of Achill.

(*Fintan*)
23. If it was thou, though it seems strange,
    Who left me in gloom, one-eyed,
    Pay me compensation (eric) for my eye,
    As law and obedience demand.

(*The Bird*)
24. Small would be the eric I would give you,
    O Fintan, son of gentle Bochra,
    That single eye [left in] thy withered head
    I would gulp down quickly in one bite.

(*Fintan*)
25. Harsh is thy chant, O great wild bird,
    Sweeter than all to wait a while,
    Since it is I who am the gentler,
    I will talk with thee about my contemporaries.

26. For five hundred years have I been blind
    As a long-sided heavy salmon,
    On lochs, on diverse rivers,
    On every rich clear-flowing sea.

27. For fifty years I was an eagle,
    Few were the birds that would fill my place;
    A hundred years happily
    I was a stately blue-eyed falcon.

28. Till the King of the Sun thought it time
    To put me in my own shape.
    Where would I get anything worthier?
    And yet I am aged today.

Fintan then gives a résumé of the changes he had witnessed in the kingdom from the time of Slainge, 'the first king of Ireland who invented
festivals', to the coming of Patrick 'of the fluent pen' in the reign of
King Laegaire. It was the death of his son Illann, as he reiterates again,
that caused him to lose his vigour and become an old man.

In return the bird recounts the battles he has seen and the preys he
has carried off from them. He taunts Fintan with the death of his
twelve sons, 'whose flesh he had under his talons', in the Battle of
Moytura Cong; and relates how he carried off the arm of the fallen
king Nuada.

37. There fell thy twelve sons;
On seeing them, dreadful the deed,
I plucked from each fresh scion,
A hand, a foot, or an eye.

. . . .

41. As I was in the midst of the carnage
I saw beside me an arm,
On each several finger of the fingers
A ring of red gold like blood.

42. Its heroic proportions, its vast size,
Alas! for him from whom that limb was severed!
Its beauty, its length, and its span,
Ruddy and beautiful were the nails.

43. A sleeve of glossy silk,
And a golden tunic sleeve,
Was around its whole length
Up to the corselet.

44. I lift it up, it was no small effort,
The hand, both flesh and blood;
I bear it with me, terrible was the distance,
To Druim Ibar of the estuaries.

45. The hand of Nuada that I found there,
The High King of the Tuatha De Danann,
It was seven years in my bird's abode:
There, O Fintan, is my story for you!

The bird then speaks of the second Battle of Moytura where fell Balor
of the Blows, and of the destruction of the Fomorians. After which

there was an era of peace and happiness, broken at last, to the delight of the flesh-seeking bird, by the heavy fighting of Lugh with his 'death-dealing fist'. Around this hero were always flocks of ravens and scald-crows, with a fine opportunity for picking bones.

Fintan, after another outburst against the bird for the loss of his sons, then takes up the tale, and relates the coming of the sons of Milesius and the division of Ireland between Eber and Eremon.

Then comes in the curious incident which we have already mentioned and which is found also in one of the prose tales.[4] The King of Ireland, Coning, was seated on his high-seat in Tara, surrounded by his nobles, when they see approaching them a man of height so lofty that he concealed from them the bright sun. In his hand he carried a branch, bearing at one and the same time nuts, apples and sloes, the Irish food of immortality. He seated himself in their midst and began to converse in his 'pure Greek speech'. They ask him who and of what country he is, and he replies that he is mighty Trefuilngidh, who had come from the East from the Paradise of Adam, and he has made a long journey westwards to the very end of the land on which the sun never sets but where all is water.

74. I walked the globe
     Alongside of every wave;[5]
     I left no inhabited spot, homestead, nor sea
     Unvisited except this land.

75. The Port of Paradise of Adam's race
     Is the Eastern threshold of the world;
     Inis Gluair, the settlement (monastery) of Brenainn,
     Is the western threshold between land and wave.

The branch that he holds in his hand satisfies all needs for human men and women, cold and hunger and thirst.

79. If thou shouldest eat it facing Northward,
     The fruit of the tree of virtues,
     The old man who partakes of it
     Straightway becomes a youth again.

80. If thou dost consume it facing South,
     The fruit of this fruiting tree,
     Thou needest have no fear of painful disease
     So long as the blackthorn lasts.

For himself the fragrance of the branch was sufficient of food and drink
and he had no need of human food.

81. He spent three days in Tara of the flocks
    Pleasantly conversing;
    Till the fair-hued host of the western land
    Gathered in one instant around him.

82. He bade farewell to the men of Fodla (Ireland),
    He went forward on his mighty course,
    He left the branch in our far land,
    A nut, a sloe, and an apple.

83. I it was who picked up the fruits
    And put them in my girdle;
    Until I had finished planting them
    None was able to do me harm.

84. I planted the three fruits
    That came to us for our help:
    Eo Rossa, the Branch of Mughna Mor,
    The old tree of Tortan of heavy hosts.

85. Here now for thee, O gentle hawk,
    A little story in return for thy visit,
    About the bright, smooth, round-topped,
    Beautiful old fort (of Tara).

Here the bird takes up the tale again, on the principle that one good
tale demands another. After giving his blessing to Fintan, he proceeds
to relate his adventures in the wars of the days of Cuchulain of the
Red Branch: of his mighty deeds of strength in those days, and the
gradual weakening of his powers as old age came upon him.

87. In the time of fair Conchobar
    Great was my renown and beauty,
    Wandering over hills and glens;
    I was king over the bird-flocks of Eire.

88. My watch and my attention chanced to fall
    On the 'Slinger' of Traigh Baile:[6]
    The man who was searching all havens,
    Cuchulain, of the Red Branch.

89. At the time when, by his treachery,
    Curoi, king of Clann Degad fell,
    I ate my fill of his blood
    After his fall in the encounter.

90. At the time that Garbh, son of Starn, fell
    By the 'Hound' [Cuchulain] who fed scald-crows;
    Two eyes of the handsome Greek
    I ate at the beginning of the good day.

91. Often I got flesh and spoils
    From Naisi who was venomous (fierce) of weapon;
    I did not taste *his* flesh or blood
    Because of his excellence in fighting.

92. The head of Cet fell to me
    After his wounding and his struggle;
    It was for me a desperate mouthful,
    His eyes were like to choke me.

93. I ate, enormous was his size,
    The body of Monodhar mac Cecht;
    I found many bodies back to back,
    From the victorious hand of Conall.

94. From the strife he did not flinch
    So long as he was alive;
    The rivers used to run blood
    From the Culgas (spear) of Conall the Victorious.

95. The spirited Fergus mac Roich:
    There was a warrior! great of stature!
    A man to fight a hundred, stubborn of valour,
    From whom I used to get gory flesh.

96. There was occasion of battle and peril
    In the wake of the hosts on the Táin;[7]
    The Rout of the Plain of Murthemne
    Was fierce and decisive enough!

97. After all that Cu of the Feats had slain
    He ceased not until his body was mangled;
    His face was drenched with blood,
    With his back against the pillar-stone of the Commor.[8]

98. I came above the warrior
    When his face was grown dark [or livid],
    To eat his eyes, not with intent of slaughter:
    I stooped my head at his outcry.

99. He felt me on his face,
    He lifted up his weakening hand,
    He put his little hero's dart
    Through my flesh at the first thrust[?]

100. I take a difficult flight
    To Inis Géidh over the furrowed sea,[9]
    I draw out of me, painful the effort,
    The hard tough shaft of the javelin.

101. The head [or barb] remained in my body,
    It tortured my heart distressingly,
    I have never been sound since then,
    And I do not conceal it, since I am old.

102. It is I who killed, great is the story,
    The solitary crane of Magh Léana,
    And the eagle of Druim Brice[10]
    That fell by me in the famous ford.

103. It is I who killed, pleasant the banquet,
    The solitary crane of grey Inis Géidh,
    It was I who chewed under my crop
    The two full-fat birds of Léithin.

104. It is I who slew
    The slender Blackfoot of Slieve Fuaid;
    The ousel of Druim Seghsa of the streams
    Died in the claws of my daughters.

105. In the time of Lugh, happy warrior,
    I often bore back to the home of my nestlings
    In my talons, without effort,
    The bodies of champions and fighting-heroes.

106. In the time of victorious Iughaine
    I had firm, powerful claws;
    Across pastures and dales
    I used to carry off a year-old boar.

107. In the time of fair Conn the Hundred-battler
Great was my fame and my comeliness;
I would bear with me afar
A fleet fawn of six months' growth.

108. In the period of Cormac mac Airt,
It was a feat of strength . . . ,
I would lift up a pig or a pigling
Aloft in the air without more ado[?]

109. I searched many-hued Meath
Before Dathi went to the East,
On every side of Tara eastwards,
Pursuing the wild fawn.

110. When I had grown old after that
I found peril and strife;
I was maddened . . .
In the time of Niall Nine-Hostager.

111. In the time of Diarmuid Donn
Son of Fergus mac Cearbhall,
I would get weary carrying a blackbird
Three or four times.

112. After all my doings in many a garth,
And after all the strife and ill I met with,
I have come hither from the west
For thine anointing, Fintan.

113. Behold me, then, departing from thee,
O Fintan, to cold Achill,
Seek thou pardon from God for me,
Tomorrow my span of life will end.

(*Fintan*)
114. Let no terror seize thee, O Bird,
Tomorrow will thy vigour be restored;
Thy soul will be in the heaven of clouds
With the chanting [?] of angels for thy tale.

115. I myself will go to meet death
On the very self-same day;
I am generous Fintan, who here am
Aged after the Fianna.

116. I believe in Christ, I will not hide it,
　　　In the High-king of the heaven of clouds,
　　　Mild Lord of the earth [lit. 'sod'] who is,
　　　Who creates both young and old.

You will have noticed that in the stanzas I have read there is a mention of various other great birds who became the prey of the voracious hawk of Achill. He speaks of having slain and devoured the solitary crane that was in Moy Léana, and the eagle of Druim Brice, the crane of Inis Géidh and the two full-fat birds of Léithin. He slew also the slender stag called the Blackfoot of Slieve Fuaid, while the blackbird or ousel of Druim Seghsa died in the talons of his daughters. 'Here,' as Dr Hyde says, 'are allusions to a whole cycle of bird and beast lore, which probably at one time had stories connected with them.' The question arises, Are any other of these stories still existing?

Dr Hyde has himself discovered one of these stories, the 'Eachtra: or Adventures of Léithin', which he found in a manuscript from Australia, but of which other copies exist in the Royal Irish Academy, Dublin. They are all much later versions than the Hawk of Achill, but run on somewhat the same lines. The conversation here takes place between an eagle called Léithin and one of her own nestlings, who asks her pitifully whether she has ever experienced so cold a night as the night just past and the present day. 'I do not remember,' was the reply, 'that I ever saw the like or the equal of them since the world was created.' But the young bird declares that there are people who do remember, even Dubhchosach, the Black-footed One of Binn Gulban, the great stag who survived the Deluge; or the white blackbird of Clonfert; or the blind salmon of Assaroc, who is undoubtedly our friend Fintan during one of his transformations. He recounts the manner in which he lost his eye much as in the 'Hawk of Achill', and asks who had sent the eagle to him for information.

Léithin replies that it was one of its own young birds, but the salmon declares that it was in fact the old crow or hawk of Achill, masquerading as a young bird. 'For its talons have got blunted with age, and its way of getting food is to go from nest to nest smothering and killing all the young and eating them.' This proves to be true, indeed, for when Léithin gets back to her nest, she finds all her birds dead and the old hawk of Achill flown away.

In his *Legends of Saints and Sinners*, pp. 40–62, Dr Hyde repeats the story of Léithin, first printed in the *Celtic Review* (June, 1915), and adds to it a folklore version of the legend, picked up in County Galway, in which again we meet with the crow of Achill, the eagle, and the blind trout of Assaroc (i.e. Fintan) as the oldest animals; but older than any of them is the old woman of Beare, whose story of her age has been tacked on to the other. 'I give you the branch (of victory), said the crow to the old woman; you are as old as the old grandmother, long ago, who ate the apples', whoever she might have been!

There is a short poem of eight stanzas from the Book of Fermoy in the British Museum (now part of Egerton 92) which I have to thank Mr O'Keeffe for copying for me (so far as it could be copied, for it is very much defaced), which I think may be the story of the white blackbird of Clonfert. In it Enaceán, an ancient bard (?), asks a talking blackbird, what had whitened its wing on its side; and the bird replies that it was Christ, who made him old, who had whitened him; and he then proceeds to relate the historical events that he had seen during his time.

He speaks of King Conchobar and the great gatherings of the Ultonians in ancient days; of Queen Meave and her expedition on the Táin bó Cualnge. Far from him now was the vigour (?) of these gatherings, for he is older than Ross son of Ruadh. He has met with Oisín son of Fionn, a man of wisdom; and with Caoilte with his Fianna; with Morgan, son of Morann, blood pouring through his body. He had witnessed the birth of Christ in the flesh. Sweet was his song from the Wood of Cuan (Taillte) when the host was destroying Troy(?). Many had been his adventures since Bran went away on his ship. He ends with a blessing on Christ who had lengthened his life, the King of Heaven of Clouds.

Yet another of this group of ancient bird-stories seems to have turned up in a seventeenth century manuscript possessed by Dr Hyde, once in the Reeves collection. It has not yet been edited. It appears to be the story of the solitary crane of Moy Léana, but it is mis-named apparently from the first lines of the two opening stanzas where the bird is addressed, 'A Chorr úd thall san léana', 'O Crane, yonder in the meadow' or 'marsh', which has suggested a likeness to the famous Irish battle of Moy Léana, with which it has nothing to do. It is a very long poem of 146 stanzas and is a conversation with a crane who speaks in reply to questions by Oisín (Ossian). She tells him that she had been a woman named Miadhach, daughter of Echdonn, but she had been changed by sorcery into a crane with the stroke of two golden wands by her father, who was jealous of her affection for her lover. For over two hundred years in all she had been wandering from oak to oak. Oisín replies by a long tale related in true Ossianic fashion about the arrival of a noble warrior from Lochlann (Norway), who lands in Ireland and plays chess with Fionn and his Fianna, with their respective wives at stake. Three times they play and the stranger is victorious and carries off the women to Norway, after which all sorts of misfortunes and adventures befall. It is a regular Ossianic legend, such as was common to both Scotland and Ireland in the later centuries.

Dr Hyde tells us that 'the crow of Achill' is a bird that every Irish speaker in the West has heard of. It is indiscriminately called a crow, a hawk, and even a raven. Mr C. Otway tells us that there is a legend in Mr Knight's work on Erris, which relates how a Viking chieftain visited Ireland, and had made love to an Irish woman, Munhanna, who had disclosed to him the secret of her husband's invincibility and had caused the Viking to slay him while he slept. On his return the woman insists on accompanying him to Norway, but he cast her off into the billows near Lough Carrowmore, where she was drowned. 'On went the cruel Northerner, glad to be rid of one who might betray him in his sleep; and a crane was now seen flapping its heavy wings over the roaring waters. It shrieked with a voice that sounded like the word "Revenge", and then she urged her flight towards the cliffs of Iniskea, where, according to O'Flaherty and other chroniclers, she stands and will stand alive and solitary until the end of time.' The author adds that the inhabitants now 'know nothing of the fated crane that old writers say is to stand there till the crack of doom; she may be there but no one ever saw her.' Dr Hyde's testimony, however, contradicts this; the memory of the story may have died out among the English speakers and have been retained by speakers of Irish.

The legend of the oldest living things is not, in Ireland, confined to animals. It may be a thorn bush, or a tree, that retains a memory of historical events, and is ever ready to recite them to an interested listener. This idea comes down to quite modern times. Raftery, the blind poet of County Mayo, has written such a poem, very long, called *Seanchus na Sgeiche*, or the 'Old Lore of the Thorn-bush', which describes how, being caught in a downpour of rain, he took shelter under a ditch in a gap in the hedge for an hour and a quarter. He was spending the time in pious reflections when suddenly the wind rose and the sun shone out and he made his way home for the night. Next morning he returns to the same spot and begins to fall out with an old thorn-tree for not having given him better shelter from the rain. The old thorn answers that it is unfair to expect much from him in the way of shelter seeing that he was created one thousand one hundred years before the Ark was made and had been living on the same spot ever since. Then obligingly he offers to while away the time by giving Raftery a little account of the history of the world, and of Ireland in particular, since that date. In 99 stanzas he fulfils his promise, beginning with Noah and ending with Cromwell.

A very similar poem, of which Raftery may have heard, is found in the British Museum (Eg. 178, Art. 35) where also a bard Seamus O'Cathain, or James Kein, took shelter under the trunk of a huge withered oak in County Roscommon and made a rhyming history of Ireland, while he was detained there, in the form of a dialogue with the tree.

We might, had we time, consider the birds of Irish folk-legend from many other points of view besides that of story-tellers and historians. There are the sea-birds at whom Cuchulain aimed his sling-stone and who turned into maidens the most beautiful that the world had ever seen. There were the lovely birds of varied plumage who flew two and two linked together with silver chains to guide the Ulster heroes to the place where Cuchulain was to be born and who, flinging off their bird-skins, showed themselves as Dechtire, his mother, and her fifty companions. There were the scall-crows and ravens into which the goddesses of war, Badb and Morrigu, transformed themselves when they followed the march of armies or hovered over a battle-field.

And there were the birds of fairyland, singing everlastingly from the pure purple trees which stand at the Eastern door of the haunts of the blest. It is but a short step from this conception to that of the birds of Paradise, where a bird of red gold with its hundred wings sings from every golden cross which guards the entries, and the splendid bird-flock sustains a perfect melody from the flowering tree of life within the heavenly bounds.

The love of animals and birds is a strong motive in early Irish Christian literature. Columba hails the bird which is winging its way from his loved Donegal across the ocean, and he bids his monks pay heed to it when it falls exhausted on the strand of Iona; swans from Killarney come at the call of Cainnech and those from Lough Foyle at the call of St Comgall. Swans sing to the monks of Colman Ela, to console them at their work, and sea-birds wing their flight to save a drowning child. A blackbird builds his nest on St Kevin's hand outstretched in prayer. The souls of the blest take the form of doves and swans; lost souls become ravens or birds of ill-omen.

Bird-souls gather in flocks around Elijah and Enoch in Paradise; they lament and beat their wings against their sides and weep tears of sorrow as he foretells the terrors of the day of doom.

But of all bird-stories perhaps the most beautiful is that told in different forms of St Brendan and St Mochaoi of Nendrum. It is not apparently a purely Irish story, for Nansen knew a Norwegian version, and there may be others. Its shortest form is that of St Mochaoi, and I will end with this.

Mochaoi, Abbot of Nendrum, in Ulster, went one day with seven score youths to cut wattles to make a church. He was himself engaged at the work, cutting timber down like the rest. He had his load ready before the others and laid it down beside him. As he awaited them, he heard a bright bird singing on the blackthorn nearby. He was more beautiful than the birds of the world. And the bird said: 'Thou workest hard, O Cleric.' 'Such work is required of us in building a church of God,' said Mochaoi. 'Who, now, is addressing me?' 'It is a man of the people of my Lord who is here, even an angel of God from heaven.' 'Hail to thee,' said Mochaoi; 'Wherefore hast thou come hither?' 'To address thee from thy Lord and to amuse thee for a while.' 'I like that,' said Mochaoi. Then the bird put its beak in the feathers of its wing, and for three hundred years did the saint remain listening to him, having his bundle of sticks by his side in the middle of the wood. The wood was not the more withered, nor did the time seem to him longer than one hour of the day. Afterwards the angel bade him farewell.

Then he went to the church, having his wattles with him, and he saw an oratory in the church which had been erected for his soul by his people. He wondered at seeing the church thus. Then he went to the dwelling, but none of them knew the other, until he himself told them his story and how he was cared for by the bird. When they heard this, they all knelt to him, and they made a shrine of the wood; and afterwards they built a church at that place where he had listened to the bird. An old poet writes:

> To Mochaoi the beautiful
> Sang the little bird,
> From the skies, from the tree-tops,
> Three melodies, fifty years in each.

The Finding of Mabon[11]

This extract, from the great *Mabinogion* tale *Culhwch and Olwen*, directly relates to the tradition of the Oldest Animals. It tells of the finding of Mabon, the divine Celtic youth, who is crucial to the fulfilment of the multiple and impossible tasks which Culhwch has been set by the giant Yspaddaden. Mabon has been lost since the beginning of time and can only be found by the chain of memory forged by animals. Mabon has a primally paradisal quality which is accessible only through the chain of the Oldest Animals; his coming brings access to innocence, truth and justice as well as the overthrow of whatever is corrupt. Caitlín Matthews has written extensively on this subject in *Mabon and the Mysteries of Britain*. This extract is from Lady Charlotte Guest's translation of *The Mabinogion*.

Now, when they told Arthur how they had sped, Arthur said, 'Which of these marvels will it be best for us to seek first?' 'It will be best,' said they, 'to seek Mabon the son of Modron; and he will not be found unless we first find Eidoel, the son of Aer, his kinsman.' Then Arthur rose up, and the warriors of the Islands of Britain with him, to seek for Eidoel; and they proceeded until they came before the Castle of Glivi, where Eidoel was imprisoned. Glivi stood on the summit of his castle, and he said, 'Arthur, what requirest thou of me, since nothing remains to me in this fortress, and I have neither joy nor pleasure in it; neither wheat nor oats? Seek not therefore to do me harm.' Said Arthur, 'Not to injure thee came I hither, but to seek for the prisoner that is with thee.' 'I will give thee my prisoner, though I had not thought to give him up to any one; and therewith shalt thou have my support and my aid.'

His followers said unto Arthur, 'Lord, go thou home, thou canst not proceed with thy host in quest of such small adventures as these.' Then said Arthur, 'It were well for thee, Gwrhyr Gwalstawd Ieithoedd, to go upon this quest, for thou knowest all languages, and art familiar with those of the birds and the beasts. Thou, Eidoel, oughtest likewise to go with my men in search of thy cousin. And as for you, Kai and Bedwyr, I have hope of whatever adventure ye are in quest of, that ye will achieve it. Achieve ye this adventure for me.'

They went forward until they came to the Ousel of Cilgwri. And Gwrhyr adjured her for the sake of Heaven, saying, 'Tell me if thou knowest aught of Mabon the son of Modron, who was taken when three nights old from between his mother and the wall.' And the Ousel answered, 'When I first came here, there was a smith's anvil in this place, and I was then a young bird; and from that time no work has been done upon it, save the pecking of my beak every evening, and now there is not so much as the size of a nut remaining thereof; yet the vengeance of Heaven be upon me, if during all that time I have ever heard of the man for whom you inquire. Nevertheless I will do that which is right, and that which it is fitting that I should do for an embassy from Arthur. There is a race of animals who were formed before me, and I will be your guide to them.'

So they proceeded to the place where was the Stag of Redynvre. 'Stag of Redynvre, behold we are come to thee, an embassy from Arthur, for we have not heard of any animal older than thou. Say, knowest thou aught of Mabon the son of Modron, who was taken from his mother when three nights old?' The Stag said, 'When first I came hither, there was a plain all around me, without any trees save one oak sapling, which grew up to be an oak with an hundred branches. And that oak has since perished, so that now nothing remains of it but the withered stump; and from that day to this I have been here, yet have I never heard of the man for whom you inquire. Nevertheless, being an embassy from Arthur, I will be your guide to the place where there is an animal which was formed before I was.'

So they proceeded to the place where was the Owl of Cwm Cawlwyd. 'Owl of Cwm Cawlwyd, here is an embassy from Arthur; knowest thou aught of Mabon the son of Modron, who was taken after three nights from his mother?' 'If I knew I would tell you. When first I came hither, the wide valley you see was a wooded glen. And a race of men came and rooted it up. And there grew there a second wood; and this wood is the third. My wings, are they not withered stumps? Yet all this time, even until to-day, I have never heard of the man for whom you inquire. Nevertheless, I will be the guide of Arthur's embassy until you come to the place where is the oldest animal in this world, and the one that has travelled most, the Eagle of Gwern Abwy.'

Gwrhyr said, 'Eagle of Gwern Abwy, we have come to thee an embassy from Arthur, to ask thee if thou knowest aught of Mabon the son of Modron, who was taken from his mother when he was three nights old.' The Eagle said, 'I have been here for a great space of time, and when I first came hither there was a rock here, from the top of which I pecked at the stars every evening; and now it is not so much as a span high. From that day to this I have been here, and I have never heard of the man for whom you inquire, except once when I went in search of food as far as Llyn Llyw. And when I came there, I struck my talons into a salmon, thinking he would serve me as food for a long time. But he drew me into the deep, and I was scarcely able to escape from him. After that I went with my whole kindred to attack him, and to try to destroy him, but he sent messengers, and made peace with me; and came and besought me to take fifty fish spears out of his back. Unless he know something of him whom you seek, I cannot tell who may. However, I will guide you to the place where he is.'

So they went thither; and the Eagle said, 'Salmon of Llyn Llyw, I have come to thee with an embassy from Arthur, to ask thee if thou knowest aught concerning Mabon the son of Modron, who was taken away at three nights old from his mother.' 'As much as I know I will tell thee. With every tide I go along the river upwards, until I come near to the walls of Gloucester, and there have I found such wrong as I never found elsewhere; and to the end that ye may give credence thereto, let one of you go thither upon each of my two shoulders.' So Kai and Gwrhyr Gwalstawd Ieithoedd went upon the two shoulders of the salmon, and they proceeded until they came unto the wall of the prison, and they heard a great wailing and lamenting from the dungeon. Said Gwrhyr, 'Who is it that laments in this house of stone?' 'Alas, there is reason enough for whoever is here to lament. It is Mabon the son of Modron who is here imprisoned; and no imprisonment was ever so grievous as mine, neither that of Lludd Llaw Ereint, nor that of Greid the son of Eri.' 'Hast thou hope of being released for gold or for silver, or for any gifts of wealth, or through battle and fighting?' 'By fighting will whatever I may gain be obtained.'

Then they went thence, and returned to Arthur, and they told him where Mabon the son of Modron was imprisoned. And Arthur summoned the warriors of the Island, and they journeyed as far as Gloucester, to the place where Mabon was in prison. Kai and Bedwyr went upon the shoulders of the fish, whilst the warriors of Arthur attacked the castle. And Kai broke through the wall into the dungeon, and brought away the prisoner upon his back, whilst the fight was going on between the warriors. And Arthur returned home, and Mabon with him at liberty.

CHAPTER FOUR

The Memory of the Ancestors

The memory of all species is potent to recall and revive all that is lost, and none more so than the memory of the ancestors. Ancestral reverence is almost absent from our present culture, but it plays a central part in the Celtic shamanic tradition.

The human condition is about forgetting and remembering. Sometimes knowledge is obscured by migration, war, pestilence and famine. Many present-day descendants of emigrants from Britain and Ireland are attempting to recontact their native homeland. Usually a strong musical or storytelling tradition survives, but not always. Complacency is the enemy of oracy: the day when a tradition becomes so obvious that everyone knows it and no one cares to take special trouble to remember it and why, when or how it is done is often the day when that tradition founders. There are frequently stories of how knowledge is lost, shipwrecked on the shores of wayward time, only to be resuscitated just before it is too late.

The shamanic solution to tribal forgetfulness is to ask the ancestors and seek their wisdom. In this section, we have three examples of how the ancestors return to help and advise. In Tuan mac Carill and Fintan, we have ancestral elders of shamanic ability. In the essay by Caitlín Matthews, which follows these texts, we draw together some of the dispersed teachings on ancestral consultation.

Tuan mac Carill's Story[1]

The story of Tuan mac Carill, great-grandson of the invader, Partholon, gives us the link between the animals and the ancestors. Tuan relates to St Finnian of Moville (d. 579), the teacher of St Columba, the successive invasions of Ireland. Tuan alone survives his race and lives through subsequent ages in the shapes of a stag, a wild boar, a hawk and a salmon, until he is caught by fishermen and served up to the wife of Cairell. He is born of her womb with full memory of all that has befallen him in past existences.

The transmigrations of Tuan are not exactly reincarnations, since he seems to retain his own nature, changing his shape during sleep. *Cormac's Glossary* cites the word *tuirgin* as a possible technical term for this transmigration, defining it as 'a birth that passes from every nature into another . . . a transitory birth which has traversed all nature from Adam and goes through every wonderful time down to the world's doom'. The *tuirgin* or 'investigative birth-seekings' of Tuan do indeed traverse the realm of animals, while retaining a human intelligence and memory. The shamanic ability to take vision-flights in the shape of animals and other species, to enter into their life, is here captured in the triumphal poetic outpourings of Tuan.

1. After Finnen of Moville had come with the Gospel to Ireland, into the territory of the men of Ulster, he went to a wealthy warrior there, who would not let them come to him into the stronghold, but left them fasting there over Sunday. The warrior's faith was not good. Said Finnen to his followers: 'There will come to you a good man, who will comfort you, and who will tell you the history of Ireland from the time that it was first colonised until to-day.'

2. Then on the morrow early in the morning there came to them a venerable cleric, who bade them welcome. 'Come with me to my hermitage,' said he, 'that is meeter for you.' They went with him, and they perform the duties of the Lord's day, both with psalms and preaching and offering. Thereupon Finnen asked him to tell his name. Said he to them: 'Of the men of Ulster am I. Tuan, son of Cairell, son of Muredach Red-neck, am I. I have taken this hermitage, in which thou art, upon the hereditary land of my father. Tuan, son of Starn, son of Sera, son of Partholon's brother, that was my name of yore at first.'

3. Then Finnen asked him about the events of Ireland, to wit, what had happened in it from the time of Partholon, son of Sera. And Finnen said they would not eat with him until he had told them the stories of Ireland. Said Tuan to Finnen: 'It is hard for us not to meditate upon the Word of God which thou hast just told to us.' But Finnen said: 'Permission is granted thee to tell thy own adventures and the story of Ireland to us now.'

4. 'Five times, verily,' said he, 'Ireland was taken after the Flood, and it was not taken after the Flood until 312 years had gone. Then Partholon, son of Sera, took it. He had gone upon a voyage with twenty-four couples. The cunning of each of them against the other was not great. They settled in Ireland until there were 5000 of their race. Between two Sundays a mortality came upon them, so that all died, save one man only. For a slaughter is not usual without some one to come out of it to tell the tale. That man am I,' said he.

5. 'Then I was from hill to hill, and from cliff to cliff, guarding myself from wolves, for twenty-two years, during which Ireland was empty. At last old age came upon me, and I was on cliffs and in wastes, and was unable to move about, and I had special caves for myself. Then Nemed, son of Agnoman, my father's brother, invaded Ireland, and I saw them from the cliffs and kept avoiding them, and I hairy, clawed, withered, grey, naked, wretched, miserable. Then, as I was asleep one night, I saw myself passing into the shape of a stag. In that shape I was, and I young and glad of heart. It was then I spoke these words:

> Strengthless to-day is Senba's son,
> From vigour he has been parted,
> Not under fair fame with new strength,
> Senba's son is an old . . .

> These men that come from the east
> With their spears that achieve valour,
> I have no strength in foot or hand
> To go to avoid them.

> Starin, fierce is the man,
> I dread Scemel of the white shield,
> Andind will not save me, though good and fair,
> If it were Beoin, . . .

Though Beothach would leave me alive,
Cacher's rough fight is rough,
Britan achieves valour with his spears,
There is a fit of fury on Fergus.

They are coming towards me, O gentle Lord,
The offspring of Nemed, Agnoman's son,
Stoutly they are lying in wait for my blood,
To compass my first wounding.

Then there grew upon my head
Two antlers with three score points,
So that I am rough and grey in shape
After my age has changed from feebleness.

7. 'After this, from the time that I was in the shape of a stag, I was the leader of the herds of Ireland, and wherever I went there was a large herd of stags about me. In that way I spent my life during the time of Nemed and his offspring. When Nemed came with his fleet to Ireland, their number was thirty-four barques, thirty in each barque, and the sea cast them astray for the time of a year and a half on the Caspian Sea, and they were drowned and died of hunger and thirst, except four couples only together with Nemed. Thereafter his race increased and had issue until there were 4030 couples. However, these all died.

8. 'Then at last old age came upon me, and I fled from men and wolves. Once as I was in front of my cave – I still remember it – I knew that I was passing from one shape into another. Then I passed into the shape of a wild boar. 'Tis then I said:

A boar am I to-day among herds,
A mighty lord I am with great triumphs,
He has put me in wonderful grief,
The King of all, in many shapes.

In the morning when I was at Dún Bré,
Fighting against old seniors,
Fair was my troop across the pool,
A beautiful host was following us.

My troop, they were swift
Among hosts in revenge,
They would throw my spears alternately
On the warriors of Fál on every side.

> When we were in our gathering
> Deciding the judgments of Partholon,
> Sweet to all was what I said,
> Those were the words of true approach.
>
> Sweet was my brilliant judgment
> Among the women with beauty,
> Stately was my fair chariot,
> Sweet was my song across a dark road.
>
> Swift was my step without straying
> In battles at the onset,
> Fair was my face, there was a day,
> Though to-day I am a boar.

9. 'In that shape, he said, I was then truly, and I young and glad of mind. And I was king of the boar-herds of Ireland, and I still went the round of my abode when I used to come into this land of Ulster at the time of my old age and wretchedness; for in the same place I changed into all these shapes. Therefore I always visited that place to await the renewal.

10. 'Thereupon Semion, the son of Stariath, seized this island. From them are the Fir Domnann, and the Fir Bolg, and the Galiuin; and these inhabited this island for the time that they dwelt in Ireland. Then old age came upon me, and my mind was sad, and I was unable to do all that I used to do before, but was alone in dark caves and in hidden cliffs.

11. 'Then I went to my own dwelling always. I remembered every shape in which I had been before. I fasted my three days as I had always done. I had no strength left. Thereupon I went into the shape of a large hawk. Then my mind was again happy. I was able to do anything. I was eager and lusty. I would fly across Ireland; I would find out everything. 'Tis then I said:

> A hawk to-day, a boar yesterday,
> Wonderful . . . inconstancy!
> Dearer to me every day
> God, the friend who has shapen me.
>
> Many are the offspring of Nemed
> Without obedience . . . to the certain King,
> Few to-day are the race of Sera;
> I know not what caused it.

Among herds of boars I was,
Though to-day I am among bird-flocks;
I know what will come of it:
I shall still be in another shape.

Wonderfully has dear God disposed
Me and the children of Nemed;
They at the will of the demon of God,
While, for me, God is my help.

12. 'Beothach, the son of Iarbonel the prophet, seized this island from the races that dwelt in it. From them are the Tuatha Dé and Andé, whose origin the learned do not know, but that it seems likely to them that they came from heaven, on account of their intelligence and for the excellence of their knowledge.

13. 'Then I was for a long time in the shape of that hawk, so that I outlived all those races who had invaded Ireland. However, the sons of Mil took this island by force from the Tuatha Dé Danann. Then I was in the shape of that hawk in which I had been, and was in the hollow of a tree on a river.

14. 'There I fasted for three days and three nights, when sleep fell upon me, and I passed into the shape of a river-salmon there and then. Then God put me into the river so that I was in it. Once more I felt happy and was vigorous and well-fed, and my swimming was good, and I used to escape from every danger and from every snare – to wit, from the hands of fishermen, and from the claws of hawks, and from fishing spears – so that the scars which each one of them left are still on me.

15. 'Once, however, when God, my help, deemed it time, and when the beasts were pursuing me, and every fisherman in every pool knew me, the fisherman of Cairell, the king of that land, caught me and took me with him to Cairell's wife, who had a desire for fish. Indeed I remember it; the man put me on a gridiron and roasted me. And the queen desired me and ate me by herself, so that I was in her womb. Again, I remember the time that I was in her womb, and what each one said to her in the house, and what was done in Ireland during that time. I also remember when speech came to me, as it comes to any man, and I knew all that was being done in Ireland, and I was a seer; and a name was given to me – to wit, Tuan, son of Cairell. Thereupon Patrick came with the faith to Ireland. Then I was of great age; and I

was baptized, and alone believed in the King of all things with his elements.'

16. Thereupon they celebrate mass and go into their refectory, Finnen with his followers and Tuan, after he had told them these stories. And there they stay a week conversing together. Every history and every pedigree that is in Ireland, 'tis from Tuan, son of Cairell, the origin of that history is. He had conversed with Patrick before them, and had told him; and he had conversed with Colum Cille, and had prophesied to him in the presence of the people of the land. And Finnen offered him that he should stay with him, but he could not obtain it from him. 'Thy house will be famous till doom,' said Tuan.

The Settling of the Manor of Tara[2]

The fulcrum of memory is central to this story. We have given this text in full because of its detailed description of the apportioning of Ireland. Each province of Ireland is characterized exactly and these qualities are still demonstrable today: those who look for a root cause of the Irish troubles could do worse than to read this text.

In this story, we read about the Feast of Tara, which all the notables of Ireland attended with their retinue, to the inconvenience of all present. How the land around Tara is to be apportioned is a task no one wants and the High King, Diarmuid mac Cerball (reigned 545–65) discovers that a wise man is hard to find. (1–6) The oldest man in Ireland is brought, Fintan mac Bóchra, grandson of Noah, who has survived from the Deluge. He gives a history of Ireland (7–9) but doubt is cast upon the reliability of his memory, so Fintan recalls the planting and harvesting of a yew tree, the oldest and slowest-growing tree in Ireland, and demonstrates his ability to arbitrate justly. (10–13) He is asked how he acquired this knowledge and relates a story about an assembly held in a much earlier reign at which a wondrous otherworldly being appeared. Trefuilngid Tre-eochair (the Strong Upholder of the Three Keys) relates the origins of the Irish

(14–19), then asks to hear what chronicles have been preserved by the *seanchais* (the wise ones, chroniclers or storytellers); the assembly shamefully admits that they have no traditions and Trefuilngid offers to teach seven *seanchais* from each quarter of Ireland. Fintan was one of these men and relates to Trefuilngid the nature of each of the provinces of the quarters. (20–8) Trefuilngid leaves with Fintan some berries which will become the great trees of Ireland. Fintan himself survives even these ancient trees. (29–30) The assembly at Tara promises to uphold the traditions related by Trefuilngid and apportions the five provinces accordingly. (31–3) Death comes for Fintan, whose funeral is attended by the spirits of Patrick and Brigit and his body is borne away like those of Elijah and Enoch.

This Middle Irish text from *The Yellow Book of Lecan* is full of Christian elements which are still recognizably partisans of the Celtic otherworldly tradition. The ancestral continuity of memory is assisted by Fintan, himself a descendant of Noah, and a primal ancestral figure. Trefuilngid Tre-eochair, who is described as an angel, if not God himself, bears the typically otherworldly branch with its nuts, apples and acorns. He is a titanic figure in the mould of Bran the Blessed, a being who upholds both the lore of the natural world and the lore of Christianity: in the mind of this story's composer, the strong linkage of ancestral responsibility unites the old and new traditions and Trefuilngid is himself an archetypal *seanchai* who is learned in both directions.

1. The Ui Neill were once in conference in Magh Bregh in the time of Diarmait son of Fergus Cerball, and this was what they discussed. The demesne of Tara seemed excessive to them, that is, the plain with seven views on every side, and they considered the curtailing of that green, for they deemed it unprofitable to have so much land without house or cultivation upon it, and of no service to the hearth of Tara. For every three years they were obliged to support the men of Ireland and to feed them for seven days and seven nights. It was in this fashion then they used to proceed to the feast of Diarmait son of Cerball. No king used to go without a queen, or chieftain without a chieftainess, or warrior without . . . or fop without a harlot, or hospitaller without a consort, or youth without a love, or maiden without a lover, or man without an art.

2. The kings and ollaves used to be placed around Diarmait son of Cerball, that is, kings and ollaves together, warriors and reavers

together. The youths and maidens and the proud foolish folk in the
chambers around the doors; and his proper portion was given to each
one, that is, choice fruit and oxen and boars and flitches for kings and
ollaves, and for the free noble elders of the men of Ireland likewise:
stewards and stewardesses carving and serving for them. Then red
meat from spits of iron, and bragget and new ale and milk water [?]
for warriors and reavers: and jesters and cup-bearers carving and serving for them. Heads-and-feet [?] next and . . . of all [kinds of] cattle
to charioteers and jugglers and for the rabble and common people,
with charioteers and jugglers and doorkeepers carving and dispensing
for them. Veal then and lamb and pork and the seventh portion . . .
outside for young men and maidens, because their mirth used to entertain them . . . and their nobility [?] used to be awaiting them [?]. Free
mercenaries and female hirelings carving and dispensing for them.

3. The nobles of Ireland were then summoned to the feast to the
house of Tara by Diarmait son of Cerball. And they said that they
would not partake of the feast of Tara until the settling of the manor
of Tara was determined, how it was before their day and how it would
be after them for all time, and they delivered that answer to Diarmait.
And Diarmait replied that it was not right to ask him to partition the
manor of Tara without taking counsel of Flann Febla son of Scannlan
son of Fingen, that is, the head of Ireland and the successor of Patrick,
or of Fiachra son of the embroideress. Messengers were accordingly
dispatched to Fiachra son of Colman son of Eogan, and he was brought
unto them to help them, for few were their learned men, and many
were their unlearned, and numerous their contentions and their problems.

4. Then Fiachra arrived, and they asked the same thing of him, namely to partition for them the manor of Tara. And he answered them
that he would not give a decision on that matter until they should send
for one wiser and older than himself. 'Where is he?' said they. 'No
hard matter that,' said he, 'even Cennfaelad son of Ailill son of
Muiredach son of Eogan son of Niall. It is from his head,' said he, 'that
the brain of forgetfulness was removed at the battle of Magh Rath, that
is to say, he remembers all that he heard of the history of Ireland from
that time down to the present day. It is right that he should come to
decide for you.'

5. Cennfaelad was then sent for, and he came to them, and they asked
him also the same thing. And Cennfaelad replied: 'It is not proper for

you to ask that of me so long as the five seniors to us all are in Ireland.'
'Where then are they?' said the men of Ireland. 'Easy to tell,' said he,
'Finnchad from Falmag of Leinster, and Cú-alad from Cruachu
Conalad, and Bran Bairne from Bairenn, Dubán son of Deg from the
province of the Fir Olnegmacht, Tuan son of Cairell from Ulster, he
who passed into many shapes.'

6. These five were then sent for, and they were brought to them to
Tara, and they asked the same thing of them, namely, to partition for
them the manor of Tara. Then each of the five related what he remembered, and this is what they said, that it was not proper for them to
partition Tara and its manor so long as their senior and fosterer in
Ireland were without the assembly. 'Where then is he?' asked the men
of Ireland. 'Not hard to tell,' said they. 'Fintan son of Bóchra, son of
Bith, son of Noah.' He was at Dun Tulcha in Kerry.

7. Then Berran, Cennfaelad's attendant, went for Fintan to Dun
Tulcha to the west of Luachair Dedaid. And he delivered his message
to him. Then Fintan came with him to Tara. And his retinue consisted of eighteen companies, namely, nine before him and nine behind.
And there was not one among them who was not of the seed of Fintan
– sons, grandsons, great-grandsons, and descendants of his was that
host.

8. A great welcome was given to Fintan in the banqueting house, and
all were glad at his coming to hear his words and his stories. And they
all rose up before him, and they bade him sit in the judge's seat. But
Fintan said he would not go into it until he knew his question. And
he said to them 'There is no need to make rejoicing for me, for I am
sure of your welcome as every son is sure of his fostermother, and this
then is my fostermother,' said Fintan, 'the island in which ye are, even
Ireland, and the familiar knee of this island is the hill on which ye are,
namely, Tara. Moreover, it is the mast and the produce, the flowers
and the food of this island that have sustained me from the Deluge
until to-day. And I am skilled in its feasts and its cattle-spoils, its
destructions and its courtships, in all that have taken place from the
Deluge until now.' And then he made a lay:

9.   Ireland, though it is enquired of me,
         I know accurately
         every colonization it has undergone
         since the beginning of the pleasant world.

Cessair came from the east,
the woman, daughter of Bith,
with her fifty maidens
and her trio of men.

The Deluge overtook them,
though it was a sad pity,
and drowned them all
each one on his height.

Bith north in Sliab Betha,
sad was the mystery,
Ladru in Ard Ladrann,
Cessair in her recess.

As for me I was saved
by the Son of God, a protection over the throng,
the Deluge parted from me
above massive Tul Tuinde.

I was a year under the Deluge
at bracing Tul Tuinde.
There has not been slept, there will not be,
any better sleep.

Then Parthalon came to me
from the east, from the Grecian land,
and I lived on with his progeny
though it was a long way.

I was still in Ireland
when Ireland was a wilderness,
until Agnoman's son came,
Nemed, pleasant his ways.

Next came the Fir Bolg,
that is a fair true tale.
I lived together with them,
whilst they were in the land.

The Fir Bolg and Fir Galion
came, it was long [thereafter].
The Fir Domnann came,
they settled in Irrus in the west.

Then came the Tuatha Dé
in clouds of dark mist,
and I lived along with them
though it was a long life.

The sons of Míl came then
into the land against them
I was along with every tribe
until the time ye see.

After that came the sons of Míl
out of Spain from the south,
and I lived along with them
though mighty was their combat.

I had attained to long life,
I will not hide it,
when the Faith came to me
from the King of the cloudy heaven.

I am white Fintan,
Bóchra's son, I will not hide it.
Since the Deluge here
I am a high noble sage.

10. 'Good, O Fintan,' said they 'We are the better for every neglect [?] which we may cause thee, and we should like to know from thee how reliable thy memory is.' 'That is no hard matter,' said he. 'One day I passed through a wood in West Munster in the west. I took away with me a red yew berry and I planted it in the garden of my court, and it grew up there until it was as big as a man. Then I removed it from the garden and planted it on the lawn of my court even, and it grew up in the centre of that lawn so that I could fit with a hundred warriors under its foliage, and it protected me from wind and rain, and from cold and heat. I remained and so did my yew flourishing together, until it shed its foliage from decay. Then when I had no hope of turning it even so to my profit, I went and cut it from its stock, and made from it seven vats and seven *ians* and seven *drolmachs*, seven churns, seven pitchers, seven *milans*, and seven methars with hoops for all of them. So I remained then and my yew vessels with me until their hoops fell off through decay and age. Then I re-made them all, but could get only an *ian* out of a vat, and a *drolmach* out of an *ian*, and a churn out of a *drolmach*, and a pitcher out of a churn, and a *milan* out

of a pitcher, and a methar out of a *milan*. And I swear to Almighty God I know not where those substitutes are since they perished with me from decay.'

11. 'Thou art indeed venerable,' said Diarmait. 'It is transgression of an elder's judgement to transgress thy judgement. And it is for that reason we have summoned thee, that thou shouldst be the one to pronounce just judgement for us.' 'It is true, indeed,' said he, 'that I am skilled in every just judgement that has been given from the beginning of the world until this day.' And then he made the following lay:

12.   I know in this way,
          no foolish one will find it,
          the first judge, boasting and no concealment,
          who pronounced without fault the first judgement.

          Judgement on the Devil over Druim Den.
          I know the manner in which it was given.
          Dear God gave it, the report spread,
          as it was the first crime, 'twas the first judgement.

          The gift divine of dear God,
          so that men should have judgement,
          the law of fair speech [i.e. Latin] was given
          to Moses, greater than every good law.

          Moses delivered, bright deed,
          the perfect judgements of the letter.
          David delivered after that
          the true judgements of prophecy.

          Fénius Farsaid, long-life [?] of favour,
          and Cai Cáin-brethach,
          by them were given, no trifling festival,
          the two and seventy tongues.

          Amairgen of the island of the Gael,
          our gold, our glory, our ray,
          Amairgen Glungel the valorous
          gave the first judgement concerning Tara.

Three kings in Liathdruim na Ler
and the four sons of Míl,
they strove for the mighty possession
of the illustrious island of Ireland.

There Amairgen pronounced for them
the most wise and fair judgement
that the sons of Míl should go out
over ten waves on the mirthful sea.

Thereupon they put out to sea,
the four sons of the king of Spain,
and they buried, a festival over the waves,
Dond, whom they left at Tech Duind.

After valiant and cunning fight
Ir was left in the rough-splintered [?] clay of the Skellig. . .

Thereupon the hosts of Eber and Eremon
departed eastwards,
and after loss of their force they occupied
Ireland, on escaping from Egypt.

Thereafter Jesus was born
from Mary maiden,
and judgements were declared with goodness,
through the pure holy new covenant.

This is enough of eloquence . . .
the little crown of the performances of fair judgements,
that the eager hosts should know,
that they might be learned in learning.

13. 'Good, O Fintan,' said they. 'We are the better of thy coming to relate the story of Ireland.' 'I remember truly,' said he, 'the progression of the history of Ireland, how it has been therein until now, and how it will be also until doom.' 'A question,' said they. 'How hast thou acquired that, and of that history what is indispensable to help us in the matter of our discussion, the settling of the manor of Tara?' 'No hard matter that,' said Fintan. 'I will relate to you meanwhile something thereon.'

14. 'Once we were holding a great assembly of the men of Ireland around Conaing Bec-eclach, King of Ireland. On a day then in that assembly we beheld a great hero, fair and mighty, approaching us from the west at sunset. We wondered greatly at the magnitude of his form. As high as a wood was the top of his shoulders, the sky and the sun visible between his legs, by reason of his size and his comeliness. A shining crystal veil about him like unto raiment of precious linen. Sandals upon his feet, and it is not known of what material they were. Golden-yellow hair upon him falling in curls to the level of his thighs. Stone tablets in his left hand, a branch with three fruits in his right hand, and these are the three fruits which were on it, nuts and apples and acorns in May-time: and unripe was each fruit. He strode past us then round the assembly, with his golden many coloured branch of Lebanon wood behind him, and one of us said to him, 'Come hither and hold speech with the king, Conaing Bec-eclach.' He made answer and said, 'What is it that ye desire of me?' 'To know whence thou hast come,' said they, 'and whither thou goest, and what is thy name and surname.'

15. 'I have come indeed,' said he, 'from the setting of the sun, and I am going unto the rising, and my name is Trefuilngid Tre-eochair.' 'Why has that name been given to thee?' said they. 'Easy to say,' said he. 'Because it is I who cause the rising of the sun and its setting.' 'And what has brought thee to the setting, if it is at the rising thou dost be?' 'Easy to say,' said he. 'A man who has been tortured – that is, who has been crucified by Jews to-day; for it stepped past them after that deed, and has not shone upon them, and that is what has brought me to the setting to find out what ailed the sun; and then it was revealed to me, and when I knew the lands over which the sun set I came to Inis Gluairi off Irrus Domnann; and I found no land from that westwards, for that is the threshold over which the sun sets, just as the Paradise of Adam is the threshold over which it rises.'

16. 'Say then,' said he, 'what is your race, and whence have ye come into this island?' 'Easy to say,' said Conaing Bec-eclach. 'From the children of Míl of Spain and from the Greeks are we sprung. After the building of the Tower of Nimrod, and the confusion of tongues, we came into Egypt, upon the invitation of Pharaoh King of Egypt. Nél son of Fénius and Goedel Glas were our chiefs while we were in the south. Hence we are called Féne from Fénius, that is the Féne, and Gaels from Gaedel Glas, as was said:

The Féne from Fénius are named, meaning without straining,
the Gaels from Gaedel Glas the hospitable, the Scots from
Scota.

Scota, then, the daughter of Pharaoh the king was given as a wife to
Nél son of Fénius on going into Egypt. So that she is our ancestress,
and it is from her we are called Scots.'

17. 'In the night then in which the children of Israel escaped out of
Egypt, when they went with dry feet through the Red Sea with the
leader of the people of God, even Moses son of Amram, and when
Pharaoh and his host were drowned in that sea, having kept the
Hebrews in bondage, because our forefathers went not with the
Egyptians in pursuit of the people of God, they dreaded Pharaoh's
wrath against them should he return, and even if Pharaoh should not
return they feared that the Egyptians would enslave them as they had
enslaved the children of Israel on another occasion. So they escaped in
the night in ten of Pharaoh's ships upon the strait of the Red Sea, upon
the boundless ocean, and round the world north-west, past the
Caucasus mountains, past Scythia and India, across the sea that is there,
namely the Caspian, over the Palus Maeotis, past Europe, from the
south-east to the south-west along the Mediterranean, left-hand to
Africa, past the Columns of Hercules to Spain, and thence to this
island.'

18. 'And Spain,' said Trefuilngid, 'where is that land?' 'Not hard to
say. It is the distance of a great prospect from us to the south,' said
Conaing. 'For it is by a view [?] Ith son of Breogan saw the mountains
of southern Irrus from the top of the tower of Breogan in Spain, and
he it is who came to spy out this island for the sons of Míl, and on his
track we came into it, in the ninth year after the passage of the
Israelites through the Red Sea.'

19. 'How many are you in this island?' said Trefuilngid. 'I should like
to see you *assembled* in one place.' 'We are not so few indeed,' replied
Conaing, 'and if thou desirest it, so shall it be done; only I think it
will distress the people to support thee during that period.' 'It will be
no distress,' said he, 'for the fragrance of this branch which is in my
hand will serve me for food and drink as long as I live.'

20. He remained then with them forty days and nights until the men
of Ireland were assembled for him at Tara. And he saw them all in one
place, and he said to them, 'What chronicles have ye of the men of

Ireland in the royal house of Tara? Make them known to us.' And they answered, 'we have no old shanachies, in truth, to whom we could entrust the chronicles until thou didst come to us.' 'Ye will have that from me,' said he. 'I will establish for you the progression of the stories and chronicles of the hearth of Tara itself with the four quarters of Ireland round about; for I am the truly learned witness who explains to all everything unknown.'

21. 'Bring to me then seven from every quarter in Ireland, who are the wisest, the most prudent and most cunning also, and the shanachies of the king himself who are of the hearth of Tara; for it is right that the four quarters [should be present] at the partition of Tara and its chronicles, that each seven may take its due share of the chronicles of the hearth of Tara.'

22. Thereupon he addressed those shanachies apart, and related to them the chronicles of every part of Ireland. And afterwards he said to the king, even Conaing. 'Do thou come thyself for a space apart that I may relate to thee and the company of the men of Ireland with thee how we have partitioned Ireland, as I have made it known to the four groups of seven yonder.' Thereupon he related it to them all again in general, and it was to me, said Fintan, it was entrusted for explanation and for delivery before the host, I being the oldest shanachie he found before him in Ireland. For I was in Tul Tuinde at the time of the Deluge, and I was alone there after the Deluge for a thousand and two years, when Ireland was desert. And I was co-eval afterwards with every generation that occupied it down to the day Trefuilngid came into the assembly of Conaing Bec-eclach, therefore it was Trefuilngid questioned me through his knowledge of interrogation:

23. 'O Fintan,' said he, 'and Ireland, how has it been partitioned, where have things been therein?'

'Easy to say,' said Fintan: 'knowledge in the west, battle in the north, prosperity in the east, music in the south, kingship in the centre [?].'

'True indeed, O Fintan,' said Trefuilngid, 'thou art an excellent shanachie. It is thus that it has been, and will be for ever, namely:

24. Her learning, her foundation, her teaching, her alliance, her judgement, her chronicles, her counsels, her stories, her histories, her science, her comeliness, her eloquence, her beauty, her modesty [lit. blushing], her bounty, her abundance, her wealth – from the western part in the west.'

'Whence are these?' said the host. 'Easy to say,' he answered.

'From Ae, from Umall, from Aidne, from Bairenn, from Bres, from Breifne, from Brí Airg, from Berramain, from Bagna, from Cera, from Corann, from Cruachu, from Irrus, from Imga, from Imgan, from Tarbga, from Teidmne, from Tulcha, from Muad, from Muiresc, from Meada from Maige (that is, between Traige and Reocha and Lacha), from Mucrama, from Maenmag, from Mag Luirg, from Mag Ene, from Arann, from Aigle, from Airtech.'

25. 'Her battles, also,' said he, 'and her contentions, her hardihood, her rough places, her strifes, her haughtiness, her unprofitableness, her pride, her captures, her assaults, her hardness, her wars, her conflicts, from the northern part in the north.'

'Whence are the foregoing?' said the host. 'Easy to say: From Lie, from Lorg, from Lothar, from Callann, from Farney, from Fidga, from Srub Brain, from Bernas, from Daball, from Ard Fothaid, from Goll, from Irgoll, from Airmmach, from the Glens [?], from Gera, from Gabor, from Emain, from Ailech, from Imclar.'

26. 'Her prosperity then,' said he, 'and her supplies, her bee-hives [?] her contests, her feats of arms, her householders, her nobles, her wonders, her good custom, her good manners, her splendour, her abundance, her dignity, her strength, her wealth, her householding, her many arts, her accoutrements [?], her many treasures, her satin, her serge, her silks, her cloths [?], her green spotted cloth [?], her hospitality, from the eastern part in the east.'

'Whence are these?' said the host. 'Easy to say,' said he.

'From Fethach, from Fothna, from Inrechtra, from Mugna, from Bile, from Bairne, from Berna, from Drenna, from Druach, from Diamar, from Lee, from Line, from Lathirne, from Cuib, from Cualnge, from Cenn Con, from Mag Rath, from Mag Inis, from Mag Muirthemne.'

27. 'Her waterfalls, her fairs, her nobles, her reavers, her knowledge, her subtlety, her musicianship, her melody, her minstrelsy, her wisdom, her honour, her music, her learning, her teaching, her warriorship, her *fidchell* playing, her vehemence, her fierceness, her poetical art, her advocacy, her modesty, her code, her retinue, her fertility, from the southern part in the south.'

'Whence are these,' said they. 'Easy to say,' said Trefuilngid.

'From Mairg, from Maistiu, from Raigne, from Rairiu, from Gabair, from Gabran, from Cliu, from Claire, from Femned [?], from

Faifae, from Bregon, from Barchi, from Cenn Chaille, from Clere, from Cermna, from Raithlinn, from Glennamain, from Gobair, from Luachair, from Labrand, from Loch Léin, from Loch Lugdach, from Loch Daimdeirg, from Cathair Chonroi, from Cathair Cairbri, from Cathair Ulad, from Dun Bindi, from Dun Chain, from Dun Tulcha, from Fertae, from Feorainn, from Fiandainn.'

28. 'Her kings, moreover, her stewards, her dignity, her primacy, her stability, her establishments, her supports, her destructions, her warriorship, her charioteership, her soldiery, her principality, her high-kingship, her ollaveship, her mead, her bounty, her ale, her renown, her great fame, her prosperity, from the centre position.'

'Whence are these?' said they. 'Easy to say,' said Trefuilngid.

'From Mide, from Bile, from Bethre, from Bruiden, from Colba, from Cnodba, from Cuilliu, from Ailbe, from Asal, from Usnech, from Sidan, from Slemain, from Sláine, from Cno, from Cerna, from Cennandus, from Bri Scáil, from Bri Graigi, from Bri meic Thaidg, from Bri Foibri, from Bri Dili, from Bri Fremain, from Tara, from Tethbe, from Temair Broga Niad, from Temair Breg, the overlordship of all Ireland from these.'

29. So Trefuilngid Tre-eochair left that ordinance with the men of Ireland for ever, and he left with Fintan son of Bóchra some of the berries from the branch which was in his hand, so that he planted them in whatever places he thought it likely they would grow in Ireland. And these are the trees which grew up from those berries: the Ancient Tree of Tortu and the tree of Ross, the tree of Mugna and the Branching Tree of Dathe, and the Ancient Tree of Usnech. And Fintan remained relating the stories to the men of Ireland until he was himself the survivor [?] of the ancient trees, and until they had withered during his time. So when Fintan perceived his own old age and that of the trees, he made a lay:

30.　　I see clearly to-day
　　　　in the early morn after uprising
　　　　from Dun Tulcha in the west away
　　　　over the top of the wood of Lebanon.

　　　　By God's doom I am an old man,
　　　　I am more unwilling than ever for . . .
　　　　It is long since I drank [?] a drink
　　　　of the Deluge over the navel of Usnech.

Bile Tortan, Eó Rosa,
one as lovely and bushy as the other.
Mugna and Craebh Daithi to-day
and Fintan surviving [?].

So long as Ess Ruaid resounds,
so long as salmon are disporting therein
Dun Tulcha, to which the sea comes
it will not depart from a good shanachie.

I am a shanachie myself before every host,
a thousand years, and no mistake,
before the time of the sons of Míl, abundance of strength,
I was bearing clear testimony.

31. So he made this lay, and remained to relate the stories of the men of Ireland even until the time he was summoned by Diarmait son of Cerball, and Flann Febla son of Scannlan, and Cennfaelad son of Ailill, and the men of Ireland also to pronounce judgement for them concerning the establishment of the manor of Tara. And this is the judgement he passed, 'let it be as we have found it,' said Fintan, 'we shall not go contrary to the arrangement which Trefuilngid Tre-eochair has left us, for he was an angel of God, or he was God Himself.'

32. Then the nobles of Ireland came as we have related to accompany Fintan to Usnech, and they took leave of one another on the top of Usnech. And he set up in their presence a pillar-stone of five ridges on the summit of Usnech. And he assigned a ridge of it to every province in Ireland, for thus are Tara and Usnech in Ireland, as its two kidneys are in a beast. And he marked out a *forrach* there, that is, the portion of each province in Usnech, and Fintan made this lay after arranging the pillar-stone:

33.   The five divisions of Ireland, both sea and land,
       their confines will be related, of every division of them.
       From Drowes of the vast throng, south of Belach Cuairt,
       to the swollen Boyne, Segais's pleasant stream.
       From white-streaming Boyne, with its hundreds of harbours
       to multitudinous cold Comar Tri nUsci.
       From that same Comor with pleasant . . .
       to the pass of the fierce Hound which is called Glas.
       From that Belach Conglais, shapely the smile,
       to broad green Luimnech, which beats against barks.

From the port of that Luimnech, a level green plain,
to the green-leaved Drowes against which the sea beats.
Wise the division which the roads have attained [?],
perfect the arrangement dividing it into five.

The points of the great provinces run towards Usnech,
they have divided yonder stone through it into five.

34. So Fintan then testified that it was right to take the five provinces
of Ireland from Tara and Usnech, and that it was right for them also
to be taken from each province in Ireland. Then he took leave of the
men of Ireland at that place, and he comes to Dun Tulcha in Ciarraighe
Luachra, where he was overcome by weakness, and he made the following lay:

Feeble to-day is my long-lived life,
decay has arrested my motion.
I change not shape any longer
I am Fintan son of Bóchra.

I was a full year under the Deluge
in the power of the holy Lord,
and a thousand pleasant years
was I all alone after the Deluge.

Then the pure bright company came
and settled in Inber Bairche.
And I wedded the noble dame
Aife, Parthalon's daughter.

I was for a long while after that
a contemporary of Parthalon
until there sprang from him thus
a vast innumerable throng.

The plague of sin reached them
in the east of Sliabh Elpa,
from it, fierce the hold,
is named Tamlacht in Ireland.

I spent thirty years after that
until the arrival of the children of Nemed,
between Iath Boirche, it was ancient,
living on grass, without contention.

On Magh Rain, with the knowledge of the Lord,
I wedded Éblenn of the radiant skin,
sister of Lugh, swiftness without treachery,
daughter of Cian and of Ethliu.

I remember, tale without tribute,
the legend of Magh Rain,
in the puissant battle of Magh Tuired
the children of Gomer wrought havoc.

It was a spreading wood, with supple branch
in the days of the Tuatha De Danann,
until the Fomorians bore it away to the east
in their boat-frames, after [the death] of Balor

. . . .

daughter of Toga of the grey stormy sea,
at that time 'twas a woman,
she from whom Sliabh Raisen is named.

Lecco the daughter of mighty Tal
and of Mid whom hostages used to magnify,
she found them on the hill, without sorrow
in the company of Mid from the south-east.

Though I am in Dun Tulcha to-day
nearer and nearer is dissolution,
the good King who hath fostered me hitherto,
'tis He that hath put weakness on me.

35. Now he was sore afflicted when he perceived signs of death approaching, but when he knew that God deemed it time for him to die, without undergoing further change of form, he then made the following lay:

I am wasted to-day in Comor Cuan,
I have no trouble in telling it,
I was born, I prospered
fifty years before the Deluge.

The bright King vouchsafed to me
that my good fortune should be prolonged,
five hundred, and five thousand years till now,
that is the length of the time.

In Magh Mais, in the secret places thereof,
where Gleoir is, son of Glainide [?],
it is there I have drunk a drink of age
since none of my co-evals remain.

The first ship, the celebration has been heard,
which reached Ireland after the transgression,
I came in it from the east.
I am fair-haired Bóchra's son.

It is from him I was born, from the lord,
the descendant of Noah, Lamech's son;
after the destruction of Cessair I have been a space
relating the story of Ireland.

Bith son of Noah before all men
was the first who came to dwell therein,
and Ladru the helmsman after that,
the first to be buried in the earth.

I give thanks to God, I am a venerable senior,
to the King who fashioned the holy heaven;
it profits me nowise, however it be,
my decay is no help to me.

Five invasions, best of deeds,
the land of Ireland has undergone.
I have been here a while after them
until the days of the sons of Míl.

I am Fintan, I have lived long,
I am an ancient shanachie of the noble hosts.
Neither wisdom nor brilliant deeds repressed me
until age came upon me and decay.

36. So Fintan ended his life and his age in this manner, and he came to repentance, and he partook of communion and sacrifice from the hand of bishop Erc son of Ochomon son of Fidach, and the spirits of Patrick and Brigit came and were present at his death. The place in which he was buried is uncertain, however. But some think that he was borne away in his mortal body to some divine secret place as Elijah and Enoch were borne into paradise, where they are awaiting the resurrection of that venerable long-lived Elder, Fintan son of Bóchra, son of Eithier, son of Rual, son of Annid, son of Ham, son of Noah, son of Lamech.

Consulting the Ancestors
by Caitlín Matthews

The Mounds of the Dead

We inherit everything from the ancestors. They have gone before us and remain the repositories of the wisdom and knowledge of our tradition. There is scarcely a people in the world who do not honour and reverence their ancestors in some way. Yet in Western society, which is furthest from its animistic and shamanic roots, ancestral veneration plays little part in daily life: this dereliction of duty is further manifest in a total disrespect for the elders of our society whose age and wisdom are summarily neglected as marginal to our concerns.

Communion with the ancestors was a feature of Celtic daily life. The realms of the dead and the living, of the otherworld and of this world overlapped in numerous ways. Perception and acknowledgement of these thresholds was most important and many protective customs surrounded the gateways of birth and death, as we shall see in Chapter 10.

Who are the ancestors? This was something all Celtic people could answer, harking back many generations, for the genealogical memory was a common heritage. One of the major duties of poets and storytellers was to be a genealogical guardian, keeping the memory of long-dead ancestors fresh in praise-songs. The ancestors were those who had gone before – the brave, the disreputable, the holy and the beautiful.

The consultation of the ancestors is more usually called necromancy, a vigorous tradition which is discernible from Aeneas to Hamlet. The major reasons for consulting the ancestors usually fall into the following categories, in order to:

1. divine or gain prophetic insight about the future
2. regain lost knowledge
3. access ancestral wisdom by oracular means
4. discover ancestral precedents for legal validation
5. reconnect one spiritual tradition with another
6. gain healing or revelation by proximity to an ancestral tomb

We have already seen examples of 2 and 4 in the 'Settling of the Manor of Tara' – a prime tale in this tradition. In this essay we briefly examine the other categories, taking into account the traditions of the severed head and the necromantic traditions of the transitory period between Paganism and Christianity.

The most common kind of intercourse is of clerics or others seeking for lost knowledge, such as when Seanchán, chief poet of Ireland, instructs his fellow poets to collect together the fragments of the great story of the *Táin* until it is perfect. It is not until they raise from his grave the spirit of Fergus mac Roich, himself a chief actor in the Cattle Raid of Cooley, that they are able to receive the whole story over the course of three days of Fergus' recitation.

Where does one go to consult the ancestors? Generally speaking, this activity was best pursued near their earthly resting place. The classical poet, Nicander of Colophon (*c.* second century AD), writes of the Celtic custom of oracular incubation by spending a night beside the ashes of the dead in order to discover the future.[3]

Cremation and urn-burial were a feature of early Celtic culture, with inhumation becoming more popular after the seventh century BCE. Among the insular Celts several forms of burial are discernible. O'Curry quotes the *Book of Lecan* on Irish burial customs:

A *fert* (a mound made of stones) of one door for a man
of science,
A *fert* of two doors upon a woman.
A *fert* with doors also for boys and maidens,
Cnocs (hill-mounds) on distinguished foreigners
Murs upon those dying of plague.

Why a mound with doors? A *fert* is understood to have been a vaulted grave-mound of stones over which earth was laid. Could the doors be in order to allow egress or access? It is important to note that a *mur* was a distinctively different structure from other forms of burial, since it was important to ensure that no one accidentally opened a plague-pit and so became infected. During the famine and typhus epidemics in Ireland in the last century, *murs* were still being dug. Clearly, *murs* were never intended to be reopened, whereas a *fert* might have been reopened to allow further interments or for other purposes.

To sit or stand upon such a mound is a foolhardy deed, one which is repeated frequently in Celtic story, invariably provoking upheaval. Conn of the Hundred Battles has two such visitations; in the first (see Chapter 8), he sits upon the height of Benn Etair mac Etgaith, bewailing his dead wife, when he encounters Becuma, a faery woman exiled from faery for her transgressions; in the second, Conn daily mounts the ramparts of Tara in case the 'people of the fairy-mounds or the Fomorians should take Ireland unawares', (see p. 254), and is transported to the deep ancestral realms in order to learn his lineage.

In *Pwyll, Prince of Dyfed*, Pwyll of Dyfed encounters Rhiannon after having purposely sat upon the Mound of Arberth, a mound which provokes either wonders or blows. In so doing he opens up an otherworldly entrance which remains stubbornly open for him and the rest of his family. Muircertach meets the faery woman, Sin (pronounced 'Shin'), on a turf mound and falls in love with her; what he does not know it that she has his downfall at heart, since he has killed her father. St Collen sets up his cell upon Glastonbury Tor and meets Gwyn ap Nudd, into whose realm he ventures with a bottle of holy water, with which he overcomes the illusion of faery appearances.[4]

Musicians who stray near the mounds of the faery frequently find themselves taken within to exchange tunes and songs, emerging many years later, richly endowed with faery music but without living friends or family to welcome them. Fear of the recent dead was widespread but, then as now, people enjoyed frightening themselves. This is a strong theme in the grisly story where Nera accepts a Hallowe'en dare and has an encounter with a hanged corpse (see Chapter 10). He too, eventually enters a faery hill.

In each of these examples, we see how strong is the association of the ancestors with the faery. It must also be stated that there is still a widespread aversion among the Irish at being in the vicinity of tombs or ancient stone monuments, since these places are associated with the faery in many minds. The continuing propitiation of the faeries in Celtic countries is due, in good part, to the fact that the ancestors and the faeries are often considered to be one and the same tribe. This notion is stronger in some parts than in others, but is derived from the idea that those who are interred in the ground become of one nature with the faery people of the hollow hills: both inhabit a dimension that is timeless and ubiquitous, accessible to mortals only on special occasions. The Gaelic name for the spirits of the dead is *sluagh sith* or the 'peaceful host' – a propitiatory euphemism. Yet the *sithean* are also the faerykind. It is not insignificant that the time when the dead and the faery are most active is at Samhain, Hallowe'en.

Samhain marks the Celtic New Year and the beginning of the agricultural year; it was and is celebrated with great fervour. In ancient times all the fires of Ireland were extinguished and relighted from the one kindled upon the hill of Tlachtga. The festival is a long-surviving one; not only has it recognizably survived as a popular folk custom within the Celtic countries, it has spread to America as 'trick or treat' and boosted the festival to a commercial pitch. But that is not all, the Celtic festival was also adopted as the basis for the Christian festival of All Souls. St Odilio of Cluny adopted it in 998 and this usage spread to the rest of the Western Christian world, possibly as an indirect result of the pastoral influence of Celtic monks who converted much of Europe. In our own time, in many Catholic countries, the day of All Souls is held in some style, notably in Mexico where the Day of the Dead is observed by the living visiting family graves to bring offerings, candles and songs, and to give family news to the departed. The festival of Samhain has been augmented in more recent times by the additional celebrations of Guy Fawkes' bonfires and fireworks on 5 November and by the remembrance of those who died in war on Remembrance Day on 11 November.

There are traditions that certain kinds of knowledge are available at the time of Samhain, the night on which the faery mounds stand wide open and when the *sidhe* come forth. In the following extract from the *Book of Lismore* (fo.96.2.1.) I have translated the meeting of a mortal man and a faery/ancestor who prophesies. This story is strongly related to that of Nera in Chapter 10.

Fingein mac Luchta was at Druim Finghein on Samhain eve . . . Every Samhain he was visited by a *ban-sidh* (faery woman) who would relate to him all the marvels and precious things in all the royal strongholds of Ireland.

'Tell me another precious thing,' said Fingein.

'Not hard,' she said. 'Three chief artefacts of Ireland were found and revealed this night. The headpiece of Briun mac Smethra: the smith of Oengus mac Urnor made it, a helmet of purplest purple from the land of *ndinnecda* [possibly India] with an apple of gold atop it. This was the size of a man's head and around it were a hundred strings of mixed carbuncle, and a hundred bright purple twists of purified red gold, and a hundred chains of white bronze in various stitchings. It has been hidden in the well of Sidh Cruachan from the Morrigan until tonight.

'Then under the earth's covering until tonight is the *fidhchell* (gaming) board of Crimtham nia Nar, which he brought out of Oenach Find, when he left with Nar the Blind-In-The-Left-Eye into Sid Buidh on an adventure, where he went under the secret places of the sea. It was hidden in the rath of Uisnech till tonight.

'The *minn* (diadem) of Loeguire mac Luchta Laimfinn, which Lén Linfhaclach mac Banbulg Banna made and which the three daughters of Faindle mac Dubroth found tonight in Sid Findachair, where it had been hidden since the birth of Conchobor of the Red Eyebrows till tonight.

Fingein has no qualms about approaching a faery woman to ask for this prophecy; she also relates to him other events which come to pass in the next twelve months.

One survival of the prophetic Samhain vigil is found in the custom of the Church Porch Watch which John Aubrey describes in his *Remains of Gentilism and Judaism*:

It is a Custome for some people that were more curious than ordinary, to sitt all night in the Church porch of their Parish on midsomer's eve . . . and they should see the apparitions of those that should die in the parish that yer come and knock at the dore. (Davidson, 1989)

This custom was practised in northern and western England and in Wales, and was widespread up until the last century; the vigil was held not only on St John's Eve, but also on St Mark's Eve (24 April), New Year's Eve and Hallowe'en – some of the major thresholds or transition points of the year. The church porch was the ideal locus for such a divination, being itself a threshold between the sacred enclosure of the sanctuary and the burial ground surrounding the church. One Somerset account of the Church Porch Watch has significant echoes of Odhran's experience (see p. 127–8):

If you watch by the gate at midnight on All Hallow's Night to see who will die within the coming year you are in danger of being the first comer yourself and you will become the 'churchyard walker' and the guardian of the graveyard until another foolhardy and impious person disturbs the Service of the Dead. (Ibid)

Keeping vigil for the dead is still observed in folk customs throughout Britain and Ireland on Hallowe'en, candles being set in windows to light the way to departed spirits (or to ward off malignant ones) and (dis)guisers going out in masks and costumes to join the mayhem and mischief of the night. On All Soul's Day (2 November), the soulers of Cheshire and Shropshire still circulate the countryside with their hobby horse, the original 'nightmare', which bears away the dead upon her back, and the old custom of soul-caking, giving a spiced cake in payment for prayers for the dead, recalls the ancient honour once shown to the ancestors.

Yet not only do the descendants keep vigil; this is also the task of certain of the ancestors. Some ancestors have no known, marked grave; one of these has become the greatest ancestor of the British, namely King Arthur. And yet he is not the only great ancestor to have been accorded the privilege of watching over the country and coming to its aid in times of need.

The Oracular Head

Another method of speaking to the dead is by oracular means. Severed heads feature strongly in Celtic lore, especially heads which speak, after the manner of Orpheus. Much claim has been made for 'a cult of the head' among the Celts, who almost certainly did not worship heads. The position is a much more subtle one, relating to the ancestors. To the Celts, the head was the seat of wisdom and of the soul. To venerate the heads of one's forebears was only a form of proper ancestral respect. To take the heads of one's enemies, was to appropriate their cunning and wisdom for the use of one's own tribe, and to deny them a place among their own kind. Many of the extant myths about heads concern ancestry and the legal precedents which underpin traditional rights.

One concerns the great British god-king, Bendigeid Bran (Bran the Blessed), who ruled Powys in North Wales. After some outrageous behaviour towards his sister, Branwen, by her Irish in-laws, he leads a raiding party to Ireland in order to rescue her. During the ensuing conflict, most of the British are slain, with only seven remaining. Mortally wounded, Bran instructs his followers to behead him and to bury the head at the White Mount (the present site of the Tower of London), there to act as a palladium against invasion. On their way to perform this sacred errand, the followers sojourn for a period of eighty-seven years at two otherworldly locations, where the head of Bran speaks to them and is as coherent as it was during life. Unaware of the passage of time, they remain thus in seclusion until one of their number opens a forbidden door and all the sorrows they have endured return to memory. Time resumes its mundane passage and the head of Bran is subsequently buried.

This legendary story has a strong traditional continuum which becomes comprehensible if we realize that the British word *bran* means 'raven'. The present folklore of the Tower of London proclaims that its resident ravens represent the sovereignty of Britain still; that if the ravens leave the Tower, then the British monarchy will fall. Bran's head watches still. In his myth we see the ancestral significance of the head and are given some notion of how deep was the fusion between the blessed ancestors and the head as the soul's shrine. During their otherworldly seclusion, Bran's followers confer with their king, receiving counsel and the healing consolation of his presence.

Bran also possesses a cauldron of rebirth, which he is obliged to give as an propitiatory honour-gift to his insulted Irish in-laws. They use it well during the conflict between Ireland and Britain, tossing their military corpses into the cauldron so that they re-emerge to fight once more, but as able-bodied warriors who can no longer speak. The dead are truly omnipresent in this tale.

The widespread tradition of oracular heads in Celtic myth points to a long practice of shamanic divination by means of a seer consulting the head of the ancestor. One of the *Welsh Triads* speaks of King Arthur going to consult the head of Bran; in this terse piece of bardic memorization, we hear only of Arthur's hubris, since he disinters the sacred palladium of his land, vowing that only he, Arthur himself, shall be its protector. We see then how the head retained memory and ancestral continuance. It also was important in establishing ancestral rights, especially where these involved powers of rulership, healing or knowledge.

Niches for severed heads are a feature of the gateway to the Celtic shrine at Roquepertuse in southern Gaul. Throughout the Celtic world, heads act as gate-guardians; stone heads are often being found today in the West Midlands, set into barns or walls, still performing their vigilant office.

Carved heads are a frequent adornment of sacred wells, to which people had recourse for their healing properties. The well of St Helens, Yorkshire, has three partially submerged heads set into the inside of the retaining wall; these can only be 'seen' by the hand. Archaeologists frequently find skulls from the Celtic era in or near wells. British folk-story retains stories about oracular heads in wells who aid heroines to fortunes. The Elizabethan dramatist, George Peele (1557–98) drew on this tradition for his play, *The Old Wives' Tale*, in which heads rise from the waters and instruct the heroine to:

> Comb me smooth and stroke my head,
> And every hair a sheaf shall be,
> And every sheaf a golden tree.

As she combs the head, she combs out both gold and wheat into her lap. Variant versions of this myth tell how the anti-heroine visits the well and spurns the ancestral head, receiving only repellent snails and slugs in her lap. This ancient story testifies to the veneration of the ancestors which, if it is respectfully upheld, will bring good fortune to the descendant, but evil fortune if they are spurned.

The screaming skulls of British and Irish folk legend – such as the skull lodged at Bettiscombe Manor in Dorset, which is about 2000 years old and probably came from Pilsdon Pen, a Celtic sanctuary within the Manor's grounds – shriek out when any attempt is made to move them. Like Bran's head, they have palladium qualities which are deeply invested in their location. Lia Fail (Stone of Fal), the stone which cries out under the rightful king, is known as the phallus of Fergus, the royal Ulster champion who is famed for his virility and regal acumen – it is an oracular stone which recognizes kings in an oracular manner, guarding the ancestral right of witness.

At what point do the recently dead enter into the realm of the great dead, the mighty ancestors? The recently dead also approach mortals, often for vengeance or appeasement, providing a fund of ghost stories that have no place here. This was one of the reasons why the far ancestors or those famed for their wisdom, holiness or efficacy are most often sought out. Clearly, the further back in time we go, the more mighty and legendary become the deeds of those who precede us. The greater the number of their collateral descendants, the greater propensity for veneration and wonder-working. And yet, there are exceptions to this rule.

The most common form of contact with the ancestors at their tombs is found in Celtic hagiography. The graves of saints quickly became the locus for miracles. One example will suffice. It comes from the *Life of St Ninian* the sixth-century apostle to the southern Picts. The *Life* tells how the parents of a boy born with distorted limbs leave him at St Ninian's tomb overnight, having prayed that their son might be cured or killed. In the middle of the night, he has a vision of a man coming towards him with a great light, commanding him to be healed. He subsequently rises up with straight limbs and pursues a career as a cleric.

It may be thought that the coming of Christianity overthrew customs requiring congress with the dead, but this is not so.

Celtic Christian Necromancy
Throughout Celtic tradition, there is a strong thread of ancestral dependence which is both connective and spiritually supporting. The interconnected Celtic clan system, with its complex lines of descent and inheritance, was frequently fragmented by feud and faction. What bound disparate family groups together was the fosterage sys-

tem, whereby the children of one tribe were fostered as the children of another. At the most superficial level, this was an unsubtle form of hostage-taking; at its most ideal level, it promoted strong kinships and loyalties which were hard to break. Many Celtic stories turn around the point of torn loyalties between blood and foster kindreds at war.

In a very profound sense, the Pagan and Christian traditions are similarly placed foster-kindred. The introduction and acceptance of Christianity was extremely gradual in Ireland, refining and adapting itself to local custom and usage. Christianity had to justify itself by every ploy in its repertoire because its practices often openly defied ancestral laws, customs and precedents. Some of these were indeed burdensome to people, such as compulsory female military service, of which Adamnan gives a chastening account – women hacking each other to pieces while their babies cling to their breasts. There were doubtless other onerous customs – blood-letting obligations, incest and widespread abuse – that Christianity sought to correct by more temperate social attitudes. But for every rotten practice, there were countless other ones which were not so easy to discount: and in these cases, it was necessary for the Church to enter into the spirit of ancestral service.

Honour for distant ancestors, a sense of family and an abiding connection to the land were central to Irish belief. The first missionaries trod carefully around these issues; but it was the native convert clergy who gradually brought about a fuller integration of the Gospels into the ancestral storytelling heritage, through their love of their own traditions. Hence, throughout the early hagiographical accounts of the saints, many ancestral consultants are resurrected by them or else kept alive beyond the natural human life-span solely in order to relate their story and to receive baptism.

The strongest motivation in these stories seems to be related to the need to bring ancestors into the family of Christ. The tradition of the Harrowing of Hell, remembered in the Apostle's Creed, 'he was crucified, dead and buried; he descended into hell; the third day he rose again from the dead', is central to this Celtic need to integrate ancestors into the Christian family. In the 'Settling of the Manor of Tara', (pp. 98–114) we have read of the oldest man alive sharing his memory with his people. This primary teaching, which connects the ignorant bards with their ancestors, is significantly conveyed by an otherworldly being during the charged and timeless moment of the crucifixion, when the ancestors are traditionally liberated from their waiting in purgatory.

There are countless stories of those who are dead, or living in the otherworld, returning to give information to the living. The commonest examples of these are when Christian saints interrogate the dead in order to learn the wisdom or story of times past. Thus St Patrick speaks to Ossian and retrieves the Fionn mac Cumhail stories while the priest, Beoan mac Innle, discovers and questions Liban who has survived for 300 years as a salmon-woman. These stories generally relate how the saint in question is the only person able to undertake such a soul-imperilling task, and how the ordinary folk are kept away. The point of this tradition, is that the ancestral stories are important to those who come after, and must be retrieved at all costs, in order to bring the ancestors into the Christian dispensation.

The literary Celtic Christian solution to tribal forgetfulness is interestingly identical to the Pagan Celtic one: necromancy – literally, divining from the dead! Of course, it is not called this and the many accounts of saints who speak to pre-Christian gods, spirits or people nearly always include the saint forbidding his followers from imitating his actions or even knowing about the material thus given. This is evident from a manuscript in Trinity College, Dublin (codex H.3.18), believed by Kuno Meyer to be as early as the eighth century. It relates the dialogue between St Columba (called Columcille here) and the spirit of a dead youth, identified as the trickster-hero, Mongan, which I translate as follows:

Some say the youth at Carn Eolairg was Mongan, son of Fiachna. Columcille said to him, 'Whence have you come, young one?'

The youth replied, 'I have come from lands known and unknown, that I may discover from you the place where knowledge and ignorance have died, the place where they were born and the place where they are buried.'

'A question for you, then,' said Columcille. 'The lake before us, what was it before this time?'

The youth replied, 'I know that. It was yellow and covered with flowers, it was green and hilly, it was full of drinking and feasting, it was rich in silver and full of chariots. I abandoned it when I was a deer; before I was a deer, I was a salmon and a seal of great endurance, and a wandering wolf. When I was a man I took a loincloth to guard the seed of my descendants, with a green sail and a red sail, steering by heart's love of my blood-lineage. Women called to me, but neither father nor mother knew I, although I conversed with the living as well as with the dead.'

Columcille asked the youth again, 'The islands to the west of us, what is underneath them?'

The youth said, 'Deep beneath them are long-haired sea-poets, and grossly pregnant sows whose utterance is tuneful, there are herds of deer, there are archetypal horses, there are twin-headed beings, there are triple-headed beings, in Europe, in Asia, in unknown lands, a green land stretching to the borders of each estuary and inlet.'

'Let that be enough,' said Columcille. And he drew the youth aside to converse with him and question him about the mysteries of heaven and earth. And while they conferred for half a day, or was it from the same hour on one day to the same the next, Columcille's monks watched them from afar.

When their dialogue came to an end, the monks observed the youth vanish from their sight. It was not known where he went. When the monks asked Columcille to share his conversation with them, he said that he could not tell them even one word of what had been said to him, for it was not a fit thing for men to be told.

How we wish they had been answered in full! In this text, we discover the spirit of Mongan, a famous transmigrator in Celtic tradition, who is said to have been an avatar of Fionn Mac Cumhail and, by prophetic inference, to be a forerunner of Christ himself. Mongan's purpose for coming to the middle realm is given as to find 'the place where knowledge and ignorance have died, the place where they were born and the place where they are buried'. The answer to this riddle is *the traditional ancestral memory* – a facility which may seem to die but which is continually being reborn. In the course of their dialogue, St Columba becomes a fresh repository or 'grave' for the ancestral traditions concerning Mongan's transmigration and the undersea world, as well as many other mysteries we are not privileged to share.

We note that Mongan uses the metaphor of sailing when describing his guardianship of his descendant's seed, a dispersal through the waters of the ages. Mongan's traditional otherworldly teacher is none other than Manannan, God of the Sea and of the otherworld, and it is of this realm that he speaks to Columba. The realm of the sea is indivisibly associated with the journey of the soul after death. Survivals of ancient death customs in nineteenth-century Ireland included 'the making of the ship'. This involved the gathering together of the deceased's male neighbours and family who then formed themselves into the shape of a ship. This custom involved much slapstick sloshing about of water and total nudity from its participants. This ancient custom was hidden from priestly eyes.

The questioning of dead or not-quite-departed ancestors for the purposes of reconnecting the tribe with forgotten stories seems then to have been admissible, at least in story, in Celtic Christian tradition. This appears to be a continuation of the druidic and bardic ability to interface with the many worlds in a shamanic way.

We are fortunate to possess an example of how the ancestral roots are laid down in the persistent tradition about St Columba and his disciple Odhran (modern Gaelic 'Oran'), which is told in the following story, related by Douglas Hyde. The island of Iona is the repository of rich legends which are tangibly manifest to any visitor. One spot particularly resonates to deep ancestral deposits of lore, notably the chapel bearing Odhran's name, Reilig Odhran. It stands next to the restored Abbey, and is the locus for many royal Scottish burials. The cobbled 'street of the dead', down which funeral processions came from the Abbey is a potent pathway in more than one reality. The early Scottish kings and the later Lords of the Isles were buried in the graveyard of Odhran's chapel, after having been 'waked' for eight days and nights.

There are two strong ancestral traditions associated with this place. One concerns the famous black stones at the base of the nearby St Martin's cross. These were traditionally the place to swear ancestral oaths. Martin Martin relates this tradition in his *Description of the Western Islands of Scotland*:

A little further to the West lie the black stones, which are so called, not from their colour, for that is gray, but from the effects that tradition say ensued upon perjury, if any one became guilty of it after swearing on these stones in the usual manner, for an oath made on them was decisive in all controversies.

Martin goes on to instance the swearing over of rights by Macdonald, Lord of the Isles to his people 'with uplifted hands and bended knee on the black stones'. Those whose vindication seemed totally justified were known to say, 'I have freedom to swear this matter upon the black stones.' This swearing on the stones is deeply connected with the 'witness of the dead', who have the power to affirm or deny guilt in the querent. What the ancestors hear, they remember.

The second ancestral tradition concerns Odhran himself. The following story is not found fully in any of the five official hagiographies of St Columba, but versions have been discovered in the Western Isles and in Nova Scotia, the exilic home of many Scots in the years following the Jacobite wars and the clearances. In this folk story Odhran is referred to as Dobhran.

Columcille began to build on Iona. He gathered together a great host of people. But all that he used to build in the day, it used to be thrown down at night. That drove him to set people to keep a watch on Iona. Every morning those men [whom he had set to watch] used to be dead at the foot of Iona. He did not continue long to set people to watch there, but since he himself was a holy man he went and remained watching Iona to try if he could see or find out what was going wrong with it. He was keeping to it and from it, and they were saying that it was on the scaur of the crag near the sea that she was, I did not see her.

He saw a *Biast* coming off the shore and one half of it was a fish and the other half in the likeness of a woman. She was old, with scales. When she shook herself she set Iona and the land a-quaking. There went from her a tinkling sound as it were earthenware pigs (jars) a-shaking. Columcille went down to meet her and spoke to her, and asked her did she know what was killing the people whom he was setting to watch Iona in the night. She said she did. 'What was happening to them?' said he. She said, 'Nothing but the fear that seized them at her appearance; that when she was a-coming to land the heart was leaping out of its cockles with them.'

'Do you know,' said he, 'what is throwing down Iona that I am building?'

'I do,' said she, 'Iona will be for ever falling so, O holy Columcille. It is not I who am throwing it down, but still it is being thrown down.'

'Do you know now any means by which I can make Iona go forward?'

'I do,' said she. 'O holy Columcille, to-morrow you shall question all the people that you have at work to find out what man will consent to offer himself alive [to be buried] under the ground, and his soul shall be saved if he consents to do that, and people shall never see me here afterwards. Iona shall go forward without any doubt.'

On the morrow he put the question to the great host of people, 'Was there any one of them at all who would consent to offer himself alive on condition that his soul should be saved in heaven?'

There was not one man of them willing to go into the grave although he was told that his soul would be saved by the decree of God. She [the *Biast*] had told him too that the grave had to be seven times as deep as the man's length.

Poor Dobhran, his brother, was on the outskirts of the crowd. He came over and stood behind his brother, Columcille, and said that he was quite willing to be offered up alive under the ground on condition that Iona might be built up by his holy brother Columcille, and he gave credence to Columcille that his soul would be saved by the decree of God.

Said Columcille, 'Although I have no other brother but poor Dobhran, I am pleased that he has offered himself to go to the grave, and that the *Biast* shall not be seen coming any more to the shore for ever.'

The grave was made seven times the height of the man in depth. When Dobhran saw the grave he turned to Columcille and asked him as a favour to put a roof over the grave and to leave him there standing so long as it might please God to leave him alive.

He got his request – to be put down alive into the grave. He was left there.

Columcille came and began to work at Iona [again], and he was twenty days working, and Iona was going forward wondrously. He was pleased that his work was succeeding.

At the end of twenty days when everything was conjectured to be going on well, he said it were right to look what end had come to poor Dobhran, and [bade] open the grave.

Dobhran was walking on the floor of the grave [when the roof was taken off]. When Dobhran saw that the grave was opened and when he heard all the world round it, he gave an expert leap out of it to the mouth of the grave and he put up his two hands on high on the mouth of the grave. He supported himself on the [edge of the] grave [by his hands.] There was a big smooth meadow going up from Iona and much rushes on it. All the rushes that Dobhran's eyes lit upon grew red, and that little red top is on the rushes ever.

Columcille cried out and he on the far side, 'Clay! clay on Dobhran's eyes! before he see any more of the world and of sin!'

They threw in the clay upon him then and returned to their work. And nothing any more went against Columcille until he had Iona finished.

What are we to make of this extraordinary story, where a Christian saint is shown engaged in a very pagan activity? The ritual interment of a body under a building or 'foundation sacrifice' in this story attests to a universal belief in the notion that no edifice will stand unless a human being's blood is cemented into it. Foundation sacri-

fices of people or, latterly, animals occurred throughout Britain and
Ireland up until the mid-nineteenth century. Odhran's is a willing
sacrifice, however; his innocence seemingly in accord with the usual
choice of victim in foundation sacrifice – normally a child or baby.

Foundation sacrifice is usually performed in edifices whose foundations break open the ground for occupation for the first time. It is
found from earliest times in Britain and Ireland, under earthworks
such as Avebury, Silbury, Cadbury and others; local legends often
speak of ancestral guardians who patrol these sites, often guarding a
great treasure. Failure to make a suitable foundation sacrifice usually
has the result of instant demolition of walls overnight and many
medieval legends surround the collapse of churches and cathedrals
due to the attention of earth spirits who have not received proper propitiation or acknowledgement. In many instances, the founding bishop or priest has to call in an angelic spirit to arbitrate in these
unseemly spiritual building disputes.

Odhran's story fulfils both these ancestral duties: he is appointed
to be the first messenger to the ancestors and he is simultaneously
appointed as a guardian. This much is clear from the fact that he
asks to be buried upright. Interment in the standing position, like
that of a watcher or guardian, is found in numerous Celtic instances:
Eoghan Bel, King of Connacht (d. 537) was buried upright, spear in
hand, facing towards Ulster, thus causing Connacht to be invincible.
The Ulstermen, discovering the cause of their defeat, caused the body
to be disintered and buried upside down elsewhere. A similar burial is
reported for a troublesome dwarf who contends with Fionn Mac
Cumhail; after rising from the grave thrice, the dwarf is subsequently
buried upside down and walks the earth no more. King Loeghaire of
Tara, refused to convert to Christianity and was buried upright.[5]

It is clear from the many mutually supporting 'lives' of St
Columba that the saint was not above a little ancestral magical practice of his own. He enters into an aggressive shamanic battle with a
Pictish druid and his prayers frequently have an immediate and salutary effect upon anyone who dares stand in his way. St Columba
comes over as a proud, headstrong and self-reliant Celt whose native
proclivities are perhaps often stronger than his Christian fosterage.
Would he, even so, have any truck with such an ancient custom? A
less Pagan and more cleaned-up version of this tradition from the
early Irish *Life* relates that Odhran was the first of Columba's monks
to die on Iona:

St Columba said, 'It would be well for us that our roots should pass into the earth here. It is permitted to you that some one of you go under the earth of this island to consecrate it.' Odhran arose quickly and thus spake: 'If you accept me,' said he, 'I am ready for that.' 'O Odhran,' said Columba, 'you shall receive the reward of this; no request shall be granted to any one at my tomb unless he first ask of thee.' Odhran then went to heaven.[6]

In a Nova Scotian version of this story, Odhran utters three sentences upon rising from the grave; the first two had been forgotten by the storyteller, but the third was *cha n'eil an iorron chomb dona agus a tháthar ag rádh*, 'Hell is not as bad as it's reported.' To which Columba rejoins: '*úir, úir air Dobhran*' – 'clay, clay upon Odhran', in case he should say too much! Columba's purpose is evidently not to allow Odhran the liberty of an ancestral oracle!

It is clear that Odhran's interment seems primarily to sanctify the ground for human occupation; but we may reach towards the true ancient purpose of this ritual and guess that his sacrifice is primarily to create an 'ancestral hot-line' which will be available to all who subsequently inhabit that site. Odhran's body consecrates the soil of Iona, while his soul remains watchful and able to grant petitions – a primacy which is not accorded to St Columba, according to the Irish *Life*.

Odhran remains watchful down the centuries, gathering to himself a company of the most renowned Scottish kings and nobles, as well as the holy monks of the Iona foundation. His story shows us the Celtic process of how ancestors are made and consulted.

At the latter end of the twentieth century, we too are part of this unfolding communion with the ancestors. They watch yet and do not slumber. They wait only to guard and to remind us that the place where knowledge and ignorance have died, the place where they were born and the place where they are buried is none other than in our own memory.

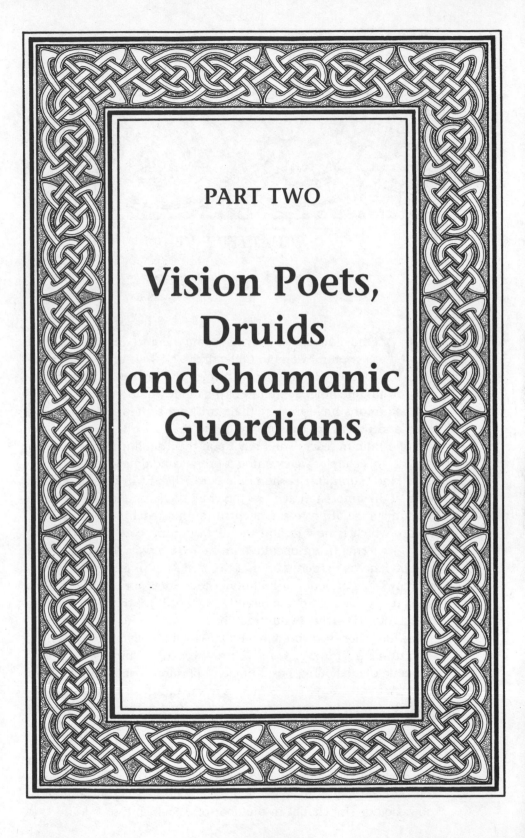

PART TWO

Vision Poets, Druids and Shamanic Guardians

CHAPTER FIVE

Initiations

W e have looked at the shamanic memory and resources of
the natural world in Celtic times. Now we turn to a consideration of the human guardians of that memory: the
poets, druids and other guardians of the Celtic tradition.

All shamans have to start their training somewhere. Some are
called and others are chosen, some find their own way without the
help of a human teacher and rely upon their guiding spirits to teach
them. In this chapter we examine a prime candidate – the Irish hero
Fionn Mac Cumhail. His shamanic career began in childhood. The
vision of the innocent and all-seeing child is a strong feature of Celtic
shamanism, relating to the deep shamanic teaching surrounding
Mabon, which is how to find the integrity and core of matter and
restore its virtue in an operative and effective way. These accounts
must be read as mystery stories of the initiation into knowledge: not
the knowledge of books or half-understood lore, but the deep gnosis
wrought of clear sight and a receptive soul. It is for this reason that a
child stands as teacher in this tradition.

The four short texts are interelated. The first tells of Fionn's childhood and upbringing. We see how he, in common with many
shamanic Celtic figures, has a hidden upbringing and gains wisdom
in a trickster-like way. This conforms to the universal shamanic tradition of the pupil having to find his or her own wisdom by stealth and
sometimes by trickery. Fionn is an interesting all-round figure, inco-
porating the elements of warrior, seer and poet. He is not just another
brainless Celtic hero hacking his way through his enemies, but an
efficient warrior, urbane, cultured and cunning. He gains his knowledge by a variety of means; his thumb is burned by the salmon of
knowledge or else caught in the door of a faery hill so that, forever

afterwards, he has only to suck his thumb in order to understand a thing. The image of the thumb-sucking adult recalls the young child in this initiatory tradition.

To Fionn also falls the task of reclaiming the Crane Bag, an otherworldly treasure of great power. He pursues it initially to avenge his father, but enters into its knowledge. The Crane Bag is a compendium of Irish magical treasures and appears and disappears like the Grail. It shifts realities and worlds, with Manannan, the God of the Sea and the otherworld, awarding its guardianship to whomsoever he wills. British tradition speaks similarly of the Thirteen Treasures of Britain, which are said to be in the wardship of Merlin.

These treasures do not have monetary worth; rather, they are spiritual objects conferring shamanic empowerment. All shamans worldwide acquire a series of objects which intrinsically represent otherworldly powers: knives for severing spiritual connections, herbs and plants for healing and giving wisdom, stones and sticks for divination, nets and strings for spirit-traps and many more. Each actual object has first been encountered upon the shamanic journey; afterwards the shaman may acquire, be given, find or make objects which manifest specific empowerments. The indigenous American people's medicine bundle is a living example of this tradition. Such collections of shamanic objects are not idly shown to others, but are carefully guarded, often for generations within a family. We must bear this in mind as we hear Caoilte's relation to his grandnephew, Oisin: the fact that both men are relatives of Fionn is important and we are privileged to overhear the mysteries of their family's guardianship.

In the third story, Fionn's daily ration of pig is stolen by the faeries. Only Fionn himself can catch the culprit and get his dinner back. In the fourth story, Fionn has trouble with the faeries yet again. He sets his heart on a *ban-sidhe*, but she desires his servant, Derg Corra. Torn between two loyalties, Derg Corra takes to the woods which is where Fionn discovers him.

The Man in the Tree, hooded and accompanied with cosmological animals, is indeed Derg Corra, but with the attributes of a threshold guardian. The blackbird, trout and stag who are with him are animals of air, water and earth respectively; each is related to the tradition of the Oldest Animals. Here Derg Corra is revealed in his otherworldly guise as a guardian of knowledge, cracking the nuts of knowledge and dispensing the apples, the fruit of eternal life and healing in Celtic tradition.

We also note that Derg Corra's exile is remarkably like that of Suibhne's (see Chapter 6), in that he seeks the uninhabited natural world in order to continue his existence.

The Boyhood Exploits of Finn[1]

There befell a meeting of valour and a contest of battle about the chief-
taincy of the *fian* and about the high-stewardship of Ireland between
Cumall, son of Trénmór, and Urgriu, son of Lugaid Corr of the
Luaigni. That Cumall was of the Corco Oche of Cúil Contuind, for to
these the Ui Tairrsig, Cumall's tribe, belonged. Torba, daughter of
Eochaman of the Erne, was the wife of Cumall, until he married
Muirne of the fair neck.

Then the battle of Cnucha was fought between them, to wit,
between Cumall and Urgriu. Daire the Red, son of Echaid the Fair,
son of Coirpre the Valorous, son of Muiredach, and his son Aed were
fighting the battle along with Urgriu. Another name for that Daire was
Morna Wryneck. So the battle was fought. Luchet and Aed, son of
Morna, met in the battle. Luchet wounded Aed, and destroyed one of
his eyes, whence the name of Goll (*i.e.* the One-eyed) clave to him
from that time forth. Luchet fell by Goll. The man who kept Cumall's
treasure-bag wounded Cumall in the battle. Cumall fell in the battle
by Goll, son of Morna, who carried off his spoils and his head, whence
there was a hereditary feud between Finn and the sons of Morna.

Hence sang the shanachie:

> Goll, son of Daire the Red, with fame,
> Son of Echaid the Fair, of valour fair,
> Son of Cairpre the Valorous with valour,
> Son of Muiredach from Findmag.

> Goll slew Luchet of the hundreds
> In the battle of Cnucha, 'tis no falsehood:
> Luchet the Fair of prowess bright
> Fell by the son of Morna.

> By him fell great Cumall
> In the battle of Cnucha of the hosts.
> 'Tis for the chieftaincy of Erin's fian
> That they waged the stout battle.

> The children of Morna were in the battle
> And the Luaigni of Tara,
> Since to them belonged the leadership of the men of Fál
> By the side of every valorous king.

Victorious Cumall had a son,
The Finn, bloody, of weapons hard:
Finn and Goll, great their fame,
Mightily they waged war.

Afterwards they made peace,
Finn and Goll of the hundred deeds,
Until Banb Sinna fell
About the pig at Tara Luachra.

Aed was the name of the son of Daire
Until Luchet with glory wounded him:
Since the fierce lance had wounded him,
Therefore was he called Goll.

Cumall left his wife Muirne pregnant. And she brings forth a son, to whom the name of Demne was given. Fiacail, son of Conchenn, and Bodbmall the druidess, and the Grey one of Luachair came to Muirne, and carry away the boy, for his mother durst not let him be with her. Muirne afterwards slept with Gleor Red-hand, king of the Lamraige, whence the saying, 'Finn, son of Gleor'. Bodbmall, however, and the Grey one, and the boy with them, went into the forest of Slieve Bloom. There the boy was secretly reared. That was indeed necessary, for many a sturdy stalwart youth, and many a venomous hostile warrior and angry fierce champion of the warriors of the Luaigni and of the sons of Morna were lying in wait for that boy, and for Tulcha, the son of Cumall. In that manner then those two women-warriors reared him for a long time.

Then, at the end of six years, his mother came to visit her son, for she had been told that he was in that place, and besides, she was afraid of the sons of Morna for him. However, she passed from one wilderness to another, until she reached the forest of Slieve Bloom. She found the hunting-booth and the boy asleep in it. And then she lifts the boy to her bosom, and presses him to her, and she pregnant at the time. It was then she made the quatrains, fondling her son:

Sleep in peaceful slumber, etc.

Thereupon the woman bade farewell to the women-warriors, and told them to take charge of the boy till he should be fit to be a warrior. And so the boy grew up till he was able to hunt.

On a certain day the boy went out alone, and saw ducks upon a lake. He sent a shot among them, which cut off the feathers and wings of one, so that a trance fell upon her; and then he seized her and took her with him to the hunting-booth. And that was Finn's first chase.

He afterwards went with certain *cairds* to flee from the sons of Morna, and was with them about Crotta. These were their names: Futh and Ruth and Regna of Moy Fea, and Temle, and Olpe, and Rogein. There scurvy came upon him, and therefrom he became a scald, whence he used to be called Demne the Bald. At that time there was a reaver in Leinster, Fiacail, the son of Codna. Then in Feeguile Fiacail came upon the *cairds*, and killed them all save Demne alone. After that he was with Fiacail, the son of Codna, in his house in Sescenn Uairbeóil. The two women-warriors came southwards to the house of Fiacail, the son of Codna, in search of Demne, and he is given to them. And then they take him with them from the south to the same place.

One day he went out alone until he reached Moy Liffey, and a certain stronghold there; and he saw the youths hurling upon the green of the stronghold there. He went to contend in running or in hurling with them. He came again the next day, and they put one-fourth of their number against him. Again they come with one-third of their number against him. However, at last they all go against him, and he won his game from them all.

'What is thy name?' they said. 'Demne,' said he. The youths tell that to the man of the stronghold. 'Then kill him, if ye know how to do it – if ye are able to do it,' said he. 'We should not be able to do aught to him,' said they. 'Did he tell you his name?' says he. 'He said,' say they, 'that his name was Demne.' 'What does he look like?' said he. 'A shapely fair (*finn*) youth,' said they. 'Then Demne shall be named Finn (the Fair),' said he. Whence the youths used to call him Finn.

He came to them on the next day, and went to them at their game. All together they throw their hurlets at him. He turns among them, and throws seven of them to the ground. He went from them into the forest of Slieve Bloom.

Then, at the end of a week, he came back to the same place. The youths were swimming in a lake that was close by. The youths challenge him to come and try to drown them. Thereupon he jumps into the lake to them, and drowns nine of them in the lake. And after that he goes to Slieve Bloom. 'Who drowned the youths?' everybody asks. 'Finn,' say they. So that henceforth [the name] Finn clave to him.

Once he went forth across Slieve Bloom, and the two women-warriors together with him, when a fleet herd of wild deer is seen [by them] on the ridge of the mountain. 'Alas!' say the two old women, 'that we cannot get hold of one of those!' '*I* can,' [says Finn], and he dashes upon them, and lays hold of two bucks among them, and brings them with him to their hunting-booth. After that he would hunt for them constantly. 'Go from us now, lad,' said the women-warriors to him, 'for the sons of Morna are watching to kill thee.'

Alone he went from them until he reached Lough Leane, above Luachair, and there he took military service with the king of Bantry. At that place he did not make himself known. However, there was not at that time a hunter his equal. Thus said the king to him: 'If Cumall had left a son,' says he, 'one would think thou wast he. However, we have not heard of his leaving a son, except Tulcha mac Cumaill, and he is in military service with the king of Scotland.'

He afterwards bids farewell to the king, and goes from them to Carbrige, which at this day is [called] Kerry, and takes military service with the king of that land. Then, on a certain day, the king came to play *fidchell*. He was prompted by Finn, and won seven games one after another. 'Who art thou?' says the king. 'The son of a peasant of the Luaigni of Tara,' says he. 'No,' says the king, 'but thou art the son whom Muirne bore to Cumall, and be here no longer, lest thou be slain [while] under my protection.'

Then he went forth to Cullen of the Ui Cuanach, to the house of Lochán, a chief smith, who had a very beautiful daughter, Cruithne by name. She fell in love with the youth. 'I shall give thee my daughter, though I know not who thou art.' Thereupon the girl slept with the youth. 'Make spears for me,' said the youth to the smith. So Lochán made two spears for him. He then bade farewell to Lochán, and went away. 'My son,' says Lochán, 'do not go upon the road on which is the sow called the Beo.' She it was that devastated the midlands of Munster. But what happened to the youth was to go upon the very road on which the sow was. Then the sow charged him; but he thrust his spear at her, so that it went through her, and left her without life. Then he takes the head of the sow with him to the smith as a bridal gift for his daughter. Hence is Slieve Muck in Munster.

After that the youth went onwards into Connaught to seek Crimall, the son of Trénmór. As he was on his way, he heard the wail of a woman. He went towards it, and saw a woman; and now it was tears of blood, and now a gush of blood, so that her mouth was red. 'Thou art red-mouthed, woman!' says he. 'Good cause have I,' says she, 'for my only son has been slain by a tall, very terrible warrior who came in my way.' 'What was thy son's name?' says he. 'Glonda was his name,' says she. Hence is the Ford of Glonda and the Causeway of Glonda on Moinmoy, and from that redness of mouth the Ford of the Red Mouth has been so called ever since. Then Finn went in pursuit of the warrior, and they fight a combat, and he fell by him. This is how he was: he had the treasure-bag with him, to wit, the treasures of Cumall. He who had fallen there was the Grey one of Luachair, who had dealt the first wound to Cumall in the battle of Cnucha.

Thereupon he goes into Connaught, and finds Crimall as an old man in a desert wood there, and a number of the old *fian* together with him; and it is they who did the hunting for him. Then he showed him the bag, and told him his story from beginning to end; how he had slain the man of the treasures. Finn bade farewell to Crimall, and went to learn poetry from Finnéces, who was on the Boyne. He durst not remain in Ireland else, until he took to poetry, for fear of the son of Urgriu, and of the sons of Morna.

Seven years Finnéces had been on the Boyne, watching the salmon of Fec's Pool; for it had been prophesied of him that he would eat the salmon of Féc, when nothing would remain unknown to him. The salmon was found, and Demne was then ordered to cook the salmon; and the poet told him not to eat anything of the salmon. The youth brought him the salmon after cooking it. 'Hast thou eaten anything of the salmon, my lad?' says the poet. 'No,' says the youth, 'but I burned my thumb, and put it into my mouth afterwards.' 'What is thy name, my lad?' says he. 'Demne,' says the youth. 'Finn is thy name, my lad,' says he; 'and to thee was the salmon given to be eaten, and verily thou art the Finn.' Thereupon the youth eats the salmon. It is that which gave the knowledge to Finn, to wit, whenever he put his thumb into his mouth, and sang through *teinm láida*, then whatever he had been ignorant of would be revealed to him.

He learnt the three things that constitute a poet, to wit, *teinm láida* and *imbas forosna* and *dichetul dichennaib*. It is then Finn made this lay to prove his poetry:

> May-day, season surpassing! Splendid is colour then. Blackbirds
>   sing a full lay, if there be a slender shaft of day.
> The dust-coloured cuckoo calls aloud: Welcome, splendid sum-
>   mer! The bitterness of bad weather is past, the boughs of the
>   wood are a thicket.
> Summer cuts the river down, the swift herd of horses seeks the

pool, the long hair of the heather is outspread, the soft white bog-down grows.

Panic startles the heart of the deer, the smooth sea runs apace, – season when ocean sinks asleep – blossom covers the world.

Bees with puny strength carry a goodly burden, the harvest of blossoms; up the mountain-side kine take with them mud, the ant makes a rich meal.

The harp of the forest sounds music, the sail gathers – perfect peace. Colour has settled on every height, haze on the lake of full waters.

The corncrake, a strenuous bard, discourses; the lofty virgin waterfall sings a welcome to the warm pool; the talk of the rushes is come.

Light swallows dart aloft, loud melody reaches round the hill, the soft rich mast buds, the stuttering quagmire rehearses.

The peat-bog is as the raven's coat, the loud cuckoo bids welcome, the speckled fish leaps, strong is the bound of the swift warrior.

Man flourishes, the maiden buds in her fair strong pride; perfect each forest from top to ground, perfect each great stately plain.

Delightful is the season's splendour, rough winter has gone, white is every fruitful wood, a joyous peace is summer.

A flock of birds settles in the midst of meadows; the green field rustles, wherein is a brawling white stream.

A wild longing is on you to race horses, the ranked host is ranged around: a bright shaft has been shot into the land, so that the water-flag is gold beneath it.

A timorous tiny persistent little fellow sings at the top of his voice, the lark sings clear tidings: surpassing May-day of delicate colours!

However, Finn went to Cethern, the son of Fintan, further to learn poetry with him. At that time there was a very beautiful maiden in Bri Ele, that is to say, in the fairy-knoll of Bri Ele, and the name of that maiden was Ele. The men of Ireland were at feud about that maiden. One man after another went to woo her. Every year on Hallowe'en the wooing used to take place; for the fairy-knolls of Ireland were always open about Hallowe'en; for on Hallowe'en nothing could ever be hidden in the fairy-knolls. To each man that went to woo her this used to happen: one of his people was slain. This was done to mark the occasion, nor was it ever found out who did it.

Like everybody else, the poet Cethern went to woo the maiden. However, Finn did not like the poet's going on that errand. At that time the name of Cumall's son was Finnéces. As they went to the wooing they formed themselves into three bands. There were nine in each band. As they went towards the fairy-knoll, a man of their people was slain between them; and it was not known who had slain him. Oircbel the poet was the name of the man that was slain there. Hence is Fert Oircbeil (the Grave of O.) in Clonfad. Thereupon they separated, and Finn went from them and . . . However, Finn thought it a grievance and a great disgrace.

He went until he came to the house of the champion Fiacail mac Conchinn, at Slievemargue. It is there his dwelling was at that time. To him, then, Finn made his complaint, and told him how the man had been slain among them in the fairy-knoll. Fiacail told him to go and sit down by the two Paps of Anu, behind Luachair. So he went and sat down between the two strongholds which are between the two Paps of Anu.

Now, when Finn was there between them, on Hallowe'en night, he saw the two fairy-knolls opened around him, even the two strongholds, their ramparts having vanished before them. And he saw a great fire in either of the two strongholds; and he heard a voice from one of them, which said: 'Is your sweet food good?' 'Good, indeed!' said a voice in the other fairy-knoll. 'A question. Shall anything be taken from us to you?' 'If that be given to us, something will be given to you in return.' While Finn was there he saw a man coming out of the fairy-knoll. A kneading-trough was in his hand with a . . . pig upon it, and a cooked calf, and a bunch of wild garlic upon it. That was Hallowe'en. The man came past Finn to reach the other knoll. Finn made a cast with the spear of Fiacail mac Conchinn. He hurled it southward from him towards Slievemargue. Then said Finn: 'If the spear should reach any one of us, may he escape [?] alive from it! I think this was a revenge for my comrade.'

That passes, till forthwith he heard a lament, and a great wail, saying:

> On the Barrow, by a sharp-pointed spear,
> Aed, Fidga's son, has fallen:
> By the spear of Fiacail, Codna's son,
> Finn has slain him . . .

Then Fiacail came to Finn, and was at the two Paps of Anu. Fiacail asked him whom he had slain. 'I know not,' saith Finn, 'whether any good has come from the cast which I have thrown.' ''Tis likely, indeed,' said Fiacail, 'that some one has been slain. It seems to me if thou do not do it to-night, thou wilt not do it to the end of another year.' However, Finn said that he had sent a cast, and that it seemed likely to him that it had reached some one. And he heard a great wailing in the fairy-knoll, saying:

> Venom is this spear,
> And venomous he whose it is,
> Venomous whoever threw it,
> Venom for him whom it laid low.

Outside the fairy-knoll of Cruachan Brig Ele Finn seized a woman in pledge for his spear. The woman promised to send out the spear if he released her. Finn let the woman from him into the knoll. Then, as she went into the knoll the woman said:

> Venom the spear,
> And venom the hand that threw it!
> If it is not cast out of the knoll,
> A murrain will seize the land.

Thereupon the spear is thrown out, and Finn takes it with him to where Fiacail was. 'Well,' said Fiacail, 'keep the spear with which thou hast done the famous deed.' Then Fiacail said the occasion was fortunate, since the man had been slain who had killed Finn's comrade. 'He whom thou hast slain here,' said he, ''tis he who used to kill every man that came to woo the maiden, because it is he who loved the maiden.'

Thereupon Finn and Fiacail went onward. Now, Fiacail had a tryst with the *fian* at Inver Colptha. Then he said to Finn that they should go home . . . since their business was finished. Said Finn: 'Let me go with thee,' says he. 'I do not wish thee to go with me,' says Fiacail, 'lest thy strength should fail thee.' 'I shall find out,' says Finn. Then they went forth. Twelve balls of lead were round the neck of Fiacail to hem his vigour, such was his swiftness. He would throw one ball after another from him, and Finn took them with him, and (yet) Fiacail's running was no swifter than Finn's.

They reach Inver Colptha. Then Finn brought all the twelve balls of lead to him, and he was pleased. That night they slept there. Then they make Finn keep watch that night, and he was told to wake the warrior if he heard any [cry of] outrage. Now, one hour of the night, as Finn was watching, he heard a cry from the north, and did not wake the warrior.

He went alone in the direction of the cry to Slieve Slanga. While Finn was there, among the men of Ulster, at the hour of midnight, he overtook three women before him, at a green mound, with horns [?] of fairy-women. As they were wailing on that mound, they would all put their hands on the mound. Then the women flee into the fairy-mound before Finn. Finn caught one of the women as she was going into the fairy-knoll of Slanga, and snatched her brooch out of her cloak. The woman went after him, and besought Finn to give her back the brooch of her cloak, and said it was not fit for her to go into the fairy-knoll with a blemish, and she promises a reward . . .

The Crane Bag[2]

I have a question for thee, Caoilte, man of the interchanged weapons: to whom did the good Crane-bag belong that Cumhall son of Tréanmhór had?

A crane that belonged to gentle Manannán – it was a treasure of power with many virtues – from its skin, strange thing to prize – from it was made the Crane-bag.

Tell us what was the crane, my Caoilte of many exploits, or, tell us, man, why its skin was put about the treasures.

Aoife, daughter of dear Dealbhaoth, sweetheart of Ilbhreac of many beauties – both she and Iuchra of comely hue fell in love with the man.

Iuchra, enraged, beguiled Aoife to come swimming, it was no happy visit: when she drove her fiercely forth in the form of a crane over the moorlands.

Aoife then demanded of the beautiful daughter of Abhartach: 'How long am I to be in this form, woman, beautiful breast-white Iuchra?'

'The term I will fix will not be short for thee, Aoife of the slow-glancing eyes: thou shalt be two hundred white years in the noble house of Manannán.

'Thou shalt be always in that house with everyone mocking thee, a crane that does not visit every land: thou shalt not reach any land.

'A good vessel of treasures will be made of thy skin – no small event: its name shall be – I do not lie – in distant times the Crane-bag.'

Manannán made this of the skin when she died: afterwards in truth it held every precious thing he had.

The shirt of Manannán and his knife, and Goibhne's girdle, altogether: a smith's hook from the fierce man: were treasures that the Crane-bag held.

The King of Scotland's shears full sure, and the King of Lochlainn's helmet, these were in it to be told of, and the bones of Asal's swine.

A girdle of the great whale's back was in the shapely Crane-bag: I will tell thee without harm, it used to be carried in it.

When the sea was full, its treasures were visible in its middle: when the fierce sea was in ebb, the Crane-bag in turn was empty.

There thou hast it, noble Oisin, how this thing itself was made: and now I shall tell its faring, its happenings.

Long time the Crane-bag belonged to heroic Lugh Long-arm: till at last the king was slain by the sons of Cearmaid Honey-mouth.

To them next the Crane-bag belonged after him, till the three, though active, fell by the great sons of Mile.

Manannán came without weariness, carried off the Crane-bag again: he showed it to no man till the time of Conaire came.

Comely Conaire slept on the side of Tara of the plains: when the cunning well-made man awoke, the Crane-bag was found about his neck.

How Finn Found Knowledge [3]

On another occasion Find[*] was in Cend Curraig. There it was customary for him to be. Every morning a man was entrusted to cook a pig for him as his day's ration. Once, then, Oisine was charged to cook it. When he deemed it time, he put it aside on the points of the fork upon the dish in the custody of his companion. Then it stuck fast. He turned about [to go] out. Oisine ran out after him beyond the Suir, namely over Ath Nemthen, beyond Ord, beyond Inniuin, beyond Fan hua Faelan to the summit of Sith Fer Femen. After he went into the fairy mound, the door was closed behind him. He left Oisine behind.

When Find's followers awakened, then he arrived.

'Where is the pig?' said Find.

'A braver man has taken it,' Oisine replied.

On the following day Cailte took it. From him it was carried off in

* Find is an alternative spelling of Finn in this text.

the same way. Thereupon he came [back].

'Where is the pig?' said Find.

'I am not braver than he from whom it was taken yesterday,' Cailte said.

'Although I go to cook it,' said Find, 'sharper is each thorn that is younger.'

He went himself to cook it, his spear-shafts in his left hand, the other hand, however, turning the pig on the points of the fork. It stuck fast. Find made a thrust at him. But only the point of the spear then attained his back. Thereupon he left the belly at Mag Tarra in Lee at Cell Ichtair (and) the breadth of the side at Toib Muicce. Seven times he leaped over the Siur.

'Open,' he said, 'before it,' [when he was] in the crown of the hill. 'Open,' he said, [running] over the [whole] length of the hill.

'Here is [something] from me!' said Find. He made a thrust at him as he went into the fairy mound, and thereby his back broke. His hand stuck fast against the door-post so that the door-valve closed on his thumb and he put it into his mouth. Therefore, some say that hence it is that Find obtained knowledge, for he used to put into his mouth the portion of his finger that had gone into the fairy mound. Their wailing was heard.

'What is that?' each said.

'Cul Dub has been slain!'

'Who has slain him?'

'Find hua Baiscni.'

They all wail.

Then he said: 'Sweet, sweet [is] the sweet little language . . .'

He carried his pig in his bosom, and apportioned it among his household.

Finn and the Man in the Tree[4]

When the fian were at Badamair on the brink of the Suir, Cúldub the son of Ua Birgge came out of the fairy-knoll on the plain of Femen and carried off their cooking from them. For three nights he did thus to them. The third time however Finn knew and went before him to the fairy-knoll on Femen. Finn laid hold of him as he went into the knoll, so that he fell yonder. When he withdrew his hand, a woman met him [?] coming out of the knoll with a dripping vessel in her hand, having just distributed drink, and she jammed the door against the knoll, and Finn squeezed his finger between the door and the post. Then he put his finger into his mouth. When he took it out again he began to chant, the *imbas* illumines him and he said [Here follows an untranslatable 'rhetoric'].

Some time afterwards they (i.e. the fian) carried off captive women from Dún Iascaig in the land of the Dési. A beautiful maiden was taken by them. Finn's mind desired the woman for himself. She set her heart on a servant whom they had, even Derg Corra son of Ua Daigre. For this was his practice. While food was being cooked by them, the lad jumped to and fro across the cooking hearth. It was for that the maiden loved him. And one day she said to him that he should come to her and lie with her. Derg Corra did not accept that on account of Finn . . . She incites Finn against him and said: 'Let us set upon him by force!' Thereupon Finn said to him: 'Go hence,' said he, 'out of my sight, and thou shalt have a truce of three days and three nights, and after that beware of me!'

Then Derg Corra went into exile and took up his abode in a wood and used to go about on shanks of deer for his lightness. One day as Finn was in the wood seeking him he saw a man in the top of a tree, a blackbird on his right shoulder and in his left hand a white vessel of bronze, filled with water, in which was a skittish trout, and a stag at the foot of the tree. And this was the practice of the man, cracking nuts; and he would give half the kernel of a nut to the blackbird that was on his right shoulder while he would himself eat the other half; and he would take an apple out of the bronze vessel that was in his left hand, divide it in two, throw one half to the stag that was at the foot of the tree, and then eat the other half himself. And on it he would drink a sip of the bronze vessel that was in his hand, so that he and the trout and the stag and the blackbird drank together. Then his followers asked of Finn who he in the tree was, for they did not recognise him on account of the hood of disguise which he wore.

Then Finn put his thumb into his mouth. When he took it out again, his *imbas* illumines him and he chanted an incantation and said: ''Tis Derg Corra son of Ua Daigre,' said he, 'that is in the tree.'

CHAPTER SIX

Shapeshifting

In this chapter we give two examples of Celtic shapeshifting traditions from Britain and Ireland. But we begin with a general overview of its traditional practice among the Celts.

Fith-Fath: Shapeshifting in Celtic Shamanic Tradition
by Caitlín Matthews

Learning the Powers

Shapeshifting is an integral part of Celtic shamanic experience. All shamans are potential polymorphs, able to assume the shape – in either the middle realms or in the otherworld, and sometimes both – of any living being.

This ability to be simultaneously part of all existences is integral to the unitive revelation of the shaman. For example, in order for Amairgin to help the Milesians conquer Ireland, he has first to commune with its total nature, so that he is able to utter his great paean of self-identification with the elements of the land itself (see Chapter 1). This is hard for the non-practitioner to understand fully, but it is closely akin to the mystic's union with all creation, as attested to in countless spiritual traditions. The difference between the two is that the mystic does not normally strive to become or appear in any other manifest shape than her own. The shaman may actively seek to appear as, or to journey to the otherworld in, another guise for various purposes, usually because the human shape is a disadvantage or because stale energy requires a substantial change.

Finding the right power which will help the shaman underlies much of shapeshifting. The shapeshifter calls upon the power of one of her animal or other helpers in order to go forth, in spirit, to transact whatever business she purposes. The projected spirit is usually invisible to others, but may be observed by people who have the Gaelic *da shealladh*, 'the two sights'. If so, the spirit-form may be shot at, causing the shapeshifter to be simultaneously wounded.

The main purposes of shapeshifting in Celtic tradition may be outlined as follows:

1. to learn from animal guises, to find information or things
2. to stalk a lover or enemy
3. to hide from someone or become 'invisible'
4. to survive in times and places when being human is dangerous
5. to become, or be enchanted into being, an otherworldly guardian.

There are also many examples of how shamans shapeshift matter in order to deceive, confuse or delay, but these cannot be dealt with here. The transformations above are usually, though not necessarily always, animal ones.

Let us look first at how shamans learn from animal guises, and find information or things. In the traditional Scottish song 'The Great Selkie of Sule Skerry', which relates the dialogue between a woman and selkie, a seal which can change into a man, we hear how he has visited her and impregnated her and now comes to collect their son, whom he intends to induct into the nature of a selkie. He prophesies that the woman will marry a gunner but that his first shot will kill the selkie and their son. This song is related to the traditions surrounding Manannan, the night-visiting God of the Otherworld, who has frequent intercourse with human women. In 'Compert Mongain' from the *Book of Fermoy*, he comes to claim his son, Mongan, and teach him the magic of the otherworld. There he remains, learning the secrets of shapeshifting until he is sixteen. He returns to his earthly family and proves to be a resourceful trickster. Manannan prophesies of his son:

> He will be a dragon before the host at the onset,
> He will be a wolf of every great forest.
> He will be a stag with horns of silver . . .
> He will be a speckled salmon in a full pool,
> He will be a seal, he will be a fair-white swan.
> He will be throughout long ages
> An hundred years in fair kingship . . .

However, despite these transformations, his time on earth will be short and he will be killed by a dragonstone and be taken to the otherworld by the White Host. Mongan is destined to enter many animal shapes in the course of his otherworldly education, although he dies in human shape. (The novelist T.H. White has his young King Arthur taught in a similar way by Merlin where he learns the tenacity of the badger, the patience of the hawk and a bird's complete disregard for human territorial boundaries.) We note that Mongan becomes animals of water, land and air, learning the qualities of each element. The ability to move through different elements is often a factor in the shaman's choice of shape. It is easier to fetch healing, for example from across the otherworldly sea by travelling in the shape of a seal than in that of a human.

In Mongan's story, we see the seeds of the shamanic understanding of different animal powers. In the British story of Math, son of Mathonwy, we read a mythic account of how transformation into animals can be used as a salutary learning experience. Math, a druidically trained king, transforms his nephews, Gwydion and Gilfaethwy, into animals for three years in order to teach them a lesson, since, urged on by Gwydion, Gilfaethwy has raped the maiden Goewin. Math causes the rapist to become a hind and Gwydion to become a stag in their first year; in the second year they switch genders again, the rapist being a boar and Gwydion a sow; in their third year, Gilfaethwy becomes a bitch wolf and his brother a dog wolf. Humiliating though this may be in itself, Math compounds the punishment, for his nephews have animal nature and mate each with the other, producing three litters from their unnatural union. Thus the rapist has to bear fawns and wolf cubs and learns for himself what it is to be female.

The foundation experience of learning from animal powers is a total entering into the nature of otherworldly reality, and is continually referenced in the work of Celtic poets. Even when the primitive shamanic practice began to fragment during the Middle Ages, this understanding remained in Celtic memory and is still retained in certain families, whose affinity with a particular animal – often a bird – is an ancestral memory of a long association with the animal powers.

Stalking the Prey

It is impossible to fathom the subtle circuitry of knowledge, the sexual pursuit and nourishment that intertwine the Celtic shamanic tradition. Intellectual and carnal knowledge have often been linked in the spiritual metaphor of the mystic's experience of divine union.

Shamans' journeys often yield parallel understandings: in otherworldly reality they experience sexual union with animals or find
themselves consuming their animals, simultaneously receiving a
steady transmission of knowledge. This happens in a Highland folk-
story, where a youth named Alasdair is sent to the Isle of Birds to
learn the language of the birds – a synonym for magical, otherworldly speech and knowledge. After three years' tuition, the boy's parents
are not much impressed by his riddling interpretation of birds' language, especially when he interprets for them the message of a
chaffinch which prophesies that Alasdair's father and mother will
humble themselves to their son. The father orders the boy's death, but
he escapes to the Isle of Birds where he quickly kills and eats the
birds, the faster to assimilate what they have to tell him.[1]

Sometimes the finding of knowledge is more of a stalking, following the desired object with the cunning of a hunter. The predatory
aspect of sexual love has similarly been frequently likened to the art
of venery. We have only to look at Gwion unwittingly receiving
knowledge from the cauldron of inspiration, being chased by
Ceridwen in many animal forms and finally being consumed and
reborn of her womb, to see that the cauldron and the womb are twin
vessels of transformation. All life bows to the needs of sexuality and
hunger; these naked needs create the shamanic stalking mentality.
For, contrary to popular expectation, shapeshifting, along with most
shamanic practice, is not undertaken solely for the benefit of the
shaman, but in order to help assuage someone's need. At no time is
this need sharper than when love strikes.

Aengus mac Og, owner of the Brugh (see Chapter 12), the god of
love and youth, dreams of a beautiful maiden and falls into a deep
lovesickness. After a long stalking of his love, he discovers that she is
Caer Ibormeith and that she spends most of her time in the shape of
a swan. He is told that she lives among a troop of 150 swans; if he
can correctly identify her, she has the choice of staying or leaving
with him. He calls her and they circle the lake in the shape of swans.
The enchantment of their musical flight causes all who hear it to fall
into slumber for three days and nights as they return to the Brugh.[2]
Here Aengus shares her shape in order to woo her.

The task of distinguishing the beloved from among 150 enchanted
others is a common theme in Celtic folk-story. It is here that the
shapeshifter comes into his own, being able to discern which is which
by going among the enchanted ones in their own form.

In an hilarious episode from the 'Compert Mongain', the hero,
Mongan, seeks to rescue his abducted wife, Dubh-Lacha, from the

King of Leinster. Mongan and his helper, Cuimne, the Hag of the Mill, appear at the court of Leinster in the shape of a beautiful couple. The King falls hopelessly in love with the woman and begs to swop wives. Mongan retreats swiftly with Dubh-Lacha, after which Cuimne resumes her original aged appearance, much to the King's disgust.

The tag which Gwion and Ceridwen play is a common pursuit on a shamanic journey, where, in the shape of his animal the shaman pursues other animals through the otherworlds in order to gain power or knowledge for another. The predatory nature of this stalking recurs in the following Scottish traditional song, in which we follow the sequence of the seasons and elements through a series of related animal transformations. 'Our Lady' and the 'Good God' in this version are titles for older deities than those of medieval convention; in other variants 'the Good God' is replaced by 'the Devil'.

> I will go as wren in spring,
> With sorrow and sighing on silent wing,
> And I shall go in Our Lady's name,
> Aye, til I come home again.
>
> Then we shall follow as falcons grey
> And hunt thee cruelly for our prey,
> And we shall go in the Good God's name,
> Aye, to fetch thee home again.
>
> Then I will go as a mouse in May
> In fields by night, in cellars by day,
> And I shall go in Our Lady's name.
> Aye, til I come home again.
>
> Then we shall follow as black tom cats,
> And hunt thee through the corn and vats,
> And we shall go in the Good God's name,
> Aye, to fetch thee home again.
>
> Then I shall go as an autumn hare,
> With sorrow and sighing and mickle care,
> And I shall go in Our Lady's name,
> Aye, til I come home again.
>
> Then we shall follow as swift grey-hounds
> And hunt thy tracks by leaps and bounds.
> And we shall go in the Good God's name,
> Aye, to fetch thee home again.

Then I shall go as a winter trout
With sorrow and sighing and mickle doubt.
And I shall go in Our Lady's name.
Aye, til I come home again.

Then we shall follow as otters swift,
And snare thee fast ere thou canst shift,
And we shall go in the Good God's name,
Aye, to fetch thee home again.[3]

This chase of prey and predator is also that of pupil and teacher or of lovers. The above song is closely related to the traditional folk song of 'The Two Magicians' in which a woman and blacksmith have a riddling debate about how he shall have, and how she shall save, her maidenhead. She is white as milk, he black as silk; she becomes a duck and he a water dog; she becomes a hare and he a greyhound; finally she becomes a sheet on a bed and he a coverlet.

The erotic elements of shapeshifting and interspecies connection that are part of this tradition seem strongly related to the major Celtic festivals. May Day, the day when the Celtic summer began, was when young people would spend the night with their lovers. More sinisterly, in the Isle of Man, the gorse was set on fire in order to flush out 'the witches, who are wont to take the shape of hares' on that day. Frazer also quotes a sixteenth-century account of how the Irish 'account every woman who fetches fire on May Day a witch . . . On May Day they kill all the hares they find among their cattle, supposing them the old women who have designs on their butter.'[4] May Day, like Hallowe'en, is the uncanny day when things happen. Disguising customs still abound at Samhain today; anciently the wearing of masks and disguises was to confound the wandering dead into imagining that the guisers were of their number and not mortals. It is at Samhain that the hardy Janet comes to disenchant Tam Lin, holding him as he changes through countless monstrous shapes until he is at last himself, a naked man, no longer thrall to the Faery Queen.[5] It would appear, from wider evidence than that presented here, that the thresholds of Beltane and Samhain are prominent points for both spirits and humans to change their shapes.

The ability to shapeshift is not solely the province of the druid or enchanter. As Dumézil says: 'Due either to a gift of metamorphosis or to a monstrous heredity, the eminent warrior possesses a veritable animal nature.' Cuchulainn's extraordinary gifts as a warrior are enhanced by his conscious drawing upon the power of the dog;

Diarmuid's tenacity is enhanced by his totemic boar; Pryderi's maternal totem is the horse and it is among foals that he vanishes and is rediscovered.

Sometimes warriors appear in strange shapes as when Fionn Mac Cumhail fights troops of men with cat-heads and dog-heads, and Art mac Conn (see Chapter 11) encounters a dog-headed individual in his otherworldly adventures. Are these warriors who are consciously drawing upon their tribal totem, or are they merely instances of the Celtic tendency to insult neighbouring tribes with the epithet 'cat/dog-heads?' In 'The Dream of Rhonabwy', in *The Mabinogion*, we see how the troops of Owain shapeshift into ravens and fall savagely upon the troops of Arthur at the same time as their respective commanders are playing a decisive board-game; the carved pieces and the troops are clearly interrelated, and the shapeshifting advantage is overthrown only by Arthur casting down the board and tumbling the pieces, powerless, to the ground.

The Goddess of War, Morrighan desires Cuchulainn for her lover. His refusal earns him her lifelong hatred, for she pursues him in numerous guises, combating him until he is overcome. She appears as a black eel, a white heifer and a grey wolf, and is wounded each time by him. She tricks him into healing her, by appearing as a decrepit hag leading a milk-heavy cow. In return for three drinks of milk, Cuchulainn blesses the giver three times, his every word a healing to the Morrighan.[6]

It is appropriate that the Morrighan, the Irish Goddess of War, should be regarded as the Celtic patroness of shapeshifting since she has a long descent down to our own times, in the person of Morgan le Fay, herself a renowned shapeshifter in the Arthurian legends.[7] As Geoffrey of Monmouth's Morgen, she is the Queen of Avalon, a healer and shapeshifter. In Malory, she retains her Morrigan-like antecedents in her jealous pursuit of Arthur's downfall.[8] In the whole of Celtic literature, there are no better stalkers than she, the mistress of life and death.

Fith-Fath and Enchantment

The title of this essay, *fith-fath*, pronounced 'fee-fawh', is a Scots Gaelic term for a charm which renders the subject invisible by making him or her appear in a different guise. It seems to have been used chiefly by hunters, warriors and travellers and is related to the Celtic protective charm called the *lorica* or breastplate charm. A Scots Gaelic *fith-fath* of this kind goes:

A magic cloud I put on thee,
From dog, from cat,
From cow, from horse,
From man, from maiden,
And from little child,
Till I again return.[9]

It seems to have been widely used by Celtic saints. The mother of St Finchua invoked it upon herself when pursued by enemies who would have raped her and aborted her unborn child.[10] But the most famous usage is by St Patrick who invokes an extensive *fith-fath* upon himself and his monks when pursued by King Loegaire's troops, rendering them all into the shape of deer. This invocation is commonly known as 'St Patrick's Breastplate' or *lorica*. It calls upon the three powers of the Trinity, the strength bestowed by the birth, crucifixion, resurrection and second coming of Christ, and the nine powers of the church's angelic protectors, apostles, confessors and virgins, before calling upon the ninefold powers of the elements:

I arise to-day
Through the strength of heaven;
Light of sun,
Radiance of moon,
Splendour of fire,
Speed of Lightning,
Swiftness of wind,
Depth of sea,
Stability of earth,
Firmness of rock.[11]

It further calls upon the powers of God to protect them and shield them against numerous enemies, among whom are mentioned 'the spells of women, smiths and druids'. It ends with a magical invocation of Christ in every direction surrounding them.

Fith-Fath, sometimes also *fath-fith*, translates as 'deer's aspect', which is interestingly the early Irish name given to St Patrick's Breastplate, the *feth-faidha*, often mistranslated as 'the deer's cry'. This seems to have been a particularly specific charm to render someone into a deer's shape, although Carmichael's research suggests that men might also be transformed into a horse or bull, women into a cat or hare.

Within the Fianna cycle we see a primal example of tradition. In a Scots Gaelic variant to the usual story, Fionn has a faery mistress whom he abandons in order to marry a human wife.[12] The faery woman puts a *fith-fath* spell upon the human woman who then turns into a deer and, pregnant with Fionn's child, retires to the wilderness. The child, Oisin, is born in human shape but retains a tuft of fawn's hair where his mother licked him. He finds acceptance among the Fianna and re-encounters his mother while on a deer hunt. She transforms into human shape, reminding him who she is and he returns to his father's kindred after singing her a warning song:

> If you be my mother and you a deer.
> Arise before the sun strikes you,
> Beware the men of the Fianna.

The major use of the *fith-fath*, then, is protective, but it is also employed in other ways. The manipulative use of shapeshifting to coerce or restrain others is part of the traditional equipment of the ancient shaman. The power to enchant others is still much feared in many parts of the world as the 'evil eye' which can overlook a person, animal or goods. The custom of invoking a protective mantle or mystical encompassment of prayer around oneself, one's animals or one's home is still common in Celtic countries (see Chapter 9).

Enchantment into a non-human shape also has the effect of preventing a person from being recognized, from operating as a full member of society, for the purposes of dispossession or in sheer vengeance. Both Etain (see Chapter 12) and the Children of Lir are enchanted into other shapes through jealousy. Etain is stricken by the rowan-tree wand of her lover's wife, Fuamnach, and turns successively into a pool of water, a worm and a fly, before being swallowed by the wife of Etar and reborn of her as Etain the second. The Children of Lir are turned by their stepmother into swans, in which shape they are fated to remain until a southern princess marries a northern prince. Three hundred years elapse before they are released.

We have already seen examples of how to survive in times and places when being human is dangerous or inappropriate, in the story of Tuan mac Carill (see pp. 93–98), who survives his race in successive animal forms, changing into these by night as the inconvenience of age comes upon him.

Liban, the daughter of Eochaid and Ebliú, is the sole survivor of her family when Loch Neagh floods. After a year in her under-lake *grianan* (solarium) she asks to be turned into a fish, the better to live in the lake. She becomes half-salmon, half-woman, while her dog becomes an otter. She is discovered 300 years later by Caoilte of the Fianna, with whom she has a hunting contest. When St Comgall sends his representative priest, Beoan, to visit St Gregory in Rome, Liban sings to the cleric and makes a rendezvous with him a year hence. She is asked then whether she wishes to be a mermaid for a further 300 years or to be baptized and die right away. At her request, St Comgall baptizes her Muirgheis ('sea-born'), she dies and is born to heaven by antlered deer.[13]

The word *tuirgin* has been used of such transmigrations, signifying an investigative circuit of existences from a single birth time. The literal meaning of *tuirgin* is 'circular birth', but in *Cormac's Glossary* it implies a fluid transmigration of the soul from form to form. The intertwining knotwork of tracery which invades most decorated Celtic objects usually involves the circuit of one or more fluid strips which follow pathways too bewildering for the eye to comprehend at first glance. So it is too with some Celtic shapeshifting. These transmigratory cycles of animal shapes seem to be associated with the ancestral teachings of the ages of the world (see Chapter 3).

The overwhelming evidence of metempsychosis (passing from one body to another at death) and metamorphosis (changing shape) derived from Celtic sources does not necessarily give us a neat parallel doctrine of reincarnation. But it is more than possible that the actual practice of shapeshifting in one lifetime may help create a bridge for the soul to pass between one soul-shrine, as the body is called, and another. Those who are able to bridge different time-scales and dimensions in this way invariably become denizens of the otherworld and may be regarded as guardians of memory, tradition and knowledge from whom later humans can learn.

Spirits of the Land and Threshold Guardians

Sometimes a shapeshifting enchantment has a semi-permanent effect which renders the subject, to all intents and purposes, a citizen of the otherworld or else into a threshold guardian. The early theriomorphic deities such as Cernunnos the antlered god, have their origins possibly in pre-Celtic times. Like the Cyclops, these figures are often monstrous, titanic, with animal propensities or features; they are often husbandmen, shepherds, swineherds, guardians of flocks, equipped with riddles and questions. The Green Knight of the medieval Gawain stories is a latter-day example of this, transformed from human into otherworldly shape by Morgan le Fay, appointed by her to keep the gates of Winter against all challengers.[14] Such figures are root threshold guardians so ancient that none remember if they ever had human ancestry. They endure as monstrous guardians of treasures or secrets who cannot be overcome unless they encounter one who has no fear of their appearance and who is willing, in turn, to take up the guardianship. Such a handing over of responsibility is a recurrent theme in Celtic tradition and brings us to the core purpose of ancestral shapeshifting stories. When Pwyll, Prince of Dyfed meets the God of the Underworld, Arawn, after having slain one of the god's deer, he finds himself under obligation to redeem his error. They swear eternal friendship and Arawn asks Pwyll to change places with him for a year in order that his enemy, Hafgan might be overcome. Pwyll spends a year in the underworld while Arawn governs Dyfed: the shape of each man is changed so that no one guesses the substitution. At the end of the year, Pwyll overcomes Hafgan on Arawn's behalf and both men return to their respective domains. For his service, Pwyll is latterly entitled Pen Annwn, Lord of the Underworld. Much of his subsequent story requires his attendance in Annwn, and he marries Rhiannon, herself a woman of the underworld. He also acquires the pigs of Annwn, a species hitherto unknown to earth.[15]

We see that shapeshifting is more subtle than we have conceived it, for it involves an exchange of power. This exchange is based on mutual respect. When one guardian transmits his secret, he also transmits his guardianship. Those who bring treasures from the depths of the underworld become porters in hell, threshold guardians who can transfer power between one realm and the next.

Many of our examples seem to be but legend and folk-tale, and yet these stories cast a long shadow, as in Ulster where a story surrounds the erection of the Black Pig's Dyke, an earthwork of human manufacture stretching originally from Donegal Bay in the west to the Newry marshes in the east. The remaining traces of it have been recently dated to AD 100, and it was doubtless erected to keep raiders out of Ulster.[16] The line of the dyke closely follows the modern border of Northern Ireland.

The root legend of its origins concerns Cian mac Cainte, father of the god Lugh. He encounters his son's enemies, the sons of Tuirenn and, not wishing to enter an unequal combat, strikes himself with a druidic wand and turns himself into a pig. The sons of Tuirenn, Iucharba and Iuchar, suppose that they will lose their prey, but their brother Brian cries 'Badly have ye acquired your learning in the city of learning when you cannot distinguish a druidical beast from a natural beast.'[17] He strikes his brothers with the druidical wand and they become hounds to chase the pig. Brian wounds the pig which begs to be allowed to return to its manly shape in order to die. Because Cian is now a man and not a pig, his honour price is accordingly higher and he prophesies that no honour price shall be higher than his will be. The Sons of Tuirenn stone him to death and hide his body, having to bury it several times before it will stay down. Lugh, Cian's son, avenges his father by demanding otherworldly and virtually unobtainable objects in compensation before killing his father's murderers.

Such is the root legend. But folk legend extends this story, telling how Cian, in black pig form, was chased right the way across the border of Ulster, casting up earth and making a trench in his furious escape. It is locally prophesied that one day the pig will return and slaughter all strangers to the north. It is also thought that houses built along the line of the dyke bring death or misfortune on their occupants. An old woman in 1953 prophesied that the pig would resume its strife and destruction two years later.[18] In 1956–7 the IRA did indeed mount a series of attacks upon the border, leading to the hastening of the present occupation of Ulster by the British Army. Truly, the Black Pig's Dyke story casts a long shadow and has demanded a high honour price!

Ultimately, the threshold guardians in enchanted shape are deeply attached to the land in which they are rooted. And when the spirits of the land make themselves manifest, then we can be sure that there are great matters afoot. The manner in which the Goddess of the Land herself shapeshifts from hag to maiden in Celtic tradition demonstrates the polymorphic nature of the land itself, which changes its mantle with the seasons from the skeletal bareness of winter to the verdant caparison of spring. She shows the manner in which threshold and otherworldly guardians validate those who behave or answer correctly (see Chapter 8).

If shapeshifting is particularly prevalent in the stories of the Scots and British, perhaps it is no wonder. The name 'Britain' is derived via the ancient word for the Britons – *Pritani*, a name which survives in the modern Welsh word for Britain, *Prydein*. In its Gaelic variant, *Pritani* becomes *Cruitni*, since Gaelic does not use the letter 'p' but substitutes the 'qu' sound.

Cruitni is the Gaelic word for Picts. There are many disputes about the origins of the Picts: some scholars think they are the original, pre-Celtic inhabitants of Scotland while others think they derive from non-Celtic Indo-European invaders. Whatever the truth, everyone remembers one fact about them, because the Romans termed them 'the painted people'. In the seventeenth century, Duald MacFirbis, who drew on a now lost source for his information, wrote, 'The *Cruitneach* (Pict) is one who takes the *cruths* or forms of beasts, birds and fishes on his face; and not on it only, but on his whole body.'[19] He was referring to the much-vaunted claim that the Picts tattooed themselves or painted themselves with woad derivatives.

The word *cruth*, meaning 'shape, form, appearance or expression', is echoed by the modern Welsh *pryd* meaning 'form, aspect or complexion'. Underlying the word we find the meaning of 'shaper', which is indeed the meaning of the Scots Gaelic word for creator. *Cruithear*. In common with many indigenous peoples of the world, the ancient British may have considered themselves to be 'the created people' or possibly, 'the shapers'. We may add one further suggestion: that they regarded themselves generically as 'the shapeshifters', so attuned to the living animal powers that they took their shapes upon their bodies, as well as upon their monuments.

The *Cruitni* or *Pritani* may indeed be the early, pre-Celtic inhabitants of Britain who knew the art of shapeshifting. They left us no written language, no texts that we can decipher; instead they bequeathed an ancestral legacy – the secret art of shapeshifting, the *fith-fath* which we can still use if we listen to the powers who also taught them.

The Shapeshifting Swineherds[20]

This, now, is the story of the two bulls, the Brown of Cuailgne, and the White-horned of Cruachan Ai, and this is the way it was with them – for they were not right bulls, but there was enchantment on them. In the time long ago Bodb was king of the Sidhe of Munster, and it is in Femen, of Slieve-na-man he was, and Ochall Ochne was king of the Sidhe of Connaught, and it is in Cruachan he used to be. They used at one time to be fighting one against the other, but afterwards they made peace, and were good friends. Now Bodb had a swineherd, whose name was Friuch, and Ochall had a swineherd whose name was Rucht, and they were friendly with one another the same as their masters. And they had the knowledge of enchantments, and could turn themselves to every shape. And when there was a great plenty of mast in Munster, the swineherd from Connaught would bring his lean swine to the south, and in the same way, when mast was plentiful in Connaught, the swineherd would bring his swine northward, and would bring them home again fat.

But after a while some bad feeling rose up between the two, for the men of Connaught and the men of Munster began to set them one against the other. So one year when there was a great mast in Munster, and Rucht brought his herd from Connaught, so soon as his comrade

Friuch had bade him welcome, he said: 'The people are all saying your power is greater than mine.' 'It is no less any way,' said Ochall's herd. 'We will soon know that,' said Friuch. 'I will put an enchantment on your swine, and even though they eat their share of mast, they will not be fat, like mine will be.' And so it happened, he put an enchantment on the Connaught swine, and when Rucht went home with them they could hardly walk at all, they were so thin and so weak, and all the people were laughing at the state they were in. 'It was a bad day for you, you went to the South,' they said, 'for your comrade has greater power than what you have.' 'That is not so,' said he. 'Wait till it is our turn to have mast, and I will play the same trick on him.'

So the next year he did as he had said, and the Munster swine pined away, so that every one said their power was the same. And when Bodb's swineherd went back home to Munster with his lean swine, his master put him out of the place. And Ochall put his herd out of his place as well, because of the swine coming back in so bad a state from Munster.

One day, two full years after that, the men of Munster were gathered together near Femen, and they took notice of two ravens that were making a great cawing. 'What a noise those birds have been making all through the year!' they said. 'They never stop scolding at one another.' Just then Findell, Ochall's steward from Cruachan, came towards them on the hill, and they bade him welcome. 'What a noise those birds are making!' he said; 'any one would think them to be the same two birds we had in Cruachan last year.' With that, they saw the two ravens change into the shape of men, and they knew them to be the two swineherds, and they bade them welcome. 'It is not right you should welcome us,' said Bodb's swineherd, 'for there will be many dead bodies of friends, and much crying on account of us two.' 'What has happened to you all through this time?' they asked. 'Nothing good,' he said. 'Since we went from you we have been all the time in the shape of birds, and you saw the way we were scolding at one another all through this year. And we were quarrelling in the same way the whole of last year at Cruachan, and the men of the North and of the South have seen what our power is. And now,' he said, 'we will go into the shape of water beasts, and be under the water for the length of two years.' And with that one of them went into the Sionnan, and the other into the Suir, and they were seen for a year in the Suir, and for a year in the Sionnan, and they devouring one another. And one day the men of Connaught had a great gathering at

Ednecha, on the Sionnan, and they saw these two beasts in the river; each one of them looked to be as big as the top of a hill, and they made such a furious attack on one another that fiery swords seemed to be coming from their jaws, and the people came round them on every side. They came out of the Sionnan then, and as soon as they touched the shore, they changed again into the shape of the two swine-herds. Ochall bade them welcome. 'Where have you been wandering?' he asked them. 'Indeed it is tired we are with our wanderings,' they said. 'You saw what we were doing before your eyes, and that is what we were doing through these two years, under seas and waters. And now we must take new shapes on us, till we try one another's strength again.' And with that they went away.

It happened a good while after that there was a great gathering of the men of Connaught at Loch Riach, for Bodb was coming on a friendly visit to Ochall. And Bodb brought a great troop with him, the most splendid ever seen; speckled horses they had, and green cloaks with silver brooches, and shoes with clasps of red bronze, and every one of them had a collar of gold, with a stone worth a newly-calved cow set in it. When Ochall saw what grand clothes and horses they had, he called to his people secretly, and asked could they match Bodb's people in dress and in horses and arms, and they said they could not. Then Ochall said: 'That is a pity, and our great name is lost.' But just then a troop of men were seen coming from the North, and black horses with them, that you would think had been cast up by the sea, and bridle-bits of gold in their mouths. And the men had black-grey cloaks, and a gold brooch at the breast of each, and a white tunic with crimson stripes, and fifty coils of bright gold round every man. And every man of them had black hair, as smooth as if a cow had licked it. And they stopped a little way off, and then the men of Connaught stood up and gave up their place to them. There was a Druid from Britain there, and when he saw them make way he said: 'From this out, to the end of life and time, the Connaught men will be under the yoke, attending on hounds and on sons of kings and queens for ever.'

Then after they had been feasting for a while, Bodb asked could any Connaught man be found that would fight against his champion Rinn, that was with him, and that had a great name, but no one knew where he came from. And at first there could no one be found, but then a strange champion came out from among the men of Connaught, and he said, 'I will go against him.' 'That is no welcome news,' said Rinn. Then they fought against one another for three days and three nights, and before the end of that time the two armies began to join into the fight, and a troop came from Leinster and joined with Bodb, and another troop came from Meath and joined with Ochall. And four kings were killed there, and Ochall among them, and then Bodb went back to Slieve-na-man. But as to the two champions, they were seen no more, and it was known they were the two swineherds. After that they were for two years with the appearance of shadows, threatening one another, the way that many people died of fright after seeing them.

And after that, they were in the shape of eels, and one went into the river Cruind, in Cuailgne; and after a while a cow belonging to Daire, son of Fachna, drank it down. And the other went into the Spring of Uaran Garad, in Connaught; and one day Maeve went out to the spring, and a small bronze vessel in her hand, and she dipped it in the water, and the little eel went into it, and every colour was to be seen on him. And she was a long time looking at him, she thought the colours so beautiful. Then the water went away, and the eel was alone in the vessel. 'It is a pity you cannot speak to me,' said Maeve. 'What is it you want to know?' said the eel. 'I would like to know what way it is with you in that shape of a beast,' she said; 'and I would like to know what will happen to me after I get the sway over Connaught.' 'Indeed it is a tormented beast I am,' he said, 'and it is in many shapes I have been. And as to yourself,' he said, 'handsome as you are, you should take a good man to be with you in your sway.' 'I have no wish,' said Maeve, 'to let a man of Connaught get the upper hand over me,' and with that she went home again.

But she married Ailell after that, and as for the eel, he was swallowed down by one of Maeve's cows that came to drink at the spring.

And it was from that cow, and from the cow that belonged to Daire, son of Fachna, the two bulls were born, the White-horned and the Brown. They were the finest ever seen in Ireland, and gold and silver were put on their horns by the men of Ulster and Connaught. In Connaught no bull dared bellow before the White-horned, and in Ulster no bull dared bellow before the Brown.

As to the Brown, he that had been Friuch, the Munster swineherd, his lowing when he would be coming home every evening to his yard was good music to the people of the whole of Cuailgne. And wherever he was, neither Bocanachs nor Bananachs nor witches of the valley, could come into the one place with him. And it was on account of him the great war broke out.

Now, when Maeve saw at Ilgairech that the battle was going against her, she sent eight of her own messengers to bring away the Brown Bull, and his heifers. 'For whoever goes back or does not go back,' she said, 'the Brown Bull must go to Cruachan.'

Now when the Brown Bull came into Connaught, and saw the beautiful trackless country before him, he let three great loud bellowings out of him. As soon as the White-horned heard that, he set out for the place those bellowings came from, with his head high in the air.

Then Maeve said that the men of her army must not go to their homes till they would see the fight between the two bulls.

And they all said some one must be put to watch the fight, and to give a fair report of it afterwards. And it is what they agreed, that Bricriu should be sent to watch it, because he had not taken any side in the war; for he had been through the whole length of it under care of physicians at Cruachan, with the dint of the wound he got the day he vexed Fergus, and that Fergus drove the chessmen into his head. 'I will go willingly,' said Bricriu. So he went out and took his place in a gap, where he could have a good view of the fight.

As soon as the bulls caught sight of one another they pawed the earth so furiously that they sent the sods flying, and their eyes were like balls of fire in their heads; they locked their horns together, and they ploughed up the ground under them and trampled it, and they were trying to crush and to destroy one another through the whole length of the day.

And once the White-horned went back a little way and made a rush at the Brown, and got his horn into his side, and he gave out a great bellow, and they rushed both together through the gap where Bricriu was, the way he was trodden into the earth under their feet. And that is how Bricriu of the bitter tongue, son of Cairbre, got his death.

Then when the night was coming on, Cormac Conloingeas took hold of a spear-shaft, and he laid three great strokes on the Brown Bull from head to tail, and he said: 'This is a great treasure to be boasting of, that cannot get the better of a calf of his own age.' When the Brown Bull heard that insult, great fury came on him, and he turned on the White-horned again. And all through the night the men of Ireland were listening to the sound of their bellowing, and they going here and there, all through the country.

On the morrow, they saw the Brown Bull coming over Cruachan from the west, and he carrying what was left of the White-horned on his horns. Then Maeve's sons, the Maines, rose up to make an attack on him on account of the Connaught bull he had destroyed. 'Where are those men going?' said Fergus. 'They are going to kill the Brown Bull of Cuailgne.' 'By the oath of my people,' said Fergus, 'if you do not let the Brown Bull go back to his own country in safety, all he has done to the White-horned is little to what I will do now to you.'

Then the Brown Bull bellowed three times, and set out on his way. And when he came to the great ford of the Sionnan he stopped to drink, and the two loins of the White-horned fell from his horns into the water. And that place is called Ath-luain, the ford of the loin, to this day. And its liver fell in the same way into a river of Meath, and it is called Ath-Truim, the ford of the liver, to this day.

Then he went on till he came to the top of Slieve Breagh, and when he looked from it he saw his own home, the hills of Cuailgne; and at the sight of his own country, a great spirit rose up in him, and madness and fury came on him, and he rushed on, killing everyone that came in his way.

And when he got to his own place, he turned his back to a hill and he gave out a loud bellowing of victory. And with that his heart broke in his body, and blood came bursting from his mouth, and he died.

The Frenzy of Suibhne[21]

In this story, Suibhne, King of Dalriadian Ireland, incurs the ire of St Ronan and finds himself translated into the nature and abilities, though not the shape, of a bird. This terrible curse causes him to dissociate himself from his normal environment and seek out wild and unfrequented places. What makes his plight so pitiable is that, during his exile as a bird, he has periods of human lucidity.

During his madness, he flees human company, taking solace in his natural surroundings, in the time-honoured manner of all shamans. He meets the Hag of the Mill, with whom he has a leaping contest. She is none other than the Cailleach na Dudain or Old Woman of the Mill who regulates the turning mill of life and death; she is frequently encountered by madmen and poets, and is the Gaelic counterpart of the British goddess Arianrhod of the Turning

Tower of Caer Sidi. Taliesin speaks of this experience of being imprisoned in her tower for three periods of initiation. It is while he is undergoing her purgative grinding that Suibhne and others come to a shamanic clarification or refinement of their abilities.

St Moling is more compassionate to Suibhne than Ronan, the cleric he originally offended, making him welcome but not seeking to restrain him. But it is Moling's swineherd, Mongan, who is responsible for Suibhne's eventual humanization, disenchantment and death.

Themes from Suibhne's story are paralleled in the legends of both Merlin and Lailokan. This story has inspired many, including the Irish novelist Flann O'Brien, whose *At Swim Two Birds* is based on Suibhne's adventures. In the version which follows the prose extracts are from the translation of T.P. Cross and C.H. Slover; the verse is translated by J.G. O'Keefe.

Suibhne son of Colmán was king of Dál nAraide.[22] One day Saint Rónán was marking the boundaries of a church in that county, and Suibhne heard the sound of his bell. When his people told him that Rónán was establishing a church in his territory, he set out in anger to expel the cleric. His wife Eorann sought to restrain him, and caught the border of his cloak, but he rushed naked from the house, leaving the cloak in her hands. Rónán was chanting the Office when Suibhne came up, and the king seized the psalter and threw it into the lake. He then laid hands on the saint and was dragging him away, when a messenger arrived from Congal Claen to summon him to the battle of Moira. Suibhne departed with the messenger leaving Rónán sorrowful. Next day an otter from the lake restored the psalter to the saint unharmed. Rónán gave thanks to God and cursed the king, wishing that he might wander naked through the world as he had come naked into his presence.

Rónán went to Moira to make peace between Domnall and Congal Claen, but without success. He and his clerics sprinkled holy water on the armies, but when they sprinkled it on Suibhne he slew one of the clerics with a spear and made a second cast at Rónán himself. The second spear broke against the saint's bell, and the shaft flew into the air. Rónán cursed Suibhne, wishing that he might fly through the air like the shaft of his spear, and that he might die of a spear-cast like the cleric whom he had slain.

Thereafter, when the battle was joined, the armies on both sides raised three mighty shouts. Suibhne was terrified by the clamour. His weapons fell from his hands. He was seized with trembling and fled in a frenzy like a bird of the air. His feet rarely touched the ground in his flight, and at last he settled upon a yew-tree far from the battle-field. There he was discovered by a kinsman, Aongus the Fat, who had fled the field after the victory of Domnall. Aongus sought to persuade Suibhne to join him, but Suibhne flew away like a bird and came to Tír Conaill where he perched on a tree near the church called Cell Riagáin. It happened that the victorious army of Domnall had encamped there after the battle. Domnall recognized him and lament-ed his misfortune.

Suibhne fled again and was for a long time travelling through Ireland till he came to Glenn Bolcáin.

> It was there that the madmen used to abide when their year of frenzy was over, for that valley is always a place of great delight to madmen. Glenn Bolcáin has four gaps to the wind and a love-ly fragrant wood and clean-bordered wells and cool springs, and a sandy stream of clear water with green cress and long waving brooklime on its surface.

In that wise he remained in Glen Bolcain until at a certain time he raised himself up [into the air] and went to Cluain Cille on the bor-der of Tir Conaill and Tir Boghaine. He went then to the brink of the well where he had for food that night watercress and water. Thereafter he went into the old tree of the church. The erenach of the church was Faibhlen of the family of Brughach, son of Deaghadh. That night there came an exceeding great storm so that the extent of the night's misery affected Suibhne greatly, and he said: 'Sad indeed is it that I was not slain at Magh Rath rather than that I should encounter this hardship'; whereupon he uttered this lay:

> Cold is the snow to-night,
> lasting now is my poverty,
> there is no strength in me for fight,
> famine has wounded me, madman as I am.

> All men see that I am not shapely,
> bare of thread is my tattered garment,
> Suibhne of Ros Earcain is my name,
> the crazy madman am I.

> I rest not when night comes,
> my foot frequents no trodden way,
> I bide not here for long,
> the bonds of terror come upon me.

My goal lies beyond the teeming main,
voyaging the prow-abounding sea;
fear has laid hold of my poor strength,
I am the crazy one of Glen Bolcain.

Frosty wind tearing me,
already snow has wounded me,
the storm bearing me to death
from the branches of each tree.

Grey branches have wounded me,
they have torn my hands;
the briars have not left
the making of a girdle for my feet.

There is a palsy on my hands,
everywhere there is cause of confusion,
from Sliabh Mis to Sliabh Cuillenn,
from Sliabh Cuillenn to Cuailgne.

Sad forever is my cry
on the summit of Cruachan Aighle,
from Glen Bolcain to Islay,
from Cenn Tire to Boirche.

Small is my portion when day comes,
it comes not as a new day's right[?],
a tuft of watercress of Cluain Cille
with Cell Cua's cuckoo flower.

He who is at Ros Earcach,
neither trouble nor evil shall come to him;
that which makes me strengthless
is being in snow in nakedness.

For seven years Suibhne wandered throughout Ireland, and then he returned to Glenn Bolcáin. There Loingsechán came to seek him. (Some say that Loingsechán was a son of Suibhne's mother, some say that he was his foster-brother, but, however that may be, he was a faithful friend, for he rescued Suibhne three times.[23]) Loingsechán found the footprints of Suibhne near the river where he used to come to eat watercress, and the trace of his passage from tree to tree in the broken branches, but he found not Suibhne. He slept one night in a hut, and Suibhne came near and heard him snore. And he uttered a lay:

The man by the wall snores: I dare not sleep like that.
For seven years since that Tuesday at Moira I have not slept for
a moment.

.   .   .   .

The cress of the well of Druim Cirb is my meal at terce.
My face betrays it. Truly I am Suibhne the Madman.

.   .   .   .

Though I live from hill to hill on the mountain above the
valley of yews, alas! that I was not left to lie with Congal
Claen.

.   .   .   .

Green cress and a drink of clear water is my fare. I do not smile.
This is not the fate of the man by the wall.

.   .   .   .

Eorann, Suibhne's wife, had gone to live with Guaire, one of the
claimants to the kingdom. Suibhne visited her and spoke of their former happiness together, of her present comfort and his misery. Their
dialogue is in verse. He reproaches her for enjoying the love of another man and the comfort of his house while her husband is an outcast,
and she protests that she would rather live with Suibhne in the wilderness than with any man of Ireland or Scotland. Suibhne tells her that
she does better to stay with Guaire than to share the life of a madman, and that he bears her no grudge. As people approach he flies
away.

Suibhne came to Ros Ercáin where he had had a house, and he
settled in a yew tree there. Loingsechán came again to capture him.
At first he pleaded with him to return home and resume the royal
comforts that had been his. Suibhne bade Loingsechán leave him to his
fate, and asked for news of his country.

'Your father is dead.' 'That grieves me,' said he. 'Your mother
is dead,' said the lad. 'Now all pity for me is at an end,' said
he. 'Your brother is dead,' said Loingsechán. 'I am sorely
wounded by that,' said Suibhne. 'Your daughter is dead,' said
Loingsechán. 'And an only daughter is the needle of the heart,'
said Suibhne. 'Dead is your son who used to call you "Father",'
said Loingsechán. 'Indeed,' said he, 'that is the drop that brings
a man to the ground.'

When Suibhne heard of the death of his son he fell down from the
tree, and Loingsechán seized and bound him, and then told him that

all his kindred were alive. Soon he recovered his reason and was king again, but he remained in the custody of Loingsechán. . . . (Cross and Slover)

Suibhne was put in Loingseachan's bed-room after his bonds were taken off him, and his sense had come back to him. The bed-room was shut on him and nobody was left with him but the mill-hag, and she was enjoined not to attempt to speak to him. Nevertheless she spoke to him, asking him to tell some of his adventures while he was in a state of madness. 'A curse on your mouth, hag!' said Suibhne; 'ill is what you say; God will not suffer me to go mad again.' 'I know well,' said the hag, 'that it was the outrage done to Ronan that drove you to madness.' 'O woman,' said he, 'it is hateful that you should be betraying and luring me.' 'It is not betrayal at all but truth'; and Suibhne said:

> Suibhne: 'O hag of yonder mill,
> why shouldst thou set me astray?
> is it not deceitful of thee that, through women,
> I should be betrayed and lured?'

> The hag: 'Tis not I who betrayed thee,
> O Suibhne, though fair thy fame,
> but the miracles of Ronan from Heaven
> which drove thee to madness among madmen.

> Suibhne: Were it myself, and would it were I,
> that were king of Dal Araidhe
> it were a reason for a blow across a chin;
> thou shalt not have a feast, O hag.

'O hag,' said he, 'great are the hardships I have encountered if you but knew; many a dreadful leap have I leaped from hill to hill, from fortress to fortress, from land to land, from valley to valley.' 'For God's sake,' said the hag, 'leap for us now one of the leaps you used to leap when you were mad.' Thereupon he bounded over the bed-rail so that he reached the end of the bench. 'My conscience!' said the hag, 'I could leap that myself,' and in the same manner she did so. He took another leap out through the skylight of the hostel. 'I could leap that too,' said the hag, and straightway she leaped. This, however, is a summary of it: Suibhne travelled through five cantreds of Dal Araidhe that day until he arrived at Glenn na nEachtach in Fiodh Gaibhle, and she followed him all that time. When Suibhne rested

there on the summit of a tall ivy-branch, the hag rested on another
tree beside him. It was then the end of harvest-time precisely.
Thereupon Suibhne heard a hunting-call of a multitude in the verge of
the wood. 'This,' said he, 'is the cry of a great host, and they are the
Ui Faelain coming to kill me to avenge Oilill Cedach, king of the Ui
Faelain, whom I slew in the battle of Magh Rath.' He heard the bellowing of the stag, and he made a lay wherein he eulogized aloud the
trees of Ireland, and, recalling some of his own hardships and sorrows,
he said:

> O little stag, thou little bleating one,
> O melodious little clamourer,
> sweet to us is the music
> thou makest in the glen.

> Longing for my little home
> has come on my senses —
> the flocks in the plain,
> the deer on the mountain.

> Thou oak, bushy, leafy,
> thou art high beyond trees;
> O hazlet, little branching one,
> O fragrance of hazel-nuts.

> O alder, thou art not hostile,
> delightful is thy hue,
> thou art not rending and prickling
> in the gap wherein thou art.

> O little blackthorn, little thorny one;
> O little black sloe-tree;
> O watercress, little green-topped one,
> from the brink of the ousel[?] spring.

> O *minen* of the pathway,
> thou art sweet beyond herbs,
> O little green one, very green one,
> O herb on which grows the strawberry.

> O apple-tree, little apple-tree,
> much art thou shaken;
> O quicken, little berried one,
> delightful is thy bloom.

O briar, little arched one,
thou grantest no fair terms,
thou ceasest not to tear me,
till thou hast thy fill of blood.

O yew-tree, little yew-tree,
in churchyards thou art conspicuous;
O ivy, little ivy,
thou art familiar in the dusky wood.

O holly, little sheltering one,
thou door against the wind;
O ash-tree, thou baleful one,
hand-weapon of a warrior.

O birch, smooth and blessed,
thou melodious, proud one,
delightful each entwining branch
in the top of thy crown.

The aspen a-trembling;
by turns I hear
its leaves a-racing —
meseems 'tis the foray!

My aversion in woods —
I conceal it not from anyone —
is the leafy stirk of an oak
swaying evermore. [?]

Ill-hap by which I outraged
the honour of Ronan Finn,
his miracles have troubled me,
his little bells from the church.

Ill-omened I found
the armour of upright Congai,
his sheltering, bright tunic
with selvages of gold.

It was a saying of each one
of the valiant, active host:
'Let not escape from you through the narrow copse
the man of the goodly tunic.'

'Wound, kill, slaughter,
let all of you take advantage of him;
put him, though it is great guilt,
on spit and on spike.'

The horsemen pursuing me
across round Magh Cobha,
no cast from them reaches
me through my back.

Going through the ivy-trees –
I conceal it not, O warrior –
like good cast of a spear
I went with the wind.

O little fawn, O little long-legged one,
I was able to catch thee
riding upon thee
from one peak to another.

From Carn Cornan of the contests
to the summit of Sliabh Niadh,
from the summit of Sliabh Uillinne
I reach Crota Cliach.

From Crota Cliach of assemblies
to Carn Liffi of Leinster,
I arrive before eventide
in bitter Benn Gulbain.

My night before the battle of Congal,
I deemed it fortunate,
before I restlessly
wandered over the mountain-peaks.

Glen Bolcain, my constant abode,
'twas a boon to me,
many a night have I attempted
a stern race against the peak.

If I were to wander alone
the mountains of the brown world,
better would I deem the site of a single hut
in the Glen of mighty Bolcan.

Good its water pure-green,
good its clean, fierce wind,
good its cress-green watercress,
best its tall brooklime.

Good its enduring ivy-trees,
good its bright, cheerful sallow,
good its yewy yews,
best its melodious birch.

If thou shouldst come, O Loingseachan,
to me in every guise,
each night to talk to me,
perchance I would not tarry for thee.

I would not have tarried to speak to thee
were it not for the tale which has wounded me —
father, mother, daughter, son,
brother, strong wife dead.

If thou shouldst come to speak to me,
no better would I deem it;
I would wander before morn
the mountains of Boirche of peaks.

By the mill of the little floury one
thy folk has been ground, [?]
O wretched one, O weary one,
O swift Loingseachan.

O hag of this mill,
why dost thou take advantage of me?
I hear thee revile me
even when thou art out on the mountain.

O hag, O round-headed one,
wilt thou go on a steed?
The hag: I would go, O fool-head
if no one were to see me.

O Suibhne, if I go,
may my leap be successful.
Suibhne: If thou shouldst come, O hag,
mayst thou not dismount full of sense!

The hag: In sooth, not just is what thou sayest,
        thou son of Colman Cas;
        is not my riding better
        without falling back?

Suibhne: Just, in sooth, is what I say,
        O hag without sense;
        a demon is ruining thee,
        thou hast ruined thyself.

The hag: Dost thou not deem my arts better,
        thou noble, slender madman,
        that I should be following thee
        from the tops of the mountains?

Suibhne: A proud ivy-bush
        which grows through a twisted tree —
        if I were right on its summit,
        I would fear to come out.

        I flee before the skylarks —
        'tis a stern, great race —
        I leap over the stumps
        on the tops of the mountains.

        When the proud turtle-dove
        rises for us,
        quickly do I overtake it
        since my feathers have grown.

        The silly, foolish woodcock
        when it rises for me
        methinks 'tis a bitter foe,
        the blackbird [too] that gives the cry of alarm.

        Every time I would bound
        till I was on the ground
        so that I might see the little fox
        below a-gnawing the bones.

        Beyond every wolf among the ivy-trees
        swiftly would he get the advantage of me,
        so nimbly would I leap
        till I was on the mountain-peak.

Little foxes yelping
to me and from me,
wolves at their rending,
I flee at their sound.

They have striven to reach me,
coming in their swift course,
so that I fled before them
to the tops of the mountains.

My transgression has come against me
whatsoever way I flee;
'tis manifest to me from the pity shown me
that I am a sheep without a fold.

The old tree of Cell Lughaidhe
wherein I sleep a sound sleep;
more delightful in the time of Congal
was the fair of plenteous Line.

There will come the starry frost
which will fall on every pool;
I am wretched, straying
exposed to it on the mountain-peak.

The herons a-calling
in chilly Glenn Aighle,
swift flocks of birds
coming and going.

I love not the merry prattle
that men and women make:
sweeter to me is the warbling
of the blackbirds in the quarter in which it is.

I love not the trumpeting
I hear at early morn:
sweeter to me the squeal
of the badgers in Benna Broc.

I love not the horn-blowing
so boldly I hear:
sweeter to me the belling of a stag
of twice twenty peaks.

There is the material of a plough-team
from glen to glen:
each stag at rest
on the summit of the peaks.

Though many are my stags
from glen to glen,
not often is a ploughman's hand
closing round their horns.

The stag of lofty Sliabh Eibhlinne,
the stag of sharp Sliabh Fuaid,
the stag of Ealla, the stag of Orrery,
the fierce stag of Loch Lein.

The stag of Seimhne, Larne's stag,
the stag of Line of the mantles,
the stag of Cuailgne, the stag of Conachail,
the stag of Bairenn of two peaks.

O mother of this herd,
thy coat has become grey,
there is no stag after thee
without two score antler-points.

Greater than the material for a little cloak
thy head has turned grey;
if I were on each little point,
there would be a pointlet on every point.

Thou stag that comest lowing
to me across the glen,
pleasant is the place for seats
on the top of thy antler-points.

I am Suibhne, a poor suppliant,
swiftly do I race across the glen;
that is not my lawful name,
rather is it Fer benn.

The springs I found best:
the well of Leithead Lan,
the well most beautiful and cool,
the fountain of Dun Mail.

Though many are my wanderings,
my raiment to-day is scanty;
I myself keep my watch
on the top of the mountains.

O tall, russet fern,
thy mantle has been made red;
there is no bed for an outlaw
in the branches of thy crests.

At ever-angelic Tech Moling,
at puissant Toidhen in the south,
'tis there my eternal resting-place will be,
I shall fall by a [spear]-point.

The curse of Ronan Finn
has thrown me in thy company,
O little stag, little bleating one,
O melodious little clamourer.

After that lay Suibhne came on to Glen Bolcain, and he was wandering through it when he encountered a mad woman. He fled before her and yet he divined that she was in a state of madness, and he turned towards her. At that she fled before him. 'Alas, O God!' said Suibhne, 'wretched is this life; here am I fleeing from the crazy woman and she fleeing from me in the midst of Glen Bolcain; dear in sooth is that place'; whereupon he said:

Woe to him who bears enmity,
would that he had not been born or brought forth!
whether it be a woman or a man that bear it,
may the two not reach holy Heaven!

Seldom is there a league of three
without one of them murmuring;
blackthorns and briars have torn me
so that I am the murmurer.

A crazy woman fleeing from her man –
however, it is a strange tale –
a man without clothes, without shoes,
fleeing before the woman.

Our desire when the wild ducks come
at Samhuin, up to May-day,
in each brown wood without scarcity
to be in ivy-branches.

Water of bright Glen Bolcain,
listening to its many birds;
its melodious, rushing streams,
its islands and its rivers.

Its sheltering holly and its hazels,
its leaves, its brambles, its acorns,
its delicious, fresh berries,
its nuts, its refreshing sloes.

The number of its packs of hounds in woods,
the bellowing of its stags,
its pure water without prohibition;
'tis not I that hated it.

(J.G. O'Keefe)

After other adventures, Suibhne went again to visit his wife, but refused to enter the house for fear that his people would confine him there. Eorann said that, since he would not stay with her, he had best be gone and not return, for she was ashamed that people should see him in his madness. In a short poem Suibhne laments the frailty of women and recalls his feats of battle when he was king. Then he flies away to Benn Boirche. (Two poems follow, the first somewhat in the spirit of Marbán's account of his life as a hermit, the second another lament for his misery.)

Then his reason returned to Suibhne and he sought to return to his people; but that was revealed to Saint Rónán, and he prayed that Suibhne might not be allowed to return to persecute the Church as he had done before. When the madman was on his way, he was beset by a fearful apparition of headless bodies and trunkless heads which pursued him through the air with frightful clamour until he escaped from them into the clouds. (Cross and Slover)

At length Suibhne came along to the place where Moling was, even Teach Moling. The psalter of Kevin was at the time in front of Moling as he was reading it to the students. In the cleric's presence Suibhne then came to the brink of the fountain and began to eat watercress.

'O mad one, that is eating early,' said the cleric; whereupon Moling
spoke and Suibhne answered him:

Moling: An early hour is it, thou madman,
for due celebration.

Suibhne: Though to thee, cleric, it may seem early,
terce has come in Rome.

Moling: How dost thou know, mad one,
when terce comes in Rome?

Suibhne: Knowledge comes to me from my Lord
each morn and each eve.

Moling: Relate through the mystery of speech
tidings of the fair Lord.

Suibhne: With thee is the [gift of] prophecy
if thou art Moling.

Moling: How dost thou know me,
thou toiling, cunning madman?

Suibhne: Often have I been upon this green
since my reason was overthrown.

Moling: Why dost thou not settle in one place,
thou son of Colman Cuar?

Suibhne: I had rather be in one seat
in life everlasting.

Moling: Miserable one, will thy soul reach
hell with vastness of slime?

Suibhne: God inflicts no pain on me
save being without rest.

Moling: Move hither that thou mayest eat
what thou deemest sweet.

Suibhne: If you but knew, cleric,
more grievous is it to be without a cloak.

Moling: Thou shalt take my cowl
or thou shalt take my smock.

Suibhne: Though to-day I am ghastly,
there was a time when it was better.

Moling: Art thou the dreaded Suibhne
who came from the battle of Rath?

Suibhne: If I am, 'tis not to be guaranteed
    what I might eat at early morn.

Moling: Whence has come my recognition,
    cunning madman, to thee?
Suibhne: Often am I upon this green
    watching thee from afar.

Moling: Delightful is the leaf of this book,
    the psalter of holy Kevin.
Suibhne: More delightful is a leaf of my yew
    in happy Glen Bolcain.

Moling: Dost thou not deem this churchyard pleasant
    with its school of beautiful colours?
Suibhne: Not more unpleasant was my muster
    the morning at Magh Rath.

Moling: I will go for celebration
    to Glais Cille Cro.
Suibhne: I will leap a fresh ivy-bush
    a high leap, and it will be a greater feat.

Moling: Wearisome is it to me in this church
    waiting on the strong and weak.
Suibhne: More wearisome is my couch
    in chilly Benn Faibhni.

Moling: Where comes thy life's end,
    in church or lake?
Suibhne: A herd of thine
    will slay me at early morn.

'Welcome in sooth is your coming here, Suibhne,' said Moling, 'for
it is destined for you to be here and to end your life here; to leave
here your history and adventures, and to be buried in a churchyard of
righteous folk; and I bind you,' said Moling, 'that however much of
Ireland you may travel each day, you will come to me each evening
so that I may write your history.'

Thereafter during that year the madman was visiting Moling. One
day he would go to Innis Bo Finne in west Connacht, another day to
delightful Eas Ruaidh, another day to smooth, beautiful Sliabh Mis,
another day to ever-chilly Benn Boirche, but go where he would each
day, he would attend at vespers each night at Teach Moling. Moling

ordered a collation for him for that hour, for he told his cook to give him some of each day's milking. Muirghil was her name; she was wife of Mongan, swineherd to Moling. This was the extent of the meal the woman used to give him: she used to thrust her heel up to her ankle in the cowdung nearest her and leave the full of it of new milk there for Suibhne. He used to come cautiously and carefully into the vacant portion of the milking yard to drink the milk.

One night a dispute arose between Muirgil and another woman in the milking enclosure, whereupon the latter said: 'the worse is it for you,' said she, 'that another man is not more welcome to you, and yet that you do not prefer your own husband to come to you than the madman who is visiting you for the past year.' The herd's sister hearkened to that; nevertheless she mentioned nothing about it until she saw Muirgil on the morrow morning going to leave the milk for Suibhne in the cowdung near the hedge at which he was. The herd's sister seeing that, came in and said to her brother: 'You cowardly creature, your wife is in yonder hedge with another man,' said she. The herd hearing that became jealous, and he rose suddenly and angrily and seized a spear that was within on a rack and made for the madman. The madman's side was towards him as he was lying down eating his meal out of the cowdung. The herd made a thrust of the spear out of his hand at Suibhne and wounded him in the nipple of his left breast, so that the point went through him, breaking his back in two. (Some say that it is the point of a deer's horn the herd had placed under him in the spot where he used to take his drink out of the cowdung, that he fell on it and so met his death.)

Enna Mac Bracain was then sounding the bell for prime at the door of the churchyard and he saw the deed that was done there; whereupon he uttered the lay:

Sad is that, O swineherd of Moling,
thou hast wrought a wilful, sorry deed,
woe to him who has slain by dint of his strength
the king, the saint, the saintly madman.

Evil to thee will be the outcome therefrom –
going at last without repentance –
thy soul will be in the devil's keeping,
thy body will be . . .

In Heaven the same will be the place
for me and for him, O man,
psalms will be sung by fasting folk
for the soul of the true guest.

He was a king, he was a madman,
a man illustrious, noble, was he;
there is his grave – bright festival –
pity for him has rent my heart.

Enna turned back and told Moling that Suibhne had been slain by his swineherd Mongan. Moling at once set out accompanied by his clerics to the place where Suibhne was, and Suibhne acknowledged his faults and [made] his confession to Moling and he partook of Christ's body and thanked God for having received it, and he was anointed afterwards by the clerics.

The herd came up to him. 'Dour is the deed you have done, O herd,' said Suibhne, 'even to slay me, guiltless, for henceforth I cannot escape through the hedge because of the wound you have dealt me.' 'If I had known that it was you were there,' said the herd, 'I would not have wounded you however much you may have injured me.' 'By Christ, man!' said he, 'I have done you no injury whatever as you think, nor injury to anyone else on the ridge of the world since God sent me to madness, and of small account should be the harm to you through my being in the hedge here and getting a little milk for God's sake from yonder woman. And I would not trust myself with your wife nor with any other woman for the earth and its fruits.' 'Christ's curse on you, O herd!' said Moling. 'Evil is the deed you have done, short be your span of life here and hell beyond, because of the deed you have done.' 'There is no good to me therefrom,' said Suibhne, 'for your wiles have compassed me and I shall be dead from the wound that has been dealt me.' 'You will get an *eric* for it,' said Moling, 'even that you be in Heaven as long as I shall be'; and the three uttered this lay between them, that is, Suibhne, Mongan, and Moling:

Suibhne: Not pleasant is the deed thou hast done,
         herd of Moling Luachair,
         I cannot go through the hedge
         for the wound thy black hand has dealt me.

Mongan: Speak to me if thou hearest,
    who art thou in truth, man?
Suibhne: Suibhne Geilt without reproach am I,
    O herd of Moling Luachair.

Mongan: If I but knew, O slender Suibhne,
    O man, if I could have recognised thee,
    I would not have thrust a spear against thy skin
    though I had seen thee harm me.

Suibhne: East or west I have not done
    harm to one on the world's ridge
    since Christ has brought me from my valiant land
    in madness throughout Erin.

Mongan: The daughter of my father and my mother
    related — 'twas no trifle to me —
    how she found thee in yonder hedge
    with my own wife at morn.

Suibhne: It was not right of thee to credit that
    until thou hadst learnt its certainty,
    alas that thou shouldst come hither to slay me
    until thine eyes had seen!

    Though I should be from hedge to hedge,
    its harm were a trifle to thee,
    though a woman should give me to drink
    a little milk as alms.

Mongan: If I but knew what comes of it,
    from wounding thee through breast and heart,
    till Doom my hand would not wound thee,
    O Suibhne of Glen Bolcain.

Suibhne: Though thou hast wounded me in the hedge,
    I have not done thee ill;
    I would not trust in thine own wife
    for the earth and its fruits.

    Alas for him who has come for a while from home
    to thee, O Moling Luachair,
    the wound thy herd has dealt me
    stays me from wandering through the woods.

Moling: The curse of Christ who hath created everyone
          on thee, said Moling to his herd,
          sorry is the deed thou hast done
          through envy in thine heart.

          Since thou hast done a dread deed,
          said Moling to his herd,
          thou wilt get in return for it
          a short span of life and hell.

Suibhne: Though thou mayest avenge it,
          O Moling, I shall be no more;
          no relief for me is it,
          your treachery has compassed me.

Moling: Thou shalt get an eric for it,
          said Moling Luachair, I avow;
          thou shalt be in Heaven as long as I shall be
          by the will of the great Lord, O Suibhne.

Mongan: It will be well with thee, O slender Suibhne,
          thou in Heaven, said the herd,
          not so with me here,
          without Heaven, without my life's span.

Suibhne: There was a time when I deemed more melodious
          than the quiet converse of people,
          the cooing of the turtle-dove
          flitting about a pool.

          There was a time when I deemed more melodious
          than the sound of a little bell beside me
          the warbling of the blackbird to the mountain
          and the belling of the stag in a storm.

          There was a time when I deemed more melodious
          than the voice of a beautiful woman beside me,
          to hear at dawn
          the cry of the mountain-grouse.

          There was a time when I deemed more melodious
          the yelping of the wolves
          than the voice of a cleric within
          a-baaing and a-bleating.

Though goodly you deem in taverns
your ale-feasts with honour,
I had liefer drink a quaff of water in theft
from the palm of my hand out of a well.

Though yonder in your church you deem melodious
the soft converse of your students,
more melodious to me is the splendid chant
of the hounds of Glen Bolcain.

Though goodly ye deem the salt meat and the fresh
that are eaten in banqueting-houses,
I had liefer eat a tuft of fresh watercress
in some place without sorrow.

(J.G. O'Keefe)

CHAPTER 7

Druids and Vision Poets

The name druid (Irish *drui*, Welsh *derwydd*) is ultimately derived from the Sanskrit root *veda*, to see or know. It is also inextricably associated with the oak (Irish *daur*, Welsh *derw* and Gaulish *dervo*). The druidic task was a shamanic one, requiring a deep and encyclopaedic knowledge of the many branches of wisdom, art and science, and an ability to interrelate the many dimensions of the otherworld. Druids, both male and female, acted as the counsellors, philosophers, shapeshifters, diviners and magicians of rulers. Among the Celts, the honour-price (a kind of insurance premium or recompense payable for insult or injury) of a druid was the same as that of a king, which may convey the awe and respect in which druids were held. The Romans rightly recognized that to overcome the Celts they must first disable their intellectuals.

After the Roman invasion of Britain, druidry was proscribed, the British druidic headquarters on Anglesey was destroyed and much of the druidic network and practice was fragmented. However, Ireland suffered no such invasion and it is for this reason that literary references to the druidic tradition of the insular Celts are frequent in the Irish texts, providing a richness of material absent from most British and Gaulish material. Its druidic practices continued into and beyond the establishment of Christianity as the major religion in the fifth century.

In Ireland, training in druidry was cellular: one druid might take a handful of students or just one or two. Trainees of a particular teacher formed certain spiritual lineages, recognizable teaching styles and practical skills – just as in Tibet individual Buddhist masters were responsible for founding certain Tibetan Buddhist lineages or orders.

Teaching was not unlike that of the poets (see Chapter 5), by means of oral instruction and practical example. As with modern university systems, students sought out druidic teachers versed in specialist skills, often travelling long distances, even overseas, to benefit from their wisdom; we see this in the story of Nede (see 'The Colloquy of the Two Sages' below), who goes to a famous school in Alba (Scotland).

Throughout the ancient Celtic world, before Christianity or political conquest entered into the reckoning, there were druidic assemblies and possibly larger teaching units or colleges. Britain and Alba seem to have had a scholastic primacy among the Celtic countries, as many Gaulish students were sent for training in Britain, just as Irish students travelled to Alba. We do not know the reason for this, just as we cannot fully understand to what extent the druids of the Celts were influenced or drew upon the skills of indigenous shamanic traditions.

The overlap of local indigenous shamanic tradition and 'official' druidic practice is difficult to judge in Britain and in Ireland. We hear of the Nemedian druid, Miach, overcoming the indigenous 'druids' by cutting out their tongues, thus effectively silencing them. This must be seen as a symbolic paradigm of what happened when the Celtic peoples arrived in Ireland: the silencing of indigenous spiritual leaders and the purloining of their sacred sites for the invaders' own use. Whether we look at Tara or Jerusalem, this pattern is repeated worldwide.

Many Indo-European scholars have pointed out the close parallels between the druid and the Hindu Brahmin priest, concluding that the mainstream Indo-European expansion of the Celts brought druidic practice to Britain and Ireland. But was a native druidry already established here?

It is beguiling to draw a parallel between the coming of Celtic druidry to Britain and Ireland and the coming of Buddhism to Tibet. When Buddhist missionaries entered Tibet in the seventh century AD, they encountered the shamanic practitioners of the Bön-Po religion. Almost immediately a subtle synthesis began whereby Buddhism acquired a particularly Tibetan flavour. The shamanic elements of Bön-Po are still discernible in modern Tibetan Buddhist practice: ritual trance and dance; the incorporation of Bön-Po spirits as Buddhist *dharma* (religious duty) protectors; a complex, exact and practical understanding of the innerworlds and an ability to journey or meditate.

Incidentally, in a peculiarly resonant parallel to the fate of British druidry in AD 64, Tibetan Buddhist practitioners suffered a severe intellectual and spiritual pogrom when China invaded Tibet in 1950. The wholesale destruction, torture and persecution of Buddhist monks, nuns and teachers may help us grasp the plight of British druids under the Romans' heel. In such times, memory is swiftly eradicated or stubbornly and secretly retained.

It is possible that earlier shamanic or druidic practitioners were incorporated within Celtic druidry in a similar way to the incorporation of Bön-Po elements into Tibetan Buddhism. That there should have been no exchange of wisdom seems unlikely. Even under the Roman dispensation, at local British shrines incorporated into Romano-British usage, indigenous shrine-guardians were encouraged to continue their important duties. It was the national and regional druidic networks that were permanently disabled.

Under Christianity, Irish druids found their practices becoming less fashionable and, although some enjoyed individual royal patronage under Pagan rulers, most found it easier to maintain status and power by becoming clerics themselves. The Celtic Christian practice of married clerics with hereditary rights, a parallel to Irish druidic practice, seems to confirm such a notion.

The decline of druidism among the Celts does not rule out those maverick individuals who continued to practise and teach. Mog Roith (see below) is a prime example. From the Irish evidence, it is clear that isolated fragments of druidic practice remained firmly embedded in the bardic teachings of the vision poets.

Classical writers give conflicting accounts of the divisions of druids, poets and seers. During the insular, pre-Roman-conquest Celtic period, we find druid, ovate (*fáith* in Ireland) and bard (*fili* in Ireland). As time, conquest and religious changes took their toll, these three roles became less defined, tending to overlap more and more. Let us look at their original definitions.

The druid was one who was proficient in the interrelation of the worlds of seen and unseen, especially for ordering the political and social patterns of life; he or she may have had the additional abilities of seer, judge, poet, prophet or philosopher. The druid often had a sacerdotal, Brahmin character as an arbiter of social rectitude.

The role of the ovate or *fáith* was that of prophet, diviner and sacrificer. The name may derive from the Indo-European root *uat*, 'to be inspired or possessed'. The ovate is defined by Strabo as an 'interpreter of nature'. The same root underlies the names Odin and Wotan.[1] Ovates worked in close association with druids among the Continental Celts, but the task of sacrificer is rarely alluded to in insular tradition where the prophetic and divinatory skills are prominent.

Bard is a word that must be clearly contextualized since it can mean a variety of things. In Ireland, a bard could imply the meanest sort of entertainer and is defined by the *Crith Gablach* as 'one without lawful learning but his own intellect'. Professional poets were called *fili*, having undergone at least a twelve-year training in poetics, prosody, versification and the arduous oral memorization of traditional stories. In the eighth year of training, the arts of prophetic invocation and shamanic knowledge-seeking were taught. Only those who reached the heights of their profession were entitled to the name *ollamh*, roughly equivalent to a very advanced doctorate in modern university parlance.

In Britain, bards were poets, with varying gradations of skill. At the top end was the *pencerdd* or chief poet who had won his chair through his commanding skills; his rank was on a par with court officials. At the bottom end was the *clerwr* or minstrel who, like the Irish bard would be attached to no household.

Bards and poets were probably originally praise-singers, but, with the erosion of the druidic and vatic roles, the poetic class subsumed many druidic and vatic skills in their social function. The prophetic arts of the poet will be examined in more detail in the next chapter. The *fili* class were probably always preoccupied with the workings of inspiration or *awen* in an often frenzied and love-sick way. Too much inspiration brings divine madness, as in the cases of Merlin and Suibhne.

Inspiration was and is a pathway between the worlds without which this world becomes a dull wasteland. In the work of Taliesin, images of fountains and running water abound, and he sings lyrically of the Mistress of Awen, Ceridwen. In 'The Colloquy of the Two Sages', between Nede and Ferchetne, we see the same preoccupation with the flowing of inspiration, this time addressed to Boann, the Mistress of the Boyne, the mystical source of poetic fervour. In 'The Three Cauldrons of Inspiration', we discover the source of inspiration and how its flow can be dispensed in a balanced way. But we begin this chapter with a study of Mog Roith and his daughter as archetypal druids.

Lord and Lady of the Wheel:
the Careers of Mog Roith and Tlachtga
by Caitlín Matthews

The Druid of the Wheel

In every tradition there are wise guardians of knowledge who endure throughout the ages, regulating its ebb and flow, sometimes venerated, sometimes forgotten. Although they start as deities of power, they eventually dwindle to mortal stature or else become the denizens of folk-tale and nightmare. In Mog Roith and his daughter, Tlachtga, we have two such guardians whose task has been forgotten and whose legend has been commuted.

In the extant texts about Mog Roith, we see an interesting instance of a druid becoming an archetypal Christian opponent. When other druids of wisdom and knowledge were long forgotten, Mog Roith remained in memory as a champion of Paganism, becoming associated with the death of St John the Baptist in apocryphal Irish Christianity, and becoming the companion of Simon Magus (Acts 8: 8–25).

But the lineage of Mog Roith is much older than these latter-day interpolations. The name means Devotee of the Wheel. O'Rahilly has suggested that Mog Roith the druid is but the last remnant of a Celtic deity, Roth, God of the Wheel. The wheel represents not only the sun, but the great cycle of years and seasons. In accordance with this background, Mog Roith lives through many ages and is the ancestor of many people. He takes military training with the woman-warrior Scathach, she who also taught Cuchulainn.

In the text of *The Siege of Druim Damhgaire* we see the fully fledged portrait of a druid in action. The most startling thing we note is that Mog Roith is blind, although this in no way affects his shamanic powers. His legend tells how one eye was lost in the Alps, becoming a 'snow-calf' or mountain, while the other was lost while stopping the course of the sun for two days. Such a loss of sight is found in the legends of particularly ancient Celtic deities, including Lugh's grandfather, the terrible Balor. It points to Mog Roith's lineage reaching into the mists of time.

Mog Roith is specifically reported as being able to fly through the air like a bird and to oversee his enemies' deeds. His shamanic equipment for this activity includes his *encennach* or bird headdress and his *roth ramach* or oared wheel, which enable him to fly through the sky. In a poem attributed to St Columba, the *roth ramach* is described as a huge ship, able to sail over sea and land alike. Both images describe the chariot or vessel of the sun, which is often called *roth fáil* or 'wheel of circling light'.

The god from whom the druid Mog Roith descends is therefore a sun deity, at odds with the manipulations of sorcery. But it is no wonder that Mog Roith's activities and legends should be so dark and full of enchantment. It has ever been the way of incoming religions to assimilate the credit of, and to vilify the practices of, the old one. This is easily seen in the widespread use of solar epithets for the Christian godhead, such as *Ard-Ri Ind Roith* or 'High King of the Wheel' and *Ard-Ri Grene* or 'High King of the Sun'. The sun is called *roth greine*, 'the sun's wheel'. Whatever is not of the sun is therefore of the darkness. The crowning irony of this displacement of the solar symbolism from Mog Roith's legend is the prophecy that the *roth ramach*, like some atomic device, shall overshadow Europe before judgement as a punishment for every country which has had a disciple who has co-operated with Simon Magus in opposition to St Peter! The Christian opposition to druidism has never been more barely stated than here.

This druidic association with Simon Magus rather rebounded on the Celtic Church when it entered into dispute with the Roman Church over local liturgical usages. The Celtic Christian tonsure, across the forehead from ear to ear, was already called the tonsure of Simon Magus, and marked out Celtic clerics from their crown-tonsured Roman brethren. In the hierarchical tussles for religious supremacy, the Celtic Church came off nearly as badly as Simon Magus himself, losing most of its power, which was devolved to Rome.

A complex legend also grew up about Simon Magus, whose practices were incorporated into a Gnostic sect which sought the 'secrets of the inner fire'; his medieval legend eventually grew into the story of Faustus.[2] According to Isidore, Simon challenged Peter and Paul to a flight to heaven; he rose in the air, but was cast down by their prayers. Here the similarity between Mog Roith and Simon is closest. Despite the damning evidence of the legends against him, Mog Roith disconcertingly turns up in the genealogies as the venerable ancestor of the two St Ciarans, St Fursa, St Molaga and St Mochuda.[3] It is not without interest that he is also called Tigernach, 'Sovereign', a title that seems to revert to his original function of Sun God. Even the juxtaposition of Mog Roith and St John the Baptist is not insignificant, since the feast of St John is held at Midsummer – the time when the sun wheel is at its most glorious.

Leaving behind the squabbles for spiritual supremacy, we turn to hard evidence for Mog Roith as shaman and druid.

The Siege of Druim Damhgaire

The long text from which the following derives has never been translated into English, and this is extracted from our unfinished translation. Most of the invocations of Mog Roith are missing from our working editions; they were probably believed by many transcribers to be too dangerous to print! We have rendered a little of what remains of them.

'The Siege of Druim Damhgaire' is a lengthy and often hilarious account of how Cormac mac Art led his army into Munster in order to exact double the tribute due to him from King Fiacha. Cormac brings his own druids, augmented by those of his faery mistress, who dry up all the water in Munster until the opposing side is about to surrender. This ill-judged expedition looks like succeeding until the Munstermen decide to call in some druidic help of their own. They engage Mog Roith at great expense to release the waters and to win the day for them.

> 'Do you know anyone in this province who is able to put our affairs in order?' asked King Fiacha of Munster.
>
> 'I do not know anyone save your own teacher, Mog Roith, who would come,' said Dil mac Dacreca. 'It was with his help that I raised you. Besides, it was he who prophesied to you, on the day of your birth, that Conn's Half [the north of Ireland] would assail you, as we have seen today, and that no one would be able to help you, if he didn't come, because it is from Sidh Cairn Breactnatan, with Ban Buanann the Druidess, daughter of Derg Dhualach, that Mog Roith has acquired wisdom over seven centuries. And there are no further enchantments that he cannot accomplish, whether within or without the *sidh*, whether on this side or the other [of the worlds], because none other, of all the inhabitants of Ireland, has ever been in flesh and bone to learn magic among the realm of the faeries save he.'

Fiacha wonders what manner of recompense the druid will require. Messengers are sent to find out and are told:

> A hundred bright white cows in milk, a hundred well-fattened pigs; a hundred strong working oxen; a hundred racehorses; fifty soft white cloaks; after the project is over, the daughter of the first lord of the East or the most prominent after him, to bear me children . . . ; the first place in the files of Munster's army for my successor who shall have in perpetuity the rank of a

provincial king . . . ; that the King of Munster should choose his counsellor from among my descendants; . . . that I am given the territory of my choice in Munster.

Dil returns to King who, with his council, agrees to this high price. Dil returns to Mog Roith who prepares to leave.

Then Mog Roith told his pupil, Cennmar, to bring to him his travelling equipment: his two noble oxen, swift as swords, from Sliab Mis, called Luath Tren and Loth Lis; his beautiful war-chariot of rowan-wood, with its shafts of white bronze, encrusted with carbuncles, its crystal doors, such that the night appeared as bright as day to those who travelled in the chariot. He also had his sword whose grip was of ivory, the blade hard and blue; his bronze lances, his two sharp five-pronged javelins of shapely wood, so easy to cast, riveted with white bronze; his brown, hornless bull-skin to stretch across the width of the chariot, on its sides and over his thighs.

With an escort of three hundred men, he prepares to choose which part of Munster's territory shall be his own. His representatives each bring him a handful of soil from each region for him to smell and make an augury over; he finally accepts the territory of Corchaille mac Con for his own due to the great number of mineral deposits in its soil. He swears his children to abide by the terms of his contract with Fiachna and sets them to demarcate his boundaries. He also choses Eimhne, daughter of Aengus Tirech, but allows her to choose whether she will marry himself or his son, Buan. She chooses Mog Roith.

All rewards having been agreed upon, Mog Roith causes the waters of Munster to flow once again by giving his magic lances to Cennmar to cast into the earth. The whole of Munster, human and animal, drinks again.

The next day, Mog Roith asked, 'What help do you need now?'

'Cast down the hill [raised by Cormac's druids],' they said, 'because it is a great affliction and calamity for us to have our enemies installed on its heights above our heads on a magic hill, while we are below them at its foot, unable to see them unless we raise our eyes thither.'

'Someone turn my face towards the hill,' said Mog Roith. This was done without hesitation. Immediately he invoked his god and his power and grew so tall that he was scarcely less high than the hill, and his head broadened so that it was as large as the high hill crowned with oak-woods, the sight of which brought terror to all who looked upon him.

It was so that he was able to see his friend, Gadhra, of Druim mac Criadhnaidhi; he who was the son of the sister of Ban Buanann, the druidess, daughter of Derg Dhualach. He came to the side and help of Mog Roith. Beautiful was his appearance that day, the side turned towards Mog Roith and towards the people of Munster, that is; for frightful and monstrous was his appearance and expression on the side which was turned towards Cormac and his armies; he was rough and spiny like a pine and as large as a royal castle. Each of his eyes was as large as a king's cauldron, and they jutted out of his head; his knees were turned backwards and his heels turned forwards. He held in his hand an iron trident; he was covered in a brown cloudy mantle, horned and bristling with bones and horns; a billy-goat and a ram followed him. All were stricken with terror who saw him in this array.

'Why are you come?' Mog Roith asked him.

'I am come,' he said, 'to bring trembling and terror to the armies so that they will scarcely have the energy of a woman in childbed when it comes to fight.'

And Gadhra took himself off in this guise to Druim Damhgaire; he made three circuits of the hill and gave three harsh cries, showing himself to the enemy so that they were seized with horror and terror; he sapped all the warriors of the best part of their strength and warrior's valour . . .

Then Mog Roith began to blow upon the hill. Each warrior from the North was unable to stay in his tent, so great was the storm; their druids did not know how it had been caused. Mog Roith blew again, saying, 'I turn and return.'

The hill disappeared altogether, enveloped in dark clouds and in a whirlwind of fog, so that the company was seized with dread at the cries of the battalions, the uproar of horses and chariots, the confusion of the shattered army resounding as the hill was reduced to its foundations. Part of the army lay plunged in frightful agony, and all gave themselves up to dejection and discouragement.

Shaken by this display, Cormac sends his druid, Colphra to fight, accompanied by his own son Cairpre Lifechair. Mog Roith is told of their coming and tells his pupil, Cennmar, to prepare for battle.

Mog Roith said to Cennmar, 'Give me my poisoned stone, my hand-stone, my hundred-battler and the destruction of my enemies.' It was given him and he began to praise it and put upon it a venomous charm and said,

I charge my hand-stone
That it be not a flying shadow;
Let it be a brand to rout the enemy,
Before the brave host of Clair [Munster].

My fiery hard stone,
Be as a red water-snake;
Woe to him around whom it coils,
Between the swelling waves.

Be as an eel of the sea, like a seal,
As long as seven ox-horns;
Be as a vulture among vultures,
To sever body from soul.

Be as an adder of nine coils
Around the body of the monstrous Colphtha.
From the ground into his head,
A smooth, spear-headed serpent.

The royal, spear-spoked wheel
Shall be a strong and galling briar;
Woe to him around whom it comes,
My fiery, vengeful dragon.

Lords and storytellers shall relate
The woe of those whom it strikes;
The proud valour of Colphtha and Lurga
It shall shatter against the rocks.

Prostrate, it shall prostrate them;
In bonds shall it bind them;
The bonds that it binds with
Like the honeysuckle-twined tree.

Their assaults shall be stayed,
Their deeds shall all fail,
Their bodies shall be wolf-fodder,
At the great ford of slaughter.

Even children will be able to bear off
Without combat, without conflict,
Their trophies and their heads,
If that is what they seek.

During the ensuing combat of Colphtha and Cennmar, Mog Roith causes stones and sands to become firebrands in every sod of earth, so that Colphtha is badly burned. To add to this cows, bulls, ants, boars and even the marsh plants become horrifyingly vocal. Colphtha sees the blind Mog Roith across the ford and realizes who has made these enchantments. 'Short your existence, the existence of your race,' utters Mog Roith. 'Henceforth I will enchant the druid.' As he says this, Cennmar places Mog Roith's hand-stone in the ford's waters where it becomes a giant conger-eel, while Cennmar himself becomes a stone. The eel fights Colphtha, breaks his arms and ties nine knots about him, sinking its teeth into his head. Cennmar transforms himself, casts one of the magical lances and Colphtha dies.

After further single combats, Cormac's druids retaliate, for in their company are three druidesses, Errgi, Eang and Engain, who shapeshift into sheep:

The sheep showed themselves the next morning. They were brown-coloured, with hard and bony heads and horny skins; their noses were of iron. They had the swiftness of the swallow, the agility of the weasel, the rapidity of birds and were able to fend off a hundred warriors during a fray.

'See, our protector!' said the Munstermen. 'See who returns in the form of three brown sheep, those who are able to plunge a hundred men into the depths of agony and death.'

'I will overthrow them for you, do not doubt it,' said Mog Roith. He asked Cennmar, 'Where are my druidic tools that I gave you for fighting these druidesses?'

'I have them,' said Cennmar. These tools were the tinder-box of Simon, the flint of Daniel, the tinder of Ether Ilcrothaig.

They were given to Mog Roith; the use of these instruments was to give the resolve of stone to the minds and hearts of the Munstermen in the hour of combat; the flaming of the fire against the same colour of the sheep.

Mog Roith struck three blows with the tinder-box against the stones. Quickly and deftly taking three stalks of the tinder, which he put in the folds of his robe, he recited a charm beginning, 'Beneath the folds of the litter a company shall rise up ...'

He said to Cennmar, 'Look at these things. What have they become?'

Cennmar looked and said, 'It is good, they are become two bitches and a dog.' He took them up to examine them, then put them down on the ground and turned their faces towards the North and the sheep.

The dogs set on the shapeshifting druidesses and breathe fire upon them so that, their fleeces on fire, they run into their own army, spreading a venomous gas. As a result, all Cormac's druids are forced to hide because their powers are useless. The sheep make for an opening in the earth but the dogs chase and devour them.

Cormac sends his chief druid, Cithruadh, to offer terms to Mog Roith, but these are refused. Mog Roith then visits his teacher, the druidess Ban Buanann (the Long-Lived Lady), in the Sidh, to ask her help in discovering how the Munstermen should continue the combat. He spends the night there and she tells him to set forth early and he will bring victory to the people of Munster. As he prepares to depart, Buan, his son, tells of a vision, which he begins to relate in the old and ancient language "A sending came to me . . ." Unfortunately we do not hear what it was.

The final showdown is between the two sets of druids, who each make up druidical fires to confound the other side. Cormac's druids get theirs going first, then Mog Roith tells Fiacha's men each to bring a handful of rowan-wood, while Fiacha himself is to bring a bundle of wood from the side of the mountain which has grown in the shade of three shelters: from the wind of March, from the wind from the sea and from the wind that causes forest fires. The firewood is carefully built up in the shape of a churn with three sides and angles and seven doors. Cormac's fire, however, is roughly stacked and has only three doors.

The fire is ready,' said Cennmar, 'Now it only needs lighting.' Mog Roith struck his tinder-box. Now the fire of the North was also ready, but all were filled with doubt and anxious haste.

Mog Roith said to the Munstermen, 'Quickly, each shave a sliver of wood from your spear-handles.' They did so and gave them to him. He then made a mixture of these with butter and laid the ball on the fire, chanting the while:

I mix a roaring, fierce fire,
Clearing woods, blighting grass,

Angry flame of powerful speed,
Rushing to skies above,
Subduing other fires' wrath,
Breaking battle on Conn's race [the North].

Tossed into the fire's heart, the ball lit with a great flame and great
uproar. Mog Roith chanted:

God of druids,
My God above
All other gods. . . .

'Now, said Mog Roith, 'bring my oxen and ready my chariot;
hold your horses ready. If the fires turn towards the North, you
must be ready to charge. If this happens, do not delay in charg-
ing, as I will do myself. If the fires come from the North, prepare to defend yourselves . . .'

As he said this, he sent a druidic wind into the atmosphere
and into the heavens, so that it formed itself into a shadowy,
dark obscurity over Cenn Claire, from which a rain of blood fell.
And Mog Roith sang, 'I send a spell with the aid of a cloud. A
rain of blood falls upon the grass . . .'

Mog Roith carefully monitors the progress of the fires by asking the
onlookers. Finally, he decides to see them for himself.

Someone brought to Mog Roith his brown hornless bull's hide,
and his *encennach*, his bird headdress, speckled with flying wings,
and his other druidic appurtenances; he rose into the air and the
heavens at the same time as the fires and he started to beat the
air, so as to turn the fires to the North, all the time chanting
this spell, 'I make the druid's arrow . . .'

Mog Roith is successful in turning the flames northwards.

Mog Roith descended then and mounted in his beautifully orna-
mented chariot, drawn by fierce and impatient oxen as fast as
the March winds, as swift as a bird. He took his brown, hornless bull's hide and turned towards the army. He sent Cennmar
to urge the Munstermen forward and all advanced with great
vigour following the druid. . . .

'What is before me?' asked Mog Roith, as they advanced. But
he already knew for he said, 'Is it not Cecht, Crota and
Cithruadh? My god has promised me that I shall transform them

into stones when they are within my reach, should I but breathe once upon them.' And he sent towards them a druidic breath so that they were transformed into stones, those that we still call Leaca Raighne today.

Cormac concedes defeat and the Munstermen, under Mog Roith's guidance, are victorious.

This text is rich in clues for druidic practice. A primary feature is the way in which Mog Roith steals a magical march every time upon his opponent druids. While Cormac's druids seem to stick to broad druidic practice, Mog Roith excels them by being more adaptive and versatile. He is highly attuned to the elements of air, earth, water and fire, proving himself a master shaman. His superior abilities clearly derive from his great experience, over seven centuries, having trained within the faery hills. Even though he excels, he is not too proud to consult his own teacher, Ban Buanann, the Long-Living Lady.

Mog Roith's costume is closely described, comprising the bull's hide and the feathered headdress or *encennach* which flies. The bull's hide is required in some kinds of prophetic work and, as such, it is Mog Roith's shamanic mantle. The bird headdress with wings is not found in any other Celtic text, although there are plenty of Celtic figures who have the power of flight. Bladud, legendary King of Bath, who is said to have introduced the magic arts into Britain, made a pair of wings but fell from the Temple of Apollo in London.[4] Morgen of Avalon is able to fly between countries.[5] Abaris, the druid, is said to fly on a druidic golden arrow and be in the service of Apollo, and we note above that Mog Roith also invokes the druidic arrow during his flight.

The twin elements of flight and shamanic or druidic practice seem strongly interlinked in the Celtic mind, remaining in memory long after other practices have been forgotten. Christian missionaries quickly made obvious connections between the shamanic flight of the druids and the semi-scriptural flying contest between Simon Magus and SS Peter and Paul.

Tlachtga, Thunderbolt-Wisdom Woman

But if Mog Roith did not meet with the Christians' approval, what did they make of his daughter, Tlachtga, she for whom 'Church legend had a hatred not found against any other of the Celtic gods and hero-ines'?[6] Tlachtga gives her name to the Hill of Ward, near Athboy, County Meath; it was here that the fires of Samhain were lit. Under

the reign of Tuthal Teachtmair, the four Celtic festivals were celebrated at the following sites, each place having its own female founder:

Festival	Place	Goddess
Samhain	Tlachtga	Tlachtga
Beltain	Uisneach	Eriu
Lughnsadh	Taillte	Tailtiu
Feis of Tara	Tara	Tea

Imbolc was celebrated domestically since it fell in the depths of winter. Keating[7] speaks of the Fire of Tlachtga, 'at which it was their custom to assemble and bring together the druids of Ireland on the eve
of Samhain to offer sacrifice to all the gods. It was at that fire they
used to burn their victims; and it was of obligation under penalty of
fine to quench the fires of Ireland on that night, and the men of
Ireland were forbidden to kindle fires except from that fire; and for
each fire that was kindled from it in Ireland, the king of Munster
received a tax . . . since the land on which Tlachtga is belongs to the
part of Munster given to Meath.'

It is significant that the Hill of Tlachtga is the assembly point for
all druids in Ireland, for we see in her the legend that Tlachtga is a
revered patroness of druidic skills. It is also appropriate that Munster
is acknowledged, since it is the home of Mog Roith. He dwells on Inis
Dairbre (Valentia Island) off County Kerry.

Tlachtga creates the dreaded pillar-stone of Cnamchaill out of a
fragment of the wheel. Cnamchaill means 'bone-damage'. It is said to
kill all who touch it, blind those who see it and deafen those who
hear it. O'Rahilly believes it to be a thunderbolt or thunderstone shot
out of the stone, a feared missile, such as Mog Roith equips his champions with in the Siege of Druim Damhgaire. We note that the blind-
ing properties of the pillar-stone seem to be evidenced in Mog Roith's
own blindness.

Tlachtga, in common with many ancient female founders of
sacred sites, is raped and dies giving birth; her triple rape at the
hands of Simon's sons is obviously a late Christian interpolation, but
there is the suggestion that she ritually lies with several partners in
the course of her career. Death through severe labour or great toil
upon a sacred site is such a common mythic theme among ancient
earth goddesses that we should not discount the presence here of an
even earlier myth. Her name itself has the roots *tlacht* or 'earth', and
gae or 'spear', which suggests that she herself has meteoric origins, in
common with many major goddesses such as Cybele, whose meteoric
stone was enshrined in Rome, and the pre-Islamic goddess Al-Uzza,

whose black stone is now venerated by countless Moslems in the Kaaba at Mecca.[8]

If this is so, we see more clearly the reason why Tlachtga's burial place becomes such a focal spot for the festival of Samhain and the propitiation of the ancestral deities. Her son's names have a palladium quality to protect Ireland. She conforms to the archetype of a black goddess, one who can kindle the fire of life from apparent deadness, one who is a touchstone of wisdom. We may speculate that in the taking of a fragment of the wheel to create the pillar-stone lies a forgotten myth, analogous to the Gnostic theft of wisdom from heaven by Sophia, or the theft of the fruit of knowledge by Eve.

If such a wisdom myth were admissible, we can see traces that support it in the extant text. Tlachtga is venerated as a supreme ancestress like her father, but as dark and enduring as he is bright and enduring. Her pillar-stone at Cnamchaill renders people deaf, blind or dead, petrifying the senses, while Mog Roith's hand-stone is able to transform or shapeshift its assailants. Theirs is the polarity of heaven and earth, sunlight and earth-shadow, sun wheel and thunderbolt. Like the *vajra dakinis* of Tibet who transmit knowledge with adamantine power, Tlachtga wields the thunderbolt charged with wisdom, leaving words of power and knowledge to her descendants in the very elements of her locus. Direct knowledge through the pillar-stone is too perilous for most, remaining as forbidden as the Tree of the Knowledge in Eden itself.

The following text, in our translation, gives a jumbled genealogy for Mog Roith and Tlachtga which we can straighten out, with the help of other texts, as follows. The female characters are in italics.

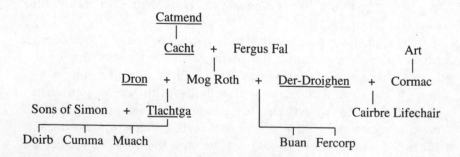

Fig. 3. *Genealogy of Mog Roith and Tlachtga*

Why was Tlachtga so called? Not difficult. Tlachtga was the daughter of Mog Roith, son of Fergus. Three sons of the magician Simon raped her.

She went with her father to learn the magic arts practised anywhere in the world. And it was she who made for Trian the Rolling Wheel, the stone in Forcathu and the Pillar in Cnamchaill. She came from the East and brought with her these things until she reached the hills of Tlachtga.

It was there she bore three sons, Doirb, Cumma and Muach, who gave their names to three regions. As long as their names are remembered in Ireland the land will not be visited by vengeful strangers.

Tlachtga Hills, splendid and high,
Foreboding doom to a great, unswerving king
Before the step which Tlachtga . . . took,
The daughter of King Roth's clever votary.
Mog Roith, the son of Fergus Fal,
The kingly and noble son of Ross.

Cacht, the daughter of the quarrelsome Catmend
Was his colourful and noble mother.
Roth, son of Rigoll was his fosterer.
This is why the name 'Mog Roith' was given him.
Two sons of Mog: Buan and [Fer-]Corb,
Were successful over armies in deeds of liberation.
She [Cacht] was the [foster] mother of the handsome sons
Of Der-Droighen, dark, strong and active,
And the real mother of Cairpre [Lifechair].
It is certain that he deceived the Hui-Bairdne.

The daughter of Mog hosted with thousands,
Tlachtga, the chosen – not that she was without feelings –
To accompany her great and noble father,
To noble Simon of sevenfold splendour.
Three sons had Simon – pleasing to look upon:
Sorrowful her struggle with their devilry.
. . . [text missing] . . . powerful.
Theirs was a powerful family, vehement and resilient.
The sons grew passionate
Towards Tlachtga at the same time,
They flowed into her body – it is no lie –
[making] descendants of beauty and lineage.

For Trian – it was no honour – Tlachtga
Created the red and swiftly mobile wheel,
Together with the great and noble Mog,
And with Simon of sevenfold splendour.
She brought with her wise sayings;
She left the moving wheel,
The finished stone of Forcarthu she left,
And the pillar in Cnamchaill.
Whoever sees it will become blind,
Whoever hears it will become deaf,
And anyone who tries to take a piece of the
Rough spoked wheel will die . . .
After the woman came from the East,
She gave birth to three sons after hard labour.
She died, the light and lively one.
This urgent, unconcealable news was to be heard.
The names of the sons were of great import . . .
Muach and Cuma and Doirb the noble.
The crowd . . . [text missing] . . .
because it is appropriate that they shall hear it:
That as long as over the stately Banba [Ireland]
The names of the three sons are remembered
As the truthful story tells . . .
No catastrophe will befall its inhabitants.
The hill where this woman from the East is buried,
To surpass all other women,
This is the name it was given:
The Hill of Tlachtga.

In Tlachtga and Mog Roith we see two fabulously venerable deities whose legends hold the memory of druidic and shamanic power. The encircling wheel of the sun encompasses all life and is of primary importance to an understanding of druidism both ancient and modern. The rays of its circuit mark the seasons of the year and fuel the growth of all living things. If the extant legends of Mog Roith and Tlachtga seem foreboding or ominous, it is to remind us that

anyone who tries to take a piece of the
Rough spoked wheel will die.

The circuit of the sun's light encompasses all beings. Its spiritual enlightenment may be bestowed, but its knowledge can never be taken or manipulated. Tlachtga and Mog Roith are the Lord and Lady of the Wheel of Life and Death, the Keepers of Druidic Knowledge, and the secrets of both lie still in their hands.

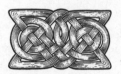

The Colloquy of the Two Sages
by John Matthews

This text, known as the *Immacallam in da Thuarad*, appears in various sources. It illustrates both the complexity of the poetic art and its shamanic qualities to the full. The ancient Irish law-tracts known as the *Senchas Mor* have it that the two poets in fact argued their case before the King, Conchobar mac Nessa. 'in a dark tongue', so that neither he nor his chieftains could understand them. 'These people,' the King's advisers declared, 'keep their judgements and their knowledge to themselves', and Conchobar, agreeing, gave out that such a state of affairs should come to an end.

The implication of this is that the shaman poets possessed a language that was intelligible only to each other, and a glance at the text is certainly enough to show that it was the speech of initiates, couched in riddling and symbolic terms which only they could have understood.

Three poets named Ferchertne are mentioned in Irish traditions: the poet who served Lebraid Lorc, the poet who served Cu-roi and Ferchertne mac Glais, poet of Conchobar mac Nessa. As to Nede, his subsequent colourful career is mentiomesd in *Cormac's Glossary*, where he has several adventures which are further described in John Matthews' *Taliesin*. The translation which follows is based on that of Dr Whitley Stokes, originally published in the learned journal *Revue Celtique* in 1905. As is often the case with translations of this period, while the translators for the most part understood the meanings of the words, they had little or no understanding of the overall *language* of the poems, or indeed what their hidden meanings were. We have therefore made our own version, based on the original Irish as well as on Dr Stokes' translation and incorporating our own understanding of the vision here preserved. While we have followed the sense of the words as closely as possible, we have occasionally compressed the

language where it is unnecessarily prolix. A brief passage at the end
of the prose introduction is omitted since it merely repeats and sum-
marizes what has already gone before.

Adne, son of Uthider, of the tribes of Connaught, had the greatest
knowledge of wisdom and poetry in Ireland. He had a son, Nede, who
went to Scotland to learn from Eochu Horsemouth, with whom he
stayed until he learned great skill.

One day the youth went forth along the edge of the sea – poets
ever believed that the brink of water was a place of revelation. And
as he stood there, he heard a sound like a wailing chant of sadness,
which seemed strange to him. So he cast a spell upon the water, causing it to reveal to him what was the matter. And the wave declared
that the wailing he had heard was for the death of his father, Adne,
whose poet's robe had been given to Ferchertne, who had taken the
ollaveship in his place.

So the youth went back home and told all of this to his tutor. And
Eochu said to him: 'Go home. You have learned well, and your knowledge shows you to be well versed in wisdom and poetry.'

So Nede went home, and with him went his three brothers, Lugaid,
Cairbre, and Cruttine. As they went, a *bolg belce* [puff ball] chanced to
cross their path. Said one of them: 'Why is it called a *bolg belce*?' Since
they did not know, they went back to Eochu and remained another
month with him. Again they set forth, and on the way chanced to
encounter a *simind* [rush]. Since they knew not why it was so named,
they went back to their tutor. At the end of another month they set
out again. A *gass sanais* [sprig of the herb sanicle] chanced to be in their
path. Since they knew not why it was named *gass sanais* they returned
to Eochu and remained a further month with him.

Now when their questions had been answered, they proceeded to
Cantire, and thence to Rind Snoc. Then from Port Rig they passed
over the sea until they landed at Rind Roisc. Thence they went over
Semne, over Latharna, over Mag Line, over Ollarba, over Tulach
Roise, over Ard Slebe, over Craeb Selcha, over Mag Eicaite, across the
river Bann, along Uachtar, over Glenn Rige, over the district of Huy
Brasil, over Ard Sailech, which is today called Armagh, and over the
elfmound of Emain [Macha].

The youth went with a silver branch over him: for such was the
usage of the *anruths* [junior pocts] and likewise a branch of gold over
the ollaves, and a branch of copper over the rest of the poets.

Thus they went towards Emain Macha, and as they went Bricriu chanced to meet them. He said that if they would serve him then Nede might become the ollave of all Ireland. So Nede gave him a purple tunic, adorned with gold and silver, and Bricriu told him to go and sit in the ollave's seat. He also told Nede that Ferchertne was dead, while in fact he was simply in the North, teaching wisdom to his pupils.

Then Bricriu said: 'No beardless boy receives the ollaveship of Emain Macha' — for Nede was still but a boy. So Nede plucked a handful of grass, and cast a spell upon it so that it became like a beard upon him. Then he went and sat in the ollave's chair and pulled his robe about him. Three colours were on the robe: a covering of bright bird's feathers in the middle, at the bottom a scattered speckling of *findruine*, while the top was a brilliant golden colour.

Meanwhile Bricriu went to Ferchertne and said: 'It would be sad, O Ferchertne, if you were to lose the ollaveship. Yet a young and honourable man has taken your place in Emain Macha.'

At this Ferchertne was angry, and hurried back to enter the hall. There he stood with his hands on the door posts . . . and on seeing Nede, he said:

> Who is this poet, wrapped in a splendid robe
> Who shows himself before he has chanted poetry?
> According to what I see, he is only a pupil,
> His beard but an arrangement of grasses.
> Who is this contentious poet?
> I never heard any wisdom from Adne's son!
> I never heard him ready with knowledge!
> A mistake it is, his sitting in this seat.

And Nede answered Ferchertne honourably:

> O ancient one, every sage tries to correct another!
> Any sage may reproach an ignorant man,
> But before he does so he should see what evil is present.
> Welcome is the piercing dart of wisdom,
> Slight is the blemish to a youth until his art is questioned.
> Step with care, O chieftain —
> You belittle me with knowledge,
> Though I have sucked the teat of a wise man.

> *Said Ferchertne*
A question, wise lad, whence have you come?

Nede answered
Not hard: from the heel of a sage,
From a confluence of wisdom
From perfection of goodness,
From brightness of the sunrise,
From the nine hazels of poetic art,
From the splendid circuits in a land
Where truth is measured by excellence,
Where there is no falsehood,
Where there are many colours,
Where poets are refreshed.

And thou, O my master, whence have you come?

Ferchertne answered
Not hard: down the columns of age,
Along the streams of Galion [Leinster],
From the elfmound of Nechtan's wife,
Down the forearm of Nuada's wife,
From the land of the sun,
From the dwelling of the moon,
Along Mac ind Oc's navel string.

A question. O wise lad, what is thy name?

Nede answered
Not hard: Very Small, Very Great,
Very Bright, Very Hard.
Angriness of Fire,
Fire of Speech,
Noise of Knowledge,
Well of Wisdom,
Sword of Song,
I sing straight from the heart of the fire.

And you, O aged one, what is your name?

Ferchertne answered
Not hard: Questioner, Declarer, Champion of Song,
Inquiry of Science,
Weft of Art,
Casket of Poetry
Abundance from the Sea of Knowledge.

A question, O youthful instructor: what art do you practice?

> *Nede answered*
> Not hard: reddening of countenance,
> Flesh-piercing satire,
> Promotion of bashfulness,
> Disposal of shamelessness,
> Fostering poetry,
> Searching for fame,
> Wooing science,
> Art for every mouth,
> Diffusing knowledge,
> Stripping speech,
> In a little room,
> Making poems like a sage's cattle,
> A stream of science,
> Abundant teaching,
> Polished tales, the delight of kings.

And you, O my elder, what art do you practice?

> *Ferchertne answered*
> Hunting for the treasure of knowledge,
> Establishing peace,
> Arranging words in ranks,
> Celebrating art,
> Sharing a pallet with a king,
> Drinking the Boyne,
> Making *briarmon smetrach*
> The shield of Athirne,
> A tribulation to all men,
> A share of wisdom from the stream of science,
> Fury of inspiration,
> Structure of mind,
> Art of small poems,
> Clear arrangement of words,
> Warrior tales,
> Walking the great road,
> Like a pearl in its setting.
> Giving strength to science through the poetic art.

Ferchertne said
A question, O youthful instructor, what are your tasks?

> *Nede answered*
> Not hard: to go to the plain of age,
> To the mountain of youth,
> To the hunting of age.
> To follow a king
> Into an abode of clay,
> Between candle and fire
> Between battle and its horrors
> Among the people of Fomor,
> Among streams of knowledge.

And you, O sage, what are your tasks?

> *Ferchertne answered*
> To go into the mountain of rank,
> The communion of sciences,
> The lands of knowledgeable men,
> Into the breast of poetic vision,
> The estuary of bountiful wisdom,
> To the fair of the Great Boar,
> To find respect among men.
> To go into death's hills
> Where I may find great honour.

A question, O knowledgeable lad, by what path have you come?

> *Nede answered*
> Not hard: on the white plain of knowledge,
> On a king's beard,
> On a wood of age,
> On the back of a ploughing ox,
> On the light of a summer's moon,
> On rich mast and food,
> On the corn and milk of a goddess
> On thin corn,
> On a narrow ford,
> On my own strong thighs.

And you, O sage, by what path have you come?

Ferchertne answered
Not hard: on Lugh's horserod,
On the breasts of soft women,
On a line of wood,
On the head of a spear,
On a gown of silver,
On a chariot without a wheelrim,
On a wheelrim without a chariot,
On the threefold ignorance of Mac ind Oc.

And you, O knowledgeable lad, whose son are you?

Nede answered
Not hard: I am the son of poetry,
Poetry son of scrutiny,
Scrutiny son of meditation,
Meditation son of lore,
Lore son of inquiry,
Inquiry son of investigation,
Investigation son of great knowledge,
Great knowledge son of great sense,
Great sense son of understanding,
Understanding son of wisdom.
Wisdom son of the triple gods of poetry.

And you, O sage, whose son arc you?

Ferchertne answered
Not hard: I am the son of the man without a father.
Who was buried in his mother's womb,
Who was blessed after his death.
Indeed, death betrothed him,
And he was the first utterance of every living one
The cry of every dead one:
Lofty Ailm is his name.

A question, clever youth: are there tidings?

Nede answered
There are indeed: good tidings:
seas fruitful,
strands overrun,
woods smiling,

wooden blades in flight,
fruit trees flourishing,
cornfields growing tall,
bee-swarms many –
a radiant world,
a happy peace,
a kindly summer,
soldiers paid,
sunblessed kings
wondrous wisdom,
battle gone,
every one to his art:
men valiant,
women sewing,
thorn-trees vigorous
treasuries full,
valour enough,
every art complete,
every good man fair.
every tiding good –
tidings always good.

And you, O aged one, have you tidings?

Ferchertne answered
I have indeed: terrible tidings,
evil times forever,
abundant leaders
but little honour,
fair judgements overturned,
the world's cattle barren,
men immodest
champions departing.
Men will be all bad:
few kings, many usurpers;
crowds of the disgraced,
all men blemished.
Chariots will smash on the track,
Nial's plains will be overrun,
truth no longer safeguard wealth.
Sentries will guard the sacred places.

Art will become buffoonery,
only falsehoods heard.
Through pride and arrogance
no one will keep his proper place,
neither rank, age, nor honour,
dignity nor art
will be served.
Even the skilled will be broken.
Kings will be paupers,
nobles condemned,
the baseborn will falter,
'till neither God nor man wins worship.
Princes, both lawful and unlawful, will perish
when the Men of the Black Spears come.
Belief will end,
offerings be stolen
houses broken open,
cells undermined,
churches burned.
Even poor storerooms be laid waste,
fruits and flowers perish,
and the King's followers
will be houseless.
Hounds will turn against their masters,
everyone will inflict a triple hurt:
by darkness, through grudging and neglect.
At the last world's ending, there will be
a plea of poverty, grudging and neglect.
Artists will quarrel,
everyone will pay a satirist
to make satires on his behalf,
all will be bound by sureties,
neighbours betray each other,
brother against brother,
drinking companions slay each other,
neither truth, nor honour nor soul in any.
Niggards will reduce everyone to their level,
usurpers will satirize each other
with storms of dark cursing,
ranks will split, clerics be forgotten,

sages despised,
music will turn men boorish,
champions will become monks,
wisdom will be turned inside out,
the lords will turn on the Church,
evil, not blessing, in their crosiers.
All relationships will be adulterous.

Peasant sons and churls will find
free will and overweening pride;
meanness, inhospitality and penury will rule
so that art becomes dark;
skilled embroidery will be
in the hands of sluts and harlots,
the garments they make without colour.

Wrong judgements will be all that lords can make,
faithlessness and anger
will be so much part of everyone,
that neither bondslave nor handmaid
will serve their masters,
neither kings nor lords
hear the prayers of their people,
neither will bailies
hear the cries of their tenants.
Tributes will go unpaid,
tenants of the church
not pay their dues,
wives not obey their husbands,
sons and daughters disobey their parents,
pupils ignore their teachers.

Everyone will turn his art to falseness,
and seek to surpass his teacher,
so that students will sit above their masters,
and there will be no shame.
when kings eat and drink
while their comrades wait,
or while farmers scoff
after closing the door
on artists who will sell their cloaks and their honour
for the price of a meal;

so that everyone eating dinner
turns away from his neighbour;
so that greed will fill every human being,
so that proud men will sell their honour
and their souls for the price of a single scruple.
Modesty will be cast away,
people condemned,
lords destroyed,
ranks despised,
Sunday degraded,
letters forgotten,
poets cease to appear.

Belief will vanish,
false judgements will manifest
through usurpers of the last world;
fruits will be burned
by strangers and rabble.
Lands will hold too many people,
districts be stretched,
forests become plains
and plains forests,
everyone will be a slave.

Thereafter will come dreadful diseases:
sudden, awful tempests,
lightning which causes trees to cry out,
winters leafy,
summers gloomy,
autumn without crops,
spring without flowers,
mortality through famine,
diseases in cattle:
staggers, murrains, dropsies, agues and lumps.

Estrays without profit,
hoards without treasure,
goods without consumers,
extinction of champions,
failure of crops,
prejudice,
angry judgements,

death for three days and three nights
on a third of all humanity,
a third of all plagues on beasts of forest and sea.

Then will come
seven years of lamentation:
flowers will perish,
in every house wailing,
outlanders consuming Erin's plains.
Men will herd men,
there will be conflict round Cnamchoill,
fair folk slain.
Daughters will lie with their fathers,
contests will be fought at sacred places,
desolation visit the heights and the plains,
the seas break their bounds
when the Land of Promise falls.
Ireland will be left
for seven years
to mourn the slaughter.

Next will come signs of the Antichrist,
to every tribe monsters will be born,
pools will flood back into streams,
horsedung will look like gold,
water taste like wine;
mountains will seem like perfect lands
bogs give birth to clover,
bee-swarms burn in the highlands,
flood-tides not withdraw for days.

Thereafter seven more dark years.
They will hide the lamps of heaven.
At the end of the world will be judgement.
It will be The Judgement, my son.
Great tidings, awful tidings,
an evil time!

Said Ferchertne
Know you, O little in age but great in knowledge, who is greater than
you?

Nede answered
Easy to say: God is above me,
and the wisest of prophets.
I know the hazels of poetry —
And I know that Ferchertne is a great poet and prophet.

The lad then knelt to Ferchertne and flung him the poet's robe, which he put from him. Nede then rose out of the poet's seat, where he had been sitting, and cast himself under Ferchertne's feet. Thereupon Ferchertne said:

Stay, great poet, wise youth, son of Adne!
May you receive glory and fame
In the sight of men and gods.
May you be a casket of poetry,
May you be a king's arm,
May you be a rock of ollaves,
May you be the glory of Emain Macha,
May you be higher than everyone!

Said Nede
May you be so, under the same titles!
Two trees springing from one root without destruction.
A casket of poetry, an expression of wisdom.
This is the perfect line of intellect:
Father from son, son from father.
Three fathers I have had:
A father in age,
A fleshly father,
A father of teaching.
My fleshly father remains not,
My father of teaching is not present,
You, Ferchertne, are my father in age!
You I acknowledge — may it be so!

There is much to consider of a shamanic nature about this work. It displays much of the learning and wisdom of the poets, who were shamans in all but name, and it shows this as deriving ultimately from the inner worlds.

Nede is presented as a type of the wondrous youth whose inspired utterances cause his critics to recognize him. Here there is more friendship and humility in the contest between the two men, who call

upon a wide range of knowledge to back up their claims. Small wonder that the King and his councillors were unable to understand what
was being said. But the text is far from nonsensical. Most of it reveals
its meaning with a little thought.

In the first verse Ferchertne throws down the gauntlet, challenging
Nede to show what wisdom he possesses. Nede replies, politely, that
while any sage may criticize a younger poet he should at least hear
what he has to say first, especially since, in this case, the youth has
had the benefit of a wise teacher of his own. Then Ferchertne asks
where Nede has come from and we have the first salvo of poetic
answers. Nede has come from a conjunction of wisdom, he has eaten
of the nine hazels of poetic art, which are said to grow above a
stream which rises in the otherworld. There, in that 'excellent land',
are many colours each one, we are told in a gloss, denoting the power
and quality of the people of that place. There poets are refreshed.

Ferchertne, challenged in turn, replies that he has travelled down
the 'columns of age' from the otherworldly place where goddesses are
to be found. He has come from the land where the sun and moon
have their home, and he is a son of Aengus (Mac ind Oic), the god of
love and inspiration. He then demands Nede's name, meaning, of
course, his poetic name. Nede's reply is full of crackling, kenning
words; he is filled with the fire of poetic insight and wisdom.

Ferchertne's poetic name is about inquiry, art, deftness with words,
abundant knowledge gleaned from questioning and long study. He
demands to know what art his young opponent practises.

Nede speaks of satire, *briarmon smetrach*, the most powerful
weapon of the poet. He promotes 'bashfulness', causes cheeks to grow
red. He also fosters the art of poetry itself, making 'polished tales' to
delight kings, paring down speech to the bare bones, ordering his
words like cattle, teaching and giving forth knowledge to all who will
listen.

Ferchertne too speaks of hunting the 'treasure of knowledge', of the
peacemaker's role, of celebrating the glory of a king whose pallet he
shares, meaning that he is as close to the king as it is possible to be.
He orders his words like warriors, and he too practises the feared art
of satire.

Nede's answer to all this is to speak of his own tasks as going to
the plain of age – that is learning the wisdom which comes with
advancing years. Yet he will remain youthful also, visiting the mountain of youth. He will follow a king into death itself, to the people of
Fomor, the otherworldly race who were the aboriginal inhabitants of
Ireland.

Ferchertne then says that he will go into the place where know-ledgeable men dwell, into the very 'breast of poetic wisdom' from which he will learn much. He, too, will face death, expecting to find great honour there.

The next exchange concerns the path by which the two poets have reached their current state of wisdom and enlightenment. Nede has crossed 'the white plain of knowledge' (another epithet for the other-world) 'on the back of a ploughing ox', which refers to the writing of lines of verse, eating of the mast, the favourite food of sacred pigs, and the rich offerings of the goddess, walking 'on my own strong thighs'.

Ferchertne has come 'on Lugh's horserod', a reference to the three inventions of the god, which are said to be draughts, ball-play, and horsemanship (or sometimes a horsewhip, as in this text). He has also come in 'a chariot without a wheelrim, a wheelrim without a chariot', which refers to the chariot of poetry itself, which can be either gentle or rough, smooth-paced or angry. The 'threefold ignorance of Mac ind Oic' is glossed thus: that 'he knew not when he would die, and what death would carry him off and on what sod he would lie'. Ferchertne seems to be applying this to himself, presumably in that all things and all futures are possible to the poet.

Nede's claims are equally modest. He is the son of poetry itself, he has the wisdom and lore that are born of knowledge, he is the child of the triple gods of poetry, glossed as 'three sons of Brighid the poetess, namely Brian and Iuchar and Uar'. There is no evidence for Brighid's three sons being gods of poetry however. Brighid herself was a triple-aspected goddess, having authority for smithcraft and medicine as well as poetry.

Ferchertne's answer is more problematical. Most contributors have chosen to interpret this verse as a reference to Christian lore. Ailm is the name of the letter A in Irish and this has been assumed to refer either to Adam, who had no father, who was buried in the womb of the earth (from which he was made) and who was blessed after his death, or to Christ as Alpha. Since the poem was copied by a Christian monk this is not surprising; possibly he substituted his own version for an originally Pagan statement. The last part of the poem takes the form of a series of prophecies, of such overwhelming dark-ness and horror that Ferchertne's vision finally overwhelms the younger man. Everything is turned upside down in this tale of horror and denial. The whole passage is full of circular references, as the poet returns again and again to the same points, the desolation of the land (Nial's plains, the plains of Erin, etc.), the reversal of the sea-sons, the failure of the very structure of society. In the lines which tell of poets having to sell their cloaks and give up their honour for a crust of bread we read a personal note, but generally the vision is apocalyptic and final in its judgement of humanity.

Finally we hear of the reconciliation between the two poets, who now seek to outdo each other in compliments, until in the end Ferchertne yields his place, and his robe, to the younger man, who in turn acknowledges him as his 'father in age'.

The whole work tells us a great deal about the bardic mysteries. The range of wisdom and the cunning use of words is considerable. We also discover that the poets claim an otherworldly origin for their inspiration, detailing the many different influences and skills necessary to practise the art. It has been suggested that this method of poetic contest was a regular practice by which bards were chosen to occupy their chair of office. Competition would have been fierce, since poets were well treated, well paid and greatly honoured. The poem as a whole is an extraordinary and brilliant evocation of the mystery of word-craft, as well as of the deep and penetrating visionary abilities of the shaman poets.

The Three Cauldrons of Inspiration
by Caitlín Matthews

The Vessels of Inspiration
The central image of Celtic shamanic tradition is the cauldron, the vessel of heat, plenty and inspiration. The Gundestrup Cauldron, a vast silver vessel discovered in Denmark and dated to the fourth or third century BCE, itself depicts a queue of warriors waiting to be deposited into a deep cauldron in an initiatory or sacrificial way. This graphic depiction is borne out in the archaeological, oral and literary testimony of the Celts from the earliest votive lake offerings to the complex weaving of the Grail stories.

As the cauldron was the primary giver of bodily nourishment, it is hardly surprising that it was also a symbol for inspiration, knowledge, wisdom and rebirth. Although no single coherent Celtic creation story has survived, there are so many references to the formation of lakes and rivers or of watery inundations scattered throughout oral lore, that we may posit a primordial tradition of a source cauldron from which all things spring.

Notable Celtic cauldrons include: the cauldron of the Dagda, which leaves no one unsatisfied; the cauldron of Diwrnach, which will not serve cowards; the cauldron of Bran the Blessed, which confers rebirth; and the cauldron of Ceridwen, which confers knowledge. These properties are also found in the cauldron's later manifestation as the Grail, conferring plenty, healing and spiritual wisdom.[9]

The prime roles of the cauldron in Celtic tradition are to bestow nourishment, to confer status and to govern the reception and dispensation of knowledge and inspiration. And it is this last role which concerns us here, since the text which follows is devoted to the mystical action of three bodily cauldrons *within* the inspired practitioner.

Inspiration (*imbas* in Ireland, *awen* in Britain), was the supreme preoccupation of Celtic poets, especially among those who had inherited the ancient prophetic and visionary arts of the ovate or *fáith* – probably the earliest form of Celtic shaman. The shamanic practices of prophecy, divination and augury seem to have remained part of the Celtic poetic tradition for many centuries after the demise of druidism. Throughout the Christian centuries, shamanic skills became further displaced from public office, remaining the function of solitary, gifted individuals whom society at large increasingly viewed as eccentric. However, seers and prophets were locally well respected, and still enjoy the same respect today in Celtic communities as they did in ancestral times.

Gerald of Wales gives us a twelfth-century account of shamanic vision in action in his *Itinerary of Wales*, where he describes prophetic and inspired individuals called *awenyddion* (literally, 'the inspired ones') who go into trance when asked questions. Their answers are given in gnomic and oracular outpourings, but they make sense and solve problems. They have to be shaken hard to return to ordinary consciousness. Gerald comments, 'They seem to receive this gift of divination through visions which they see in their dreams. Some have the impression that honey or sugary milk is being smeared on their mouths.' The *awenyddion* seem to be direct descendants of the British ovates (Welsh, *ofyddion*).

But within the Gaelic tradition, seership and the shamanic abilities of finding and healing were maintained by the poetic class. Shamanic methods of procuring inspiration were still being used in seventeenth-century Scotland in order to train poets, as Martin Martin's *Description of the Western Islands of Scotland* relates:

> I must not omit to relate their [the poet's] way of study, which is very singular. They shut their doors and windows for a day's time, and lie on their backs, with a stone upon their belly and plaids about their heads, and their eyes being covered, they pump their brains for rhetorical encomium or panegyric; and indeed they furnish such a style from this dark cell, as is understood by a very few.

This method of study is paralleled in Ireland, as related by the Marquis of Clanricarde in his *Memoirs* of 1722, where he describes visiting a poetic school. It was open only to the descendants of poets and was situated well away from disturbances of any kind. The House of Memory was a low hut, with 'no windows to let in the day, nor any light at all used but that of candles. The professors gave a subject suitable to the capacity of each class . . . the said subject having been given over night, they word it apart each by himself upon his own bed, the whole next day in the dark, till at a certain hour in the night, lights were brought in, they committed it to writing.' Each student then dressed and gave a performance of his work to his teacher, and was given a fresh subject to study in the dark.

The houses of darkness were the incubation chambers of inspiration and vision. The use of darkness and isolation are still central to shamanic practice worldwide. But what happens in that darkness? What is sought? What visions are discovered? These are the secrets of the shaman, who practises the long craft of learning how to discern and interpret the Ariadne's thread of vision that snakes through the darkness and silence. We note that the *awenyddion* are asked to solve problems or find information, that the trainee poets are given a subject to meditate upon while lying on their beds or reclining. Shamanic vision cannot be pursued without purpose. Celtic seers and poets were connected with a specific database of traditional wisdom; they were not mediums arbitrarily drawing upon unconnected or irrelevant data. The kindling of vision for both poet and seer derived from the inspiration of the otherworld and was fuelled by human need – these are the basic constituents of the quest for all people.

In our own time, where direct sources of inspiration are mocked and marginalized, such a fundamental trust seems misplaced. Yet all artists learn to trust the imagination as the seed-bed of inspiration, training it to receive the eternal truth and the deep knowledge of the otherworld.

The Celtic otherworld is a reality which transcends but also inter-sects the ordinary reality we call 'everyday life'. It is not dislocated from ordinary reality but continually interrelates with it, feeding it and drawing from it, acting as a deep resource of wisdom. Every cul-ture has its own imaginal realm: Hebrew Qabala calls it the world of Briah, the creative realm; Platonism calls it 'the realm of archetypes'; Jungian theory calls it 'the collective unconscious'. The Celtic other-world is not necessarily analogous to these, however; it remains a place where the essential inspiration of the universe is freely avail-able.

The Celtic otherworld was and is accessible through that burning glass of the soul, the imagination. The original sense of the word 'imagination' has become warped into meaning 'a faculty to dream up illusory things'. But the imagination is nothing less than our door-way to the otherworld, it is the prime faculty of shamanic conscious-ness through which come the dreams, visions and ideas which we in turn implement in ordinary reality. We have to learn to trust the information that our meditations give us, trusting our imagination and our dreams, and sifting the answers the otherworld gives us.

All societies need their gifted ones, their artists and mystics: with-out them, the land becomes weary and disenchanted. Traditional Celtic society enshrined the maintenance of otherworldly enchant-ment by supporting its gifted people. What is enchantment? Like imagination and other terms, it has lost its currency. To enchant is literally 'to en-chant', 'to infuse with song'. The tradition of the pri-mal note by which creation comes into being is well attested in many spiritualities. The first utterance of the gods gives forth vibrations and harmonies whose interweaving causes variety within creation. These vibratory rates are distinguished by colour, number and qualitative functions which influence the whole of our life. Music is the first ordering of chaos. When the music of enchantment ceases to sound, chaos returns.

There is a strong tradition that druidic and monastic foundations both maintained 'perpetual choirs of song' which perpetuated Britain's sacred order. In Pagan Celtic tradition, these were undoubt-edly the poets and bards whose voices were trained to utter the enchantment of the otherworld. They maintained the song-lines of our land with sacred story. The primacy of oral utterance in Celtic tra-dition overturns our modern reliance on written theory.

This oracular method of comprehension is frequently accompa-nied by images of water, for the myths which accompany the sources of Celtic inspiration are nearly all to do with cauldrons and watercourses, wells, springs and spas – all the natural containers and features which hold or receive water. These myths, taken to their ultimate medieval flowering, feed the stream of the Grail texts.

The deities who preserve and foster inspiration are invariably female – Boann, Ceridwen and Brighid. In a complex water-laden myth, Taliesin imbibes the liquor of the cauldron of inspiration, is reborn of Ceridwen's womb, is cast upon the waters and is drawn forth by his patron Elphin, who is searching the weir for salmon.

The source of the Boyne, named after the goddess Boann, is described as 'a shining fountain, with five streams flowing out of it . . . Nine hazels . . . grew over the well. The purple hazels dropped their nuts into the fountain, and five salmon which were in the fountain severed them, and sent their husks floating down the streams.' We are told that these are, 'the five streams of the senses, through which knowledge is obtained. And no one will have knowledge who drinks not a draught out of the fountain itself and out of the streams. The folk of many arts are those who drink of them both.' [10] These are none other than the *aois dána*, the inspired poets. There is a tradition that the unworthy cannot approach this mystical source of the Boyne, that four cup-bearers pace about it, guarding it and dispensing the water only to the truthful of heart.

Yet the water images are also balanced by those of heat and fire, for the flow of inspiration is contained and heated within the cauldron to produce a more fervent liquid. The Danann goddess, Brighid, is chief among those who dispense wisdom. In insular Celtic tradition, she (usually in the guise of her namesake, St Brigit of Kildare) is the one who is invoked to keep the hearth-fire and to keep the soul in safety. Geoffrey of Monmouth speaks of Taliesin being under the aegis of Minerva, with whom Brighid is closely identified in Romano-Celtic usage. Both Brighid and Ceridwen have the reputation of being the mistresses of inspiration and wisdom.

The emblem adopted by reformed branches of druidism for the outpouring of *awen* is three drops from which three rays flow forth. These three drops can be seen as the three hot splashes which Gwion Bach catches on his finger before becoming transformed into the all-wise Taliesin, whose rays of inspired knowledge stream out throughout the world.

In the following text, we find a similar sacred triplicity, three guardian vessels of inspiration which govern the reception and dispensation of the otherworld's generous gift.

Fig. 4. The Awen

The Three Cauldrons:
a new translation with commentary by Caitlín Matthews

This fifteenth century treatise on poetry, found in an Irish legal codex, records rare and unusual details about the metaphysics of inspiration, of which we might otherwise have been ignorant. Most extant Irish poetic lore is technically concerned with the poet's craft of composition, but the material contained in this text reveals new insights into poetic education and the human response to creativity.

The text is found complete in only one edition, MS TCD MS H.3.18. pp. 53a1–57b5, and was transcribed in the original by Annie Power into *Anecdota from Irish MS. vol 5*; she entitled it 'The Cauldron of Poesy'. I have entitled this text 'The Three Cauldrons.'

Transcribed in the fifteenth or sixteenth century at Druim Goll (unlocated), it is basically intended as an instruction for young poets upon inspiration and the poetic art, but it has important correlatives for anyone interested in the practical applications of Celtic shaman-ism since it describes the vessels of inspiration within the body. Along with our students, we have worked practically with this text and found that it provides a useful way of identifying and understanding the flow of physical, artistic and spiritual energy.

Two sections of the text are put into the mouths of fabulously ancient poets, Amairgin and Nede mac Adne, whom we met in 'The Dialogue of the Two Sages'. As we have seen, Amairgin was the poet-ic spearhead of the Milesian invasion of Ireland, while Nede mac Adne was the chief *ollamh* (doctor of poetry) under the Ultonian king, Conchobhar mac Nessa. So might educators instruct young poets today by putting seminars into the mouths of Shakespeare and Chaucer.

The text is complex and sometimes highly technical, but we have attempted to clarify it by means of the glosses and by diagram. The text is followed by a discussion of its contents. The four divisions of this text have been retitled; a gloss follows each extract in which poet-ry is numbered by line and prose by sentence.

1. Amairgen's Song of the Three Cauldrons

My own cauldron, cauldron of warming,
God-given from the mysterious elements;
ennobled is each belly from
which pours forth the oral utterance.

5. Amairgin White-knee am I,
   blue tattooed shank and beard of grey.
   My cauldron of warming serves up
   multiplicity of forms
   and many-coloured verse.

10. Not equally does God distribute
    gifts to each person:
    but some inclined, some prone, some supine,
    some empty, some half-full,
    some full of knowledge like Eber and Donn,

15. creating their verse
    with innumerable chantings,
    in masculine, feminine, and neuter,
    in signs denoting double consonants,
    long vowels and short vowels;

20. thus is its function metrically declared,
    by the votary of this cauldron.
    I sing of the cauldron of knowledge,
    whence the law of each art is dispensed,
    which gives boundless treasure,

25. which magnifies each artist in general,
    which gives each person its gift.

3–4. All people have the cauldron of warming, but those who use their vital vessel to heat verses are especially worthy. The metaphor of belly (as a heater) is sustained here, and may be compared with the parallel of traditional Chinese medical philosophy which declares the bodily cavity to be a triple vessel of warming.

7–9. on the 'colour of poetry'. A textual gloss gives the following: 'black is satire, speckled is warning (for not having paid the poet's fees), white is praising.'

10–21. These seem to speak of the Cauldron of Vocation.

14. Eber and Donn were sons of Mil. Eber succeeded to southern Ireland, while Donn died in the storm which brought the Milesians to Ireland. He is buried at Tech Duinn, off south-western Munster.

17–19. These are the components of the poet's metrical craft.

2. The Lore of the Three Cauldrons

1. Question: is the source of poetic art in a person's body or soul? 2. Some say the soul, since the body is one with it. 3. Others say the body, since it stems from a fitting source, from father and grandfather, but it is truer to say that the source of poetic art is in each person's body, though in every second person it is absent: in the other it appears.

4. What then is the source of poetic art and every other knowledge? 5. Not hard. 6. Three cauldrons are engendered with each person: the Cauldron of Warming, the Cauldron of Vocation and the Cauldron of Knowledge.

7. The Cauldron of Warming is born face up in a person first of all; from it learning is distributed to all people in early youth. 8. The Cauldron of Vocation, then, increases after it has been activated; it is originally present on its side in each person. 9. The Cauldron of Knowledge is originally positioned upside down, and it distributes many artistic gifts, besides poetry.

10. The Cauldron of Vocation, in every second person, is upside down in unenlightened people; it is on its side in those who practise bardic and poetic skills; it is upright in the masters of knowledge and learned art. 11. The reason why every person does not attain the same level of proficiency is because the Cauldron of Vocation is upside down for them until it is converted by sorrow or joy.

12. Question: how many divisions of sorrow are there which will convert it? 13. Not hard, there are four: longing, grief, the pangs of jealousy, and the exile of pilgrimage for God's sake; it is within that these four are experienced, though they are produced [caused] from without.

14. There are two chief divisions of joy by which joy can overturn the Cauldron of Knowledge: divine and human. 15. Human joy has four divisions, thus: the force of sexuality; the joy of health; the joy of attaining poetic privilege after long study; joy at the approach of *imbas* amassed by the nine hazels of fair fruitfulness in Segais of the *sidhe*, which hurtles upstream along the Boyne in a ram's-head bore, swifter than a three-year old at the racetrack, in the middle of June each seventh year.

16. Divine joy, however, brings special grace to convert the Cauldron of Knowledge, turning it upright so that there are sacred and secular prophets, commentators upon both holy and practical matters alike, who speak words of grace and perform miracles, whose pronouncements are precedents and judgements, becoming the pattern of all speech. But it is from without that these qualities make the cauldron upright, although they are produced within.

1. Many Irish treatises begin with this question: this is undoubtedly a successor to the oral examination of students by poetic teachers in the bardic schools.
3. The hereditary ability theory is passed over in favour of potential ability in everyone.
5. This modest answer is commonplace in such discussions and usually precedes a lengthy exposition or answer.
6. Each person possesses these three vessels. The original Irish titles of cauldrons are: *Coire Goiriath* Cauldron of Warming – the warmth of piety, service or cherishing is intended here; *Coire Ernma*, Cauldron of Vocation – the meaning includes a course of action, apprenticeship or vocational tendency; and *Coire Soís*, the Cauldron of Knowledge.
9. The Cauldron of Knowledge distributes. The function of distribution was ascribed to people of high degree: to a king, chieftain or ruler, to a host or hostess, to divine powers. In the poems of Taliesin, the divine being is described as 'the Distributor'.
10. The cauldron is upright for *anruths*; the term *anruth* roughly corresponds to one whose level of proficiency is that attained by a master of arts. The doctor of philosophy would be an *ollamh*.
14. Although the Cauldron of Vocation is turned by grief or joy, the text speaks only of the action of sorrow upon it. The action of joy is ascribed to the Cauldron of Knowledge, possibly because the Cauldron of Vocation is activated by the quest for harmony – it moves because its subject wishes to find the source of comfort, inspiration, wholeness. The Cauldron of Knowledge turns by joy because the Cauldron of Vocation is itself tilted by the search.
15. This first joy is given literally in the original as 'the pleasure of jealousy at cuckolding'; we have rendered it as above, as this seems merely a euphemism for 'fornication'. Since the treatise is doubtless intended for the young poet who would not have the income to support a wife until after his final examination, it seems to suggest that the young man might find his pleasures among young women married to older men.

Imbas means 'inspiration' which, for the Irish poet, was the vehicle of his poetic course. The Well of Segais, near the source of the Boyne, had nine hazel trees which dropped their nuts into the river, where they were eaten by the Salmon of Knowledge. Every poet identified himself with this salmon, and recognized the Boyne, its patroness Boann, and the nine hazels of knowledge with high respect, as his privileged inscape whence all poetic inspiration came.

16. We note that both sacred and secular scholarship is held in equal esteem and is held to proceed from the self-same Cauldron of Knowledge, in both cleric and poet.

3. The Cauldron of Vocation

Hear the words of Nede mac Adne:
the Cauldron of Vocation sings
with insights of grace,
with measures of knowledge,
5. with streams of inspiration;
[as] an estuary of wisdom,
a confluence of knowledge,
a stream of dignity;
[giving] exaltation of the lowly,
10. mastery of eloquence,
royal discernment,
sovereign insight,
a poetic lineage
to cherish students;
15. [it is] where laws are regulated,
where meanings are recited,
where musical runs are chanted,
where knowledge is propagated,
where the free-born are taught,
20. where the bound are set free,
where the nameless win fame;
where praise is related
by measured regulation,
by distinct degrees,
25. with pure measures of immunity,
with the eloquence of sages:
a confluence of scholarship;
the noble brew in which is boiled

the stock of each knowledge –
30. it is established by rote,
     it is enriched by diligence,
     it is fermented by inspiration,
     it is overturned by joy,
     it manifests through sorrow;
35. it is an enduring power
     whose protection never ebbs.
     Thus sings the Cauldron of Vocation.

38. Question: what is the *ermae* [vocational trend]? 39. Not difficult: a noble course of achievement, or a noble returning, or an artistic vocation, i.e. it confers knowledge and freedom and status [upon the subject] after it [the cauldron] has turned.

This poem concerns the Cauldron of Vocation which can be overset according to what comes into it. The sustained metaphors of accumulations of water, by way of poetic inspiration, learning and practical knowledge of poetic craft, suggest that the *aois dána* knew exactly what would make the Cauldron of Vocation move! Although pride at the poet's final status as supreme over all other beings runs through this poem, it is also made clear that this vocational trend is not merely the gift of noble people, but can also be attained by those of unfree or serf status, since the possession of such artistic gifts inherently ennobles their possessor.

3–8. The sustained metaphor of the cauldron's outpourings is one of water growing from trickles to a vast body of water.

9–11. The metaphor suggests the amplification of all students from poor to noble status.

13. Line 9 speaks of the *doeir or daer*, 'unfree' or bond-person's status. Here it is contrasted with the *saer* or 'free' class of person. The metaphor suggests the ennobling of the unfree, by the giving of a new genealogical background – the spiritual lineage of poets. This metaphor is continued in the next line.

15–27. The cauldron is the 'school-room' for the learning of many arts.

16–17. The whole of Irish learning was memorized by means of reciting words by rote which would have been chanted on sustained musical runs or patterns.

25. The immunity of the poet from certain laws was upheld throughout Ireland; to injure a poet, whether by violence or by insult, was to put oneself to great expense and to expose oneself to the shamanic

skills of a satirist. In his youth, Fionn Mac Cumhail once apprenticed himself to a poet so that he might enjoy poetic immunity from attack when his family were under threat of feud.

4. The Nine Gifts of the Cauldron

The Cauldron of Vocation
gives and is replenished,
promotes and is enlarged,
nourishes and is given life,
5. ennobles and is exalted,
requests and is filled with answers,
sings and is filled with song,
preserves and is made strong,
arranges and receives arrangements,
10. maintains and is maintained.
Good is the well of measure,
Good is the abode of speech,
Good is the confluence of power:
it builds up strength.
15. It is greater than any domain,
It is better than any inheritance.
It numbers us among the wise,
And we depart from the ignorant.

This poem enumerates the nine gifts of the Cauldron of Vocation, which may be seen as analogous to the gifts of the nine hazels of the Well of Segais – the source of all poetic inspiration. The dual function of the cauldron is clearly stated: this vessel, active within all who are aware of their creative resources, both gives out to others in the physical world and is replenished by the inner world. This is an important realization in the creative arts: that the practice of one's art is not to empty oneself, but to be filled again. There is no diminution in either quality or quantity of the personal gift.

By the nine gifts of the cauldron, the poet becomes a mediator for the people who seek him or her out. The exact relationship between the nine gifts enumerated here and the three cauldrons is not established.

The Function of the Three Cauldrons

We are used to considering the archetypal cauldron or Grail as the object of quest, but our first realization on reading this text is that these cauldrons are conceived of as being within each person. Many people have asked whether there is a Celtic equivalent of the Hindu chakra system. No such parallel exists, yet this text suggests that the three cauldrons have a close metaphysical relationship to the reception and dispensation of inspiration. Let us examine their functions and possible locations within the body.

Coire Goiriath – The Cauldron of Warming

This vessel is born and operative in every person; it is the foundation vessel which maintains vital energy and power, as well as preserving the cultural nourishment which each person receives in their upbringing. It provides the essential nurture which all human beings require. It is upright in all people.

Coire Ernmae – The Cauldron of Vocation

This vessel is inverted in some people who have no apparent gifts or skills. In those who are aware of their gifts it is positioned on its side, like a receiver or satellite dish. In those who are fully enlightened it is in the upright position. It can, however, be turned from its inverted position by either joy or sorrow. It gives a rich selection of gifts to those in whom it is operative, helping them interface with ordinary and non-ordinary reality.

Coire Soís – The Cauldron of Knowledge

This vessel is originally positioned in an inverted manner. Like the *Coire Ernmae*, it can be turned by joy or sorrow, and there is some suggestion that the *Coire Ernmae* may actually need to be fully operative before the *Coire Soís* turns. In those who are spiritually operative or enlightened, it is upright and has the greatest capacity for spiritual and artistic gifts.

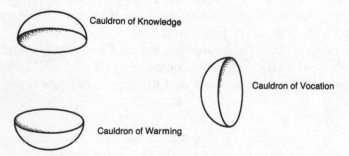

Cauldron of Knowledge

Cauldron of Vocation

Cauldron of Warming

Fig. 5. Positions of the cauldrons at birth

In most people, only the first is operative, and the second is inverted over it, indicating a closed circuit of experience. In poets and other inspired people, the second cauldron is turned on its side, as a kind of receiver of experience. In spiritual people, the third cauldron is also operative. The turning or conversion of the two upper cauldrons – the Cauldrons of Vocation and Knowledge – is rather mysterious. The text implies that the Cauldron of Vocation's position determines one's creative responsiveness. The action of this cauldron may be demonstrated by any person in love! The text implies that the Cauldron of Vocation may in turn activate the Cauldron of Knowledge for those whose disposition is to follow a spiritual path.

The alignment of the three cauldrons is obviously critical to the reception and dispensation of inspiration. Each acts as an essential vessel of nurture for the whole being: if one is inoperative, then the physical, emotional or spiritual health is impaired. The following table is offered as a possible schema underlying the philosophy of the three cauldrons:

CAULDRON:	Warming	Vocation	Knowledge
LOCATION:	belly/womb	heart/solar plexus	head
HEALTH:	vitality/physical	emotional/psychic	spiritual

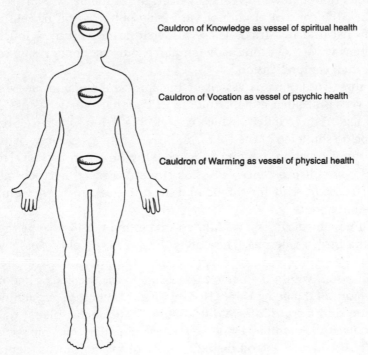

Cauldron of Knowledge as vessel of spiritual health

Cauldron of Vocation as vessel of psychic health

Cauldron of Warming as vessel of physical health

Fig. 6. Location of the cauldrons within the body

This theory is supported by a close study of Celtic attitudes to the body. The head is of paramount importance to the Celts, being the seat of the soul, the oracular link with the ancestors, and honoured above all other bodily parts. It follows that the Cauldron of Knowledge should be located in the brain, the organ of wisdom. If this is so, then the two other cauldrons must be in a position to cause it to become upright. The text speaks tellingly of how the Cauldron of Vocation is inverted or righted by the effects of the emotions of joy and sorrow, which are felt within the heart or solar plexus – the part of the body which we automatically defend when physically or emotionally assaulted. The Cauldron of Warming seems to belong to the womb or belly, the vessel of life itself and its maintainer.

In our own culture we accord emotional, physical and spiritual characteristics to different organs and bodily locations. We speak of being cowardly or 'lily-livered'; of someone being of similar temperament or 'of one's own kidney'; of 'taking things to heart'; of 'having the gall' to attempt audacities; of 'venting one's spleen' when giving way to anger; of 'having the stomach for something'; of 'yearning with one's bowels' when expressing compassion for someone. In the West, we still locate knowledge in the head and the emotions in the heart, and, although we have mostly disregarded the belly as the seat of vitality, the concept of *hara* or vital belly power is still upheld in the Far East and in Africa. These understandings subconsciously affect the way we move, our body language, our emotional responses and spiritual comprehension.

The three cauldrons as vessels of the spirit are comparable with similar vessels of other esoteric traditions: Lurianic Qabala speaks of the ten sephiroth or spheres which contain the living essences of the divine being shattered at the Fall. Qabalists, by means of pious living and spiritual devotion, attempt to mend what has been broken. The sephirotic vessels are conceived of as simultaneously macrocosmic and microcosmic, scattered throughout the universe and active within humankind at once.

In Chinese medical lore, we find an interesting parallel to the theory of the three cauldrons. The bodily energies are held to be governed by the Triple Heater (or Warmer or Burner), described as 'three burning spaces' within the body; these relate to the organs located in these regions of the body: Upper Heater – heart and lungs, regulating breathing and circulation; Middle Heater – stomach, spleen, gall bladder, liver and small intestine, regulating digestion, enzyme secretion, bile production, blood detoxification, absorption of nutrients; Lower Heater – kidneys, bladder and large intestines, regulating the separation of nutrients, the excretion of unused waste, and regulating temperature, lymphatic and the immune systems.

Interestingly, *The Yellow Emperor's Classic* likens the Upper Heater to a mist, the Middle Heater to a foam and the Lower Heater to a swamp, demonstrating the understanding of three heaters as central to the alchemical distillation process.

The doctrine of the Hindu chakras has a vast literature and is only tangentially of interest to this study, although it is possibly the better known of the systems mentioned here. The chakras are conceived of, not as vessels, but as regulating wheels through which both physical and subtle energies revolve. The most interesting parallel with the three cauldrons is that the chakras are simultaneously receivers as well as maintainers of energy.[11]

It is evident that the teachings contained in the Three Cauldrons text are not unique; they point to a universal understanding of the subtle and vital energies of life itself. Let us turn now to its shamanic application.

The shamanic application of the cauldrons

Shamanic practice concerns the kindling, harnessing and distribution of spiritual heat. The original Siberian word shaman, in Tungus, implies great heat or warming. We may also recall the origins of the word enthusiasm, which comes from the Greek 'the inspiration of the gods.' This task of warming is specifically related to shamanic work, where failing vitality, flagging enthusiasm or spiritual coldness are remedied.

The Cauldron of Warming, *Coire Goiriath*, has the basal meaning of heat or warmth, but also includes the warmth of the service or piety of a person. It is significant that in the Welsh story of Culhwch and Olwen from the *Mabinogion* a character called Gwyddolwyn Gorr appears – this name means 'the little Irish dwarf'. His function is far more interesting than the accidental similarity between his epithet of *gorr* (mutated from *corr*, Welsh for 'dwarf') and Irish *goire*, for he possesses bottles which will preserve the heat of whatever liquid is put within from the eastern extremity of the world to its western edge. Gwyddolwyn Gorr's thermal ability may be related to the guardianship of the Cauldron of Warming.

Shamanism is an alchemical craft which uses the available ingredients of a situation, illness or problem; it diagnoses the cause and distills the remedy by directly accessing the spirit world. The alchemical interrelation of the three cauldrons is upheld by its alchemical guardians. In the story of Taliesin, Ceridwen's cauldron is kept brewing for a year and a day, its ingredients gathered by her in accordance with 'the arts of the books of the *fferyllt*'. The *fferyllt* are the ancestral alchemists of British tradition, beings who maintain the spiritual heat of the land. Their abode is in the high places of Snowdonia at Dinas Affaraon, the Fortress of the High Powers, where they are associated with the governance of the dragons, the symbolic guardians of the energy of the land.[12]

The alchemical transformation of raw emotion into fodder for inspiration is clearly outlined in the Three Cauldrons. In an anonymous bardic poem of eighteenth-century Ireland, the poet speaks of his bardic school as the place of three forges: the house of memorizing, the house of reclining and the house of the critic, where the study, inspiration and exposition of poetry were sequentially learned:

> The three forges wherein I was enclosed
> Brought me delight of mind;
> That I cannot revisit these three forges
> Wears away my mind's treasury.
>
> (Author's translation)

The gnostic 'arousal of inner fire', like the Hindu notion of raising the *kundalini* has been associated, by the profane, solely with sexuality. Within esoterical tradition, this arousal of inner fire is about contacting and aligning with the source of divine inspiration, so that the practitioner becomes a lightning rod of revelation. All who encounter that practitioner become aware of divine potentialities within themselves; suddenly all things are possible, miracles happen. The power flowing through such an individual is so great that even being in her presence is itself a revelation. So, within Celtic tradition, vision poets were vessels of prophecy and inspiration, able to answer questions and transmit knowledge.

The flowing of blessings and knowledge is central to the shamanic task: if it were not, then people would long ago have ceased to consult shamans. The giving of gifts or blessings is also a function of Celtic cauldrons, as we find in the Cauldron of Annwn, the British underworld. Arthur goes on quest for this vessel, which is warmed by the breath of nine maidens. This ninefold sisterhood is found throughout Celtic tradition as the guardians of the arts, both spiritual and mundane.[13] Here, images of water and fire combine in their final alchemical fusion. The waters that flow between the worlds are contained within the cauldron, but it is by the breath of the otherworldly fire guardians that the liquid is heated. The ninefold sisters are the supreme dispensers of inspiration whose breath inspires the brew of the cauldron, bestowing the ninefold gifts upon it. They come down to us as faery godmothers, dispensing birth-gifts, but that function primarily belongs to their mistress, none other than Brighid, Goddess of Inspiration.

The giving of nine gifts is inextricably bound up with Brighid in Gaelic lore, where she is frequently invoked to bless new-born children. Brighid has three aspects governing smithcraft, healing and poetry. Each aspect dispenses three gifts which promote the livelihood, health and inspiration of the individual. At birth, in the West Highlands of only hundred years ago, a child would be passed across the fire three times, then carried about the fire deosil three times before receiving 'the midwife's baptism' of water:

> A small wave for your form
> A small wave for your voice
> A small wave for your speech
> A small wave for your means
> A small wave for your generosity
> A small wave for your appetite
> A small wave for your wealth
> A small wave for your life
> A small wave for your health
> Nine waves of grace upon you.
> Waves of the Giver of Health.

The blessing of fire and water is traditional to Brighid, who is the midwife's protector.

Brighid is thus a being who has nine separate spiritual appearances and blessings which are ubiquitously invoked through Celtic lore, as here where Nede mac Adne relates his mystical ancestry in 'The Colloquy of the Two Sages':

> I am the son of poetry,
> Poetry, son of reflection,
> Reflection, son of meditation,
> Meditation, son of lore,
> Lore, son of research,
> Research, son of great knowledge,
> Great knowledge, son of intelligence,
> Intelligence, son of understanding,
> Understanding, son of wisdom,
> Wisdom, son of the three gods of Dana.

The three gods of Dana, are taken to be Brighid's three sons by Tuireann, son of Ogma: Brian, Iuchar and Iucharba, who are revered here as the progenitors of a spiritual lineage to which all poets belong. Brighid is often fused with the ancient Celtic ancestress, Dana. We may set these nine 'ancestors' side by side with the nine gifts enumerated in 'The Nine Gifts of the Cauldron' from the Three Cauldrons text.

POETRY:	sings and is filled with song
REFLECTION:	maintains and is maintained
MEDITATION:	preserves and is made strong
LORE:	promotes and is enlarged
RESEARCH:	requests and is filled with answers
GREAT KNOWLEDGE:	gives and is replenished
INTELLIGENCE:	arranges and receives arrangements
UNDERSTANDING:	nourishes and is given life
WISDOM:	ennobles and is exalted

As no part of either text has been reordered to form this poetic riddle, we may conclude that both teachings derive from a unitive source. The exact relationship between the nine gifts and the three caudrons is not definitively established in our text, but the juxtaposition of the two poems in this manner reveals a shamanic core practice and philosophy that would be hard to fault. Much of Celtic poetic evidence is often highly technical, theoretical and riddled with the selfish introversion of the professional, specialist clique. This text reveals to us a whole and practical framework which gives and receives in equal measure. This speaks eloquently of a preserved shamanic tradition which we can utilize today.

There are a variety of ways in which this text can be used practically. When we first discovered and translated it, we made a shamanic journey to discover the status of our own cauldrons. We were shown how the position and vitality of the cauldrons could be diagnosed by rattling and singing, or intuited in conversation with people. A journey could be made to check the health of one's own cauldrons; it was also possible to find and confer with one's own cauldron guardians who could then give advice as to how one could change things.

Our general findings from working shamanically with this text have shown the following. The Cauldron of Warming maintains the body: if it were inverted, the subject would be extremely ill or dead! It indicates bodily sickness by its liquor being discoloured or badly smelling or the cauldron itself being corroded. The Cauldron of

Vocation oscillates a great deal and can change position several times in a short period. It is evident when someone's vocational cauldron is inverted: there is a lack of vital sparkle or interest in the subject, which is troubling. If it is inverted for a long period, soul-fragmentation and soul-loss can occur. This cauldron can appear almost mercurial or flower-like, with the sensitivity of a wind-mobile or solar-triggered plant. The Cauldron of Knowledge's capacity for spiritual awareness seems to be dependent upon the position of the Cauldron of Vocation, and the subject's ability and willingness for selfless service to the universe. During an emotional upset, which inverts the Cauldron of Vocation, an upright Cauldron of Knowledge can also flip over. It is also possible to meditate upon each cauldron and gain further information about their personal application.

In transmitting these secrets the keepers of this teaching granted us an inestimable gift of shamanic heritage. Almost none of the subtle teachings have survived in textual form because they were orally transmitted. Owing to the cultural isolation of Ireland, the ancestral respect for the vision poet and the manner in which ancient shamanic teachings were incorporated into the medieval Irish poetic curriculum, we have a treasured teaching which is beyond price.

PART THREE

The Bright Knowledge

CHAPTER 8

Prophecy and Divination

The Celtic Art of Divination
by Caitlín Matthews

In any society, the ability to augur, divine or prophesy is highly respected. The prophet or diviner is able to provide information by entering into communion with the otherworld and the spirits who inhabit those realms. Such divination remains a prime shamanic skill, although many forms of divination – those that use a series of symbolic analogues which do not involve trance – are not shamanic.

The major Celtic means of providing otherworldly information may be outlined as follows:

1. the second sight
2. dreams (involuntary or ritually incubated)
3. studying divinatory patterns (birdsong, Ogam, stones etc.)
4. ritual augury (the *frith*)
5. prophecy by psychometry, trance-song or ritual meal

Many of these methods overlap. Seership or the second sight is commonly found throughout the Celtic world today. Seers have the gift (or affliction, depending on your viewpoint) of *da shealladh*, literally 'having two sights'. This gift cannot be denied or turned off, enabling the seer to see both ordinary and non-ordinary reality simultaneously: a truly disconcerting and frightening gift! Martin Martin, writing in the seventeenth century, records his encounter with this ability among the Western Highlanders:

The second-sight is a singular faculty of seeing an otherwise invisible object without any previous means used by the person that sees it for that end; the vision makes such a lively impression upon the seers, that they neither see nor think of any thing else except the vision, as long as it continues . . . The seer knows neither the object, time nor place of a vision, before it appears; and the same object is often seen by different persons, living at a considerable distance from one another.

He relates an incident that befell a family with whom he lodged:

Archibald MacDonald happened to be in the village of Knocknow one night . . . and told the family that he had just then seen the strangest thing he ever saw in his life: to wit, a man with an ugly long cap always shaking his head; but that the strangest of all, was a little kind of a harp which he had, with four strings only, and that it had two hart's horns fixed in the front of it. All that heard this odd vision fell a-laughing at Archibald, telling him he was dreaming . . . [But] within three or four days after, a man with the cap, harp etc. came to the house [answering] the description of them at first view; he shook his head when he played, for he had two bells fixed to his cap. This harper was a poor man and made himself a buffoon for his bread, and was never before seen in those parts, for at the time of the prediction he was in the Isle of Barray, twenty leagues distant from that part of Skye.[1]

Such exact information-giving is usual in Gaelic seership, but those who have the second sight rarely find their gift personally useful. Can the second sight be accounted as a shamanic skill? As it is involuntary and the spirits seem to come at will to the subject, it may depend upon the personality of the seer and his or her willingness to co-operate. Eilidh Watt, a contemporary Gaelic seer, speaks of her own experience thus:

I may be directed to answer prayers at some inconvenience to myself. I may miss a bus and have to make a detour to meet the person involved. A chain of trivial events may lead me to a particular person. On occasion I become very restless and feel that there is somebody whom I must visit . . . When I arrive, my convenience is taken for granted, and I am there to nurse, fill in forms or dissuade from suicide. I am left feeling that I am expendable. On the other hand, I by nature am prepared to be expended in the interest of my fellows.[2]

The seer is often aware of a guardian spirit which accompanies him or her. This *coimimeadh* or co-walker, is mentioned by Robert Kirk in his seventeenth-century study of second sight and the faery, *The Secret Commonwealth of Elves, Fauns and Fairies*:

> [This] Co-walker [is] every way like the man, as a twin-brother and companion, haunting him as his shadow and is oft seen and known among men, resembling the original . . . [It] was often seen, of old, to enter a house; by which the people knew that the person of that likeness was to visit them within a few days.[3]

Eilidh Watt speaks from her own experience:

> I believe that I have a co-walker, and am sometimes of the opinion that there may be more than one, each possibly with different functions.[4]

The combination of the co-walker with the second sight and a willingness to be helpful to one's community would certainly define someone as a shaman, although this combination is not always present in seers.

The commonest form of divination which may be practised involuntarily by anybody is dreaming to discover information. The use of shamanic incubation is dealt with in Chapter 10. Here, we will briefly consider further ways in which dreaming secures information. The dreams of non-shamanic people often have divinatory, predictive or helpful content. 'The Dream of Maxen Wledig' from the *Mabinogion* details how Maxen falls asleep in Rome and travels to Britain in his dream, where he discovers a woman with whom he falls instantly in love. With a mass of landscape information and corroborative detail, he awakens and sends out messengers to discover the whereabouts of his bride. She is discovered in North Wales, recognized from the information of his dream, and subsequently becomes his wife.

We see similar cases of precognitive dream throughout Celtic lore, but the most striking use of the dream as a shamanic journey is in the druidic custom of the *tarbh feis*, wherein the druid eats and drinks of the broth of a freshly killed bull, wraps himself in its hide and lies down within it to obtain a problem-solving vision.

The seventeenth-century historian, Keating, writes about the divinatory habits of druids, drawing on oral tradition:

As to the druids, the use they made of the hides of the bulls offered in sacrifice was to keep them for the purpose of making conjuration, or laying *geasa* on the demons; and many are the ways in which they laid *geasa* on them, such as to keep looking at their own images in water, or gazing on the clouds of heaven, or keep listening to the noise of the wind or the chattering of birds. But when all these expedients failed them, and they were obliged to do their utmost, what they did was, to make round wattles of the quicken [rowan] tree, and to spread thereon the hides of the bulls offered in sacrifice, putting the side which had been next the flesh uppermost, and thus relying on their *geasa* to summon the demons to get information from them, as the conjurer does nowadays in the circus; whence the old saw has since been current which says that one has gone on his wattles of knowledge (*cliataibh fis*) when he has done his utmost to obtain information.[5]

Geasa (singular *geas*) are prohibitions or binding duties which are normally laid upon a person at birth by a seer. To break a *geas* is to forfeit one's luck and ultimately one's life. Here, Keating speaks of the druids laying *geasa* upon 'demons', by which he means spirits.

It is unclear from this and from other texts whether 'sleep' is to be taken literally, or whether a trance state of consciousness is intended. The technical vocabulary of vision tends to be restricted among those who do not practise it themselves. The shamanic trance journey is normally undertaken in waking consciousness, but, the imbibing of a single food, probably after fasting, suggests here that the digestion of the meat is intended to aid the vision, and that the subject may indeed be asleep as a result of a full stomach.

The ancient druidic *tarbh feis* had its Scottish equivalent in the *taghairm*, whereby the diviner wrapped himself in a newly slaughtered ox-hide and lay behind a waterfall or near a tidal inlet; wrapped in the 'cloak of knowledge', the seer would seek the answer in the roar of the water and from the spirit of the slain animal: surely a practice that precluded any slumber! Highland Gaels who practised this form of divination or who were seers were termed *taibhsear* or 'spirit-seer'.

The variety of druidic divinatory methods which is hinted at in the extract from Keating are certainly reflected throughout the tradition.

Classical writers mention three prevalent Gaulish customs of divination. Diodorus writes horrifically of ovates divining from the throes of dying captives, purposely stabbed above the diaphragm: by the way the victim fell, the convulsions of the limbs and the flow of the blood certain things could be construed. Diodorus also writes of the Celtic practice of ornithomancy, the observation of the flight of birds. This method was widely used by the Etruscans and Romans, but it is not known whether druids made a preliminary division (*templum*) of the sky.

The observation of animals has long been a source of divination. The Celts may well have bred certain animals for sacred rather than culinary purposes, as is hinted at in Julius Caesar's list of taboo animals: 'Hares, fowl, and geese they think it unlawful to eat, but rear them for pleasure and amusement.' Why did he write this?

The hare brings the sun back out of the ground by his leaping in March – the time of Easter or of the Spring Equinox. Hare-coursing with greyhounds may have ancient divinatory antecedents. The hare was sacred to the goddess Andraste of the Iceni, of whom Boudicca sought an augury by loosing a hare from her garment and distinguishing the outcome of the battle by its manner of flight.

The goose is quick to react to strangers and has long been kept as an aggressive guardian of boundaries. A goose appears on the frieze overlooking the skull-shrine at the Gaulish sanctuary of Entremont and the remains of geese have been found interred with warriors. We may assume that the honking of geese in migratory flight may have contributed to its being seen as a threshold animal which pointed the way between the worlds.

Chickens' eggs may have been used in druidic divination, as may the manner in which they scratched for grain. We know only that the cockerel appears as companion bird of Mercury in Romano-British reliefs, as well as appearing on Celtic coins.

Despite Caesar's comment that the Celts did not eat these three animals, their remains do turn up in archaeological sites of the period, especially the bones of fowl. Divining is like gambling, in that any created thing may be used to divine by or gamble upon. Perhaps it is here that we find the hairline division between the two in the sports of hare-coursing and cock-fighting where chance and fate seem intertwined.

The chief source of divination seems to have been weather-watching. The druids were certainly as weather-wise as any modern meteorologist. A glance at the Coligny Calendar, a bronze Gaulish tablet of the first century AD, shows that the druids spent at least five years watching the weather every day and night in order to arrive at the listing of favourable and unfavourable days from the random combinations of meteorological conditions, which are contributed to the omens inscribed upon the tablet. *Neldoracht* or cloud watching is described in 'The Siege of Druim Damgaire' where druids of both sides view the day and the weather, watching the sky closely, for information which will determine the day's actions.

The full details of these practices have not come down to us, but, though the modern practitioner would be forgiven for not wanting to restore human or animal sacrifice, there is no reason why some of these might not be recovered shamanically. We must note however that most of these methods are non-shamanic, relying as they do upon symbolic analogues or traditional omens and portents, rather than upon shamanic vision, for their outcome.

Throughout this book we have made much mention of Brighid, who is a central figure to the Celtic vision world. The augury or *frith* of Brighid is an important form of divination, and is listed separately from common divinatory methods, since it has been used not only to provide portents for the coming season but also to discern information shamanically at long distance. To understand the position of Brighid, let us look at this extract from *Cormac's Glossary*:

> Brighid — a poetess, daughter of the Dagda. She is the female sage, woman of wisdom, or Brighid the Goddess whom poets venerated because very great and famous for her protecting care. She was therefore called 'Goddess of Poets'. Her sisters were Brighid the female physician, and Brighid the female smith; among all Irishmen, a goddess was called 'Brighid'. Brighid is from *breo-aigit* or 'fiery arrow'.

Here, Cormac carefully records all he knows of Brighid of the Tuatha de Danann. The veneration of Brighid extended throughout the insular Celtic world: she was known as Brigantia in Britain, and, after the myths of the Goddess Brighid and St Brigit of Kildare were virtually fused together, she is known as St Ffraid in Wales and St Bride in Scotland. Cormac's etymology of 'fiery arrow' is ingenious but incorrect, as Brighid comes from the Sanskrit *brahti*, 'high one'.

In Celtic Christian lore, St Brigit becomes the midwife and foster-mother of Christ, and the perpetual helper and friend of Mary. The Gaelic method of the *frith* was said to derive from the loss of Christ by Mary in the Temple:

> The augury which Brigit made for her Foster-Son:
> She made a pipe of her palms:
> 'I see the Foster-Son by the side of the well,
> Teaching the people without doubt.

Sometimes the augury is made by Mary:'

> The augury made by gentle Mary for her Son,
> The Queen of Virgins looked through her palms:
> 'Did you see the King of Life?'
> The Queen of Virgins said that she saw.[6]

This method of curling the hands to form a 'seeing-tube' seems to have been used by *frithirs* for discovering lost people and animals, or to discover the health of an absent being. The use of the palms is also widespread in Irish Gaelic usage, where the palms are used to provide a 'seeing-space' or *tabula rasa*, to block out the light or to focus the seer. Here, real shamanic vision was employed to discover the unknown. At the turn of the century, a Lewis man emigrated to Australia and was not heard of for three years; his wife consulted a *frithir* who went into a trance and replied that her husband had moved his abode, that he had not prospered but that he would write to her now. Three months later a letter arrived from him asking whether his wife had consulted the seer, Mary MacNeill, on such a day and hour. He reported seeing and speaking with the *frithir* and had been prompted to write home as a result.[7] Sometimes the *frithir* used a divinatory stone, probably held or carried during the *frith*; such a 'little stone of the quests', of red quartz, was given into the possession of the collector, Alexander Carmichael: the very same one used to help discover the body of Donald Maclean of Coll, after being drowned in the Sound of Ulva.

But the usual practice of the *frith* was undertaken by the *frithir*, fasting, on the first Monday of the quarter, at sunrise, with bare head and feet. It was done in order to divine the portent for the coming quarter. Special prayers to invoke Mary and Brigit and to welcome the *frith* were said while walking deosil round the household fire three times. Then, with closed or blindfolded eyes, the *frithir* went to the threshold of the house, placing one hand on either jamb with prayers to grant the request which occasioned the *frith*. Then, with open eyes, he or she looked steadfastly ahead and noted all that he or she saw.

The signs are called *rathadach* (lucky) or *rosadach* (unlucky). A man or beast rising up indicates improving health, lying down denotes ill health and death. A cockerel coming towards the *frithir* is fortunate, while other approaching birds indicate news. A duck indicates safety for sailors, while a raven indicates death. A rhyme about horses and the *frith* survives:

> A white horse for land,
> A gray horse for sea,
> A bay horse for burial,
> A brown horse for sorrow.[8]

The role of *frithir* was believed to be inherited; the name has survived as the surname Freer, which is held to be the title of the astrologers of the kings of Scotland.

Among the gifted people of the Celts, memory was supreme: without it there could be no knowledge. But if the memory circuits were accidentally erased, then there were ways of retrieving memory – through the shamanic techniques of *teinm laegda* or 'decoding by means of verse', *dichetul do chennaib* or 'psychometric composition' and *imbas forosna* or 'inspiration of tradition'. These three techniques were called the Three Illuminations, since they threw light on dark matters. These are the primary shamanic skills employed by the *filidh* poet, who derived from this lore the additional ability of prophetic and magical insight. The Three Illuminations called upon the ability to analyse things by means of visionary and prophetic poetry, by psychometric touch and by spirit-vision flight.

The need to know the origin, source or precedent for things reflects the word-hunger of the Celt which twines its way sinuously and exploratively through philological complexities which leave the non-Celt baffled. Those who have read and enjoyed James Joyce's *Finnigan's Wake*, Dylan Thomas's *Under Milk Wood* or David Jones' *Anathamata* have revelled in these waters. *Cormac's Glossary* is the earliest attempt at an etymological dictionary of names and their origins; it is found in *The Yellow Book of Lecan*, the work of a monastic author of about the ninth or tenth century, who describes and defines the Three Illuminations from a Christian standpoint.

Imbas Fosonai – the inspiration of tradition, the knowledge that discovers whatever the poet wishes to know. It is done like this: the poet chews a piece of flesh from the red pig, or of cat or dog and after so chewing puts it on the flagstone behind the door. He pronounces an invocation over it and offers it to his spirits. He calls his spirits to him and if they do not reveal the matter immediately he sings incantations over his two palms and calls the spirits again to keep his sleep undisturbed. Then he lays his palms over his cheeks and so falls asleep in this posture. He is watched to ensure that nothing interrupts him until the matter is revealed to him; this may be a minute or two or three, or as long as necessary. Patrick abolished this practice along with *tein-ma laegda*, for he judged that those that practised these methods should merit neither heaven nor earth, because it renounced one's baptismal vows. The practice of *dichetal do chennaib* he alone allowed, since it was not necessary to make offerings to spirits, for the revelation comes straight away from the ends of the poet's fingers.

This important text reveals the true shamanic nature of the poet. Here the poet makes a meat offering to the spirits, which he shares, then sings in order to call the spirits and to discover some unknown matter. If this does not work, he lies down and covers his eyes with his hands in order to make a shamanic journey. Cormac clearly does not understand the necessity for darkness and imagines that the hands and cheeks are somehow significant. The duration of this journey seems rather short when compared with the worldwide shamanic spirit-flight examples, which can last from a few minutes to several hours, but the attunement of the *filidh* seems total and the results are quickly shown in most examples of this method. From this information, we see that the *tarbh feis* is itself a form of *imbas forosna*.

We note that the co-operation of animal spirits is a major part both of the *tarbh feis* and of *imbas forosna*, where the skin and meat of an animal are respectively employed. In shamanic practice, it is impossible to use or eat the physical remains of an animal without also communing with its spirit. The kinds of animal that are used in these methods, as far as we can establish from Cormac's disjointed definition – the pig, cat, dog and bull – are domesticated species which have an established relationship with humankind. It is more usual for shamanic animal helpers to be of untamed species, but we must remember that some domestic animals in the Celtic era still retained a healthy wild streak and were not comparable to our tame pets or factory-farmed livestock. The method was presumably undertaken after preparatory fasting. The chewing of the meat, which may have been raw or undercooked, would certainly release the brain's endorphins, readying the *filidh* for oracular utterances.

Dichetal do chennaib, the psychometric method of divination is revealed in another part of *Cormac's Glossary*:

Coire Breccain – 'Breccan's Cauldron' . . . Now Breccan son of Main, son of Niall of the Nine Hostages, had fifty curraghs trading between Ireland and Scotland, until they fell at one time into the cauldron there, and no one ever knew of their destruction until Lugaid, the Blind Poet, came to Bangor, and his people went to the strand of Inver Bece and found a bare small skull there. They brought it to Lugaid and asked him whose head it was. He said, 'Put the end of the poet's wand upon it.' This was done and Lugaid said, 'The tempestuous waters of the whirlpool destroyed Breccan. This is the head of his dog.'

This little snippet reveals a little more of the shaman poet's art. Here, Blind Lugaid practises *dichetal do chennaib*, receiving information about a long-dead man and his companions through touching the skull of Breccan's dog with his poetic wand. We have already seen (Chapter 7) how the blind druid Mog Roith discerned the best earth in Munster from touch and smell. Knowledge is kindled in darkness, where the shamanic senses are honed to discern and track the resonances of spiritual presence.

Writing as a cleric in the ninth century, Cormac has little to say of the druid-kind, but he does associate their magic with poetry in this definition of druid: '*drai* – an enchanter. It is through the art of poetry that he makes his incantations.' What manner of poetry is this? Shamanic methods of trance-singing are found worldwide, and seem to have been particularly widespread in the Celtic world. The *filidh* utilized a form of vocal tracking called *teinm laegda*, 'the decoding of the poem', which involved trance-singing to come at unknown information. The *filidh* sang over the subject, communing with its soul-life or energy-field, and sang aloud the images, impressions and metaphors that came to him: following the thread of the poem/song, the *filidh* was able to arrive at a solution. We find an example of this in the following extract from Cormac:

Orc Treith – literally 'spirited piglet' or 'young salmon', a kenning for a king's son. . . . It happened that Fionn mac Cumaill's fool, Lomna, saw the champion Coirpre lying with Fionn's woman. The woman swore him to silence, but Lomna could not deceive his master, so he carved an ogam on a four-square rod and alluded to the betrayal thus: 'An alder stake within a silver fence. Deadly nightshade in a bunch of cresses.' . . . Fionn read and understood, putting the woman from him. The woman set Coirpre to kill Lomna. Coirpre beheaded the fool and left his

body lying there. 'Whose is this body without head?' cried the
fianna. Fionn put his thumb in his mouth and spoke through
teinm laegda,

> He has not been killed by people,
> Nor by the people of Leinster,
> Nor by a wild boar,
> He has not been killed by a fall,
> He has not died on his bed,
> Lomna! This is Lomna's body!

Fionn tracked Coirpre with dogs, and found him with Lomna's
head on a pole, preparing fish to eat. Coirpre gave no fish to the
head nor to the *fianna*, so Lomna said, 'A white-bellied salmon
(*orc*) has come out of a small fish indeed!'

This elliptical tale reveals how the poetic skill of the great hero, Fionn,
finds Lomna through the shamanic art of *teinm laegda*. The repetitive
diagnosis of the situation finally culminates in the identification of
the body as Lomna's. The head of the dead Lomna itself provides its
own *teinm laegda* in identifying his murderer as a 'small fish'. This
story also reveals the allusive art of ogam – the inscription of strokes
upon a rod, employed by poets to send messages without them being
detected by the unlearned. Lomna, by use of the poet's 'dark language' of ogamic allusion, loyally and discreetly reveals the decep-
tion which dishonours his master.

Fionn's magical thumb, which once touched the salmon of knowledge itself, is also pressed into service to solve this mystery. Does
Fionn utilize *dichetal do chennaib* here as well as *teinm laegda*? *Dichetal
do chennaib* or 'psychometric composition' is also referred to as 'com-
posing on the finger ends'. Was there a poetic method of enumeration
or elimination of possibilities which the *filidh* practised in such cases,
using the fingers as reference points to the 'dark language' of shamanic interpretation? We know that, apart from any psychometric application, the joints of the fingers were utilized in *dichetal do chennaib*, for
Cormac further says: 'When [the poet] sees the person or thing before
him he makes a verse at once with his finger ends, or in his mind
without studying, and composes and repeats at the same time.' This
suggests that the fingers kept a reckoning of points under consideration. It is possible, as Robert Graves has suggested, that the table of the
hand, with its finger joints were used as a mnemonic method of recalling associative images by use of the poetic alphabet, the Ogam, in
much the same way as we keep count by using our fingers.

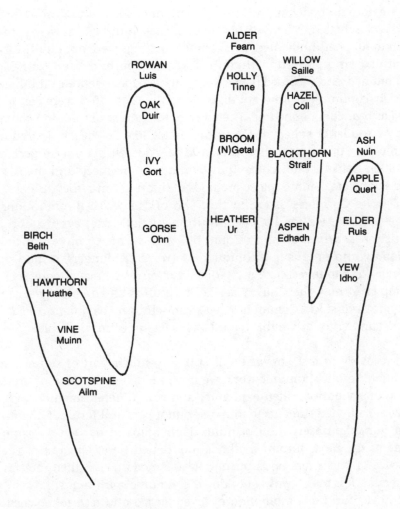

Fig. 7. *The Hand as Mnemonic Ogam Aid*

As each Ogam letter had enumerable poetic kennings or allusions, the trained *filidh* would have been able to touch the appropriate finger or joint to reconnect with the associative Ogam letters, thus 'activating' shamanic vision by invocatory means. See *The Celtic Shaman* by John Matthews for some of these kenning lists.

Although *teinm laeghda* and *imbas forosna* were outlawed by St Patrick, since baptismal vows require Christians to renounce the influence of any spirit but that of the Trinity, which the invocation of spirits clearly contradicts, it is interesting that Patrick is less finicky about *dichetal do chennaib* as a means of discovering unknown things. Why should this be so?

We note that each of the Three Illuminations is oracular in nature and is closely tied into mystical and poetic teachings which were common to all poets and gifted ones. These teachings were not lightly disregarded since, through them, all knowledge had been gained, maintained and recorded. Genealogy, knowledge, science and otherworldly communion were not divisible to the Celts: they were considered as branches of one tree. The voice of the ancestral tradition could not be suddenly stilled. If Christian clerics like St Patrick desired a foothold in this society then they had to acknowledge the respected tradition-holders, and realize that divination, prophecy and the second sight were commonplace methods of information-retrieval.

Despite Cormac's assertion that two of the Three Illuminations were banned, we see little diminution in their use, even among Christian saints such as St Columba, who seems to have utilized visionary and prophetic incantations to ward off dangers, to punish enemies and to investigate mysterious matters. We have already seen (Chapter 4) how the Church desired to graft itself completely on to the ancestral stock. Columba reveals himself to be as ardent a *filidh*, satirist and visionary in this regard as his Pagan country-people.

The recovery of lost knowledge is still very much part of shamanic tradition. In our shamanic work, we have made use of many of these forms of divination, often experimenting with different methods. We have encouraged students to find and adapt personal forms of divination from the observation of natural phenomena as well as using some of the more formal methods mentioned here. Obviously, the practice of *imbas forosna* is unsuitable for modern use: there are far easier and less messy ways of taking a shamanic spirit-flight.

I have found a combination of *teinm laegda* and *dichetal do chennaib* most practical, especially when diagnosing physical illness and in cases of soul wandering. I begin by singing a variable series of tones over the reclining subject until I am able to tune into his or her 'note' – the spiritual resonance of his or her energy field. As I do this, I stretch out my hands over the subject or sometimes hold a monochord (a long sound-board over which is stretched one tunable metal string). Using my hand or the monochord's vibrating wooden body, I begin to pick up impressions which I then allow to pass to my lips as song. This forms in an incantatory way, building and weaving into a story or journey, especially if I am shamanically tracking a fragmented soul-part. During this process, my spirit takes flight and I begin to journey, simultaneously singing what I experience.

Afterwards, subjects are often struck by the apt nature of the images and the synchronicity of the path which is followed in the singing; they often experience strong physiological changes or immediate spiritual relief from their trouble as a result of the song alone. This is unsurprising, since the interaction of the *teinm laegda* and *dichetal do chennaib* plumb the subject's physical energy field, allowing me to travel shamanically to the time and place wherein the solution or healing lies hidden. The way is opened by sound vibrations and unfolds in impressions which directly relate to the subject's experience and to no other traditional or shamanic criteria. In direct contradiction of Patrick's ban, I always invoke my helping spirits before undertaking this combination of the Three Illuminations!

The use of divination to discover unknown, lost or hidden matters continues to intrigue humankind, and has certainly not been lost among Celtic seers and shamanic practitioners. Whether the seer is innately gifted with the second sight or seeks the enlightenment of problems by asking the help of trees, animals, weather or other omens, answers may still be readily sought by those who are committed enough to ask the question.[9]

The Sovereign Prophecy

Some of the most striking texts about methods of prophecy and divination occur in stories relating to the sovereignty of the land. Celtic royal succession was not determined by primogeniture but by tribal election of the most suitable candidate drawn from the royal blood lineage. The selection and election of sovereigns was an onerous duty which devolved to druids and vision poets, since only the shamanically able might discover the candidate's mystical suitability.

In the following selection of texts, we discover a series of methods by which the sovereign is chosen or confirmed by:

1. the *tarbh feis*, incubation in a bull's-hide
2. the Stone of Fál, locus of inauguration
3. the confirmation of the Goddess of Sovereignty
4. the direct command of an angel
5. the direct command of the god Lugh.

Baile in Scail *or* The Apparition of the Shadow[10]

Conn Cet Chathach (Conn of a Hundred Battles) ruled over northern Ireland in the second century AD. In this important story, Conn has two encounters with the agents of sovereignty: the Stone of Fál, known as the Lia Fáil, and the god Lugh, who appears partnered by the Goddess of Sovereignty herself.

One day Conn was in Tara after the other kings had departed. He went on to the rampart of Tara preceded by his three druids, Mael, Bloc, and Bluiccniu, together with Eochu, Corbb, and Cesarn the *fili*. For it was his custom to mount the rampart every day lest the people of the fairy-mounds or the Fomorians should take Ireland unawares. He saw a stone at his feet and trod upon it, and it screamed so that it was heard throughout Tara. Conn asked the *fili* why the stone had screamed and what manner of stone it was. The *fili* asked for a delay of fifty days and three. At the end of that time through his power of divination he was able to answer. *Fál* (i.e. *fo-ail* 'under-rock', i.e. 'a rock under a king') was the name of the stone. It had come from Inis Fáil to Tara in the country of Fál. It would go to Teltown where a fair of games would always be held, and any prince who should not find it on the last day of the week of the Fair of Teltown would die within the year. The number of cries that the stone had uttered under Conn's feet signified the number of kings of his seed who should be over Ireland. 'Tell them to me then,' said Conn. 'I am not destined to tell them to you,' said the druid.

A great mist came around them so that they lost their way. They heard the sound of a horseman approaching, and then he made three casts against them. The *fili* called out a warning against violation of the king's person. The horseman ceased from casting, and welcomed Conn and bade him go with him to his dwelling. They came to a plain where there was a golden tree. There was a house thirty feet long with a ridgepole of white gold. They went into the house and saw a girl seated in a chair of crystal, wearing a gold crown. In front of her was a silver vat with corners of gold. A vessel of gold stood beside her, and before her was a golden cup. They saw the Phantom himself on his throne, and never was there seen in Tara one as wonderful as he.

He spoke to them and said: 'I am not a phantom and I am not a spectre, and I have come after death to be honoured by you, and I am of the race of Adam. My name is Lug son of Ethniu son of Smretha son of Tigernmar son of Faelu son of Etheor son of Irial son of Érimón son of Míl of Spain. And I have come to tell you the span of your sovranty and of that of every prince that will come of you in Tara for ever.'

The girl was the Sovranty of Ireland and she gave food to Conn, the rib of an ox and the rib of a hog. The ox-rib was twenty-four feet long and eight feet from the arch to the ground. The hog's rib was twelve feet long and five feet from the arch to the ground. When she went to serve the ale, she asked to whom the cup of red ale (*dergflaith*) should be given, and the Phantom answered her. When he had named every prince from the time of Conn onwards, Cesarn wrote them down in *ogam* on four staves of yew. Then the Phantom and his house disappeared, but the vat and the vessel and the staves remained with Conn. And so men speak of The Vision and Adventure and Journey of Conn of the Hundred Battles, and The Phantom's Frenzy.

Here we find Conn, accompanied by his druids and poets, about a kingly and sacred task – the magical defence of the land from the incursions of faery. The custom of climbing sacred hills occurs frequently in Celtic story and is pivotal to subsequent encounters with the Goddess of the Land. In the *Mabinogion*, Pwyll ascends the Mound of Arberth and spies Rhiannon, herself a representative of sovereignty. Celtic rulers are inaugurated upon mounds, raised up high so that all can identify them.

Here, in the sacred landscape of Tara, Conn discovers the Lia Fáil by stepping upon it. He asks his *filidh*, Cesarn, why it shrieks out under him. Whenever we encounter shrieking stones in Celtic story, we may be sure that we are hearing the voice of the land, calling out in primal response. This theme runs throughout the Celtic tradition and finally lodges in the Grail legends where the Celtic inauguration stone becomes the Seat Perilous, which shrieks out if an unworthy knight sits upon it. The Lia Fáil derives from the island of Fáil and travels (on a regular yearly basis, presumably) to Teltown where an annual *oenach* or fair is held; this grew out of the original funeral games of Tailtiu, Lugh's foster-mother, who is very important in the bestowal of sovereignty. The ruler who fails to find the stone there (or attend the festival) by the last day of the fair will die within a year. Cesarn asks for an inordinately long time to find an answer for Conn. However, despite this delay, neither he nor the druids can tell the king how many of his descendants will rule Ireland.

It is at this point that the deeper answer manifests. Conn and his sacred retinue corporately enter the mist of vision wherein they have their extraordinary encounter with the 'horse's mouth' of sovereign information. They enter the otherworld by passing the threshold guardian, travel to the plain where stands a golden tree, symbol of the otherworld, and find the dwelling of Lugh. Lugh himself appears like a high king, and Conn is spectacularly honoured to be served by none other than Sovereignty herself. He is given the gargantuan ribs of the two staple beasts – the ox and the pig – rather than the more usual joint of the thigh, which was the king's portion of an animal.

Lugh Samildanach, the many-gifted god who helps the Tuatha de Danann, is the shadow or spirit of the title: he appears throughout Irish lore as a helper of heroes. Many scholars have linked him with the northern god Odin. Both are concerned with the fortunes of war, are multi-gifted, have raven messengers and have occasion to shapeshift into eagles; both are associated with hills and high places. Odin is lord of Valhalla; Lugh is high-king of the otherworldly hall.[11]

This connection is particularly relevant to this text since Odin is linked with the function of the shamanic seeress or *seidhkona*, who traditionally sits in a high chair and gives oracular information while a small women's chorus chants a trance-inducing song. The *seidhkona* speaks with the aid and inspiration of Odin. In 'Baile in Scáil', the two otherworldly protagonists are Lugh and the Goddess of Sovereignty, who sits in a crystal chair with the vessels of inspiration and sovereignty before her, which return from the vision as manifestations of his otherworldly sacring.

Here the oracle is given by Lugh, while Sovereignty pours the royal liquid which confirms kingship. The king-list is recorded in Ogham by the *filidh*, Cesarn, on yew-staves, the most enduring of woods. We note that the whole vision is brought about by Conn asking a question about the Lia Fáil.

Niall of the Nine Hostages[12]

Niall of the Nine Hostages was High King of Ireland from 379 to AD 405. The story of his candidacy and acceptance into the kingship is told here. Niall is championed by two men: Torna, a poet, and Sithcenn, a smith who happens also to be a prophet. Together they enable him to overcome the tests of kingship. However, it is Niall himself who succeeds in the final testing at the hands of Sovereignty herself.

Eochu Muigmedón, king of Ireland, had five sons, Brian, Ailill, Fiachra, Fergus and Niall. Mongfind ('Fair Hair') daughter of Fidach was his queen and the mother of four sons, but Niall was the son of Cairenn Chasdub daughter of Scal the Dumb, king of the Saxons. Mongfind hated Niall and his mother, and inflicted much hardship upon Cairenn, who was compelled to draw water from the well. Even when she was pregnant with Niall she was compelled to do it, and the child was born in the open as she lay beside her pail. She dared not take up the child, but left it there, and none dared take it up for fear of Mongfind. Then Torna the Poet came by and took up the child, and he foresaw all that was to come. He took him and reared him, and neither he nor the child came to Tara until Niall was of age to be king.

> Then Torna and Niall came to Tara. Cairenn met them as she was carrying water. Niall said to her: 'Leave that menial work!' 'I do not dare,' said she, 'on account of the queen.' 'My mother shall not be a servant,' said he, 'and I the son of the king of Ireland!' He took her with him to Tara, and dressed her in a purple robe.

Mongfind was angry and called upon Eochu to judge between his sons as to who should succeed him. He referred the matter to Sithchenn the smith, who was a prophet. Sithchenn set fire to a forge in which the five sons were at work. Niall came out carrying the anvil, Brian brought the hammers, Fiachra brought a pail of beer and the bellows, Ailill brought the weapons, and Fergus a bundle of kindling with a stick of yew in it. Sithchenn greeted Niall as the victor, and appraised the others according to their merits. Fergus was pronounced sterile, and hence the proverb 'a stick of yew in a bundle of kindling'.

> One day the five sons went hunting and they lost their way in the forest and were enclosed on every side. They lit a fire and cooked some of their game and ate till they were satisfied. They wanted water,

and Fergus set out in search of it. He found a well, but there was an
old woman guarding it. She was as black as coal. Her hair was like a
wild horse's tail. Her foul teeth were visible from ear to ear and were
such as would sever a branch of green oak. Her eyes were black, her
nose crooked and spread. Her body was scrawny, spotted and diseased.
Her shins were bent. Her knees and ankles were thick, her shoulders
broad, her nails were green. The hag's appearance was ugly.

> 'You are horrible,' said the lad. 'Ay,' said she. 'Are you guard-
> ing the well?' said the lad. 'Ay,' said she. 'May I fetch some
> water?' said the lad. 'Ay,' said she, 'if you give me one kiss on
> the cheek.' 'No!' said he. 'You shall have no water from me,'
> said she. 'I give my word,' said he, 'that I would rather die of
> thirst than kiss you.'

Fergus returned without water, and each of the brothers went in turn.
Only Fiachra spoke temperately to the hag, and she promised that he
would visit Tara. And that came true, says the story, for two of his
descendants, Dá Thí and Ailill Molt, became kings of Ireland, but none
of the descendants of the other three.

At last it was Niall's turn to go. When the hag asked him for a kiss,
he consented and lay down with her. Then, when he looked upon her,
she was as fair a girl as any in the world. She was as white as the last
snow in a hollow. Her arms were full and queenly, her fingers long
and slender, her legs straight and gleaming. She had two golden shoes
on her bright little feet, and a precious purple cloak about her, held
by a silver brooch. Her teeth were like pearls, her eyes large and
queenly, her lips of Parthian red.

> 'You are fair, woman,' said the boy. 'Ay,' said she. 'Who are
> you?' said the boy. 'I am Sovranty,' said she. And she said this:
> 'King of Tara, I am Sovranty. I shall tell you its virtue. Your
> seed shall be over every clan. There is good reason for what I
> say.'

She bade him return to his brothers with the water, and told him that
he and his race would be kings of Ireland for ever, except for Dá Thí
and Ailill Molt and one king from Munster, namely Brian Bórama. As
he had seen her, horrible at first and beautiful in the end, so also is
sovranty; for it is most often won by war and slaughter, but is glorious in the end. He was to give no water to his brothers until they
granted him seniority over them, and that he might raise his weapon

a hand's breadth above theirs. He returned with the water and exacted the promise as the maiden had taught him.

The brothers returned to Tara, and as they put up their weapons, Niall placed his a hand's breadth higher than theirs. Eochu asked tidings of them, and Niall told their story. Mongfind inquired why it was not Brian, the eldest, that spoke. They answered that they had given seniority to Niall, and the first right to the kingship. Sithchenn announced that they had forfeited it for ever, for Niall and his descendants would ever hold dominion over Ireland.

That came true, for none held the kingship of Ireland from Niall onward, save one of his children or descendants, down to Mael Schechlainn son of Domnall, except in revolt. And twenty-six kings of the Uí Néill of north and south held it, ten of the race of Conall and sixteen of the race of Eogan.

This powerful story gives us an early portrait of the Goddess of the Land, Sovereignty. She appears first as a hideous hag, but it is only in the arms of a candidate who unconditionally accepts her that she changes into her true otherworldly guise. If he cannot accept the land, with all its imperfections and internal difficulties as it really appears, he stands no chance of being a true king.

Niall needs the championship of the two seers, Torna and Sithchenn, since his mother is a Saxon captive who, as a mere concubine, has little standing at the court of Eochu Muigmedon, the King. Niall's half-brothers look to stand a far better chance of the kingship than he. Torna sponsors Niall as foster-father, bringing him to the attention of his father. From a variant text we know that it is Sithchenn, the prophet-smith, who prepares the two tests: the rescue of the forge-equipment and the boys' manhood testing in the forest alone at night.

Cairenn, Niall's mother, can be seen as the representative of Sovereignty since she is set to work as a slave at the well. Niall's righteous anger on her behalf and his desire to clothe her in the royal garments due to her status, honours the Goddess of the Land, simultaneously revealing the true ugliness of Mongfind's cruelty.

A full study of the faces of the Celtic Goddess of Sovereignty can be found in *Arthur and the Sovereignty of Britain* by Caitlín Matthews.

The Birth of Conaire[13]

The following story is taken from a long text, *The Destruction of Da Derga's Hostel*, which gives a graphic account of the *tarbh feis*, the shamanic choosing of the king and the onerous *geasa* which are placed upon him. Conaire is the grandson of the faery woman, Etain ni Etar. His otherworldly birth and tragic ending are both in the hands of the *sidhe*, the faery-kind, who bring about his conception and cause him to break his *geasa* and go to his death.

At the point when we join the story, Etain ni Etar has come from the *sidhe*, married King Eochaid Fedlech (also called Airim) and borne him a daughter, also called Etain. The second Etain is married to Cormac of Ulster.

After the end of a time Cormac, king of Ulster, 'the man of the three gifts,' forsook Eochaid's daughter, because she was barren save for one daughter that she had borne to Cormac after the making of the pottage which her mother — the woman from the fairy-mounds — gave her. Then she said to her mother: 'Bad is what thou hast given me: it will be a daughter that I shall bear.'

'That will not be good,' said her mother; 'a king's pursuit will be on her.'

Then Cormac again wedded his wife, even Etain, and this was his desire, that his own daughter should be killed. So Cormac would not leave the girl to her mother to be nursed. Then his two thralls took her to a pit, but she smiled a laughing smile at them as they were putting her into it. Then their kindly nature came to them. They carried her into the calfshed of the cowherds of Eterscel great-grandson of Iar king of Tara, and they fostered her till she became a good embroideress; and there was not in Ireland a king's daughter dearer than she.

A fenced house of wickerwork was made by the thralls for her, without any door, but only a window and a skylight. King Eterscel's folk espied that house and supposed that it was food that the cowherds kept there. But one of them went and looked through the skylight, and he saw in the house the dearest, most beautiful maiden! This was told to the king, and straightway he sent his people to wreck the house and carry her off without asking the cowherds. For the king was childless, and it had been prophesied to him by his wizards that a woman of unknown race would bear him a son. Then said the king: 'This is the woman that has been prophesied to me!'

Now while she was there next morning she saw a bird on the skylight coming to her, and he left his birdskin on the floor of the house, and went to her and captured her, and said: 'They are coming to thee from the king to wreck thy house and to bring thee to him perforce. And thou wilt be pregnant by me, and bear a son, and that son must not kill birds. And Conaire, son of Mess Buachalla shall be his name'; for hers was Mess Buachalla, 'the Cowherds' Fosterchild.'

And then she was brought to the king, and with her went her fosterers, and she was betrothed to the king, and he gave her the value of seven bondmaids and to her fosterers a like amount. And afterwards they were made chieftains, so that they all became lawworthy, whence are the two Fedlimids the stewards. And then she bore a son to the king, called Conaire son of Mess Buachalla, and these were her three urgent prayers to the king, – the nursing of her son among three households; that is, the fosterers who had nurtured her, and Mane Honeywords, and herself the third; and she said that such of the men of Erin as should wish to do aught for this boy should give securities to those three households for the boy's protection.

So thus he was reared, and the men of Erin straightway knew this boy on the day he was born. And other boys were fostered with him, to wit, Fer Le and Fer Gair and Fer Rogain, three sons of Donn Desa the champion.

Now Conaire possessed three gifts, – the gift of hearing and the gift of eyesight and the gift of judgment; and of those three gifts he taught one to each of his three foster-brothers. And whatever meal was prepared for him, the four of them would go to it. Even though three meals were prepared for him each of them would go to his meal. The same raiment and armor and color of horses had the four.

Then King Eterscel died. A bull-feast was prepared by the men of Erin in order to determine their future king; that is, a bull was killed by them and thereof one man ate his fill and drank its broth, and a spell of truth was chanted over him in his bed. Whomsoever he would see in his sleep would be king, and the sleeper would perish if he uttered a falsehood.

Four men in chariots were on the Plain of Liffey at their game, Conaire himself and his three fosterbrothers. Then his fosterers went to him and summoned him to the bull-feast. The bull-feaster, in his sleep, at the end of the night had beheld a man stark-naked, passing along the road of Tara, with a stone in his sling. 'I will go in the morning after you,' said Conaire.

He left his fosterbrothers at their game, and turned his chariot and his charioteer and fared to Dublin. There he saw great white-speckled birds, of unusual size and color and beauty. He pursued them until his horses were tired. The birds would go a spearcast before him, and would not go any farther. He alighted, took his sling out of the char- iot, and went after them until he reached the sea. The birds betook themselves to the waves. He went after them and overcame them. The birds quit their birdskins, and turned upon him with spears and swords. One of them protected him, and addressed him, saying: 'I am Nemglan, king of thy father's birds; and thou hast been forbidden to cast at birds, for here there is no one that should not be dear to thee because of his father or mother.'

'Till today,' said Conaire, 'I knew not this.'

'Go to Tara tonight,' said Nemglan; ''tis fittest for thee. A bull- feast is there, and through it thou shalt be king. A man stark-naked, who shall go at the end of the night along one of the roads of Tara, having a stone and a sling — 'tis he that shall be king.'

So Conaire fared forth naked; and on each of the four roads where- by men go to Tara there were three kings awaiting him, and they had raiment for him, since it had been foretold that he would come stark- naked. Then he was seen from the road on which his fosterers were, and they put royal raiment about him, and placed him in a chariot, and he took sureties.

The folk of Tara said to him: 'It seems to us that our bull-feast and our spell of truth are a failure, if it be only a young, beardless lad that we have visioned therein.'

'That is of no moment,' said he. 'For a young, generous king like me to be in the kingship is no disgrace, since the taking of Tara's sureties is mine by right of father and grandsire.'

'Excellent! excellent!' said the host. They set the kingship of Erin upon him. And he said: 'I will take counsel of wise men that I myself may be wise.'

He uttered all this as he had been taught by the bird-man at the sea, who had said this to him: 'Thy reign will be subject to a restric- tion, but thy bird-reign will be noble, and these shall be thy taboos:

'Thou shalt not go righthandwise round Tara and lefthandwise round Mag Breg.

'The evil-beasts of Cerna must not be hunted by thee.

'And thou shalt not go out every ninth night beyond Tara.

'Thou shalt not sleep in a house from which firelight is manifest outside after sunset, and in which light is manifest from without.

'And three Reds shall not go before thee to Red's house.

'And no rapine shall be wrought in thy reign.

'And after sunset a company of one woman or one man shall not enter the house in which thou art.'

'And thou shalt not settle the quarrel of thy two thralls.'

Now there were in Conaire's reign great bounties, to wit, seven ships in every June of every year arriving at Inver Colptha, and oak-mast up to the knees in every autumn, and plenty of fish in the rivers Bush and Boyne in June of each year, and such abundance of good-will that no one slew another in Erin during his reign. And to every one in Erin his fellow's voice seemed as sweet as the strings of lutes. From mid-spring to mid-autumn no wind disturbed a cow's tail. His reign was neither thunderous nor stormy.

Conaire's mother, Mess Buachalla, 'the cowherd's fosterchild', is saved from Cormac's cruel abandonment by kind cowherds who take her into the land of Eterscel of Tara. There, in her secret hut, she is visited by a shapeshifting otherworldly being who fathers Conaire upon her. However Eterscel believes Conaire to be his natural son.

At Eterscel's death, a *tarbh feis* is instituted to discern the true king-ly successor. At the same time as the bull-feaster is upon his shaman-ic journey, Conaire is visited by one of his otherworldly father's bird-people, Nemhglan ('The Clear Heavens'), who tells him to go stark naked to Tara with only a stone and sling in his hand. It is so that the druid bull-feaster perceives Conaire in his vision and returns to inform everyone to look for such a man.

Nemhglan returns at Conaire's inauguration to utter a series of onerous *geasa* which restrict the king's freedom. Such *geasa* were incumbent upon kings and other individuals of high destiny. They probably derive from ancient ancestral taboos and conditions negoti-ated during shamanic visions. Despite the harmonious beginning of his reign, Conaire breaks all his *geasa* in a fearful revenge engineered by the people of the *sidhe* because Conaire's grandfather has destroyed one of their mounds.

The unity of king and land is total in Celtic tradition. A fortunate and well-attuned king brings peace and prosperity. Because Eochaid violates a faery mound, unjustly imposing his earthly sovereignty upon faery sovereignty, his grandson, Conaire suffers in his place. This relationship of land and king is even further accentuated in the medieval Grail legends where, if the king is wounded, the land becomes wasteland.

The Glass Book of Kings[14]

The problem of choosing and inaugurating suitable kings was not just a Pagan one. The role of the druidic seer devolved to Christian clerics like St Columba who, in the following extract, finds himself just as entangled in tribal politics as the laymen. Columba had thrown in his lot with the Irish Dalriadan settlers in the Western Highlands. When King Conaill of Kintyre died in 574, his tribally appointed *tanaiste* or successor was Eoghan, his cousin. Columba supported him but his vision gave him another successor.

At another time, when the illustrious man was staying in Hinba island [Eilean-na Naoimh?], one night in an ecstasy of mind he saw an Angel of the Lord sent to him, who held in his hand a book of glass of the Ordination of Kings, and when the venerable man had received it from the Angel's hand, at his command he began to read it. And when he refused to ordain Aedhan as king according to the direction given to him in the book, because he loved Iogenan his brother more, the Angel, suddenly stretching forth his hand, struck the Saint with a scourge, of which the livid mark remained on his side all the days of his life, and he added these words, saying: 'Know thou for certain that I am sent to thee by God with this book of glass, that according to the words which thou hast read in it thou mayest ordain Aedhan to the kingship – and if thou art not willing to obey this command, I will strike thee again.' When, therefore, this Angel of the Lord had appeared for three successive nights, having in his hand that same book of glass, and had pressed the same commands of the Lord concerning the ordination of that king, the Saint obeyed the word of the Lord, and sailed across to the isle of Iona, and there, as he had been commanded, ordained as king Aedhan, who arrived there at that same time. And during the words of ordination he prophesied future events regarding his sons and grandsons and great-grandsons, and laying his hand upon his head, he ordained him and blessed him.

Cuimine the Fair, in the book which he wrote concerning the virtues of St Columba, thus said that St Columba began to prophesy as to Aedhan and his posterity and his kingdom, saying: 'Believe, O Aedhan, without doubt, that none of thy adversaries will be able to resist thee unless thou first do wrong to me and to those who come after me. Wherefore do thou commend it to thy sons, that they also may commend to their sons and grandsons and posterity, lest through evil counsels they lose from out their hands the sceptre of this realm.

For in whatever time they do aught against me, or against my kindred who are in Ireland, the scourge which I have endured from the Angel in thy cause shall be turned upon them, by the hand of God, to their great disgrace, and men's hearts shall be withdrawn from them and their enemies shall be greatly strengthened over them.'

Now this prophecy has been fulfilled in our times in the battle of Roth, when Domhnall Brecc, grandson of Aedhan, devastated without cause the province of Domhnall, grandson of Ainmire. And from that day to this they are in decadence through pressure from without – a thing which convulses one's breast and moves one to painful sighs.

It is seldom that shamans are called upon to wrestle with spirits in such a way. In his life, Columba is revealed to be a very human man of great pride and self-conviction. The humbling of his tribal and opinionated behaviour is to be scourged by an angel. If this hagiographical account seems overtly redolent of extreme Christian penitential practice, we have only to turn to *The Sick Bed of Cuchulainn* where we find that exactly the same fate is accorded to the great warrior, Cuchulainn, who is whipped mercilessly by two faery women until he suffers massive soul-loss. Columba is stricken for not obeying the spirit who commands him.

The glassy book of kings which he sees in his vision seems to owe more to the *liber vitreus* of *Revelations* than to any indigenous vision, but crystal is a substance which appears frequently as a medium of vision and otherworldly help in Celtic tradition. Successive cultures and beliefs may change the content of shamanic vision, but they do not change the manner or potency of the vision itself.

The portents and visions surrounding the inauguration of monarchs and leaders are enduring, seen by non-visionary people in their dreams, clearly perceived by seers: we have only to look at the portents surrounding the careers of world leaders to see the truth and clarity of this in our own times.

The Tale of the Ordeals[15]

Prophetic skills and shamanic visions are not acquired without effort, and this often takes the form of tests or trials visited upon the would-be initiate by otherworldly beings. In the text that follows, the full title of which is 'The Tale of the Ordeals. Cormac's Adventures in the Land of Promise, and the Decision as to Cormac's Sword', a number of these tests and trials are listed.

The setting is the court of Cormac mac Art, one of the most famous kings of ancient Ireland. It is here that we find the reference alluded to in 'The Colloquy of the Two Sages' (Chapter 7) to the dark speech of the poets, which only the initiated could understand. It is for this reason that we find Cormac declaring that the poets should lose their right to make judgements – presumably since the inspired utterances, acquired by shamanic trance or journey, were so obscure as to hinder the meting out of judgement.

However, the text then goes on to list the ordeals, which are clearly considered more worthy and appropriate means of arriving at the answer to questions regarding truth or falsehood. It will be noticed that in five of the examples listed a vessel of some kind is involved, and that the ordeal consists either in burning the hand or tongue, or in drinking water which has been heated in such a vessel. All of this points very directly to the idea of the cauldron as an initiatory vessel concerned with knowledge and truth. There is an aura of shamanistic and poetic activity in all of these cases, and we get a very clear indication of the close links between these two disciplines – so much so, indeed, that we might be close to the truth if we say that the bardic way was the primary expression of shamanism in the late Celtic world.

The ordeal which refers to Cormac's Cup of Truth provides an excuse to tell the story of how he came by the cup, and in so doing we have one of the most interesting accounts of an otherworldly visit and of the ability of the *sidhe* to provide their own methods of judgement.

In all, this is an important text which offers valuable insights into working of the Celtic mind.

Once upon a time, a noble illustrious king assumed sovranty and sway over Ireland: Cormac grandson of Conn was he. At the time of that king the world was full of every good thing. There were mast and fatness and seaproduce. There were peace and ease and happiness. There was neither murder nor robbery at that season, but every one [abode] in his own proper place.

Once, then, the nobles of the men of Ireland happened to be drinking the Feast of Tara with Cormac. And these are the kings who were enjoying the feast, even Fergus the Black-toothed and Eochaid Gunnat, two kings of Ulster: Dunlang son of Enna the Hero, king of Leinster: Cormac Cas, son of Ailill Bare-ear, and Fiacha Broad-crown, son of Eogan, two kings of Munster: Nia the Great, son of Lugaid Firtri, who was the son of Cormac's mother, and Aed son of Eochaid son of Conall, two kings of Connaught: Oengus Bloody-spear king of Bregia: Fera-dach son of Asal son of Conn the Champion, king of Meath.

At that time the men of Ireland used to proceed to assemblies and great meetings in this wise: every king with his royal robe around him and his golden helmet on his head, for they used to wear their kingly diadems only on a field of battle. Splendidly did Cormac enter that great meeting, for excepting Conaire son of Etarscél, or Conchobar son of Cathbad, or Oengus son of the Dagda, his like in beauty had never come. Distinguished, indeed, was Cormac's appearance in that meeting. Hair-braids slightly curled, all-golden upon him. He bore a red shield with engraving and with *míla* of gold and bow-ridges of silver. Around him was a mantle purple . . . folded. A jewelled brooch of gold on his breast. A necklace of gold round his throat. Around him was a white-hooded shirt with a red insertion. A girdle of gold with gems of precious stone over him. He wore two golden shoes of network with buckles of gold. In his hand [he carried] two golden-ringed spears with many clasps [?] of bronze. He was, moreover, shapely, fair, without blemish, without disgrace. Thou wouldst deem that a shower of pearls had been cast into his head. Thou wouldst deem that his mouth was a cluster of rowan-berries. Whiter than snow was his nobly-built body. His cheek was like a forest-*forcle* or a mountain-foxglove. Like blue-bells were his eyes: like the sheen of a dark-blue blade his eyebrows and his eyelashes.

Such then was the shape and semblance in which Cormac fared to that great meeting of the men of Erin, and they say that that convention is the noblest ever held in Erin before the Faith. For the rules and laws which were made in that meeting shall abide in Erin for ever.

The nobles of the men of Erin declared that every man should be arranged according to what was due to himself, both kings and ollaves and fools and landholders and soldiers, and every class besides. For they were sure that the arrangement made in Erin at that meeting by the men of Fodla[16] would be that which would abide therein for ever. For poets alone had judicature from the time that Amairgen Whiteknee the poet delivered the first judgment in Erin till the dialogue, in Emain Macha, of the two Sages, even Fercertne the Poet and Nede son of Adna, concerning the ollave's robe of office. Obscure to every one seemed the speech which the poets uttered in that discussion, and the legal decision which they delivered was not clear to the kings and to the (other) poets. 'These men alone', say the kings, 'have their judgement and skill and knowledge. In the first place, we do not understand what they say.' 'Well then', says Conor, 'every one shall have his share therein from today forever. But the judgment which is proper to them out of it shall not pass away[?]. Every one shall take their shares of it'. So the poets were then deprived of their judicial power save only what was proper to them; and each of the men of Erin took his share of the judicature: as there are the Judgments of Eochaid son of Luchta, and the Judgments of Fachtna son of Senchaid, and the Wrong Judgments of Carat-nia Tesctha, and the Judgments of Morann Mac main, and the Judgments of Eogan son of Durthacht, and the Judgments of Doet Nemthenn, and the Judgments of Brig Ambae, and Diancecht's Judgments concerning Leeches.

And though these had been previously [settled], the nobles of the men of Erin at that time prescribed the measure of advocacy and speech to every one in accordance with his dignity, as they are in the Bretha Nemed.

Howbeit each man again encroached on the other's profession, until that great meeting was held by Cormac. So in that great meeting they again separated the men of each art from the others; and every one of them was ordained to his own art.

The nobles of the men of Erin were requesting Cormac to ordain his proper right to every one in Tech Midchuarta. This, then, was the solution which Cormac invented, namely, to place on the fire the Five-fist Caldron which was in Tara, – it was a *coire aisicain* or *ansirc* – and to put into it swine and beeves, and to sing over it an incantation of lords and poets and wizards.

It was a caldron of this kind that used to be of old in every hostel of the royal hostels of Erin. And this is why it was called *coire aisic* 'caldron of restitution', because it used to return and to deliver to every company their suitable food.

For however long the food might be therein, until the proper company would come, it would in nowise be spoiled. Moreover, no boiled [meat] was found therein save what would supply the company, and the food proper for each would be taken thereout. It was this kind of caldron that Cormac then had at Tara.

Now each in turn was brought up to that caldron, and every one was given a fork-thrust out of it. So then his proper portion came out to each, to wit, a thigh to a king and to a poet, a chine for a literary sage, a shinbone for young lords, heads for charioteers, a haunch for queens, and every due share besides. Wherefore in that assembly his proper due fell to each.

Moreover the Twelve Ordeals were published by them. These are what they had to decide truth and falsehood. And here they are:

> Morann [Mac máin's] Three Collars:
> Mochta's Adze:
> Sencha's Lot-casting:
> The Vessel of Badurn:
> The Three Dark Stones:
> The Caldron of Truth:
> The Old Lot of Sen son of Aige:
> Luchta's Iron:
> Waiting at an Altar:
> Cormac's Cup.

Morann Mac Main's Collar

Morann son of Carpre Cat-head, of the race of the peasants was he. Carpre Cat-head assumed the kingship of Ireland, and he slew all the nobles of Ireland save three boys, namely Corp Bare-ear and Tibraite Tírech and Feradach Findfechtnach, who were carried off in their mothers' wombs, and were born in Scotland. Now Carpre, Morann's father, had a cat's snout, and every son that was born to him used to have a blemish, and so then he killed them. Carpre had a famous wife and of a noble race. She gave him this advice: to hold the Feast of Tara, and to summon to it the men of Erin in order that they might make prayer to their gods so that, may be, some profitable children might be given him. He held the Feast, and the men of Ireland were at it till the end of three months; and in each month they all used to fast and to pray a prayer to God that prosperous offspring might be born of Carpre and his wife. And that was done then, in spite of him, because he was a wicked man. So then the wife conceived, and bore a man-child, and it seemed as if he were all one hood [?] from his two shoulders upwards, and no mouth was seen in him, nor any (other) apertures. Said the queen: 'I have borne a *maen* [mute]. He is equal [?]

to thy other son. [This] is the blessing of the men of Ireland to thee
their enemy!' 'Take him,' says Carpre, to his steward, 'tomorrow to
the slough and drown him.' That night a man of the fairy-mound
appeared to the boy's mother and said to her: 'It is to the sea that the
child must be taken, and let his head be placed on the surface till nine
waves come over it. The boy will be noble: he will be king. "*Morann*"
this shall be his name' (he was *mór* 'great' and he was *find* 'fair').

The steward is summoned to her and she told him this. Then the
boy was taken to the sea and is held against the surface. When the
ninth wave came to him the membrane that surrounded his head separated and formed a collar on his two shoulders. Thereat he sang a lay
and said:

> Worship, ye mortals,
> God over the beautiful world!
>
> .   .   .   .
>
> .   .   .   .
>
> .   .   .   .   .   wherein is a festival with joyance
> with my forgiving God,
> Who formed about clouds a heavenly house.

Now the steward did not kill the boy, and he durst not take him with
him for fear of the king. So he delivered him to the king's cowherd.
He went home and declared that to the king and the queen, and [the
king] adjudged that the boy should be killed. The king said of him that
maen [treachery] would come of him, even of that boy. Wherefore he,
the son of Carpre Cennchait, is called 'Morann mac main.' A covering of gold and silver was made round that membrane, and thus it
became the 'Collar of [Morann] Mac main'. If he round whose neck it
was put were guilty, it would choke him. If, however, he were innocent, it would expand round him to the ground.

Morann Mac Main's Second Collar

Morann had another collar, namely, a circlet that he had, like a wood-
en hoop. That circlet he got from Ochamon the Fool on Síd Arfemin.[17]
For he sent him into that [fairy-mound], and thereout Ochamon
brought that little collar. He saw in the fairy-mound that it was the
thing [used] there in distinguishing between truth and falsehood. Now
that collar used to be put round the foot or the hand of the person
[whose guilt was in question], and if he were false it would close itself

round him till it cut off his foot or his hand. But if he were innocent it would not close itself round him.

Morann Mac Main's Third Collar
Then there was another *Sín Morainn* 'Collar of Morann'. Morann of the Great Judgments went to Paul the Apostle, and brought from him an epistle and wore it round his neck. So when Morann returned from Paul and went to his fortress he chanced to meet one of his bondmaids at the fortress-gate. Then when she saw the epistle round his neck she asked him: 'What collar (*sín*) is that, O Morann?' 'Truly,' says Caimmin the Fool, 'from today till doom it shall be [called] Morann's *sín*' [collar]. Now when Morann used to deliver judgment he would put the epistle round his neck, and then he would never utter falsehood.

Mochta's Adze
Namely, an adze of brass which Mochta the Wright possessed. It used to be put into a fire of blackthorn [until it was red-hot], and the tongue [of the accused] was passed over it. He who had falsehood was burnt. He who was innocent was not burnt at all.

Sencha's Lot-casting
That is, a casting of lots which Sencha son of Ailill practised. He used to cast two lots out of fire, one lot for the king and one for the accused. If the accused were guilty the lot would cleave to his palm. If, however, he were innocent, his lot would come out at once. Thus was that done: a poet's incantation was recited over them.

The Vessel of Badurn
That is, Badurn the name of a king. Now his wife went to the well, and at the well she saw two women out of the fairy-mounds, and between them was a chain of bronze. When they beheld the woman coming towards them they went under the well. So she went after them under the well, and in the fairy-mound she saw a marvellous ordeal, even a vessel of crystal. If a man should utter three false words under it, it would separate into three [parts] on his hand. If a man should utter three true words under it, it would unite again. Then Badurn's wife begged that vessel from the folk of the fairy-mound. It was given to her. So *that* was the vessel which Badurn had for distinguishing between falsehood and truth.

The Three Dark Stones

That is, a bucket was filled with bogstuff and coal and every other kind of black thing, and three stones were put into it, even a white stone and a black stone and a speckled stone. Then one would put his hand therein, and if the truth were with him, he would bring out the white stone. If he were false, he would bring out the black stone. If he were half-guilty, he would bring out the speckled.

The Caldron of Truth

That is, a vessel of silver and gold which they had to distinguish between truth and falsehood. Water was heated therein until it was boiling, and then [the accused person's] hand was dipt into it. If he were guilty the hand was scalded. But if he had no guilt no harm was done to him. For these are the three things most used by the heathen, to wit, the Caldron of Truth, and Equal Lot-casting, and Waiting at an Altar. Hence has [the practice] still grown with the Gael of casting lots out of reliquaries.

The Old Lot of Sen

That is, the lot-casting of Sen son of Aige, that is, to cast into water three lots, to wit, the lord's lot and the ollave's lot and the lot of the accused. If he, the accused, had guilt his lot would sink to the bottom. If, however, he were innocent it would come to the top.

Luchta's Iron

That is, Luchta the wizard went to study in Brittany, and there he saw a strange thing [used] for discerning truth and falsehood, namely, an iron was hallowed by the wizards, and then cast into a fire until it became red, and then it was put on the palm of the accused. Now if guilt were with him the iron used to burn him. But it did him no harm unless he were guilty. Thereafter Luchta told them that it would be needed 'for us, the men of Erin,' saith he, 'to distinguish between truth and falsehood'. Luchta afterwards brought with him his hallowed iron, and it was [used] in distinguishing between truth and falsehood. Hence then [the ordeal of] the hallowed iron is still continually practised by the Gael.

Waiting at an Altar

That is, a proof which they used at that time to distinguish between truth and falsehood, namely, Waiting at an Altar, that is, to go nine

times round the altars, and afterwards to drink water over which a
wizard's incantation had been uttered. Now if [the accused] were
guilty the token of his sin was manifest upon him. But if he were innocent [the water] would do him no harm. Now Cai Cainbrethach, – the
pupil of Fenius Farsaid, the twelfth, or the seventy-second, disciple of
the school which Fenius collected from the Greeks in order to learn
the many languages throughout the countries of the world, – it was
that Cai who brought this ordeal from the land of Israel when he came
to the Tuath Déa, and he had learned the law of Moses, and it was he
that delivered judgments in the school after it had been gathered
together from every side, and it is he that ordained the 'Judgment of
Cai.' It was that same Cai, moreover, who first ordained in Erin the
Law of the Four Tracks, for only two of the school came to Erin,
namely, Amergin White-knee the poet and Cai the judge. And Cai
remained in Erin until he had outlived nine generations, in consequence of the righteousness of his judgments, for the judgments which
he used to deliver were judgments of the Law of Moses, and therefore the judgments of the Law are very abundant in the Fénechas. They
were judgments of the Law [of Moses], then, that served for Cormac.

Cormac's Cup

Cormac's own Cup, then, was a cup of gold which he had. The way
in which it was found was thus:

One day, at dawn in Maytime, Cormac, grandson of Conn, was
alone on Múr Tea in Tara. He saw coming towards him a warrior
sedate [?], greyhaired. A purple, fringed mantle around him. A shirt
ribbed, goldthreaded next [?] his skin. Two blunt shoes of white
bronze between his feet and the earth. A branch of silver with three
golden apples on his shoulder. Delight and amusement enough it was
to listen to the music made by the branch, for men sore-wounded, or
women in child-bed, or folk in sickness would fall asleep at the melody
which was made when that branch was shaken.

The warrior saluted Cormac. Cormac saluted him.

'Whence hast thou come, O warrior?' says Cormac. 'From a land,'
he replied, 'wherein there is nought save truth, and there is neither
age nor decay nor gloom nor sadness nor envy nor jealousy nor hatred
nor haughtiness.'

'It is not so with us,' says Cormac. 'A question, O warrior: shall
we make an alliance?'

'I am well pleased to make it,' says the warrior.

Then [their] alliance was made.

'The branch to me!' says Cormac.

'I will give it,' says the warrior, 'provided the three boons which I shall ask in Tara be granted to me in return.'

'They shall be granted,' says Cormac.

Then the warrior bound [Cormac to his promise], and left the branch, and goes away; and Cormac knew not whither he had gone.

Cormac turned into the palace. The household marvelled at the branch. Cormac shook it at them, and cast them into slumber from that hour to the same time on the following day.

At the end of a year the warrior comes into his meeting and asked of Cormac the consideration for his branch. 'It shall be given', says Cormac.

'I will take [thy daughter] Ailbe today,' says the warrior.

So he took the girl with him. The women of Tara utter three loud cries after the daughter of the king of Erin. But Cormac shook the branch at them, so that he banished grief from them all and cast them into sleep.

That day month comes the warrior and takes with him Carpre Lifechair [the son of Cormac]. Weeping and sorrow ceased not in Tara after the boy, and on that night no one therein ate or slept, and they were in grief and in exceeding gloom. But Cormac shook the branch at them, and they parted from [their] sorrow.

The same warrior comes again.

'What askest thou today?' says Cormac.

'Thy wife', saith he, 'even Ethne the Longsided, daughter of Dunlang king of Leinster.'

Then he takes away the woman with him.

That thing Cormac endured not. He went after them, and every one then followed Cormac. A great mist was brought upon them in the midst of the plain of the wall. Cormac found himself on a great plain alone. There was a large fortress in the midst of the plain with a wall of bronze around it. In the fortress was a house of white silver, and it was half-thatched with the wings of white birds. A fairy host of horsemen [was] haunting the house, with lapfuls of the wings of white birds in their bosoms to thatch the house. A gust of wind would still come to it, and still the wind would carry away all of it that had been thatched.

Then he sees a man therein kindling a fire, and the thick-boled oak was cast upon it, top and butt. When the man would come again with another oak the burning of the first oak had ended.

Then he sees another fortress, vast and royal, and another wall of bronze around it. There were four houses therein. He entered the fortress. He sees the vast palace with its beams of bronze, its wattling of silver, and its thatch of the wings of white birds.

Then he sees in the garth a shining fountain, with five streams flowing out of it, and the hosts in turn a drinking its water. Nine hazels of Buan grow over the well. The purple hazels drop their nuts into the fountain, and the five salmon which are in the fountain sever them and send their husks floating down the streams. Now the sound of the falling of those streams is more melodious than any music that [men] sing.

He entered the palace. There was one couple inside awaiting him. The warrior's figure was distinguished owing to the beauty of his shape and the comeliness of his form and the wondrousness of his countenance. The girl along with him, grown-up, yellow-haired, with a golden helmet, was the loveliest of the world's women. Her feet are washed without being observed. [There was] bathing on the partition without attendance of any one, but the [heated] stones [of themselves went] into and [came] out [of the water].

Cormac bathed himself thereafter.

As they were there after the hour of none they saw a man coming to them into the house. A wood-axe in his right hand, and a log in his left hand, and a pig behind him.

''Tis time to make ready within,' says the warrior; 'because a noble guest is here.'

The man struck the pig and killed it. And he cleft his log so that he had three sets [?] of half-cleavings. The pig is cast into the caldron.

'It is time for you to turn it,' says the warrior.

'That would be useless,' says the kitchener; 'for never and never will the pig be boiled until a truth is told for each quarter of it.'

'Then', says the warrior, 'do thou tell us first.'

'One day,' says he, 'when I was going round the land, I found another man's cows on my land, and I brought them with me into a cattle-pound. The owner of the cows followed me and said that he would give me a reward for letting his cows go free. I gave him his cows. He gave me a pig and an axe and a log, the pig to be killed with the axe every night, and the log to be cleft by it, and there will [then] be enough firewood to boil the pig, and enough for the palace besides. And, moreover, the pig is alive on the morning after, and the log is whole. And from thence till today they are in that wise.'

'True, indeed, is that tale,' says the warrior.

The pig was turned [in the caldron], and only one quarter of it was found boiled.

'Let us tell another tale of truth,' say they.

'I will tell one,' says the warrior. 'Ploughing-time had come. When we desired to plough that field outside, then it was found ploughed, harrowed and sown with wheat. When we desired to reap it, then [the crop] was found stacked in the field. When we desired to draw it into that side out there, it was found in the garth all in one thatched rick. We have been eating it from then till today; but it is no whit greater nor less'.

Then the pig was turned [in the caldron], and another quarter was found to be cooked.

'It is now my turn,' says the woman. 'I have seven cows,' says she, 'and seven sheep. The milk of the seven cows is enough for the people of the Land of Promise. From the wool of the seven sheep comes all the clothing they require.'

At this story the third quarter [of the pig] was boiled.

'It is now thy turn,' they say to Cormac.

So Cormac related how his wife and his son and his daughter had been taken from him, and how he himself had pursued them until he arrived at yonder house.

So with that the whole pig was boiled.

Then they carve the pig, and his portion is placed before Cormac. 'I never eat a meal,' says Cormac, 'without fifty in my company.' The warrior sang a burden to him and put him asleep. After this he awoke and saw the fifty warriors, and his son and his wife and his daughter, along with him. Thereupon his spirit was strengthened. Then ale and food were dealt out to them, and they became happy and joyous. A cup of gold was placed in the warrior's hand. Cormac was marvelling at the cup, for the number of the forms upon it and the strangeness of its workmanship. 'There is somewhat in it still more strange,' says the warrior. 'Let three words of falsehood be spoken under it, and it will break into three: Then let three true declarations be under it, and it unites [?] again as it was before.' The warrior says under it three words of falsehood, and it breaks into three. 'It is better to utter truth there,' says the warrior, 'for sake of restoring the cup. I make my declaration, O Cormac,' saith he, 'that until today neither thy wife nor thy daughter has seen the face of a man since they were taken from thee out of Tara, and that thy son has not seen a woman's face.' The cup thereby became whole.

'Take thy family then,' says the warrior, 'and take the Cup that thou mayst have it for discerning between truth and falsehood. And thou shalt have the Branch for music and delight. And on the day that thou shalt die they all will be taken from thee. I am Manannan son of Ler,' says he, 'king of the Land of Promise; and to see the Land of Promise was the reason I brought [thee] hither. The host of horsemen which thou beheldest thatching the house are the men of art in Ireland, collecting cattle and wealth which passes away into nothing. The man whom thou sawest kindling the fire is a young lord, and out of his housekeeping he pays for everything he consumes. The fountain which thou sawest, with the five streams out of it, is the Fountain of Knowledge, and the streams are the five senses through the which knowledge is obtained [?]. And no one will have knowledge who drinketh not a draught out of the fountain itself and out of the streams. The folk of many arts are those who drink of them both.'

Now on the morrow morning, when Cormac arose, he found himself on the green of Tara, with his wife and his son and daughter, and having his Branch and his Cup. Now that was afterwards [called] 'Cormac's Cup', and it used to distinguish between truth and falsehood with the Gael. Howbeit, as had been promised him [by Manannan] it remained not after Cormac's death.

Now rules and laws and duties were ordained at that meeting, and the men of Erin's councils were determined. Three preeminent assemblies used to be held at that time, namely, the Feast of Tara on Allhallowtide — for that was the Easter of the heathen, and all the men of Erin were at that meeting, helping the king of Erin to hold it — and the Fair of Tailtiu at Lammas, and the Great Meeting of Uisnech on Mayday. Seven years lasted the preparation for the Feast of Tara, and still at the end of seven years then used to be a convention of all the men of Erin at the Feast of Tara, and there they would determine a jubilee, namely, the Rule of Seven Years from one Feast of Tara to another. And he who broke those rules was a mortal enemy and was banished from Ireland, with this exception that manslayings were permissible in these [eight] places, to wit, Sligo Midluachra, the Ford of Fer-Diad, Áth cliath, Belach Gabráin, Áth n-Ó, Cnám-choill, Conachlaid and the Two Paps of Ánu. If it were in one of these places that any man avenged his wrong no retaliation was made upon him.

Then the king of Erin appointed his soldiers over the men of Erin.

He appointed thrice fifty royal champions over them to maintain his rule and his discipline and his hunting. He gave the headship of all and the grand-stewardship of Erin to Find grandson of Baiscne.

A famous deed was also done by Cormac then, namely, the compilation of the *Saltair Cormaic*. The old men and the historians of the men of Ireland, including Fintan son of Bochra and Fithel the Poet, were gathered together; and [then] the synchronisms and the pedigrees were recorded in writing, and the careers of their kings and princes, and their battles and contests, and their antiquities, from the beginning of the world down to that time. Wherefore this, the Psalter of Tara, is a root and a foundation and a source for Erin's historians from thence to the present day.

Great, then, and not to be told was Cormac's control over Erin at that time. The hostages of Erin were in his hand. One of them was Socht son of Fithel, son of Oengus, son of Glangen, son of Sech, son of Socht, son of Fachtna, son of Senchaid, son of Ailill Cestach, son of Rudraige.

Out of the Book of Navan cecinit.

Socht had a wonderful sword, with a hilt of gold and a belt of silver: gilded was its guard, diverse-edged its point (*éo*). It shone at night like a candle. If its point (*rind*) were bent back to its hilt it would stretch [back again] like a rapier. It would sever a hair [floating] on water. It would cut off a hair on [a man's] head, and without touching the skin. It would make two halves of a man, and for a long time one half would not hear or perceive what had befallen the other. Socht said that it was the Hard-headed *Steeling*, Cúchulainn's sword. They held this sword to be a tribal bequest [?] both of fathers and grand fathers.

At that time there was a famous steward in Tara, even Dubdrenn son of Urgriu. The steward asked Socht to sell him the sword, and told him that he should have a ration of the same meal as he [Dubdrenn] had every night, and that his family should have, every day, four men's food in sub-payment for the sword, and the full value thereof, at his own award, after that. 'No,' says Socht; 'I am not competent to sell my father's treasures while he is alive.'

For a long time they went on thus, Dubdrenn seeking and thinking about the sword. Once upon a time he brought Socht to a special drinking-bout. Then Dubdrenn begged the cupbearer to press wine and mead upon Socht until he became drunk. Thus was it done, so that Socht knew not where he was, and so he fell asleep.

Then the steward takes the sword and went to the king's brazier, Connu.

'Art thou able,' says Dubdrenn, 'to open the hilt of this sword?'

'Yea, I am able,' says the brazier.

Then the brazier sundered the sword, and in the hilt he wrote the steward's name, even Dubdrenn, and set the sword again [by Socht] as it was before.

So things remained for three months after, and the steward kept on asking for the sword, and he could not [get it] from Socht. At last the steward sued for the sword, and fulfilled all the requirements of the suit, and declared that the sword was his own, and that it had been taken from him. Then Socht pleaded that he himself had a prescriptive title to the sword and its trappings [?] and ornament, and, moreover, that he had an equitable right to it.

Socht went to consult Fithel and to request him to take part in that action, and to bring his father to defend [his claim to] the sword. 'No,' says Fithel: 'act for thyself in thy causes. It is not I who will ever arbitrate for thee, for greatly dost thou put thyself and take thyself [?] in thy causes; and [it is] not to say truth without falsehood. Falsehood is opposed in falsehood . . .'

The right is done, and Socht is allowed to prove that the sword is his, and Socht gives the oath that the sword was a family treasure of his, and that it belonged to him.

Said the steward. 'Well, in sooth, O Cormac: yon oath that Socht has uttered is perjurous.'

'What proof hast thou', says Cormac, 'that the oath is false?'

'Not hard to say,' quoth the steward. 'If the sword is mine, my name stands written therein, covered up and concealed in the hilt of the sword.'

Socht is summoned to Cormac, who told him what had been said. 'It will be a short story till this is known,' says Cormac. 'Let the brazier be summoned to us,' quoth he. The brazier comes, and breaks open the hilt, and the steward's name was found written therein. Then a dead thing testified against a living, value being ascribed [?] to the writing.

Said Socht: 'hear ye this, O men of Erin, and Cormac with you! I acknowledge that this man is the owner of the sword. The property therein, together with its liabilities, passes from me to thee.'

'I acknowledge,' says the steward, 'property therein, together with its liabilities, passes from me to thee.'

Then said Socht: 'This is the sword that was found in my grandfather's neck, and till today I never knew who had done that deed. And do thou, O Cormac, pass judgment thereon.'

'Thy liability,' says Cormac [to the steward], 'is greater than [the value of] this [sword].'

Then seven *cumals* are adjudged by Cormac [as compensation for the slaying of Socht's grandfather], and also restitution of the sword.

'I confess', says the steward, 'the story of the sword.' And then he relates the whole tale of it in order, and the brazier tells the same tale concerning the sword. Cormac then levied seven *cumals* from the steward, and other seven from the brazier. Said Cormac: '*Mainech* etc. This is true', says Cormac: 'yon is Cúchulainn's sword, and by it my grandfather was slain, even Conn the Hundred-battled, by the hand of Tibraite Tírech, king of Ulaid, of whom was said

> With a host over valiant bands
> Well did he go to Connaught.
> Alas that he saw Conn's blood
> On the side of Cúchulainn's sword!'

With that they, even Cormac and Fithel, decided the case, and it was Cormac that ensnared [Socht], and Cormac obtains by [his] decision the sword as a wergild for Conn. Now neither battle nor combat was ever gained against that sword and against him who held it in his hand. And it is the third best treasure that was in Erin, namely [first], Cormac's Cup, and [secondly] his Branch, and [thirdly] his Sword.

So that tale is the tale of the Ordeals, and of Cormac's Adventures in the Land of Promise, and of Cormac's Sword.

The wise declare that whenever any strange apparition was revealed of old to the royal lords, – as the ghost appeared to Conn, and as the Land of Promise was shown to Cormac, – it was a divine ministration that used to come in that wise, and not a demoniacal ministration. Angels, moreover, would come and help them, for they followed Natural Truth, and they served the commandment of the Law. It was a divine ministration, moreover, that freed the men of Erin at Uisnech from the Great Bardic Company, without leaving it to them.

CHAPTER 9

Healing and Soul-Restoration

Healing plays a major part in shamanic work. In this chapter we consider the healing of body and soul, drawing on a wide variety of scattered sources in order to build up a substantial background of lore for further consultation.

We may classify healing methods into five categories, some of which have both physical and shamanic possibilities:

1. The patient is given to eat or drink (herbs, medicines, foods, potions etc.).
2. Something is put into or taken out of the body (surgery, shamanic extraction or retrieval).
3. The frame of the body is manipulated or given external aids (bone-setting, exercise, prosthetics, etc.).
4. Outside forces are brought to bear upon the body (water, steam, music, X-rays, spiritual healing).
5. The body is influenced by the mind or spirit and thus healed (psychotherapy, prayer, spiritual healing).

The last category is dealt with in the second essay in this chapter and the others are covered in the first. Neither attempts to give a full or exhaustive coverage of healing methods, but concentrates on the specific areas of evidence which provide shamanic information.

Healing Among the Celts: The Children of Airmed

by Caitlín Matthews

Humankind's attempt to find wholeness and harmony underlies all methods of healing. Yet sometimes that wholeness itself is fragmented, as we find in modern Western notions of health, which have concentrated predominantly upon healing the physical frame, neglecting the emotional and spiritual correlations of illness. Among indigenous peoples past and present, the complete interrelationship of body and spirit is universally understood, and is formally recognized in the healing methods used: physical treatment is accompanied by prayers and invocations, diagnosis is aided, in the case of shamanic practitioners, by vision journeys to ask for spiritual help and to find applicable cures.

Not all illnesses among the Celts were treated shamanically, of course, although a consciousness of the spiritual cause of illness and a willingness to interact with otherworldly help seem to be the hallmarks of the Celtic healer. It is said of the Ulster physician Fingen, for instance: 'Now such was his skill that by the vapours that arose from a house he could tell how many were ill in that house, and with what disease they were afflicted'.[1]

Who was responsible for the healing process? Between the early centuries AD and the Middle Ages, the craft of physician and surgeon was a hereditary and professional one. Although male physicians predominated, we have historical accounts of female practitioners, both professional and non-professional. Practical and theoretical training were recognized by qualification and legal privileges. Apart from the professional doctors, there were also unqualified, though not unskilful, healers or leeches who performed minor cures.

The physician had a *lés* or medicine bag in which local treatments, salves and potions would have been carried. There are accounts in *Táin bo Cuailgne* of how the doctors came out at the end of each day's engagement to tend the wounded with their *lésa*. We know that doctors used herbs, cautery, trephination, cupping and probing, Caesarean delivery and a variety of other methods both familiar and forgotten. Unqualified healers relied heavily upon herb-lore, bloodletting and spellcraft, leaving surgical operations to professionals, since the legal redress against them might be severe.

The Brehon law was clear about the healing process. The patient's family was responsible for paying the board and keep of the doctor in attendance, but if the cure was not successful, then the doctor reimbursed the family. Similarly, if after the prescribed 'testing time', a wound or injury did not heal satisfactorily (a head fracture, for example, was considered to be healed by three years), then the doctor was liable to pay for the injury as if he himself had caused it. This principle of 'no cure, no payment' seems to have obtained in Ireland, at least. We have far less information on early healing in other Celtic countries.

There is provision in Brehon law for hospitals, supported by local tribes. Patients with the means paid for their keep and treatment; those who could not were accorded charitable status and injured parties were maintained by their assailants. The hospital or *forus tuaithe* ('territorial house') was regulated by enlightened means: cleanliness and good ventilation were maintained by four open doors, with a channel of water running through the middle of the floor.[2]

The work of unprofessional healers maintained health at local levels in remote areas, supplementing herb-craft and cures with fairy blessings and healing spells which were handed down to their children. It is these skills which have survived best down to our own times.

Physicians attended to bodily ailments, but were not slow to call in collegial help from the druidic classes as, later, they would call in the clergy. Myriad forms of soul-sickness were considered to be the natural province of the gifted ones, whose skills in divination, augury and spirit-lore were frequently brought to bear upon a problem, as we shall see in the next essay.

The Healing Divinities

Various Celtic deities are associated with healing. Brighid is patroness of healing, smithcraft and poetry. Goibniu, the smith, is understood to have magical healing powers. Diancecht and his family are accorded the status of supreme physicians and surgeons, healers of contagion, disease and injury, while Aengus mac Og appears in the supreme role as a healer of souls. Specific local deities appear in a variety of healing roles throughout the Celtic world, wherever the spirits of nature are divinized by virtue of their healing properties.

In West Munster, the life spark was believed to be governed by the goddess Aine. She has been identified with Anu, the great mother ancestor of the Danann gods. Her cult is localized to County Limerick, where, at Cnoc Aine (Aine's Hill) she was still worshipped in the last century upon Midsummer's Eve when local people carried torches of hay and straw. After invoking Aine na gClair (Aine of the Wisps), they would return to their fields and wave the torches over the crops and livestock. Among herbalists and folk-healers, Aine was held to be responsible for the vital spark of life which they understood traversed the entire body every twenty-four hours. No blood-letting was undertaken on days associated with Aine (the Friday, Saturday and Sunday before Lughnasadh Day were sacred to her) as it was believed that the vital spark would flow away and leave the patient dead.[3]

Anu is the source-mother of the gods, a figure so ancient that she is the womb of life, the high one herself. In her more approachable shape of Aine, she offers us fresh insight into the nature of our life: we find her name means 'delight, pleasure, agility, melody'; she is the sparkle and vitality of life itself. Her sister, Grian, is Goddess of the Sun, the vitality of the day itself. Aine herself is the seed of the sun which inhabits our veins, making its own circuit through our blood, even as the sun takes her own diurnal circuit through the heavens. Notions of a female sun and a male moon are common in north-western Europe, perhaps indicating a more primal understanding of solar and lunar influences.

The healing branch of the Tuatha de Danann comprises Diancecht and his family. We hear about them in the 'Second Battle of Mag Tuiread', where the king, Nuadu, has lost his hand in battle – a terrible blemish, possibly disqualifying him from the kingship. Diancecht and his son Miach go to work in this original case of Celtic prosthetics which simultaneously throws up the first instance of professional medical etiquette.

> Now Nuadu was in his sickness, and Diancecht put on him a hand of silver with the motion of every hand therein. That seemed evil to his son Miach. Miach went to the hand which had been replaced by Diancecht, and he said, 'Joint to joint of it and sinew to sinew,' and he healed Nuadu in thrice three days and nights. The first seventy-two hours he put it against his side, and it became covered with skin. The second seventy-two hours he put it on his breast . . . That cure seemed evil to Diancecht. He flung a sword on the crown of his son's head and cut the skin down to the flesh. The lad healed the wound by means of his skill. Diancecht smote him again and cut the flesh till he reached the bone. The lad healed this by the same means. He struck him a third blow and came to the membrane of his brain. The lad healed this also by the same means. Then he struck the fourth blow and cut out the brain, so that Miach died, and Diancecht said that the leech himself could not heal him of that blow.
>
> Thereafter Miach was buried by Diancecht, and herbs three

hundred and sixty-five, according to the number of joints and
sinews, grew through the grave. Then Airmed opened her
mantle and separated those herbs according to their properties.
But Diancecht came to her, and he confused the herbs, so that
no one knows their proper cures unless the Holy Spirit should
teach them afterwards. And Diancecht said, 'If Miach be not,
Airmed shall remain.'[4]

It was widely believed that the body had 365 joints, sinews and members – information that is recorded in the eighth-century religious
tract *Na Arrada*. We see that Miach knows the traditional chant for
healing sprains, an example of which is given below.

An alternative version of the story is given in the story of the Fate
of the Children of Tuirenn, where we learn of the watchman of Tara,
a youth with only one eye. Two doctors come to Tara and offer to put
the eye of a cat in place of his lost eye. 'This turned out to be a convenience and an inconvenience for him: for when he wished to sleep or
take rest, then the eye would start at the squeaking of the mice and
the flying of the birds, and the motion of the rushes; and when he
wished to watch a host or an assembly, it was then it was surely in
deep repose and sleep with him.'

Their reputation comes to the attention of Nuadu the King, who
invites them in. The doctors, called Miach and Ormiach, treat the
King's arm, expelling a chafer beetle from it. Miach makes a new
arm, but the Tuatha de Danann prefer an arm of flesh and the only
one the right length is that of Modan the swineherd (whose occupation makes him unclean and thus an unsuitable candidate). The
people suggested that the bones of Nuadu's own arm might be better
employed in any healing. Miach asks Ormiach, 'Do you wish to set
the arm, or to go to bring herbs for the purpose of putting flesh upon
it?' Ormiach prefers to set the arm, and Miach goes for the herbs.

While Ormiach favours a straight medical solution, it is Miach
who prefers the magical and somewhat Frankinstein-esque remedy of
regrowing the flesh with herbal means. In both these stories, Miach
virtually incubates the dead hand, in one against his own flesh and
in the other by the application of herbs.

Sometimes deities themselves find healing at mortal hands. It is
one of the features of the hero Cuchulainn's powers that only he can
heal those whom he has wounded. Having refused the patronage and
love of the goddess Morrighan, Cuchulainn finds himself forced to
fight with her. He wounds her three times and she retires, but that is
not the end of the business:

In the counterfeit presentment of an old crone, Ernmas's daughter, the Morrigu, came and appeared as milking a cow of three teats. The aim of her coming thus being that of Cuchullin she should have relief; for of all such as at any time he might have hurt, save and except that in the curing of them also he had a hand, none might recover and live. He then with thirst being in extremity, craved of her a drink and she gave him such measure as one teat yielded. 'May this be to the giver's profit,' he said, and the Morrigu's injured eye was whole. He begged the yield of another teat; she let him have it, and he pronounced a blessing on that bestowed it. Yet again he begged a draught, and she gave him the third teat. 'The full blessing of both *dée and an-dée* be upon it!' he said. Now the people of power at that time they rated as *dée* and the people of ploughing as *an-dée*. The end of the matter was that hereby the Morrigu was healed completely.[5]

We note that Cuchulainn heals the Morrigan by means of three blessings in exchange for three draughts of milk. The final blessing mentions the *dé* and the *an-dée* – 'the gods and the not-gods'. This curious expression is glossed in *Coir Anmann* as follows: 'the *dé* were the poets and the *an-dée* were the husbandmen . . . These were the gods, the magicians.'[6] This perhaps gives us some notion of the regard in which the druidic classes were held.

Here Cuchulainn merely gives a blessing, revealing to us the power of the word in Celtic tradition. In an oral society, the power of the word was supreme. The *filidh* accessed a great power through their study of poetic form, memorizing many treatises, stories, poems, ancestral and judicial lore etc. The utterance of the first word on a subject, whether it be about a legal precedent or a newly born child, was considered to be significant and binding. When Rhiannon's lost son is restored to her, having been raised by foster-parents under the name of Gwri Gwallt Euryon (Gwri of the Golden Hair), she cries out, 'At last my anxiety (*pryder*) is over!' Pendaran Dyfed, an elderly family member, advises that the boy should be named Pryderi. When Rhiannon rejects this suggestion, Pryderi's father equitably replies, 'It is more fitting for the boy to take his name from the words his mother first uttered when she had good news of him.'[7]

'The king's truth' was the supreme law which every ruler had to uphold, or prove forsworn of his inaugural oath. The word of the druidic classes was considered to be even more binding, which is why it was desirable that only people of great probity became judges, prophets or *filidh*, since they could wreak havoc. The power of the poet's satire could bring not only public shame after the fashion of today's media-hounding, but could raise blisters on the person satirized. By the sixth century, there was much disquiet about the power of poets to demand high fees of patrons and to behave as though they owned the world; this was mixed with a good measure of fearful respect. The council of Druim Ceat (AD 575) was partly convened to curb the influence of the poets and restrict their god-like power.

The power of the word to bless or curse was due not to the form of words used, but to the intention behind it. It is thus that the continuity of the word in Celtic society is retained to this day. In Ireland, on entering a house, it is still usual to call a blessing upon all within it, or to pass on implements to a fellow worker with a blessing on the work being done. The chain of good health and harmony is thus forged for the good of all, creating a circuit of blessing as vital as the life-seed of Aine circulating in our veins.

Charms and Remedies of the Celtic Christian World

Most of the material under consideration was transcribed in the Celtic Christian era by clerics. Whatever the religious differences between converts to Christianity and their Pagan fellows, the tribal tradition was a conservative one, not given to vast changes from ancestral precedent: by and large historical events and stories were faithfully transcribed as orally related. The overlap between one tradition and the other is perhaps most strongly marked in the area of health. Whenever one religious tradition supersedes another, there will always be a pooling of helpful spirits: gods of new and old alike will be invoked.

Ever seeking out ways to weave together the indigenous tradition with Christianity, clerics capitalized on the most enduringly popular stories in the search for local Christian heroes. One such incident comes in 'The Cattle Raid of Cooley', where Conchobor mac Nessa is felled by a sling-shot ball made out of Mesgegra's brains. Fingen, the physician, is sent for:

> 'Well,' said Fingen, 'if the ball be extracted from thy head, thou wilt die at once. But if thou suffer it to remain, I can restore thee to health, only thou wilt retain the blemish of it.' . . . [Conchobor's] head was then healed, and it was stitched with a thread of gold, because Conchobor had golden hair. And the physician warned the king to be cautious and not to allow himself to be roused to anger or to passion, nor to ride henceforth on horseback, not to run.[8]

Injuries to the head, then as now, constituted a severe threat to life and, to the Celtic mind, to the soul. The eminently sensible advice offered by Fingen is overset by a significant event. Conchobor lives a restricted life until one day nature itself is wracked by a series of convulsions: his druids tell him that these events signal the distant crucifixion of a man born on the same night as the King himself. In a quixotic attempt to defend the King of Heaven, King Conchobor rushes into a copse, hacking at the trees until his frenzy causes the slingshot to start out of his head, and his brains to come away. Here the Celtic sense of injustice is invoked as Conchobor attempts to defend one whom he can only understand as a fellow nobleman, beset by foes and ignominiously nailed up to die without retinue. His soul literally 'rushes to his head', causing a fatal rupture of the wound.

Protection of the head was still a preoccupation with the Irish cleric who wrote down the following charm against headache in the eighth century in the monastery of St Gall:

Caput Christi	the head of Christ
Oculus Isaiae	the eyes of Isaiah
Frons nassium Noe	the forehead and nose of Noah
Labia lingua Salomonis	the lips and tongue of Solomon
Collum Temathei	the neck of Timothy
Mens Beniamin	the mind of Benjamin
Pectus Pauli	the heart of Paul
Iunctus Iohannis	the understanding of John
Fides Abrache Sanctus	the faith of holy Abraham.
Sanctus, Sanctus	Holy, holy,
Dominus Deus Sabaoth	Lord God of Hosts.

(After you have sung this, spit into your palm and smear it round both temples and occiput, then sing *paternoster* thrice and sign yourself on the crown of the head with a cross, and then make this sign on your head: U.) (Author's translation)

This charm combines a pseudo-liturgical litany of spiritual help with the prophylactic qualities of spittle. The double signing of the head, both with a cross and a horn-like symbol on the forehead shows how old and new traditions were conservatively combined – just in case! This litany of protection may have been derived from earlier usage, invoking other spirits; repetitive and cumulative charms abound in Celtic lore.

Modern Irish folk medicine has preserved the 'measuring of the head' to remove headaches. Healers take a cord around the forehead with the ends crossing at the back of the head. The ends are then brought forward, crossed under the chin and brought up over the cheeks to the crown of the head. All the while, the healer diagnoses the plates of the skull and presses upon those that need pressure, almost in the manner of a cranial osteopath.[9] The recitation of a charm similar to the one above may accompany this skill, which is only passed down to family members.

A charm for the removal of a thorn is found in another extract from the St Gall MS. Interestingly it mentions both Christ and Goibniu:

> Nothing is higher than heaven,
> Nothing is deeper than the sea.
> By the words Christ uttered from the Cross,
> Remove this thorn from me.
> More sharp is Goibniu's wisdom,
> May Goibniu's spear be far removed!

> (Lay this charm in butter and keep it from water. Smear some all round the thorn, but not on the point or the wound. If there is no thorn in actuality, then one of the two front teeth will be lost.) (Author's translation).

This charm seems to associate two sets of mystical symbolism: the spear which Longinus thrusts into Christ's side causes a flow of blood and water to gush forth, 'the river of life' by which salvation is effected. Similarly, Goibniu is wounded while making spears that cannot miss; Ruadan, a Fomorian spy, takes one and casts at Goibniu, who slays his assailant and makes his way to the miraculous well of Slane which makes all wounds whole.

Another charm from the same MS vaunts itself as a specific against various ailments and refers to Diancecht; although a salve is mentioned here, there is no clue as to its composition, indicating perhaps that it was so well known as to need no explanation:

> I save the nearly dead. Against burping, hiccups, against sudden tumour, against haemorrhage caused by iron, against fire's burns, against wounding, against gorging like a dog, against withering: three nuts that bind, three sinews that weave.

> I strike down disease, I vanquish blood-flow — let it not be a chronic tumour!

Wholeness be upon the place where Diancecht's salve is smoothed! I put my trust in the salve which Diancecht bequested to his family, that it brings wholeness wherever it is applied.

(Recite this while your palms are full of water when washing, and then put it [the water or the written charm?] into your mouth, inserting the two fingers next to the little finger into your mouth, each held apart.) (Author's translation.)

These instructions are confused, but they remind us of Fionn's way of putting his thumb under his tooth to obtain wisdom. The insertion of the fingers as stated produces a channel for spirit entry or egress. Both charms are early examples of Christianized folk-medicine invocations.

We can compare the magical application of spittle as witnessed in this Pagan Irish charm for healing wounds caused in battle, animal bites or poison:

The poison of a serpent,
the venom of a dog,
the sharpness of the spear
does no good to man.
The blood of one dog,
the blood of many dogs,
the blood of the hound of Fliethas —
these I invoke.
It is not a wart to which my spittle is applied.
I strike disease,
I strike wounds,
I strike the disease of the dog that bites,
of the thorn that wounds,
of the iron that strikes.
I invoke the three daughters of Fliethas against the serpent.
Benediction on this body to be healed;
benediction on the spittle;
benediction on him who casts out the disease.[10]

The daughters of the goddess Flidias, protector of beasts, is pertinently invoked to combat the dangers of the hunt in this charm. She who is the protagonist of the *Tain bo Flidias*, drives a deer-harnessed chariot and milks wild does for her offspring. The pre-historic and Ice Age memory of reindeer herding lingers in the remote goddesses of Celtic tradition for both Flidias and the Cailleach Beare are associated with the skills still practised by the Saami peoples of Lapland. Neither goddess enjoyed a healthy reputation among Celtic Christians as both the Cailleach and Flidias are possessed of inordinate sexual capacity. We note that in this charm, as in the Christian charm against the thorn, it is the ancient deities who are invoked against venom and infection.

Some ills have no physical cure. In these cases, the practice of pilgrimage to a sacred site, whether a saint's tomb or a natural land feature with healing properties, is the common recourse. The physical effort involved in a pilgrimage is matched by the spiritual motivation: for someone who is severely ill, a pilgrimage carries its own special healing grace. From modern Celtic practices at pilgrimage sites we see that, on arrival at the site, it is usual to make a *turas* or circuit, always sunwise, around the well, stone or tomb, saying prayers or invocations. Nowadays, in Catholic areas, decades of the rosary are said at the stations or prescribed locations at a site.

It is still common practice to tie a rag or clootie upon a tree or bush near the site, as a token of one's petition for healing. It is believed that as the cloth fades and withers, so will the illness in question. In Ireland the tying of the rag is accompanied by the words '*Air impidhe an Tigherna mo chuid tinneas do fhagaim am an air so*' – 'By the intercession of the Lord, I leave my portion of illness in this place.'[11] Other objects are frequently left, usually whatever is in the petitioner's pockets: these offerings are not stolen or moved, since the thief might also bear away the malady.

The sanctity and efficacy of these sites is respected still, as I saw when I visited Sancreed Well in Cornwall in 1993. The thorn tree above the well-head was covered with clooties of cloth and paper, the shelves inside the well-head were adorned with flowers and candles, and pilgrims from other countries were visiting it, despite the difficulty of access. It is but one of many healing sites which survive in full usage until today.

The Healing Waters

The primacy of water in Celtic tradition is attested in the preponderance of healing springs and wells. Wherever springs emerge, Anu, the great mother of gods, is venerated and acknowledged under a variety of titles. While the two most common dedications for wells in Britain and Ireland are Bridewell and St Anne's Well, remembering Anu and Brighid, the continued veneration of water has passed into the guardianship of the saints, many of whom are Christianized deities and spirits.

Some wells and springs had powers to cure infertility while others cured specific illnesses of parts of the body. A rare account of the fertility rites performed at an Aberdeenshire well in the last century is given by one who, as a boy, naughtily hid in the bushes to watch a woman's ritual:

> Three barren women and the auld wife came into the hollow
> . . . The auld wife went doun on her knees on the flat stone at
> the side of the spring and directed the women . . . They took
> off their boots, their hose, and syne they rolled up their skirts
> and petticoats till their wames [abdomens] were bare. The auld
> wife gave them the sign to step round her and one after the
> other, wi' the sun, round the spring, each one holding up her
> coats like she was holding herself to the sun. As each one came
> anent her, the auld wife took up the water in her hands and
> threw it on their wames . . . Three times round they went . . .
> Then they dropped their coats to the feet again, syne they
> opened their dress frae the neck and slipped it off their shoul-
> ders so that their paps sprang out. The auld wife gave them
> another sign. They doun on their knees afore her, across the
> spring; and she took up the water in her hands again, skirpit
> [sprinkled] on their paps, three times the three.[12]

The mystic ninefold anointing is the *toradh* or fruitfulness of Anu which descends to her daughters wherever the holy healing waters well up.

In 'The Second Battle of Mag Tuiread', while the earthly warriors are readying their weapons and druidic warriors their magical skills, the healers set to work to put 'fire into the warriors who were slain'. Diancecht, with his sons Octriuil and Miach, and his daughter Airmed, sing spells over the well of Slane. 'Now their mortally wound-ed men were cast into it as soon as they were slain. They were alive when they came out. Their mortally wounded became whole through the might of the incantation of the four leeches who were about the well.' Shortly after Goibniu has been healed in the well, the Fomorians conspire together and cast stones into the well so that it becomes a cairn instead. The well is also named Loch Luibe, because Diancecht put every herb in Ireland into the well. [13]

This is reminiscent of the Cauldron of Rebirth which is brought from a lake in Ireland by Llassar Llaes Gyfnewidd and Cymeidu Cymeinfoll, and which is given back by Bran of Britain to Matholwch of Ireland in recompense for an insult. The tradition of the life-restoring vessel continues into medieval lore in the shape of the Holy Grail. But whether a cup or a cauldron is employed, the essential healing element is the liquid which is contained by the vessel.

The heating of an iron house to destroy enemies within is a frequent feature of Celtic stories; like an inverted cauldron, such a structure is said to destroy otherworldly invaders and mortal foes alike in the tales of 'Branwen, Ferch Llyr' and 'the Intoxication of the Ulstermen'. But the heating of a house to bring healing rather than destruction was a major feature of Celtic healing.

The use of the *teach an alais* or sweat-house has not survived past the nineteenth century but was once widespread in Ireland and probably in other parts of the Celtic world. Remains of beehive huts made of dry-stone walls covered in clay and turf were still visible and their use still remembered when Wood-Martin wrote in 1902. The sweat-house was used primarily for relieving the effects of rheumatism or other diseases, and for purification from infection. Many had stone seats within which were covered with straw or grassy sods upon which the subject sat or lay. The house was heated by a variety of means, by igniting a peat fire in the hut's centre and clearing the ashes before entry. In County Monaghan, people remembered how hot bricks were heated in a fire then carried into the house in a creel in which herbs had been placed, especially when inhalation was a part of the cure. Folk memory tells of how children may be bathed in a bath of lusmore or fairy-thimble (also known as foxglove or *digitalis purpurea*) if they seem to suffer a wasting sickness due to being overlooked by the faeries.

A sweat-house in County Tyrone had a small opening in the roof and a low doorway; both were covered by flag-stones when the subjects were inside. A contemporary account tells us:

> When men used it as many as six or eight stripped off and went in, when all openings were closed except what afforded a little ventilation. A person remained outside to attend to these matters. When they could suffer the heat no longer, the flag was removed, and they came out and plunged in a pool of water within a yard or two of the sweat-house, where they washed, got well-rubbed and put on their clothes. In case of women, they put on a bathing dress whilst using the bath, and generally omitted the plunge. . . . The constructor was a cooper. He once came to me on crutches, having contracted rheumatism from lying on a damp bed. After four sweats he was quite well again, and continued so until his death.[14]

Having been often asked about 'Celtic sweat-lodges' by those who like to find similarities or parallels with Native American traditions, I can only proffer the above information. No details of accompanying spiritual practices have survived to my knowledge. The prevalence of sweat-houses and their association with the Celts may be indicated by Professor H. Hennessy's experience in Prague and Nuremburg in 1879 where he encountered 'turkish baths' under the local name of *Römische-Irische bader*, 'Roman-Irish baths'.

Sweat-houses were frequently sited near springs or rivers. The only natural hot-water springs in Britain, at Bath, were held by the Celts in the highest esteem and the site was dedicated to Sul, the Goddess of the Sun's Eye. When the Romans conquered Britain, they concurred with this view and built over the native shrine a temple complex dedicated to Sulis-Minerva, fusing the native goddess with their own one.

Spas and mineral springs enjoy periods of popularity, sometimes becoming fashionable watering places like Bath in the eighteenth century, but it is not simply a question of fads. People are always drawn to the healing properties of water. Whether they seek saline waters for inflammatory and congestive disorders, or red chalybeate waters with their tonic and restorative powers, or sulphur waters for skin complaints, rheumatism and arthritis, water has the power to heal and our Celtic ancestors knew it. The many healing wells which are still in use in Britain and Ireland are testimony to its properties, and they are places of pilgrimage and prayer, true fountainheads of healing. They remain places where individuals go on pilgrimage, seeking as much for the well at world's end or the vessel of the Grail as for the health of their bodies.

Animal Healing

For the Celts, animals were their wealth and any sickness among them was treated immediately. A fund of animal-healing lore exists. It is outside the scope of this book, but I give two examples to demonstrate how shamanic healing methods were used.

For sprains, in people or animals, the practitioner placed a woollen thread with nine knots in it (the *snaithnean*) into his or her mouth while reciting an invocation such as the following Scots Gaelic charm:

> Bride went out
> One morning early
> With a pair of horses:
> One broke his leg,

With great pain,
It was torn asunder:
She put bone to bone,
She put flesh to flesh,
She put sinew to sinew,
She put vein to vein;
As she healed him
May I heal this.
          (Author's translation)

The thread is then placed about the beast's tail. If the beast is to recover, the practitioner of the charm herself begins to feel ill.[15] The *snaithnean* is also used, with other words, against the evil eye. Variant sprain charms call also upon Christ and Odin throughout Scotland, depending on the nature of the Christian or Scandinavian influence on the locality.

Curative talismans were commonly employed to ward off disease in animals. The famous Connoch or Murrain Caterpillar Charm found at Timoleague Abbey in County Cork is the form of a caterpillar cast in silver with a series of amber and azure-coloured crystals embedded into it. It resembles the larvae of a hawk-moth (*genus Sphingidae*), which is common in Ireland. All caterpillars seem to have been regarded as particularly pernicious and causers of cattle murrain and were summarily killed if seen. The healer would place this silver talisman into a drinking trough and encourage the afflicted beast to drink. The use of helping spirit animals in healing is common in shamanic work. Taking the evidence of extant Celtic charms, there seems to have been a genuine revulsion against serpents, beetles and insects in general. It is thus all the more amazing that the Connoch talisman should have been employed as a helper.

Such Celtic agricultural lore may survive in pockets wherever traditional farming methods are practised. The special watering places with healing properties are still visited by anxious stockmen from the Fountain of Barenton in the forests of Broceliande in Brittany, to the remote springs and wells of Ireland and Scotland.

The Heritage of the Healers

After the breakdown of classical Irish society from the twelfth century onwards, the practices which have been described here also waned. Professional doctors increasingly incorporated a wider spectrum of European medical practice during the Middle Ages. The Brehon laws, which had supported tribal provision for the sick and a series of compassionate strictures designed to protect the patient's rights, gradually broke down as a Norman judiciary was imposed upon Irish society, primarily protecting the strong and privileged and penalizing the disenfranchized native. Medieval monastic hospitals and hostels were maintained only until the Reformation, at which point health provision severely declined. During this dark period it was the experienced healers and their descendants who continued to practise their skills.

Armed with a battery of herbal lore, faery wisdom and apocryphal Christian blessings, the healer was often the last bastion of protection from illness. Wood-Martin gives a portrait of a nineteenth-century herb doctor or wise woman:

> Over her cabin door a horse-shoe is nailed for luck. Beneath the salt-box is a bottle of holy water to keep the place purified and to ward off crickets (the supposed harbingers of bad luck.) A bunch of fairy flax lies on the top of the salt box; sown into the folds of the wise woman's scapular is a four-leafed shamrock, an invaluable specific for rendering fairies visible to the human eye. Over the door, beds and over the cattle in the byre hang branches of withered yew, and when the cows calve the wise woman ties a red woolen thread about their tails to protect them from being either over looked or elfshot by the fairies.

To such as her, desperate families would appeal for healing. Her stock-in-trade were the simples and decoctions familiar to modern herbalists and to our own grandmothers, who had few patent medicines to call upon.

Several Irish families retain their hereditary reputation for healing, including the *Icidhe* or the O'Hickeys, whose family were physicians to the O'Briens of Thomond, and the O'Shiels, doctors to the MacMahons of Oriel. The family of the Lees were traditionally doctors and physicians. In the late seventeenth century, Muirchetach O Laoi was taken by the faeries to an otherworldly island off Galway where he obtained a book of healing lore which is still preserved today in the Royal Irish Academy of Dublin. Richly illustrated, it contains a series of cures in Irish, translated from Latin text-books.[16] Another such book was compiled by the Physicians of Myddfai in Wales; they were the descendants of the otherworldly Lady of Llyn y Fan Fach. The book contains herbal cures commonly practised by country people.

Many healing skills are alleged to pass from mother to son, or from father to daughter, or else are inherited by the seventh child of a seventh child. Diarmuid MacManus gives an account of such a healer called Biddy Cosgary living in the village of Killeaden, County Mayo, in about 1902. She performed miracle cures for eye ailments. Her method on being approached for help was to take a cup and saucer to a nearby well and fill the cup. Returning, she made her client sit opposite her and look at her as well as they could. Taking a sip of the water, she would roll it around her mouth and mumble invocations, then bend forward, and spit the water from her mouth into the saucer, and the offending eye obstruction would appear floating in the liquid. She never touched her clients. Her reputation was considerable and two beneficiaries of her treatment were personally known to MacManus: both maintained that the obstruction vanished as Biddy spat out the water into the saucer. This process is similar to many shamanic extraction methods worldwide.

Biddy was interviewed by MacManus's grandmother. She informed her that the cure could only be done on Mondays and Thursdays and might only be attempted nine times in total. Biddy was reluctant to speak about the spirit or goddess who helped her, merely referring to her as 'the saint of the eye'.

> 'My charrum is given from a man to a woman and from a woman to a man. 'Tis only praying to the Blessed Virgin and the Saint of the Eye. Sure, yis, there is a Saint of the Eye up in heaven. Well, when anyone come to me, a good neighbour or a well wisher . . . and ask me would I cure the eye for thim, thin I should bring a drop of spring water from the well and to take it in my mouth and to kape me mouth closed and say those prayers and worruds to the Blessed Virgin and the Saint of the Eye. Then, savin your presence, I let the water down out of me mouth into a white plate and you'll see in that water whatever injury is in the eye. And to do that three times. It mightn't come the first time . . . There did a letter come over out of England to me and told me that a young boy I knew . . . got something in to his eye that hurted it, and the eye was keeping bad. Well, I tuck and done the charrum for him. And the first drop of water I let down out of me mouth what was in it but a big piece of grass.'[17]

The boy wrote stating the hour and day of his relief which was simultaneous with Biddy's long-distance extraction.

Some ancient skills remain in Celtic countries today. There are families still practising the ancient healing skills of bone-setting, animal-doctoring, herb-craft and the shamanic gift of spell-craft and healing. Certain individuals are natural repositories of healing, and their touch or blessing can cure. The seventeenth-century 'stroker', Valentine Greatrakes, cured sores, cancers, deafness, dim sight and obstructions by touch alone. I am personally acquainted with one such practitioner, an Irishwoman whose aunt also possessed the skill. Her healing touch is activated in the presence of illness or discomfort: her hands tingle and grow hot, able to draw out pain and bring healing. I can personally testify to her ability, as she touched my own recently sprained ankles in such a way that I was able to walk again with confidence.

Such skills are not commonly noticed as they fall outside the orthodoxies of our society, yet these healers enjoy considerable respect; in the case of traditional bone-setters or those with the healing touch, for example, people assemble from miles around to find the relief their doctors have been unable to provide. Seers and other gifted people enjoy a vast clientele.

A true understanding of the surviving extent of Celtic healing methods cannot be gained without an extensive survey of practitioners and their results. The heritage of shamanic methods certainly remains in the widespread use of spiritual invocations, charms and other practices. The indigenous and ancient practices, as elsewhere in the world, have acquired the clothing of Christian saints; but the intention to heal, whatever names are invoked, remains true. It is Diancecht himself who prophesies the fate of Celtic healing: 'If Miach be not, Airmed shall remain.' The great professionals are no more, yet Airmed has many descendants who practise their hidden skills with faith and vision today.

The Circuits of the Soul in Celtic Tradition
by Caitlín Matthews

The Nature of the Soul in Celtic Tradition

Celtic spiritual wholeness is defined by three conditions: *cràbhadh* – the trust of the soul, or devout observance; *creideamh* – the heart's consent, or belief; *iris* – the mind's pledge, or faith.

When these three are as one, then there is true strength and power within the *coich anama*, or the soul-shrine, as the body is termed. The body is like the cover of a triptych which unfolds its panels to reveal a landscape full of wonders. The complicit triad of soul, heart and mind are encoded throughout the Celtic tradition in the shamrock, in the triple spiral of Newgrange, in triadic sayings and memorizations, in the triple pattern of dots which infill illuminated missals and testaments. It is believed that the triple obsession of the Celtic peoples even had a determining effect upon the eventual doctrine of the Trinity, which was formulated in the fourth century by the Gaulish bishop St Hilary of Poitiers in his *De Trinitate*.

The trinity of soul, heart and mind are strong in harmony, yet they can be shattered if they are not in union. Doubt, distrust and neglected observances are the pathways to madness, heartsickness and soul-fragmentation. No wonder a great deal of Celtic ritual is concerned with weaving stout defences or *loricas* against such occurrences.

It is an elusive business, trying to define the soul in Celtic tradition. *Anam*, the Gaelic for soul implies life's vigour, and is related to *anal*, the breath. The soul wanders in and out of life, and in and out of consciousness. When you want someone to bestir themselves, you say 'Take your soul to yourself'. The soul is in the blood and the breath, its mortal house is the skull; when it is out of the body, it can travel in many animal shapes to the realms of faery and of the ancestors. But the soul is intimately moved by the mind and the heart, and cannot often be seen separate from either. The integrity of the mind, the desire of the heart, the love of the soul, are each vulnerable to attack. They are intimately associated with the three cauldrons which contain the body's vitality, its emotions and intelligence (see Chapter 7).

Ultimately, the Celtic soul cannot be conceived as one and the same as the classical or Christian soul – a total unitive entity subordinate to the divine spark of the spirit, but superior to the body and its faculties. The predominant Western notion of the soul seems to include the personality and divine identity that inspirit a body, but definitions are often vague.

Classical writers are often brought forward to testify to the druidic philosophy of the Celtic soul. Ammianus Marcellinus says of the druids:

> [They] were of loftier intellect, and bound by the rules of brotherhood as decreed by Pythagoras's authority, exalted by investigations of deep and serious study, and despising human affairs, declared souls to be immortal.

Alexander Cornelius Polyhistor writes that:

> The Pythagorean doctrine prevails among the Gauls' teaching that the souls of men are immortal, and that after a fixed number of years they will enter into another body.

Lucan's outrageously propagandist *Pharsalia* is less respectful of druidry, but even he writes:

> Truly the peoples on whom the Pole Star looks down are happy in their error, for they are not harassed by the greatest of terrors, the fear of death. This gives the warrior his eagerness to rush upon the steel, a spirit ready to face death, and an indifference to save a life which will return.

Valerius Maximus wrote of the Gauls:

> They lent sums of money to each other which are repayable in the next world, so firmly are they convinced that the souls of men are immortal.[18]

The classical soul-expectation was a darkness of twittering ghosts in Hades, Dis, Erebus or the blessed light of the Elysium fields. The Christian soul-expectation is not dissimilar: a damned eternity of hell, or a cleansing period in purgatory followed by a blissful eternity in heaven. The Celtic soul-expectation was clearly different, more mobile and fluid, with no fixed destination. The druidic belief in the transmigration of souls from body to body has often been compared with reincarnation, but is it really the same? Reincarnation involves the soul inhabiting a new human body; in transmigration or metempsychosis the soul may inhabit any living body, animal or human.

Let us settle on that mysteriously useful Irish word *tuirgen* (plural *tuirgente*) as the circuit of births, 'the birth that passes from every nature into another . . . a transitory birth which has traversed all nature from Adam and goes through every wonderful time down to the world's doom' as *Cormac's Glossary* has it. Each *tuirgen* is conceived as having 'the nature of one life', each component of one's being is the same, only the body is different. I therefore contend that the Celtic definition of the soul comprises the trinity of soul or psyche, heart and mind within the soul-shrine of the body.

Attack the soul-shrine or its triadic components and a soul-part detaches itself, leaving the whole weakened. This condition, known as 'soul-loss' is a commonly recognized problem in indigenous societies. Soul-loss is caused by illness, assault, shock or fright, and manifests as vitality-depletion, mental disorientation and dispiritedness. It is a shamanic task to find and return the missing soul-fragment. But it is an everyday business to guard, protect and maintain the soul from such dangers.

This concept of a multi-faceted soul seems strange to the Western mind, yet it is a common one throughout the world, especially among animistic peoples. As we shall see, the multiple soul plays a special part in Celtic tradition.

The *Tuirgen* of the Soul

There is a Gaelic folk-story riddle which is relevant to the *tuirgente* of the soul: 'Who is the birth that has never been born and never will be?'[19] In an endless cycle of births, it is hard to discover where the soul itself is born. Magical opportunities for the soul's conception outside wedlock and normal sexual relations are common in Celtic lore. Conception by eating an animal which has a human soul within it figures strongly: Etain's mother conceives her daughter by swallowing the fly in whose form Etain has been enchanted; Tuan mac Carill is in salmon form when he is swallowed by the wife of Carill; Gwion shapeshifts into a grain of wheat and is eaten and born of Ceridwen.

Conception is often accompanied by the visit of an otherworldly husband or spirit. Manannan is one of the chief night-visiting lovers of Celtic tradition, engendering the druidic hero Mongan upon Kentigerna.[20] Otherworldly fathers visit the mothers of Merlin and Conaire. Otherworldly women, like Rhiannon and Modron, seek out mortal lovers in order to conceive a child. This custom of actively seeking out a partner from the borders of the otherworld is even remarked upon by St Augustine, who says of the women of Gaul that they are visited by woodland spirits, '*sylvani* and Pans.'[21] Faeries, ancestors and deities figure among the engenderers of children in Celtic lore.

Conception can be caused by a significant act, as when Arianrhod steps over Math's staff to prove her virginity. Unfortunately for her, the staff is a druidic one which causes truth to manifest, revealing that she is not a virgin; she not only conceives from the semen she has recently received, but bears twin sons in one instant in full view of the court! Even where sexuality is denied, nature provides a window for the soul's conception. A staggering number of mothers of future saints have their vows of chastity overthrown by rape, such as Non, mother of St David or Taneu, St Kentigern's mother, who is cast into the sea in a sealed box with her child in a Danaë-and-Perseus-like way for the audacity of her pregnancy. Maelduin, hero of a *immram* (wonder-voyage cycle) is the son of a raped nun.

Celtic anti-conception measures for virgins must therefore have included extreme care in what was eaten, in bathing or exposure to moon or sunlight and in guarding the thoughts lest faery lovers be evoked. Yet even locking up virgins did little good, as we see from the conception of Conaire by Mess Buachalla, whose otherworldly lover comes through the skylight in bird form.

Guarding against soul-loss was a primary concern for mothers of newborn babies. Martin Martin describes the carrying of fire deosil around a woman after childbirth and around unbaptized children; he was told by midwives that

. . . it was an effectual means to preserve both the mother and the infant from the power of evil spirits, who are ready at such times to do mischief and sometimes carry away the infant, and when they get them once in their possession, return them poor meagre skeletons; and these infants are said to have voracious appetites, constantly craving for meat. In this case it was usual with those who believed that their children were thus taken away, to dig a grave in the fields upon quarter-day, and there to lay the Fairy Skeleton til next morning; at which time the parents went to the place where they doubted not to find their own child instead of this skeleton.[22]

In the *Proceedings of the Synod of Cashel*, 1172, Benedict of Peterborough mentions that, in Ireland, a child's father might, in accordance with ancient custom, immediately immerse the child after birth three times in water, or, if a rich man, in milk.[23] But the lustration of the newborn was a druidic custom, one which in after-eras was performed by midwives. Ninefold lustration in water to gift the infant with beneficial qualities was still being practised in the Western Highlands in this century.[24] Water and fire dedicated the child to mortal life. These elements were both present in Christian baptism, reinforced by the promise of salvation. The ceremonial passing on of ancient, pre-Christian skills, such as healing, was normally performed before baptism, since the skill might not 'take' after the recipient had been baptized.[25]

Among the West Highland Gaels, unbaptized infants were not buried in the churchyard but consigned to remote burial spots, usually after sunset and before sunrise. It was believed that such children had no soul, but only a spirit or *taran*, which entered into the rock to become *mac talla*, the son of the rock, the Gaelic name for 'echo'.

It is not insignificant that the Gaelic words for soul (*anam*) and name (*ainm*) are so similar. Children were guarded from faery abduction by having a childhood name. The adult name would be given when they were of an age to have performed deeds which marked them. In this way, Cuchulainn's childhood name was Setanta; only after he had slain Culainn the smith's hound, and had to substitute himself as a human guard-dog, did he gain his adult name – *cu chulainn*, 'the hound of Culainn'. St Columba's birth name was Crimthann (Gaelic for 'wolf'); his nominal volte-face succinctly reveals his soul's struggle, for he took for his clerical name the Latin word for dove.

Blood was held to be of the soul. Even the sucking of someone's blood created ties of kinship. When Cuchulainn accidentally wounds Dervorgil, an otherworldly woman with whom he is deeply in love, he sucks out a sling-stone from her wound, declaring, 'I cannot wed thee now, for I have drunk thy blood. But I will give thee to my companion here, Lugaid of the Red Stripes.'[26] Such a blood-friendship or *crocodaig* was intentionally practised from earliest times; a blood covenant was made and broken between Branduff, King of Leinster and the King of Ulster in AD 598 in an attempt to overthrow the High King of Ireland.

The Elizabethan poet, Edmund Spenser, witnessed the drinking of blood while on campaign in Limerick. He watched the foster-mother of an executed man, 'take up his head whilst he was being quartered and suck up the blood that ran from it, saying that the earth was not worthy to drink it, and steep her face and breast with it, at the same time tearing her hair, and crying out and shrieking most terribly.'[27] The drinking of blood seems to have been an attempt to capture the departing soul and give it a fresh opportunity to reincarnate: significantly, most instances of blood-drinking at death are performed by women in Celtic tradition.

We still inadvertently guard against soul-loss in many ways even today, as when we cover our mouths when we yawn to prevent the soul from escaping, or when we bless people when they sneeze. The breath is one of the abodes of the soul, along with the blood and the hair.

The life of the soul is often circumscribed by extraordinary safeguards and restrictions. The Welsh Llew is born prematurely of his mother Arianrhod. His uncle, Gwydion, a cunning druid, takes up the infant and incubates him in a chest within his chamber. Llew's subsequent career is as ill-starred as his birth. Because of the shame of his birth, Llew's mother, Arianrhod, refuses to acknowledge him, and lays a terrible set of *geasa* which virtually condemn him to non-existence: she wills that he have no name or arms, unless she herself gives them, both of which Gwydion tricks her into doing. She finally wills that he have no wife of human stock. Gwydion and Math make him one out of flowers, but the conjured wife, Blodeuwedd, loves another. She causes Llew to reveal the fated manner of his death, which he foolishly does. Setting up the extraordinarily complicated conditions of his demise takes her a year and then she begs him to relieve her anxiety about his death by showing her how difficult it would be to accomplish. Llew steps neatly into the trap and is slain, as fated, with a spear thrown by Blodeuwedd's lover.

Llew, however, does not die; he passes into the shape of a moulting eagle and perches at the tree's top until Gwydion locates him and bardically sings him down. He restores Llew to his human guise and once more has the task of restoring him to full strength. This complex story is almost an index of the soul's life and Celtic belief. In many ways, Llew is the original 'boy without a father'. He also fits the Gaelic folk-story riddle: 'Who is the birth that has never been born and never will be?' His origins are unknown and he seems unable to die.

Rituals and invocations to keep the soul in the soul-shrine are commonplace. The Gaelic *sian* is an invocation bestowing invulnerability in battle; the famous Death-Lifting *Sian* of St Patrick was frequently sent for by Irish soldiers in the nineteenth century, in the belief that wearing it about them would protect them from being shot:

> The victory of the green tree.
> The sap of the sharp branches, within you!
> Blessing upon the soul and body
> Of each one who recites the Marthainn on himself!
> May your holy angel be with you,
> May you not fear the King of the Fallen![28]

The invulnerability of the soul, so believed in by the ancient Celts, seems to have obtained among later warriors of their kindred. The coat of MacLeod of Bearnaray in Harris, over whom the *sian* had been said before the battle of Culloden, was found to be full of bullet-holes, yet not one bullet had pierced his flesh. Belief in the *sian* to fend off danger was implicit:

> No spear shall rive thee,
> No sea shall drown thee,
> No woman shall wile thee,
> No man shall wound thee.
>
> The mantle of Christ Himself about thee . . .
> From the crown of thy head
> To the soles of thy feet . . .
> Thou shalt go forth in the name of thy King,
> Thou shall come in in name of thy Chief,
> To the God of life thou now belongest wholly,
> And to all the Powers together.[29]

The *sian* is similar to the breastplate charms, also called loricas or *sciathlúireacha*, of which St Patrick's Breastplate is perhaps the most familiar. (See Chapter 6.) But although such devices may have given confidence in tight places, death eventually called the soul onto the hidden path of its *tuirgen*.

The Paths of the Dead

The Gaelic custom of the *treoraich anama* or soul-leading seems to be the sole survival of a Celtic Christian duty now considered an entirely sacerdotal task: the conducting of the soul from life into death. Carmichael notes that the soul-leading prayer over the dying one was invariably said by the *anam-chara* or 'soul-friend', not by a cleric. The concept of soul-friendship is deeply lodged in Celtic Christianity; a soul-friend was a spiritual director, sometimes but not always a confessor. The Celtic Church, like the Eastern Orthodox Churches today, believed that soul-friendship was established by the Holy Spirit, that it was not extinguished by death; lay people, under this system, could play an important role in helping and strengthening souls.

In the Gaelic soul-leading, soul-friends helped to direct the soul from the body, through their prayers and presence. They prayed to Christ and St Michael to take the soul and prepare its path. At the point when the soul left the body, it was seen ascending as a bright ball of light and the soul-friend proclaimed:

> Now is the pitiful soul set free
> Outside the soul-shrine;
> Christ of the encompassings, thy blessing
> Surround my love in your good time.
>
> (Author's translation)

The soul is often seen in the shape of a butterfly or moth in Celtic countries, in common with the folk belief of many regions. But where was the soul bound and what was its expectation?

Inhumation of Celtic bodies in pre-Christian times was often accompanied by the burial of grave-goods to be used in the otherworld, suggesting that the deceased's afterlife was intended to follow a similar course to this one. The magnificent burial site of a European Celtic chieftain found at Hochdorf, Germany, in 1968 is dated to 550 BCE. The tomb contained an iron couch, a waggon, eating and hunting utensils and toilet articles.[30] Despite his gorgeous apparel, he was incongruously furnished with a birch-bark hat which rather validates the traditional Scots Border ballad 'The Wife of Usher's Well' in which the woman's three sons come home to her after death,

> and their hats were o' the birk.

> It neither grew in syke nor ditch,
> nor yet in ony shough;
> but at the gates o' paradise,
> that birk grew fair enough.

The birch, the first of the trees to cover the land when it emerged from the Ice Age, the first tree in the Ogam alphabet, the tree of beginnings, appears here in a hat which only the dead wear, as a soul-covering for the journey to be taken.

Some Irish burial sites have yielded shoes which could never have been worn, since they were joined together or were made of metal. Were these special footwear for the soul's journey?[31] Otherworldly beings like Manannan are described as wearing 'two blunt shoes of white bronze between his feet and the earth' signifying his ability to walk between the worlds.[32] The very rich may not have needed such footwear since chariot-burials in both the Marne and eastern Yorkshire attest to a belief that the deceased would be able to drive to his or her destination.

But what were the paths through the afterlife? The passage of the soul after life was a preoccupation of Celtic people in both Pagan and Christian times, and the routes that the soul took along traditional paths are embedded in both custom and folklore. Following the suggestion of the Rees brothers,[33] in my 'Celtic Book of the Dead', I posited the use of the *immrama* or wonder-voyage stories as a possible soul-route.[34] In traditional Irish storytelling, it was customary for stories of famous births to be told at lyings-in, of abductions and wooings at weddings, of mighty deeds of arms at times requiring courage. The *immrama* stories, which relate encounters upon a series of islands, seem to have been told to help prepare the soul for its wanderings after death.

The Voyage of Maelduin, for example, visits thirty-three islands which provide a coherent map of the otherworld. Thirty-two of them fall into four categories of encounter – the physical challenges of existence, the purification of the emotions, the clarification of the soul and the realization of otherworldly wisdom – and the thirty-third island marks the path of assimilation and return. See *The Celtic Book of the Dead* for a full exposition.

This *immram* tradition was adopted by the Celtic Church to illuminate the soul's quest. *The Voyage of St Brendan* leads to the promised land of saints, a sight of paradisal existence before death. Both St Brendan and Maelduin returned homewards, but the early hero, Bran mac Febal, still wanders through the many islands of the otherworld.

Purification of the soul was not only a Christian preoccupation. There is a long streak of native asceticism in the Celtic soul which permeates ancient and later lore. There is ample evidence to suggest that the ancient festival of Imbolc, associated with Brighid, was one of purification and preparation for the coming year.[35] The *immrama* stories present challenges which excoriate the body, and cleanse the soul, emotions and reason. The very physicality of these challenges was present in the excessive penitential exercises of the Celtic Church, and is reflected today in the endurance required in the barefoot pilgrimage to the summit of the mountain of Croagh Patrick, County Mayo or the three-day fast upon St Patrick's Purgatory on Lough Derg.

Many traditional Celtic paths of the dead have become fused with Christian eschatological ideologies, notably purgatory, the place of purification, where souls are cleansed before passing on into the glory of paradise. After the Reformation, when Catholic prayers and masses for the dead were removed from Protestant practice, the human hunger for the purification of dead souls was unappeased. In Wales, the ancient Celtic concept of a ritual scapegoat was remembered and instituted in the sin-eater. Known only now from Welsh Border tradition, the sin-eater was probably drawn from an unfortunate or unlucky family living on the verges of the community, the role descending hereditarily in the scapegoated family. The sin-eater's duty was to ritually take on the sins of a dead person by eating food placed upon the corpse's chest. The departed soul would then be pure and free to pass on, while the sin-eater's burden would be passed on in an eternity of tribal can-carrying. John Aubrey also alludes to this custom in his *Remains of Gentilism and Judaism*. Matthew Moggridge of Swansea described sin-eating in the region of Lladebie in the early nineteenth century:

> When a person died, his friends sent for the Sin-Eater of the district, who on his arrival placed a plate of salt on the breast of the defunct, and upon the salt a piece of bread. He then muttered an incantation over the bread, which he finally ate, thereby eating up all the sins of the deceased. This done, he received his fee of 2/6d and vanished as quickly as possible from the general gaze; for it was believed he really appropriated to his own use and behoof the sins of all those over whom he performed the above ceremony. He was utterly detested in the neighbourhood – regarded as a mere Pariah – as one irremediably lost.[36]

A description of a Welsh Border funeral in 1671 relates: 'There stood upon the coffin a large pot of wine, out of which everyone drank to the health of the deceased, hoping that he might surmount the difficulties he had to encounter in his road to Paradise.'[37] I am reminded of the Celtic Christian decoration, which occurs in many illuminated texts, of a pair of peacocks drinking from a vase, signifying eternal life. From the rich burial site of a Celtic nobleman, discovered in Hochdorf, Germany in 1968, where a cauldron full of mead was discovered, to the solemn and taciturn Welsh ceremony which was still upheld until recently, and the expansive and sociable Irish 'wake', drinking over the corpse seems to have been a ancient Celtic custom for helping the soul upon its road.

In the Second Vision of Adamnan, we are told that the soul visits four places before passing on: the place of birth, the place of death, the place of baptism and the place of burial – the fourfold stations of temporal and Christian life. P.W. Joyce relates a story in which an Irish woman dying in Liverpool at the end of the nineteenth century begged to know from the priest whether she would be permitted by God to visit Ireland on her way to heaven, showing that this practice was still partially current. Could this fourfold visitation of the passing soul not be part of a much earlier practice which might have included the deceased's home, the place of birth and death, as well a visitation to the realm of the ancestors?

The traditional North Country song 'The Lyke Wake Dirge' details the soul's progress over a prickly moor of whin-bushes onto the bridge of dread through a place of fire: those who have given shoes to the barefoot pass over the moor well-shod, just as those who have given food to the hungry are not burned. In the fifteenth-century Scottish tale 'Tomas of Ersseldoune', the Faery Queen herself details five possible roads for the soul, combining both traditional and Christian venues: over a mountain to the heaven of the purified soul, under a hill to the joys of earthly paradise, under a green plain where uncleansed souls are purified, to a deep valley where burn the fires of hell, and to a fair castle on the high hill which is the land of Faery.[38]

The Celtic faery tradition contains a wealth of lore about the nature of the soul, helping us to understand the complexity of its wandering circuit through the maze of many lives. It retains knowledge of soul-theft and restoration, and magical protection of the soul and of its double, the hidden soul.

The Hidden Soul and the Double

In an Irish fifth-century prayer for long life, we encounter a strange invocation:

> I invoke the Silver One, undying and deathless;
> may my life be enduring as white-bronze,
> may my double be slain.[39]

The Silver One in question has not been authoratively identified, although Nuada, the Silver-handed, may be intended, seen as an immortal spirit. But what interests us here is the concept of the 'double' or *riocht* (Scots Gaelic, *tamhasg*), for the soul-form of a living human. This Celtic idea of the soul having a double is widespread throughout the tradition.

The Rev. Robert Kirk, writing in the seventeenth century, speaks of the double as the *coimimeadh* or co-walker:

> [Seers] avouch that every Element and different state of being, has in it animals resembling those of another element . . . They have told me they have seen . . . a double-man, or the shape of the same man in two places . . . They call this Reflex-man a *coimimeadh* or Co-Walker, every way like the man, as a twin-brother and companion, haunting him as his shadow and is oft seen and known among men, resembling the original, both

before and after the original is dead . . . If invited and earnestly required, these companions make themselves known and familiar to men, otherwise, being in a different state and element, they neither can nor will easily converse with them.[40]

Those with the sight are accustomed to see the *riocht* of the soul, which may appear like an astral body or else be so manifest that the seer can barely distinguish between the two. The *riocht* or co-walker is frequently seen as a presager of death, and its bilocation causes great remark or fear. The modern Scottish seer, Eilidh Watt, speaks of visiting her brother in her sleep by sending out her own *coimimeadh*; the next morning, her sister-in-law phoned at the behest of her brother who, on having seen and spoken with his sister's *riocht*, determined that she must be dead and was most distraught.[41]

Few people are so skilled as this seer, able to send forth their double at will; only a great shock or the approach of death itself will cause their *riocht* to be manifest to others. This is brought about by the sudden or gradual loosening of the ties of life upon the soul, causing part of it to fragment out. In the presence of a person who is agitated or grieved, I have discerned the *riocht* as an identical shape imperfectly superimposed upon the body itself. Here we touch upon the manner in which the soul 'escapes the body' when danger threatens, a factor we will explore further below.

Side by side, and often entangled, with the idea of the double, is the animistic notion of the hidden or exterior soul. The hidden soul is exterior to the soul-shrine and its contents; its existence is usually bound up or shared with another form of life. This brings us into the area of shamanic spirits as helpers or life-companions. A child's soul-life is often parallel with that of another being – often animal or tree. While the animal or tree lives, the child lives; but their fates are intertwined, and if one suffers damage or death, the other is also wounded or killed. Thus, the life of Diarmuid O' Duibhne is fatally entwined with that of his half-brother, who was saved from death by being turned into a boar. When Diarmuid slays this boar, his own life seeps away. Individuals who have such a shared or hidden soul are usually obliged by *geas* never to harm the parallel animal or tree, as was the case with Conaire and his bird kindred (see chapter 8).

There are numerous cases of the soul's double or spirit-helper being seen just before death. A common death-herald is the bird. Many Irish people express great dread of unusual bird activity near or in their houses, since they recognize this as a death-omen for one of their family. The death-herald or way-shower may appear as a *bean-*

sidhe, a faery woman who bewails impending death in certain families who have relations or soul-friends with the local faery-kind. Faery alliances are commonplace in Celtic lore, a reciprocal arrangement whereby faery and mortal parties enter into agreements for mutual benefit, service being required by one from the other. The work of R.J. Stewart to re-establish such contracts between faeries and modern practitioners is based upon the identification of co-walkers as faery allies and animal spirits. (See R.J. Stewart, *Earth Light*.)

The many stories of transmigration or shapeshifting that occur in Celtic tradition relate to the shamanic ability to send the soul into any shape – only one who is most skilled can track and catch the hidden or shapeshifted soul. The shamanic ability to take the *feth fiada* or 'deer's aspect' upon oneself, brought one within the otherworld, making one invisible to others.

In Celtic shamanic practice, the soul's shrine is hidden or wrapped up in many levels of protective lore. The home of the soul is strictly guarded and never divulged. Celtic folk-story retains the memory of druidic practice in numerous stories relating to a series of titanic beings or giants. Possessed of primordial skills which are druidic in origin, the giant can only be overcome if his soul is discovered. Needless to say, like any skilled shaman, he disperses his soul into many different elements, places and animals, so that no hiding place can result in soul-loss. His soul leaps from shape to shape, changing nightly like a password in a stronghold, so that no one can catch him unawares.

The Irish folk-story 'Blamainn, Son of Apple' tells of a formidable giant whose soul is cunningly hidden thus: under a flagstone on the hearth is a sheep, in its belly a duck, and in the duck's egg lies the soul. It is found and overcome by the hero only with the help of a dog, a falcon and an otter. The dog pulls out the sheep, the falcon catches the duck while the otter takes the egg from the sea where it falls and crushes it. [42]

In other tales, the giant figure is cast as a *gruagach* or 'hairy one', understood to be either a brownie or an enchanter. There is such a strong tradition of the *gruagach* as a teacher of magical skills that it is possible to see a folk-memory of druidry in these tales. In 'The Fisherman's Son and the Gruagach of the Tricks', the *gruagach* apprentices a boy for a year and day to learn his tricks. After springing his boy from the *gruagach*'s service, the fisherman profits by his son's new-found arcane knowledge to earn some money. However, the *gruagach* attempts to regain his apprentice. In a dazzling succession of shapeshiftings, the boy becomes a ring in a fire, a spark in a wheat barrel and a grain of wheat; the *gruagach* and his eleven sons become twelve pairs of tongs, twelve men and twelve cocks. Finally, the boy becomes a fox and bites off their heads. Such rapid shapeshiftings are earnests of soul-searchings, where one attempts to overcome the other.[43]

In the Scots Gaelic story 'Manus', Manus appeals on behalf of his twelve men to the white *gruagach* for permission for the men to marry the *gruagach*'s twelve sisters. On the way home to ratify this event, the *gruagach* cries out that he is slain.

'What ails thee?' said Manus.

'There is a stone in the burn, and there are three trouts (sic) under the stone, and they are in thy wife's apron. As long as the trouts should be alive I would be alive, and thy wife has one of them now in the fire.'[44]

It is only by slaying a horned, venomous beast and bringing the *gruagach* its blood that Manus is able to revive his friend, who dies, since his soul is hidden in the three trout and they have been cooked and consumed.

It is evident from these stories and other traditions that the soul of the *gruagach*, descendant of druids and *filidh*, is well hidden against unwary assaults. It can inhabit or possess exterior objects and other living beings while the *gruagach's* body is simultaneously animated. Such beings seldom appear under their own name, being called 'the Knight of the Riddles' or 'the Gruagach of the Tricks'; often the revealing of their name causes their soul and magical services to be subdued to the finder's will, as in the case of such stories as 'Tom, Tit, Tot', a Rumplestiltskin parallel.

In 'Culhwch and Olwen', Culhwch wishes to marry the giant's daughter. Although he injures the giant, Culhwch cannot overcome him until he has completed a series of thirty-nine impossible tasks. Chief among these is to fetch shears and a comb which lie between the ears of a monstrous ravening boar, Twrch Trwyth. Only when these are brought and Yspaddaden is shorn and shaved can he finally be overcome, for the power of his soul lies in his hair. Similarly, Blathnait ties her husband Cairpre to the bed by his hair, so that Cuchulainn, her lover, may kill him.

Hair and thread, as well as the utensils pertaining to them, acquire specific soul-endangering qualities. It was considered dangerous among Scottish Gaels for a man to cut his own hair for 'to raise scissors above his own breath' was to endanger his life's thread. Women should not comb their hair at night, for every dropped hair was believed to endanger the life of a relative at sea. Hair as the soul's home is common in worldwide tradition. Hair or nails are required as the 'witness' in radiology, where they are subjected to radionic frequencies which are said to heal at great distances.

The soul's life was often implacably hidden in other body parts or objects. Celtic midwives' ritual concerning the disposal of both navel string and afterbirth reinforce the belief in the exterior soul. If the afterbirth was not properly burned or buried under a tree, the mother might have no other children: the reasoning was that the ejected placenta was still considered to be a vessel for life. Like the ritually twisted swords and purposely broken votive offerings thrown into lakes in early Celtic times, the placenta was returned to the elements so that it could not be reused. In the Highlands, navel strings were ground to powder and given to the child to drink in water, so that only the child might imbibe the vitality of its own life-cord. Both navel strings and afterbirth were approved folk-cures for sterility, implying that these objects were vital vehicles for soul-life.

A talismanic object often acted as a hidden soul, as in the case of Arthur's sword, Excalibur, whose scabbard prevented loss of blood. It is so clearly wound up with his life that only when Excalibur is returned to the lake of its origin is Arthur's soul able to pass into the realm of Avalon, the dwelling place of the Lady of the Lake.

Anything which was knotted, wound or woven held soul-power. Even the band that secured the spinning wheel should not be left on overnight, and the spancel (a short hobbling band that stopped beasts from straying) was treated with great caution. Women wore a *sianchrios* or holy belt around their waists when pregnant to bring spiritual benefit to unborn children.[45] Even today the women of Aran weave a *crios* or belt for their men. They also knit distinctive figures into Aran jerseys with charged names such as 'the ladder of life', symbolizing the spiritual path, and 'the crooked road', a zig-zag stitch symbolizing the ups and downs of married life.

The thread of life quite literally runs throughout Celtic art, first in metal and stonework, and later in the illuminated pages of missals and testaments. The weaving thread of Celtic knotwork symbolizes the soul's path through life, encoding certain qualities and powers into the object so decorated. These patterns are not mere decoration but meaningful pathways which hold soul-life and can help to lead it back when it strays.

Soul-Loss and Soul-Wandering

As we have seen, the Celtic soul is a great wanderer; it especially strays when it is exposed to shock, illness or distress. The term 'soul-loss' should be more properly called 'soul-fragmentation', for a loss of all soul parts signals death. Soul-loss may involve mental disorientation, emotional deadness or psychic depression; in severe cases, it may involve loss of consciousness, as in 'The Sick-Bed of Cuchulainn'.

This story gives a highly informative account of a common Celtic problem – the irruption of one reality into another, causing soul-fragmentation. This normally comes about when an individual is careless or disrespectful to certain spirits, most often the faery. In this story, Ulster is celebrating the feast of Samhain when a flock of unknown birds lands on a nearby lake. The Ulsterwomen provoke their men into catching a pair of them each. Cuchulainn goes forth to pursue the most beautiful pair, which are yoked by a chain of red gold. He casts at one and hits its wing, but it promptly vanishes and the other flies away. Vexed at the failure of his legendary skills,

> Cuchulainn departed, and rested his back against a stone pillar, and his soul was angry within him, and sleep fell upon him. Then he saw two women come to him; the one of them had a green mantle upon her, and upon the other was a purple mantle . . . The woman in the green mantle approached him, and she laughed a laugh at him, and she gave him a stroke with a horse-whip . . . then the other approached him . . . and struck him in the same way; and for a long time were they thus, each of them in turn coming to him and striking him, until he was all but dead.[46]

His companions discern that he is having a vision and realize that he should not be wakened. He returns to consciousness and asks to be put to bed, where he remains for one year without speaking. As Samhain returns, the faery man, Angus mac Aed, comes to Cuchulainn and tells him that his two faery daughters, Liban and Fand, could heal him, and that Fand loves him dearly. Cuchulainn sits up and relates his vision and goes to the pillar-stone where he originally rested. There the green-cloaked woman, Liban, commands his presence in Faery to kill her husband's opponent, promising Fand as a reward. Too weak to oblige, Cuchulainn sends his charioteer, Laeg, to discover the dispositions of the otherworld, returning to bed.

Cuchulainn's wife, Emer, succinctly sums up the situation:

His illness is the work of the fairy folk,
Of the women of Mag Trogach.
They have beaten thee,
Then have put thee into captivity;
They have led thee off the track.
The power of the women has rendered thee impotent.

After Laeg's return and the exhortations of Emer, Cuchulainn goes into the otherworld himself and kills the faery's opponent. He sleeps with Fand for a month and arranges to meet her again. Emer brings the women of Ulster to the tryst to support her prior claim to his love. Fand is overcome by their pleas and returns to faery with her former husband, Manannan. Cuchulainn goes mad with lovesickness, sleeping rough and going without food or drink. Eventually, Conchobar

sent out his learned men and his people of skill, and the druids of Ulster to find Cuchulainn, and to bind him fast and bring him with them to Emain. And Cuchulainn tried to kill the people of the skill, but they chanted wizard and fairy spells against him and they bound fast his feet and his hands until he came a little to senses. Then he begged for a drink at their hands, and the druids gave him a drink of forgetfulness, so that afterwards he had no more remembrance of Fand nor of anything else that he had then done; and they also gave [the drink] to Emer that she might forget her jealousy, for her state was in no way better than the state of Cuchulainn. And Manannan shook his cloak between Cuchulainn and Fand, so that they might never meet together again throughout eternity.

In this story, Cuchulainn is twice smitten by soul-loss: once when he hunts the birds who are really faery women, and once when Fand leaves him. When Liban and Fand come to him and whip him he appears to his companions to be in a deep vision. This whipping is very significant in worldwide shamanic practice. The Yanomani Indians of the Amazon conclude the exorcism of a spirit-possessed person by flogging him gently with wild pepper stalks to complete the process;[47] in Egyptian folk-medicine, exorcisms are still accompanied by often severe beating of the subject; in medieval Europe, beating the possessed was a common 'treatment'. Cuchulain's beating at otherworldly hands robs him of his powers just as conclusively as his love-longing for Fand rends his reason from him.

Jealousy was a strong and overriding cause of soul-displacement.

Brehon law undertook that any injury sustained by a second wife on the first day of her coming into the household of an established first wife was not a convictable offence. Emer's condition is said to be as bad as that of her husband, but it is jealousy of Fand that has caused it.

We have mentioned the power of the word to injure as when the poet's satire caused blisters on the face of a foe. In the story of 'The House of the Two Milk Pails' (see Chapter 12) the girl Curcog is insulted so grossly by Finbarr that she becomes unable to eat the faery food of her foster-father. Her soul-loss works in the reverse manner to that of Cuchulainn's, for she gradually fades out of the faery land of her home into mortal realms.

Sometimes grief itself causes soul-loss. When Diarmuid O'Duibhne is slain by the boar of his *geas* in the Fionn cycle, his foster-father, Aengus Og berates himself:

'Ah! why did I abandon thee to be decoyed to thy doom by the guileful craft of Finn? By my neglect has thou suffered, O Dermat; and now, indeed, I shall for ever feel the bitter pangs of sorrow!'

Then Angus asked Grania's people what they had come for. And when they told him that Grania had sent them to bring the body of Dermat to Rath-Grania, he said:

'I will bring the body of Dermat with me to Bruga of the Boyne; and I will keep him on his bier where he shall be preserved by my power, as if he lived. And though I cannot, indeed, restore him to life, yet I will breathe a spirit into him, so that for a little while each day he shall talk with me.'[48]

The grieving Grania, Diarmuid's beloved, has no body to bury: a cause of soul-loss known to the widows of combatants and the families of disaster victims alike, for a known grave equates with a peaceful soul and the relief of mourning. An unburied body only delays the soul's departure.

Collective soul-loss happens when a whole people suffer national grief, the shame of conquest, the deprivations of famine and sickness or war. War is one of the major causes of collective soul-loss in any generation. As the social dislocation of returned war veterans today testifies to their shock at the atrocities witnessed or endured in the field, so we find similar instances of Celtic battle shock. We saw how Suibhne becomes *geilt* or 'mad' in Chapter 6. The effect of battle fatigue upon the soul was even recorded as one of the 'wonders of

Ireland' in a Norse book *Kongs Skuggsjo* (Mirror of Kings) in 1250: 'There is also one thing which will seem very wonderful about men who are called *geilt*.' The author describes how men run mad out of battle and live in the woods so that feathers grow on their bodies and, though they are not quite able to fly, they nevertheless possess animal speed; they 'run along the tops of the trees almost as swiftly as monkeys or squirrels'.[49] The cause of Merlin's madness is from horror at the Battle of Arfderydd.

Sometimes collective soul-loss is brought about by an ancestral curse. The Ulsterman's *noinend* or nine-fold curse is brought about by the humiliation of the goddess Macha, at the hands of the Ultonian king. Having been forced to run a race against the King's horses when heavily pregnant, Macha gives birth to twins at the finishing post and vents her curse on Ulster: that each man who heard her shrieks would suffer the pains of childbirth for five days and four nights at the time of their greatest need – a curse that was to descend to the ninth generation!

Such a soul-binding curse was greatly feared; it was but one way in which the soul might be stolen.

Soul-Theft, Soul-Binding

Soul-theft occurs when an individual purposely attempts to intimidate or steal the vitality, goodness or virtue of another, or to bind the soul to their service. Soul-theft is most often attributed to the evil eye, when the vitality and energy of a living being is sapped by an 'overlooker' who is jealous of its powers. Jealousy is one of the strongest motives for soul-theft – a manipulative readjustment of the life-force which is much feared and which is a major feature of Celtic protective invocations.

Most soul-stealing in Celtic tradition seems to be laid at the door of the faeries. There is a double-edged relationship between mortal and faery in Celtic tradition: reciprocal respect and mutual aid can easily slip into jealous overlooking, theft and greed. The faeries expect respect and exact retribution if the rules of common inter-species politeness are transgressed. The felling of a faery tree or even the siting of a building can have dire consequences. Diarmuid MacManus relates the story of Michael O'Hagan, in a village in County Mayo, who, in order to accommodate his growing family, had extended his house in such a way as to block the path between two neighbouring faery forts. Over the next few weeks his children began to die, first the eldest, then the second, third and fourth children. The doctor could not diagnose or cure the mysterious complaint with which they had all been stricken. With but one child remaining to him and the boy likely to die, O'Hagan consulted the local wise woman, Mairead ni Heine. She immediately saw what was wrong with the house and bade him demolish the extension forthwith. Working all night with a pick-axe, he finished the job at dawn to find that his son was already improved. This event happened in 1935 and the circumstances were corroborated by the doctor and O'Hagan's neighbours.[50]

Celtic mothers are careful not to praise their children's qualities in case the faeries become jealous and overlook the child.

Changelings are substitutions of healthy children for wizened-looking faery infants. From a number of stories it would appear that faeries seldom reproduce themselves and so steal human children to replenish their own stock. Changelings give themselves away by their unnaturally precocious behaviour or long memory, such as remembering local afforestations or the rising and falling of rivers over many centuries. The traditional way to unspell a changeling is to boil an eggshell of water on the fire; the changeling exclaims, 'Well in all my days I never saw water that boiled like that before!' Another method is to place the infant on a shovel and thrust it into the fire so that the faery are forced to substitute the original child. It is interesting that both methods utilize fire and water – the traditional saining elements used by midwives over newborn children – for the elements cannot lie.

Sometimes the faery steal away an adult human to serve in their realms. In such a way is Tam Lin taken by the Faery Queen. He is intended to become a faery sacrifice, but his pregnant sweetheart, Janet, comes to the crossroads at Halloween to meet the faery procession and retrieve the soul of her beloved. She pulls Tam Lin from his horse and holds him fast as he undergoes a series of terrifying shapeshiftings until he stands once more in her arms as a naked man.[51]

Celtic soul retrievals often involve much bargaining. In *The Mabinogion*, Manawyddan patiently undergoes a series of trials in order to release Pryderi and his mother, Rhiannon, from the otherworld, where they have been trapped by Llwyd Cilcoed, a faery being. Manawyddan craftily catches one of the mice which have been eating his harvest and makes to hang it from a miniature gallows, knowing full well that Llwyd will come to save it. Manawyddan refuses to release the mouse, which is really Llwyd's own wife, until Pryderi and Rhiannon are released from their servitude in the otherworld. From the context of the story, it becomes clear that the imprisoned pair have been doing the work of draught horses.

Sometimes the subject will be stricken by the faery stroke like Cuchulainn, bed-ridden and seldom conscious. Coma indicates massive soul-loss, for the soul is unable to return fully to the body, remaining trapped in shock or else imprisoned by spirits. Sleep, that simulacrum of death, was bound about with its own customs. It was considered dangerous to rouse someone from a nightmare without calling their name, for to do so might cause a wandering spirit to inhabit the body rather than its true occupant.

There was great fear of ghosts, the souls who returned to their homes and refused to go upon their *tuirgen*. The feast of Samhain, held in honour of dead ancestors, was bound about with precautions so that the stray souls of the recently dead should not be attracted but sent quickly upon their way. In Christian times, prayers for the dead are said for the repose of such souls. Lanterns are still set in windows to guide lost souls. A corpse and its possessions were not allowed to remain long in mortal places. In Ireland, the ceremonial burning of the dead's bedding often took place upon faery mounds, in a manner reminiscent of Romany funerals where the deceased's possessions and caravan are burned, the object being to leave nothing in this world which might become a spirit-house for a stray soul or ghost to inhabit.

The evil eye was essentially the look of envy which could take the soul-life or goodness from a person or animal. It was particularly guarded against in the Western Highlands on the first Monday of the quarter, since that was the day when the men and women of the *frith* made their augury (see Chapter 8). Cows were kept indoors, lest the augurer of the *dubh-cheilg* or 'black guile' spirit away their milk with the help of the *droch shuil* or evil eye. Charms were made,

> Against peering-eyed women,
> Against keen-eyed men,
> Against blear-eyed slender ones,[52]
> Against seven phantom faires.

The thwarting of the evil eye is done by blessing water taken from beneath a bridge where both living and dead cross over and anointing the ears of the afflicted beast or person, being careful not to mention their name during the blessing. The evil is reflected back on the sender with,

> May it lie upon their virile sons,
> May it lie upon their nubile daughters,
> May it lie upon each of their worldly joys
> That they themselves love best.

It is also thwarted by the charms of the knots.

The power of the knot to bespell another is widespread as a shamanic method of sorcery. A long and difficult labour necessitates the loosening of all knots in the room. The soul about to be born cannot otherwise come into being. It was believed in Scotland that a couple getting married should have no knots about them, including shoe-laces or fastenings; if any were present upon their persons during the wedding, they would be unable to conceive a child. All such were carefully undone at the beginning of the service and retied afterwards.[53]

The comb is frequently the agent of soul-enchantment, since it restrains or catches the hair, in which the soul is believed to lie. Many ballads in the north-western European tradition speak of this, notably 'Willie's Lady'. In this song, Willie's Lady is in labour: he promises his mother many wondrous rewards in return for a child born well and healthy, but his mother, a witch, despairs of the labouring woman's life. The household spirit, Billie Blin, a brownie or *gruagach*, advises him to make a waxen baby and bid his mother come to the christening, then to stand near the church door to see what she says. Sure enough she curses:

> Oh wha has loosed the nine witch knots
> That was amo that ladie's locks?
>
> And wha has taen out the kaims of care
> That hands amo that ladie's hair?
>
> And wha's taen down the bush o woodbine
> Tha hang atween her bower and mine?
>
> And wha has killd the master kid
> That ran beneath that ladie's bed?
>
> And wha has loosed her left-foot shee
> And lotten that ladie lighter be?

Accordingly, Willie rushes home and performs all these actions speedily and his wife is safely delivered immediately.[54] The emblem of the comb upon Pictish symbol stones bespeaks a powerful matrilineal presence, for she who had the power of 'the kaims of care' and the mirror which reflects back enchantment held regnal power supreme.

The Tasks of the Dead

We have seen how the soul may wander into other realms or enter other shapes voluntarily, how it can become imprisoned. When a soul is trapped in the otherworld or voluntarily offers itself for service, we enter the murky ground of necromancy.

Many enchantments practise a soul-binding which traps souls to particular locations, as in the case of treasure-guardians, or to ancestral grave-mounds where a foundation sacrifice has been performed in order to maintain a cemetary guardian. We have already noted the atavistic custom of appointing dead spirits as guardians. In the Highlands it was believed that the last person buried in the graveyard kept watch (*an fhaire chlaidh*) until the next new arrival.

R.J. Stewart recounts his encounter through seership with the spirit of such a guardian at a grave-mound in Jersey.

> The King suggested quite jovially that the process was voluntary, but implied a system of family obligation which could not be avoided, or a system which cast out those who did not merge when their time was due. This shocking occurrence was the greatest 'loss of Earth-root' that anyone could visualize . . . Once the inner integration process had occurred, the chamber was then used for consultation and initiation. Entry was madethrough a tiny crawl passage, usually kept sealed and guarded by a restrained soul.[55]

Such voluntary guardians have a special place as soul-bearers of the people in this tradition. They have walked the ancestral pathways and their purpose is to act as way-showers for the living and the dead. Such figures as Bran or King Loegaire who seek to guard their land, become imbued with great reverence as soul-bearers for a whole country. Specific voluntary guardians may act as *psychopompoi* at death. Several of these are discernible as threshold guardians on the borders of the otherworld in the *immrama* tradition.[56]

King Arthur is said to 'change his life'; he does not die, since the King and the land are one. His immortality is assured as long as the land has need of him, according to tradition. This and an even older guardianship are remembered in the custom of keeping ravens at the Tower of London: if they leave the Tower, the sovereignty of Britain is supposed to crumble. Ravens were the birds of Bran the Blessed, whose head was buried at the site of what is now the White Tower as a palladium against foreign invasion; according to Welsh lore, Arthur disinterred that head and took over the guardianship himself. Each country has such national and local ancestral guardians.

Several Celtic apologists have refused to credit our ancestors with the practice of human sacrifice, regarding the numerous classical accounts as Roman propaganda, yet the evidence, both textual and archaeological, testifies otherwise. The dedication of a human sacrifice was the offering of a soul, usually for the purpose of binding the victim to the service of a deity or to propitiate the deity against drought or murrain.

A suitable candidate for sacrifice, in druidic eyes, would be one who was kin to none. Druidic sacrifice for propitiatory or divinational purposes seems to have involved strangers or prisoners of war – any person outside the tribal framework, on whose behalf no legal redress could be sought; anyone who had put himself outside the law was no longer a recognized being. The many instances of the theme of 'a boy with no father' in Celtic lore, both Christian and Pagan, perhaps bespeaks this. Although the sacredness of motherhood as a kinship factor is an indigenous and Pictish belief which permeated pockets of Celtic settlement in Britain and Ireland, the sacrifice of an innocent child as foundation cement crops up frequently in the stories.

There is a strong belief in Celtic lore in zombies – reanimated bodies which are serviceable because their souls are bound. The Cauldron of Rebirth which appears in 'Branwen, Daughter of Llyr' is used by the Irish to resurrect their own dead soldiers; they arise to fight the next day, but they cannot speak.

The *Foras Feasa ar Eirinn* describes how the Tuatha de Danann sojourned in Boetia and there learned all their magic. It so happened that the Syrians made war on the Athenians, and both sides engaged in daily skirmishes. But the bodies of the Athenians who were slain would be fighting the next day, because the Danann put spirits into the same bodies to restore them'. The Syrians consulted their own druid who counselled them to set watch on the battlefield and to thrust a spit of rowan through the bodies of the dead. If the bodies were truly inspirited by their own souls, they would remain incorruptible, but if they were inhabited by the souls of demons then the bodies would immediately decay.[57]

We note that the identical method for rendering the undead inoperative is used in Irish as in Transylvanian tradition – a stake through the torso! Rowan is the wood most commonly utilized in Celtic tradition to ward off evil from faery or otherworldly sources. The traditional Scots saying, 'Rowan tree and red thread, hold the witches to their speed', testifies to an old ritual or protection.

A common Celtic method for ridding oneself of spirit-possessed guests is to construct an iron house and burn them to death. This death by the inverted cauldron of an iron house seems to polarize the rebirth within a cauldron. From the cauldron of souls, many were called back into the same family once again. The naming of a child by the name of a revered ancestor was called *togail an ainm* or 'raising the name', and was practised widely among the Celts. If such a child died early, it was unlucky to pass the name on again.[58]

Souls were the currency of life, providing the credit on which others lived. The redemption of souls by the payment of other souls underlay the practice of sacrifice long before Christianity itself subscribed to it, making it a central tenet of faith. This concept even extended to the animal world in early Celtic times, as Arrian tells us:

> Some of the Celts are obliged to make annual sacrifices to Artemis. Others offer the goddess a hoard or treasure which is made up thus: for a hare that they have caught they place two obols on the heap; for a fox a drachma, for the fox is a crafty creature always lying in ambush and is the scourge of hares; for a wild goat four drachma because it is a much bigger animal and more valuable game. The next year, when Artemis' birthday comes round again, they open the hoard and with the sum collected they buy a victim, a sheep, goat or a calf if there is enough money. Once sacrifice has been made and the first fruits offered to the huntress, according to their respective customs, they regale themselves and their dogs. On that day the dogs are even crowned with flowers to emphasize that the festival is given in their honour.[59]

Although Arrian writes of Artemis here, he intends us to understand a Celtic goddess with Artemisian qualities. The redeeming of wild animal souls by the offering of a domestic animal is not unlike the Gaulish ritual of the *pharmakos* or scapegoat, by which collective soul-burdens and other calamities requiring purification were atoned or paid for in the coin of life. Servius, preserved in a fragment of Petronius, relates:

> Whenever an epidemic broke out at Marseille, one of the poor of the town offered himself to save his fellow citizens. For a whole year he had to be fed with choice food at the town's expense. When the time came, crowned with leaves and wearing consecrated clothes, he was led through the whole town; he was heaped with imprecations, so that all the ills of the city were concentrated upon his head, and then he was thrown into the sea.[60]

Sometimes this collective purification of the soul was put upon the shoulders of one person in the Celtic rite of abandonment: put into a boat with a knife and water but without oars, sail or rudder, the subject was set adrift upon the mercy of the wave. Such exile was the normal punishment for incest, a crime which brought shame upon the whole tribe.

The exile or soul-journeying of one for the good of many is a central element of the Celtic quest (see Chapter 11). The quest to find an object which will restore the dead or heal the wasteland is of paramount importance. From the finding of the cauldron of rebirth to the quest for the Holy Grail, the healing of the soul-shrine and the restoration of its contents is a driving Celtic concern.

Reanimating the Soul-Shrine

Once the soul is out of its soul-shrine, how may it be brought home? The common theme to all methods is that of finding the thread or track of the soul and coaxing it home by some manner, that the triple spiral be once more ravelled up into its original configuration.

We have noted how a thread symbolized the soul's life; in the Highland charm called 'Eolais an T-Snaithnean' ('The Wisdom of the Threads') a triple thread was a method of disenchantment from soul-loss caused by the evil eye. It was used extensively upon animals, but may also have been used on people. Animal souls were believed to be stolen by the faery or by envious individuals and might ail as a result. The triple woven or plaited thread was put into the mouth while reciting the invocation and then tied around the animal's tail. If the beast was to recover, the person applying the thread was believed to feel some brief passing over of the illness to themselves. An Orkney coda for this custom was to say,

> Nine knots upo' this thread
> Nine blessings on thy head;
> Blessings to take away thy pain,
> And ilka tinter of thy strain.[61]

That the healing of soul-loss from the evil eye frequently brought a temporary symptomatic recoil upon the healer is witness to the extreme care which must be taken when doing such work. Restoring soul-parts to the soul-shrine was dangerous work which involved the healer in basic self-protection and scrupulous spiritual and physical cleanliness. Such a state of grace might only be arrived at by the healer's continuous recourse to spiritual help and by the implementation of daily practices of attunement. Such grace was believed to reside in those who by age or special virtue manifested a shining soul.

Many saints who revive the seemingly dead or who cast out spirits of illness, despair or doubt, are venerated still as spiritual helpers against similar conditions today. The Saxon saint, Dunstan of Glastonbury, casts out intrusive spirits; the measuring of St Gobhnat's statue in Ballyvourny with a length of wool restores full health; St Dympna restores those suffering from mental breakdown. The lively belief in these and other saints is more familial than ecclesiastic in nature, an appeal to dear ancestral helpers who by-pass the spiritual bureaucracy of the Church.

There is a widespread awareness that it is not by means of personal shamanic powers that soul-retrieval is achieved, but with the help of deities and spirits. Even when they have done all they can to heal Cuchulainn and Emer of love and jealousy, the druids and *filidh* appeal to Manannan himself who shakes his cloak of forgetfulness between the pair, that they might be restored to their former relationship.

Music plays the central role in Celtic soul-restoration, forming the most subtle net to help the soul-parts reassemble. There are numerous examples of the silver branch's ability to bring the sleep of vision or forgetfulness. Manannan, God of the Otherworld, has 'a branch of silver with three golden apples . . . delight and amusement enough it was to listen to the music made by the branch, for men sore-wounded, or women in child-bed, or folk in sickness . . . [they] would fall asleep at the melody which was made when that branch was shaken.'[62]

After their disastrous struggle with the Irish, the seven Britons who accompany the head of Bran the Blessed make for Harlech. During their meal the three birds of Rhiannon appear:

> and began singing unto them a certain song, and the songs they had ever heard were unpleasant compared thereto; and the birds seemed to them to be at a great distance from over the sea, yet they appeared as distinct as if they were close by, and at this repast they continued seven years.[63]

The song of Rhiannon's birds lifts their sorrow into an awareness of the otherworld, giving them respite from grief and a chance to understand the events that have passed from a different perspective, for Bran's head converses with them. The Irish goddess Cliodna, wife of Manannan, also has three birds: one blue with a crimson head, one crimson with a green head, and one speckled with a golden head which give guidance, entertainment and the sleep of forgetfulness.

These three birds are related to the three harp-strains which grant three releases in Irish tradition: Suantrai bringing sleep, Geantrai bringing joy, and Goiltrai granting tears. We note that the threefold nature of the soul is restored by those same conditions which cause the three cauldrons of the subtle body to move: joy, sorrow and repose (see Chapter 7).

In 'The Second Battle of Mag Tuiread', the Tuatha de Danann rescue Uaitne, the Dagda's harper, who has been carried off by the Fomorians:

> They reached the banqueting-house in which were Bres son of Elotha, and Elotha son of Delbaeth. There hung the harp on the wall. That is the harp in which the Dagda had bound the melodies so that they sounded not until by his call he summoned them forth; when he said this below:
>
> Come Daurdabla!
> Come Coir-cethair-chuir!
> Come summer, Come winter!
> Mouths of harps and bags and pipes!
>
> Now that harp had two names, Daur-da-bla 'Oak of two greens' and Coir-cethair-chuir 'Four-angled-music.'
> Then the harp went forth from the wall, and killed nine men, and came to the Dagda. And he played for them the three things whereby harpers are distinguished, to wit, sleep-strain and smile-strain and wail-strain. He played wail-strain to them, so that their tearful women wept. He played smile-strain to them, so that their women and children laughed. He played sleep-strain to them, and the company fell asleep. Through that sleep, the three of them escaped unhurt from the Fomorians.[64]

We hear about this technique again in 'The Cattle Raid of Fraech' and discover that the three harp strains derive from the goddess Boann:

> 'Let the harpers play to us,' said Ailill to Fraech. 'Indeed, let them so!' said Fraech. The harps were covered with otterskins, with ornaments of Parthian leather worked in gold and silver. The interior covers were of kidskin, white as snow, with dark grey eyes in the centre. About the strings themselves was a covering of linen, white as swansdown. The harps were of gold and silver and white bronze, with animal shapes of snakes, birds and

dogs in gold and silver upon them. When the strings were vibrating these animal shapes would make circuits about the men. The harpers played then and twelve men in that house died of weeping and sorrow.

The three harpers were handsome and melodious, and they were, moreover the play [i.e. offspring] of Uaitne. These three famous men were three brothers, Goltraiges, Gentraiges and Suantraiges. Boann of the *sidhe* was their mother. When that woman was in labour the first time, she was in weeping and sorrow because of the sharpness of her pains; the second birth was followed by smiles and joy because of the pleasure of her two sons; finally she found sleep and quietness because of the heaviness of the last birth. So it was that they were named for the three strains of music. Afterwards, Boann awoke from her sleep and said, 'Receive your three sons, O passionate Uaitne, for the music of sleep and laughter and sorrow will affect the cattle and women or Ailill and Maeve that bring forth young.'

(Author's translation)

The healing sleep obtained in incubation is dealt with in Chapter 10, but we cannot pass over the role of sleep as healer, especially in the extraordinary example of Cuchulainn. In the defence of Ulster, the hero takes no sleep whatever between Samhain and Imbolc (from 31 October to 1 February). Overcome by exhaustion and wounded beyond measure, Cuchulainn lies totally spent. His charioteer, Laegh, spies a wondrous figure coming towards them. 'Tis one of my faery kin that comes to succour and solace me.' It is none other than Lugh, his otherworldly father, who bids him: 'Sleep then, Cuchulainn, and by the grave in the Lerga slumber deeply, until three days with their three nights be ended. During which space, upon yonder host I myself will exercise my skill in arms.' While he sleeps thus, Lugh 'laid balsams and healing herbs of fairy potency, so that as he slept, nor knew that which was wrought in him, the hero made a good recovery. In the period of his soul's absence, Cuchulainn's appearance has been upon Lugh who has stoutly defended Ulster.'[65]

The voice itself was a healing oracle, able to call souls from beyond the otherworld back into the soul-shrine. Classical writings and Gaulish inscriptions alike speak of the *gutuater*, the 'keeper of the [people's] voice'. The *gutuater* appears in Caesar's writings as an 'inciter of war', but Le Roux and Guyonvarc'h favour the interpretation of 'invoker of the gods', one whose specialist role may have included an incantatory rallying of the tribal soul.[66]

On a more personal level of healing, we see the effect of Taliesin's voice upon the deranged Merlin in Geoffrey of Monmouth's *Vita Merlini*. In a brilliant remembering of Merlin's fragmented soul, Taliesin recites to him a bardic creation of the universe, which simultaneously contextualizes Merlin's place in his own time and place.[67] When Llew is struck by Gronw's spear, he does not die, but passes into an eagle's shape, until his soul is coaxed back into the human body by Gwydion, who sings *englynnion*, shamanic verses that echo the divinatory quality of *teinm laegda*. The singing home of the soul is perhaps the crowning glory of the *filidh*, skilled in divinatory verse and visionary journeying.

The ultimate soul-restoration is that which is undertaken on behalf of the land and of all that lives upon it. The wasteland which is brought about by war, political corruption or natural disaster is symptomatic of the land's soul-loss. Through earthly quest and otherworldly search, by deeds of arms and shamanic discovery, Celtic heroes and wise ones seek for ways to re-ensoul their land, ever looking for helpers and way-showers.

The primary soul-guardians of Celtic tradition are Aengus and Brighid. As we have seen, Aengus Og is able to breathe the soul back into the body of Diarmuid, whom he keeps guarded in the Brugh. He also makes a soul-house for the wandering shape of Etain to inhabit, until Fuamnach the enchantress creates a high wind to blow Etain out into the world again. Aengus is concerned with the harmony which should be within the soul-shrine, and his otherworldly home at Newgrange is inscribed with the triple spiral which is the three-fold template of the soul. Brugh na Boyne itself acts as an otherworldly soul-shrine, an abode where lost souls can refresh themselves before taking up their *tuirgin* once more.

Similarly, the threefold protection offered by Brighid is related to the triple Celtic soul: as the Lady of Smithcraft, Healing and Poetry, she is concerned with the weaving together of the mental, emotional and psychic strands which make life worthwhile. Celtic people have always invoked her to wrap her mantle of protection around them, for her mantle is nothing less than the web of life which defines the soul-shrine. The mantle of Brighid is invariably woven by the recitation of the *caim*, an 'encompassing' or protective prayer which acts as a palladium against a variety of dangers. Any suitable form of words may be used, but normally Brighid's name and that of other saints and the Trinity are invoked, and vulnerable parts of the body named and protected.

Caim means 'loop' or 'bend', but its specialist meaning is 'sanctuary' or 'protective circle', which is how the practitioner uses it. The traditional way to make the *caim* is for the encompasser to stretch out the forefinger of the right hand, keeping it towards the subject, while walking sunwise around her and saying the *caim*. It may also be made upon oneself.

The *caim* was made in all seasons and circumstances, around people, houses, animals, around the very fire itself which represented the vitality of life. As her family prepared to sleep, the Gaelic mother would breathe these words over the fire as she banked it in for the night:

> I smoor the hearth
> As Brighid the foster-mother would smoor it.
> The holy name of the foster-mother
> Be upon the hearth and the herd,
> Be upon each of my household.
> The encircling of God upon myself and the hearth,
> The encircling of God upon myself and the floor,
> Upon each herd and flock,
> Upon each of my household.

> (Author's translation)

As she said this, she would spread the embers into a circle, and divide it into three equal heaps with a central heap. To make the holy name of the fostermother, she placed three turfs of peat between the three heaps, each one touching the centre, and covered it all with ash. Such smooring customs and invocations are still performed in the West of Ireland. And so the protection of Brighid is wrapped about the house and its occupants, preserving the threefold integrity of the soul.

We have forgotten many of the common soul-protections of our ancestors which maintained the triple spiral within the soul-shrine. But as Western medical and worldwide shamanic understandings draw closer together in identifying the spiritual causes of physical sickness, mental illness and emotional trauma, so we can rediscover modern ways in which we can honour and protect the mind, soul and heart within the soul-shrine that it stray no more.

CHAPTER 10

Dreams and Visions

The use of dreams and visions as a means of discovering the prognosis either of future events or those which took place at a distance in time or space is well attested among the Celtic peoples. It is also an important part of the skills practised by contemporary shamans the world over. In this chapter we begin with an essay on the subject of dream incubation, evidence for the practice of which has been discovered at several sites in Britain. This is followed by a story from Irish tradition which illustrates the activity of augury.

The story revolves around the danger and horror surrounding the festival of Samhain, the Celtic New Year, our modern Hallowe'en. Then, as now, it is the night on which the faery-hills are opened, when the way between the worlds is very busy with otherworldly traffic, when spirits abound. Even in modern folk customs surrounding this ancient Celtic festival, it is not a night to go out unless one is in disguise to confuse the spirits. Mischief is abroad and only the foolhardy, brave or well protected go out. However, the hero accepts a dare to put a withy round a hanged man's foot on Samhain eve. His subsequent adventures reveal the time-lapse which accompanies any foray into the otherworld – something which is often experienced on a shamanic journey, which can seem to take no time at all or much longer than the clock records.

Nera's fortitude in accomplishing this feat is offset by the vision that he has of the destruction of the royal dun of Cruachan. He gains otherworldly knowledge of the *sidhe* and so averts the vision. However, as with many such gifts, Nera himself does not finally return from the *sidhe*, but falls out of his own world into theirs.

Here, as in other tales of Celtic myth, the visionary gift is seen as a two-edged sword, one which can bring great insight, but which can also cause trouble for the participants.

Incubation and the Dream Quest
by John Matthews

Auguries

The search for omens and their meaningful interpretation is one that has long been recognized as a major concern of humans. Ellen Ettlinger sums this up precisely:

> The life of primitive man depended upon his unceasingly vigilant attitude towards the phenomena of nature. Among these were uncanny incidents, strange coincidences or vivid dream-impressions which took hold of his imagination. By pure intuition and without any analogy man interpreted a stirring natural happening as a warning of trouble ahead. Similar or recurrent experiences caused the attribution of . . . forboding to a particular event. The newly won knowledge was passed on to the medicine-man who handed the facts and the meaning of the 'omen' down to his successor. As time went on the functions of the medicine-man gradually separated more and more from each other and developed along their own lines. Magicians, diviners, leeches, judges, and poets emerged and were initiated into the omen-language in order to satisfy the requirements of their respective activities.[1]

The first principle of which we become aware when the subject of precognition among the Celts is studied, is the importance of dreams in which the subjects learn something of considerable import to their circumstances. A typical example of this is to be found in the Irish text of 'The First Battle of Moytura' in which the arrival of the Tuatha de Danann is perceived by King Eochaid in the following manner:

> 'I saw a great flock of black birds', said the king, 'coming from the depths of Ocean. They settled over all of us, and fought with the people of Ireland. They brought confusion on us, and destroyed us.' [And he said to his Druid, Cesard]: 'Employ your skill and knowledge, and tell us the meaning of the vision'. Cesard did so, and by means of ritual and the use of his science the meaning of the king's vision was revealed to him: and he

said: 'I have tidings for you: warriors are coming across the sea, a thousand heroes covering the ocean; speckled ships will press in upon us; all kinds of death they announce, a people skilled in every art, a magic spell; an evil spirit will come upon you, signs to lead you astray . . . they will be victorious in every stress.'[2]

Two factors become immediately apparent from this: First that the King recognises his dream as important, implying that precognitive dreaming was a normal matter; and secondly that he requires an interpreter for the meaning of the dream – in this case, the druid Cesard. A third factor, that the symbolism of the dream involved creatures (specifically birds) and water (the sea) will be seen to possess an importance of their own.

Prognostication from the actions of animals or birds are well attested in Celtic literature, and were a part of a substantial shaman-ic tradition in Britain and Ireland. Two treatises preserved in a Middle Irish MS in the Library of Trinity College Dublin (codex H.3.17), refer specifically to the interpretation of the flight patterns and songs of the raven and the wren – birds long recognized as sacred in Celtic myth. Of the raven, it is said that if it calls

. . . from above an enclosed bed in the midst of the house, it is a distinguished grey-haired guest or clerics that are coming to see thee, but there is a difference between them: if it be a lay cleric [?] the raven says *bacach*; if it be a man in orders it calls *gradh gradh*, and twice in the day it calls. If it be warrior guests or satirists that are coming it is *gracc gracc* it calls, or *grob grob*, and it calls in the quarter behind thee, and it is thence that the guests are coming. If it calls *gracc gracc* the warriors are oppressed to whom it calls.

Of the wren we are told:

If it be between thee and the sun, it is the slaving of a man that is dear to thee . . . If it be at thy left ear, union with a young man from afar, or sleeping with a young woman. If it call from behind thee, importuning of thy wife by another man in despite of thee. If it be on the ground behind thee, thy wife will be taken from thee by force. If the wren call from the east, poets are coming towards thee, or tidings from them.[3]

The observations here are of a very general kind and are perhaps not to be taken too literally; however, they do indicate the divinatory importance of birds and suggest that at one time the practice was both more sophisticated and more precise.

Apart from this there were a number of specific kinds of omen which occurred frequently, notably before a battle: weapons that shrieked or cried aloud, the appearance of the Washer at the Ford (see below) or the behaviour of animals – notably horses or dogs. Among the death omens which surrounded the last days of the great Irish hero Cuchulainn is that in which he is offered a vat from which to drink before departing for battle. Hitherto this had always been a sign of certain victory for him, but on this occasion he finds the vat filled with blood.

Dreams

By far the most significant documentation of augury concerns precognitive dreams, not only of the kind discussed above, which are primarily spontaneous, but also self-induced visions, which may be brought on in a number of ways, including the position of the sleeper, bodily contact with other men or women, and contact with the skin of an animal on which the sleeper lay to have his or her dream.[4]

Several texts mention the positioning of the sleeper between two pillar-stones, as in the case of the Irish hero Cuchulainn, who could not sleep inside a house until a special bed was built for him at the behest of the King. First two tall stones were erected, then the bed was placed between them. Cuchulainn was then able to sleep – although when he heard 'the groans of the Ulstermen', his comrades, in a battle, he stretched forth and broke both the stones. Another text mentions Condla Coel Corrbacc resting on an island 'leaning his head against a pillar-stone in the western part of the island and the feet against a pillar-stone in its eastern part'.[5]

Neither character is described as having any vision or dream in this instance, but it seems likely that the depiction of this unusual method of sleeping, with its east – west orientation, once held a greater significance as the position assumed by the seeker after dreams of predictive visions. Elsewhere we read that when the druids wished to make an important prognostication, and having tried all other methods available to them, they made 'round hurdles of rowan, and spread over them the hides of sacrificed bulls with the fleshly side uppermost'.[6] Whence it was said, remarks the historian Keating, that 'anyone who had done his utmost to obtain information . . . that he had gone onto his hurdles of knowledge'.[7]

The importance of sleeping on the skin of a particular beast is well attested throughout Celtic literature. The best-known example is in the story of 'The Dream of Rhonabwy' from *The Mabinogion*, in which the hero is in pursuit of an actual historical figure, known to have lived in the Middle Ages in Wales. Seeking shelter one night in the dank and evil-smelling hut belonging to a hag, Rhonabwy sleeps on a yellow bull's hide and dreams a long and astonishingly complex dream of the hero Arthur and his men, who are all depicted as larger than life and much saddened by the fact that Wales has come to be occupied by such little men![8]

Apart from the obvious shamanic nature of this idea, it is clearly a reminder of the *tarbh feis* practised by the Irish druids. In this, after having sacrificed a (usually white) bull and made a broth from its flesh, the druid wrapped himself in the freshly flayed skin and slept a profound sleep, in which he would dream the answer to a great question – usually the secession of a king or something of equal importance.

The eating of the sacrificed creature's flesh suggests a further connection with methods of prognostication described in *Cormac's Glossary*. Among the techniques mentioned is *Imbas Forosna*, (see Chapter 8).

The manner in which this relates to worldwide shamanic practice is discussed in John Matthews' *Taliesin: the Shamanic and Bardic Mysteries in Britain and Ireland*, but it is worth noticing that among the Okinawa, as among the Esquimaux, the Wintu and Shasta tribes of North America, and the African Zulus, shamans frequently receive their 'call' in the form of dream or vision, and that often animals or birds are involved as in the examples of raven and wren lore quoted above.[9]

The practice of sleeping on a hide was attested as late as the eighteenth century, by Martin Martin. He describes the rite known as *taghairm* as follows:

> A party of men, who first retired to solitary places, remote from any house . . . singled out one of their number, and wrapp'd him in a big cow's hide, which they folded about him, his whole body was covered with it except his head, and so left in this posture all night until . . . [he gave] the proper answer to the question in hand.[10]

This wrapping of the dreamer in a hide recalls the descriptions of patients at the Asklepion, who were wrapped in tight bandages, from which they were symbolically cut free after their incubatory period as a sign of their healed state. The objectives here are different, but the method of obtaining the vision once again curiously similar. We do not know whether this was practised as a mimesis of the swaddling clothes of small children, whose fontanelles would still be open to allow the ingress of spirits and visions, but this is a factor to be considered.

Finally, we must mention the idea of physical contact as a further means of enhancing the visionary state. We do not know if the priests of the Asklepion were present or watched over the patient during their incubatory sleep; it would seem, on the whole, unlikely. However, in most of the accounts from Celtic literature, the sleeper is described as being watched over by his friends, or by the druids who initiated his state of being. In some cases they are described as chanting 'a spell of truth' over the sleeper; in others as being near at hand and shaking him awake after his period in a darkened room. Often there are four guardians mentioned, as in the description of the bull-feast mentioned above. Elsewhere, in the text known as 'The Voyage of Bran', one of the characters is described as ascending every day to the top of the royal rath with his three chief druids in order 'to view all four points of the heavens that the *sid* [faery] men should not rest upon Ireland unperceived by him . . .'[11]

We may guess from this that a watch was to be maintained at all times over the sleeper to ensure that his sleeping or wandering spirit was not carried off into the otherworld, as might happen all too easily at that time.

Whether or not the guardians were actually touching the sleeper is not stated, but in several other texts such contact is specifically noted. In 'The Mabinog of Math Son of Mathonwy' for instance we learn that Math spent most of his time with his feet in the lap of the royal foot-holder; while in a later story a child who is experiencing difficulty in remembering the Psalms has only to sleep with his head resting on the knees of the Irish St Aengus in order to awake with the entire canon of the scripture secure in his memory!

This seems to point to the idea of the passing on of knowledge by direct contact with the master. It is no large step from here to the idea of knowledge gained from the dead, who were frequently consulted on matters of import, and who could be contacted by either visiting their graves or summoning them in necromantic fashion. The Roman author Tertullian states (*De Anima* 27) that the Celts were given to sleeping on the tombs of their ancestors in order to receive knowledge and inspiration. The same idea was current among the Norse; places where the dead rested were regarded as sanctuaries and the act of sleeping upon them as likely to result in a revelatory experience.

Incubation

The method of obtaining information from inner sources (primarily the otherworld) most often attested to, not only among the Celts but in a much wider sphere, is that of the incubatory sleep. This is especially true of ancient Greece, where the temples dedicated to Asklepios concerned themselves specifically with the healing of ailments through this method. Here the sufferer, after being suitably prepared, slept in a special cell in a part of the temple called an *abaton*, and there dreamed a dream in which he or she either received a visitation from the god himself, whose touch brought healing; or else was instructed in a method of self-cure – sometimes cryptically and in a form requiring interpretation, although this does not seem ever to have been done by the priests of the temple.[12]

To early man, who saw sickness as a reflection of spiritual health, if a person suffered from a physical ailment (except loss of limbs or wounds acquired in war) there must be something wrong with his soul. For this reason Asklepios, who became the God of Physicians, was seen not only as a healer, but also as a 'saviour' god, whose actions were intended to counteract those of other deities whom the patient might have offended, or whose observance he or she might in some way have neglected. Incubatory sleep was the god's principal method of working his cures – much as in modern psychoanalysis, where the patient is encouraged to discover the disaffection in his or her soul through the study or interpretation of his dreams.

Unlike the modern practice however, the dreams were seen as specifically emanating from the god, and the whole process took place within a specific *temenos*, the sacred precinct of the god (the word *incubare* is translated as 'sleeping in the sanctuary'). The resultant dreams (and few seem not to have experienced something) either effected an immediate cure or gave a method by which this might be achieved.

Preparation for the ritual of dreaming was also carefully controlled. After undergoing rites of purification, involving a lustral bath and preliminary sacrifices to the god (usually of a cockerel), the patient went to sleep in the place 'not to be entered by the unbidden'[13] It appears that he or she underwent some period of waiting, until 'called' by the priests, or even by the god himself, to enter the *abaton*. The importance of preparedness is stressed in every account of the Asklepiae; if the patients were not in a proper state of mind they were likely either not to experience a dream or to have one which was unsatisfactory. Those who did so were likely to be sent away, perhaps to try again later on, after a further period of preparation.

It is also clear that the incubatory sleep took place at night, an important point for our argument in the light of the emphasis on absence of light by the Celtic poets and prophets, who frequently gave their precognitive visions after being enclosed in a dark place, watched over by friends or priests, and afterwards brought forth into bright light. It is apparent that patients at the Asklepion who failed (perhaps from excitement or pain) to sleep at all, received some kind of direct vision of the god, in which they were instructed as to how they might achieve healing, in the same way as if they had experienced a dream.

Asklepios himself appears to have begun life as a mortal physician who, taught by the centaur Cherion, was struck down by Zeus after he had successfully raised the dead. A still earlier account suggests a more shamanic personality, in which his name is Aischabios and he is represented by totemic animals – the dog and the snake. The latter continued to be Asklepios' theriomorphic form, so that whenever a new Asklepion was founded, one of the sacred snakes kept in the temple was taken there to be installed with due ceremony.[14]

The Asklepiae were generally founded near groves of trees or springs, indicating their connection with both the elements and the underworld. As Dr Chadwick has noted in her study of dreams in ancient Europe:

> The most striking features which these dreams share in common . . . are (1) that they generally relate to the underworld . . . and (2) that they are for the most part shared with the rest of the community.[15]

This in itself indicates the chthonic nature of the Asklepiae, and of the god himself, and it of course also recalls the accounts of sleeping on the graves of dead heroes or druids in order to obtain dreams in which their wisdom could be plumbed. That this was a very central aspect in the design of temple precincts where incubatory sleep took place is demonstrated by the account of the Greek historian and geographer Pausanias, who personally experienced initiation into the mysteries of Trophonios, an early Greek hero who became deified and took on many of the aspects of Asklepios. Initially he was shown to have lived in a cave at Lebadeia in Boetia, again an indication of chthonic aspects. Pausanias' account makes this even more apparent.

> When a man decides to go down to Trophonios, he first lives a certain number of days in a building which is consecrated to Good Fortune (Fortuna) and the Good Spirit (Agathadaimon).

> Living there he purifies himself and uses no hot water; his bath is the river Herkyna.[16]

The initiate is then bathed in the river Herkyna and anointed by pubescent boys, called the *Hermai*.

> From here he is taken by the priests, not straight to the oracle, but to the water-springs, which are very close together. Here he must drink the water of Forgetfulness, to forget everything in his mind until then, and then the water of Memory, by which he remembers the sights he sees in his descent.

After a period of worship here, he is taken to the mountainside above a sacred wood, which is surrounded by a circular platform of white stone, about 5 feet high. On this are bronze posts which are linked by bronze chains. Passing through the doors down into a chasm, the initiate descends through the kiln-shaped orifice of the earth, descending 20 feet by means of a ladder. On floor level here is a small passage 1 foot high and 2 feet wide to admit the initiate. The man going down lies on the ground with honey cakes in his hands and pushes his feet into the opening and then tries to get his knees in. The rest of his body is immediately dragged after his knees, as if some extraordinary deep, fast river was catching him in a current and sucking him down. From here on, inside the second place, people are not always taught the future in one and the same way: one man hears, another sees as well. Those who go down return feet first through the same mouth.

> When a man comes up from Trophonios the priests take him over again, and sit him on the throne of memory, which is not far from the holy place, to ask him what he saw and discovered.

Pausanius' account says that only one person had ever been killed here. He himself had passed these dangers and wrote from personal experience. All who consulted the oracle had to write down their story on a wooden tablet and dedicate it to the shrine. Such a collection of testimonies would be most interesting to read.

That mysteries such as these were once current among the Celts is evident from accounts in widely scattered sources. As these are pieced together we begin to see a pattern emerging.

Clearly water was seen as a conductor of healing or information from beneath the ground. Numerous instances could be quoted from Celtic literature in which omens or precognitive dreams are vouchsafed beside rivers or springs. In the poetry of the Welsh poet Taliesin (a probable contemporary of Merlin) there are more references to water than to any other element, and this can be seen to reflect the complex matter of visionary insight as it connects with both darkness and light, as in the story of Nechtan's Well. Those who looked into the well unprepared were at once blinded by a light from within, but its waters also gave inspiration to those who had undergone the necessary preparation (as in the case of the visitors to the Asklepiae).[17]

Examples of omens received at or by rivers include the following from 'The Siege of Howth'.[18] In this the King, Mes-Gegra, and his charioteer have paused behind the main body of the army to rest awhile. The charioteer sleeps first and while he is watching Mes-Gegra sees a large nut floating downriver. Seizing it the King cuts it in half and eats the kernel. As he looks he sees the charioteer 'lifted up in his sleep from the ground'. When the man wakes the King asks how he is: 'I have seen an evil vision' replies the charioteer and asks about the nut. A quarrel then breaks out and the King is severely wounded and the charioteer killed. Although the connection between the dream and the nut is not made clear, we should remember that the nut is invariably connected with visionary insight, and of course once again we have the themes of precognition and water.

Badbh, the Irish War Goddess, announced the approaching death of eminent heroes by taking the form of the Washer at the Ford, who was to be seen washing out bloody clothes or blood-stained armour in the river near the site of a forthcoming battle – a possible memory of a time when priestesses, trained in the arts of prophecy, kept watch at fords or springs and were called upon to give prognostications before battle was joined.

There is no clear evidence for the existence of incubation temples in Britain or Ireland, but one site at Lydney, Gloucestershire, has caused more than one commentator to suggest that it may have been put to just such a use – the inference being that if one such temple were operative in this country others may well have existed of which we have no current knowledge.

The site is of Romano-British provenance and was built between AD 364 and 367. It was excavated by Sir Mortimer Wheeler in the 1940s and found to possess a building consisting of several small cubicles. It was then noticed that the ground plan of the temple complex bore a marked resemblance to the layout of the Asklepion at Epidavros, including a bath-house and dormitories. Casts representing a disfigured hand and a heavily pregnant woman were also discovered at the site, suggesting that these may have been representations of the ailments suffered by those who attended the temple. At Epidavros, similar effigies were found in profusion, having been hung up in the temple as thank-offerings by patients who had been cured.

All of this led Wheeler to suggest that:

> Here, then, we seem to have a recurrent feature of some of the principal classical shrines of healing, and we may provisionally regard the Lydney building as a member of this series. On this line of thought it may be that the Long Building was indeed an 'abaton', used to supplement the 'chapels' in the temple itself for the purpose of that temple-sleep through which the healing-god and his priesthood were wont to work.[19]

If we accept this suggestion, the question arises as to whether the Lydney temple was the province of a native god, or was a copy of the classical foundations.

The dedication of Lydney was undoubtedly to the Celtic god Nodens, of whom little is, unfortunately, known. The presence of a priestly diadem at the site has led some commentators to the belief that he was a solar deity, a belief substantiated by the great Celticist Sir John Rhys,[20] who also pointed out the probable links between Nodens, the Irish Nuada Argetlam (Nuada of the Silver Hand) and the Welsh Llud Llaw Eraint (a title applied to Nodens in the hero list from 'Culhwch and Olwen' in *The Mabinogion* – both of whom derive from an earlier Brythonic version, Ludons Lamargentios. Nuada was, of course, the possessor of an artificial hand, made for him by the Smith-God Creidne with the help of the Leech-God Dian Cecht. Llud can be identified with Llyr Lledyeith (Half-speech). These are interesting as they suffer from physical defects, and are connected with a god who may have been responsible for a healing temple.

However, the diadem mentioned above, which depicts the god in a chariot drawn by horses and surrounded by nereids and spirits of the winds, suggests not so much a solar deity as a god of the sea. William Bathurst, who first drew attention to the Lydney site in 1831, translated the name Nodens as 'God of the Abyss' or 'of the Depths'[21], a suggestive appellation since it suggests connections both with the sea and with the chthonic depths with which, as we have seen, Asklepios was identified. Interestingly, like Asklepios, Nuada was eventually struck down by a bolt of lightning, at the battle of Mag Tuired. Llyr was also connected with the sea, and together these watery references recall the provenance of so many Celtic dream visions beside streams or rivers – although this analogy should not be pressed too far.

It is possible, then, that we have in the figure of Nodens a native equivalent of Asklepios, and on the site at Lydney a British, Romano-

Celtic temple where incubatory sleep was practised. We have seen from the evidence presented above that the idea of sleep as a means of discovering information or precognitive vision was common among the Celts. That a tradition of shamanism was also current at least as late as the sixth century AD is also certain. The combination of these two strains of thinking and belief make it more than likely that the idea of incubatory sleep for healing purposes would have been readily acceptable; although whether it was imported from the classical world or already existed is less certain. However, one final piece of evidence does remain, which suggests that it may well have been current at least in Ireland.

We discussed the use of sweat-houses in Chapter 9. The similarity between these structures and the ancient howes or burial chambers of Britain and Ireland is marked. Martin Brennan first drew attention to this in his book *The Boyne Valley Vision*. He notes that steam baths were an ancient and well-attested method of inducing an altered state among the shamans of many parts of the world. The combination of this idea with that of incubatory sleep and the Celtic love of augury suggests a very strong argument in favour of there being such practices in these islands, perhaps from a very early date.

I would like to end this essay on a personal note. A few years ago, while suffering from a bout of 'flu, I received a visit in dream state from an inner guide who communicated to me a specific method of helping myself to recover quickly. I had virtually forgotten about this until a few weeks ago, when I was again laid low with a virus. Lying in bed, suffering alternate bouts of hot and cold. I began to dream lucidly. I recalled the previous instruction clearly. I must seek and find a pattern of negative promises: for example, 'I promise to feel very much *more* ill in a moment'; 'I promise to bite my thumb very hard when I wake up'. When I had successfully established this pattern I would awake refreshed. It proved extremely difficult to do. The tendency was to think: 'I will feel *better* when I awake': 'I will *not* bite my thumb hard on waking'. But eventually I was able to discover the right pattern, helped by a specific symbol which remained in my mind until I had finished. I then woke up feeling a great deal better.

The symbol looked like this:

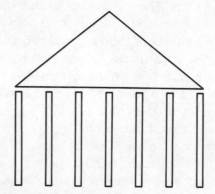

Fig. 8. The healing temple

Subsequent meditation on this has revealed more of the image: that of a temple portico, with seven pillars and a wide entrance standing open before me. It does not require too great a stretching of one's credulity to believe that this is an image of the healing temple – whether the mother foundation of Asklepios or the native one at Lydney. Either way, it suggests to me very powerfully the continuing efficacy of incubatory sleep, as it was, I believe, once practised in these islands.

To end, here is an incubatory invocation to be recited by the priest or priestess of the shrine over the sleeper. It was written by Caitlín Matthews, after a discussion of the material presented above:

> Learn to the gifted with the night,
> With the words of wisdom.
> From the depths of darkness' dazzling
> The story will rise
> As a circling snake.
>   May the sacred curve
>   of Her arm enfold you!
>   May the stars of Her
>   dark veil cover you!
>   May your sleep be founded
>   in the deep night of Her own lap!

The Adventures of Nera
translated by Kuno Meyer[22]

One Halloween Ailill and Medb were in Rath Cruachan with their whole household. They set about cooking food. Two captives had been hanged by them the day before that. Then Ailill said: 'He who would now put a withe round the foot of either of the two captives that are on the gallows, shall have a prize for it from me, as he may choose.'

Great was the darkness of that night and its horror, and demons would appear on that night always. Each man of them went out in turn to try that night, and quickly would he come back into the house. 'I will have the prize from thee', said Nera, 'and I shall go out. Truly thou shalt have this my gold-hilted sword here', said Ailill.

Then this Nera went out towards the captives, and put good armour on him. He put a withe round the foot of one of the two captives. Thrice it sprang off again. Then the captive said to him, unless he put a proper peg on it, though he be at it till the morrow, he would not fix his own peg on it. Then Nera put a proper peg on it.

Said the captive from the gallows to Nera: 'That is manly, O Nera!' 'Manly indeed!' said Nera. 'By the truth of thy valour, take me on thy neck, that I may get a drink with thee. I was very thirsty when I was hanged.' 'Come on my neck then!' said Nera. So he went on his neck. 'Whither shall I carry thee?' said Nera. 'To the house which is nearest to us', said the captive.

So they went to that house. Then they saw something. A lake of fire round that house. 'There is no drink for us in this house', said the captive. 'There is no fire without sparing in it ever. Let us therefore go to the other house, which is nearest to us', said the captive. They went to it then and saw a lake of water around it. 'Do not go to that house!' said the captive. There is never a washing- nor a bathing-tub, nor a slop-pail in it at night after sleeping. 'Let us still go to the other house', said the captive. 'Now there is my drink in this house', said the captive. He let him down on the floor. He went into the house. There were tubs for washing and bathing in it, and a drink in either of them. Also a slop-pail on the floor of the house. He then drinks a draught of either of them and scatters the last sip from his lips at the faces of the people that were in the house, so that they all died. Henceforth it is not good [to have] either a tub for washing or bathing, or a fire without sparing, or a slop-pail in a house after sleeping.

Thereupon he carried him back to his torture, and Nera returned to Cruachan. Then he saw something. The dun was burnt before him, and he beheld a heap of heads of their people [cut off] by the warriors from the dun. He went after the host then into the cave of Cruachan. 'A man on the track here!' said the last man to Nera. 'The heavier is the track', said his comrade to him, and each man said that word to his mate from the last man to the first man. Thereupon they reached the sid of Cruachan and went into it. Then the heads were displayed to the king in the sid. 'What shall be done to the man that came with you?' said one of them. 'Let him come hither, that I may speak with him', said the king. Then Nera came to them and the king said to him: 'What brought thee with the warriors into the sid?' said the king to him. 'I came in the company of thy host', said Nera. 'Go now to yonder house', said the king. 'There is a single woman there, who will make thee welcome. Tell her it is from me thou art sent to her, and come every day to this house with a burden of firewood'.

Then he did as he was told. The woman bade him welcome and said: 'Welcome to thee, if it is the king that sent thee hither'. 'It is he, truly', said Nera. Every day Nera used to go with a burden of firewood to the dun. He saw every day a blind man and a lame man on his neck coming out of the dun before him. They would go until they were at the brink of a well before the dun. 'Is it there?' said the blind man. 'It is indeed', said the lame one. 'Let us go away', said the lame man.

Nera then asked the woman about this. 'Why do the blind and the lame man visit the well?' 'They visit the crown, which is in the well', said the woman, 'viz. a diadem of gold, which the king wears on his head. It is there it is kept'. 'Why do those two go?' said Nera. 'Not hard to tell', said she, 'because it is they that are trusted by the king to visit the crown.' 'One of them was blinded, the other lamed'. 'Come hither a little', said Nera to his wife, 'that thou mayst tell me of my adventures now'. 'What has appeared to thee?' said the woman. 'Not hard to tell', said Nera. 'When I was going into the sid, methought the rath of Cruachan was destroyed and Ailill and Medb with their whole household had fallen in it'. 'That is not true indeed', said the woman, 'but an elfin host came to thee. That will come true', said she, unless he would reveal it to his friends. 'How shall I give warning to my people?' said Nera. 'Rise and go to them', said she. 'They are still round the same cauldron and the charge has not yet been removed from the fire.' Yet it had seemed to him three days and three nights since he had been in the sid. 'Tell them to be on their guard at Halloween coming, unless they come to destroy the sid. For I will promise them this: the sid to be destroyed by Ailill and Medb, and the crown of Briun to be carried off by them'.

[These are the three things, which were found in it, viz: the mantle of Loegaire in Armagh, and the crown of Briun in Connaught, and the shirt of Dunlaing in Leinster in Kildare.]

'How will it be believed of me, that I have gone into the sid?' said Nera. 'Take fruits of summer with thee', said the woman. 'Then he took wild garlic with him and primrose and golden fern. And I shall be pregnant by thee', said she 'and shall bear thee a son. And send a message from thee to the sid, when thy people will come to destroy the sid, that thou mayest take thy family and thy cattle from the sid'.

Thereupon Nera went to his people, and found them around the same caldron; and he related his adventures to them. And then his sword was given to him, and he staid with his people to the end of a year. That was the very year, in which Fergus mac Roich came as an exile from the land of Ulster to Ailill and Medb to Cruachan. 'Thy appointment has come, oh Nera', said Ailill to Nera. 'Arise and bring thy people and thy cattle from the sid, that we may go to destroy the sid'.

Then Nera went to his wife in the sid, and she bade him welcome. 'Arise out to the dun now', said the woman to Nera, 'and take a burden of firewood with thee. I have gone to it for a whole year with a burden of firewood on my neck every day in thy stead, and I said thou wert in sickness. And there is also thy son yonder'. Then he went out to the dun and carried a burden of firewood with him on his neck. 'Welcome alive from the sickness in which thou wast!' said the king. 'I am displeased that the woman should sleep with thee without asking'. 'Thy will shall be done about this', said Nera. 'It will not be hard for thee', said the king. He went back to his house. 'Now tend thy kine today!' said the woman. 'I gave a cow of them to thy son at once after his birth'. So Nera went with his cattle that day.

Then while he was asleep the Morrigan took the cow of his son, and the Donn of Cualgne bulled her in the east in Cualgne. She [the Morrigan] then went again westward with her cow. Cuchulaind overtook them in the plain of Murthemne as they passed across it. For it was one of Cuchulaind's *gessa* that even a woman should leave his land without his knowledge. [It was one of his *gessa* that birds should feed on his land, unless they left something with him. It was one of his *gessa* that fish should be in the bays, unless they fell by him. It was one of his *gessa* that warriors of another tribe should be in his land without his challenging them, before morning, if they came at night, or before night, if they came in the day. Every maiden and every single woman that was in Ulster, they were in his ward till they were ordained for husbands. These are the *gessa* of Cuchulaind]. Cuchulaind overtook the Morrigan with her cow, and he said: 'This cow must not be taken'.

Nera went back then to his house with his kine in the evening. 'The cow of my son is missing', said he. 'I did not deserve that thou shouldst go and tend kine in that way', said his wife to him. On that came the cow. 'A wonder now! Whence does this cow come?' 'Truly, she comes from Cualgne, after being bulled by the Donn of Cualgne', said the woman. 'Rise out now, lest thy warriors come', she said. 'This host cannot go for a year till Halloween next. They will come on Halloween next: for the fairy-mounds of Erinn are always opened about Halloween'.

Nera went to his people. 'Whence comest thou?' said Ailill and Medb to Nera, 'and where hast thou been since thou didst go from us?' 'I was in fair lands', said Nera, 'with great treasures and precious things, with plenty of garments and food, and of wonderful treasures.' 'They will come to slay you on Halloween coming, unless it had been revealed to you'. 'We shall certainly go against them', said Ailill. So they remain there till the end of the year. 'Now if thou hast anything in the sid', said Ailill to Nera, 'bring it away'. So Nera went on the third day before Halloween and brought her drove out of the sid. Now as the bull calf went out of the sid, viz. the calf of the cow of Aingene (Aingene was the name of his son), it bellowed thrice. At that same hour Ailill and Fergus were playing drafts, when they heard something, the bellowing of the bull calf in the plain. Then said Fergus:

> I like not the calf
> bellowing in the plain of Cruachan,
> the son of the black bull of Cualgne, which approaches,
> the young son of the bull from Loch Laig.

> There will be calves without cows
> on Bairche in Cualgne,
> the king will go a . . . march
> through this calf of Aingene.

[Aingene was the name of the man and Be Aingeni the name of the woman, and the appearance which this Nera saw on them was the same as that which Cuchulaind saw in the Tain Bo Regamna.]

Then the bull calf and the Whitehorn meet in the plain of Cruachan. A night and a day they were there fighting, until at last the bull calf was beaten. Then the bull calf bellowed when it was beaten. 'What did the calf bellow?' Medb asked of her neat-herd, whose name was Buaigle. 'I know that, my good father Fergus', said Bricriu, 'it is the strain which thou sangest in the morning'. On that Fergus glanced aside and struck with his fist at Bricriu's head, so that the five men of the draft-board that were in his hand, went into Bricriu's head, and it was a lasting hurt to him. 'Tell me, O Buaigle, what did the bull say?' said Medb. 'Truly, it said', answered Buaigle, 'if its father came to fight with it, viz. the Donn of Cualgne, it would not be seen in Ai, and it would be beaten throughout the whole plain of Ai on every side'. Then said Medb in the manner of an oath: 'I swear by the gods that my people swear by, that I shall not lie down, nor sleep on down or flockbed, nor shall I drink butter-milk nor nurse my side, nor drink red ale nor white, nor shall I taste food, until I see those two kine fighting before my face'.

Thereafter the men of Connaught and the black host of exile went into the sid, and destroyed the sid, and took out what there was in it. And then they brought away the crown of Briun. That is the third wonderful gift in Erinn, and the mantle of Loegaire in Armagh, and the shirt of Dunlaing in Leinster in Kildare. Nera was left with his people in the sid, and has not come out until now, nor will he come till Doom.

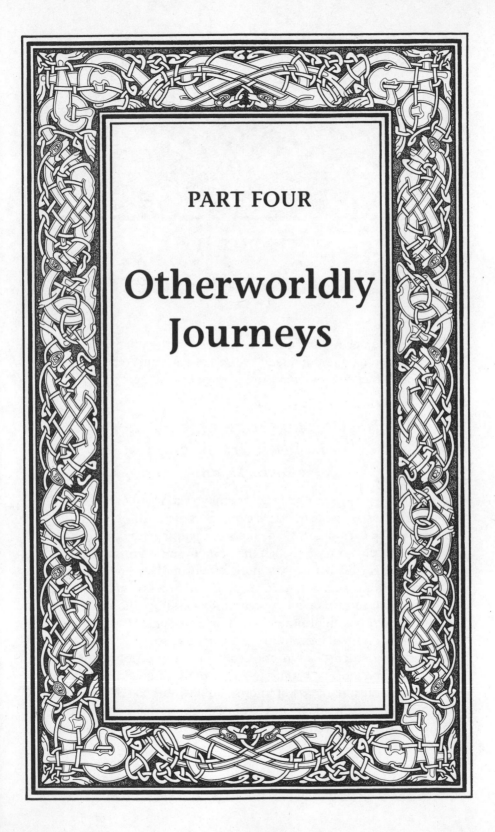

PART FOUR

Otherworldly Journeys

CHAPTER 11

The Journey Quest

I n this chapter we examine the journey to the otherworld in the context of the quest and read two sets of adventures in which mortal and otherworldly realms are bridged from either side.

The Quest as Shamanic Journey in Celtic Tradition
by Caitlín Matthews

In Chapter 9 we assessed the soul's ability to move about outside the body. To what extent is the classic and purposeful shamanic journey present in Celtic tradition? The shamanic journey may be defined as a non-physical journey in which the *riocht* or soul-shape of a shaman travels from earthly reality into many otherworldly regions.

There is little doubt that, in early Celtic times, druids and *filidh* were very skilled at moving between the worlds by shamanic means in order to discover information, healing or wisdom. After the onset of Christianity and the dismantling of Celtic spiritual practice, the *filidh* continued to practise the prophetic, divinatory and healing skills which required shamanic journeying. From the Middle Ages onwards, there is a distinct falling off of information relating to shamanic practice. The ancient wisdom or journeying ability was not, however, entirely lost by seers and may have remained in oral tradition in places few have thought to look.

Living at the latter end of the twentieth century, we have few direct links with the practices of our ancestors. The examples of Celtic journey methods given throughout this book lie scattered throughout the literary evidence which, though helpful and corroborative, are often incomplete. Moreover, in such an oral tradition, we cannot expect to find hard evidence of shamanic practice in written testimony. Where else can we look? The academic answer to this question is short: if there were such a shamanic tradition, it can only be inferred from textual evidence which at best must be considered with great caution. The shamanic answer is ruthlessly practical: make a journey and ask the ancestors – an answer not likely to appeal to academics, since subjective experience is rarely trusted as a criterion for anything!

If textual sources are to be considered suspect in support of a lively oral tradition, then let us turn to the surviving oral tradition for evidence. Could the shamanic journeying of our ancestors have influenced accounts of the otherworld as related by storytellers, so that storytellers incorporated this knowledge into a collective tradition which was inspirational to many people?

The storyteller (Gaelic, *seanchai*: Welsh, *cyfarwydd*) descends from the *aois dana*, the gifted people, who chronicled the history, events, lineage and stories of the tribe. The storyteller plays a prime role in the survival of Celtic tradition because, without such rememberers, we would find little inspiration in our heritage. Memory is central to druidic and bardic wisdom, all teachings being given orally and recited over and over by rote until memories retained them. The twelve-year bardic curriculum included the learning of 350 stories, often the length of a novel. Such feats of memory might be considered fantastic were it not for the fact that surviving Celtic storytellers in the nineteenth and twentieth centuries were still able to recite one story over several evenings of telling. [1]

What has the storyteller to do with the shamanic journey? Shamanic practice involves a shaman's otherworldly search by means of a journey for a variety of different reasons: to gain information, healing or wisdom; to commune with the spirits of the ancestors, or with animal and plant allies; to bring healing to the sick by the restoration of virtue, fertility or vital energy; to seek for collective tribal empowerment for a people bereft of leadership; or to find lost objects or souls. On returning from such a soul-journey, the shaman then relates the experience, if it has not already been simultaneously sung aloud, to the one seeking the information, healing or empowerment. Such a relation details the places visited, the beings encountered, the nature of the information received and the action or advice required to implement, solve or heal whatever has been the purpose of the journey.

We know that Gaelic storytellers had a fund of different categories of stories which were told under particular circumstances: births (*coimperta*) were told at confinements, wooings (*tochmarca*) were told at weddings etc. From the many categories of tale, the ones which most echo the shamanic vision journey are the voyages (*immrama*) and the adventures (*echtrai*).

The *echtra* (plural *echtraí*) or adventure story is invariably one of quest, leading into the otherworld and back. Like the shamanic journey, it involves a purpose, an otherworldly visit or series of visits, through significant landscapes where beings are encountered who give advice, offer challenge or ask questions; the quester invariably returns with solutions, healing objects, or knowledge which will release hidden potentials.

Parallel to this tradition is the Gaelic *immram* or voyage quest, whereby a hero is called to penetrate to the furthest west in order to find wisdom, healing or paradise. For the Celtic peoples, the lands westward over the Atlantic have ever been the regions of the Blessed Isles, the happy otherworld from which faery visitants, empowering objects and supra-human wisdom derive. As with the Grail quest, the *immrama* are found in both pre- and post-Christian traditions, testifying to their importance, which may have been remnants of a once-coherent 'book of the dead' teaching, preparing people for states of existence after death, similar to the Tibetan *bardo* wisdom.

The relationship of the *echtraí* and *immrama* stories to actual shamanic experience is actually closer than many might think. The Celtic storytellers did not create fiction, as modern novelists do: they were in the business of relating the history of characters and events as load-bearing myths which sustained the tribe and people. Plain history relates the bald facts occuring in linear time and physical space, but myth contextualizes characters and events in relation to otherworldly time and space.

Our society is obsessed with the rationalization of myth, and is gratified when archaeology 'proves' myths to be 'merely historical'. However, such discoveries as Schlieman's identification of Troy and the recent excavation of the site of Emain Macha show how faithful remembrance and skilful storytelling are actually prime forensic tools for rediscovery. Without Homer's *Iliad* and the Ulster Cycle, neither site could have been historically contextualized or even sought out. Behind these arguments is the fact that *the story itself* combines knowledge of historical events with their relationship to otherworldly events. Time is interpenetrated by timelessness, space by sacred locus.

Our conclusion, therefore, is that the traditional Celtic story holds a knowledge of shamanic journey experience by virtue of the fact that it describes the Celtic otherworld in ways that are consistent with the numerous shamanic witnesses of Celtic lore. Common themes, tasks and journeys continually recur in ways that are independent of narrative conventions:

1. a situation in mortal realms requiring resolution or healing
2. a prior contact by an otherworldly being, providing help or patronage in mortal realms, often caused by alliance requiring reciprocation
3. exile/journey from home to seek for an object/help/wisdom etc.
4. recontact with an otherworldly being for advice/guidance
5. overcoming/passing of threshold guardians or adversaries
6. location of object/wisdom/healing
7. return with object to vindicate actions and restore

Most of these themes occur in some combination in most shamanic journeys and in the *echtraí* and *immrama*. The difference between the two story genres is that, generally speaking, the *echtra* is undertaken on behalf of others, while the *immram* is a more personal quest, often requiring a total spiritual transformation. Thus, Art mac Conn goes to the otherworld to restore his father's honour and heal the land of blight; Bran mac Febal sails to the Blessed Isles to re-establish a faery alliance in the Land of Women; Laeg goes to faeryland to restore Cuchulainn's spirit; Maelduin starts his voyage as a quest for his father's murderer, but completes it with total knowledge of the otherworld and so changes himself that he can offer forgiveness rather than vengeance; the adventures of Nera into faeryland are brought about by his taking up a Samhain dare to place a withy around the foot of a hanged man, but he concludes by attempting to save his people from faery invasion.

The alliance or patronage of an otherworldly being establishes a mode of transferral between the worlds: faery women invite Bran mac Febal and Connla to the otherworld; Manannan co-ordinates the journey to wisdom for Cormac mac Airt; Aed Abrat comes from faeryland to invite Cuchulainn thither, although Laeg goes in his place; the white deer opens the otherworldly gates to Pwyll. Sometimes the invitation is a trap, and the otherworldly being in question is a spiritual foe, like the white boar which lures Pryderi and Rhiannon to otherworldly imprisonment.

In order to seek the object, healing or solution, the hero must forego earthly life for a temporary interval and be detached from tribe and family – a difficult and dangerous condition, akin to being outlawed, without nominal existence or honour-price. That the exile of voyage overseas was likened by Celtic monks to 'the white martyr-dom', gives us some notion of the high regard in which the purlieus of home were held. The shaman's voluntary act of taking a soul-jour-ney is similarly about responding to a need greater than one's own, in order to bring resolution to land, tribe or family.

The landscape through which the journey-quest travels is of great significance. Celtic cosmologies are complex and varied, presenting otherworldly glimpses of a chequer-board of local variants which sel-dom follow one unified codifiable system. The Irish otherworld is most frequently entered by passage overseas or under the earth, by means of mound-entry. Exposition of the British otherworld cosmology, as adduced from the poems of Taliesin, is given extensively in John Matthews' *Taliesin, Bardic and Shamanic Mysteries*. The borders of the otherworld are patrolled by threshold guardians whose riddles must be answered correctly or who must be challenged and overcome if the journeyer is to pass further within. Cunning, skill or familiarity with the guardians assists the traveller.

Once within the otherworld, the landscape radically changes and announces the fact. Trees in simultaneous leaf and flame, rivers of fire, herds of giant beasts and other wonders abound. A frequent fea-ture of both Irish and British otherworlds is the chequer-board field with black sheep on white squares and white sheep on black squares, as perceived by both Peredur and Maelduin. This image is encoun-tered on the verges of the worlds, where the realms reverse out like a photographic negative. Otherworldly inhabitants are fantastically huge or small, endowed with magical abilities. They must be treated with respect or they can be dangerous. But in the heart of the other-world there are no such dangers, only a blessed immortal land whose buildings are of precious metals, crystals or birds' feathers.

It is usually within this deep heart that the object, knowledge or quality sought is discovered. Cormac finds the cup of truth, Maelduin and his men discover a lake conferring life, the destined wives of Culhwch and Art are found, the healing draught of life is discovered by Diarmuid. The return is usually swift and the application of the object of the quest effective.

To demonstrate let us briefly outline one such complete itinerary in demonstration. In the quest of Art to find Delbchaem (see below), he travels overseas in a faery coracle, arriving at a paradisal island where he is greeted by a faery woman, Creide, a seer, and is refreshed and instructed by her in the rest of his quest. Creide's dwelling, appearance and actions accord with those of a shamanic guide. Although Art does not know her, she is well aware of him, and is able to warn him of dangers that threaten him. This is the itinerary she gives him:

> across an ocean of sea-monsters
> through a wood of spear-points
> across an icy mountain
> through a glen of poisonous toads
> across a mountain of lions
> across an icy river over a narrow bridge guarded by a giant to a dark house in a wood where seven hags and bath of molten lead await him

Here he must encounter two women – one with a cup of poison, one with a cup of wine – one of which he must choose from before entering a palisade of bronze, each stake set with a severed head, before slaying Delbchaem's mother, the dog-headed Coinchenn. He accomplishes all this and returns home to banish Becuma and become king in his father's place.

Prime among the many stories of the sacred journey is the Grail Quest which has its origins in pre-Christian Celtic myth as the cup or cauldron which restores life, health, nourishment and courage. This is one of the longest on-going stories which has survived from oral tradition to medieval transcription, and which has been updated in every generation since. It details the personal spiritual progress from ignorance to mature wisdom. The dangers of the quest often manifest as monstrous or deluding phantoms which beset the traveller. Spiritual perspicacity and resourcefulness are pressed to their limits in the dark wood, the perilous voyage, the mysterious Grail castle. The aim of the quest is the Grail which regenerates all things – sometimes seen as a healing cauldron, sometimes as the Cup of the Last Supper. Whichever is achieved, the Grail does not solely transform its finder, but is achieved for the benefit of all. This is the prime impulse and teaching of the quest tradition which is found throughout all levels of the Celtic tradition.[2]

Such are the chief features of the traditional stories which accord with the shamanic journey. Knowledge of otherworldly cosmologies and the assistance of spiritual guides and helpers were an integral part of early Celtic practice. The traditional pathways of the shamanic journey began at the gateways between the worlds, gateways which were known by every person, although not everyone was willing or qualified to travel in their *riocht* through these gates. The soul-journey was a specialist practice, requiring formal tuition by those who had made such journeys, and who could teach from personal experience.

A major reason for the twelve-year bardic and druidic training now begins to emerge: just as the formal pathways of meditation are taught in the context of complex inner cosmologies in Tibetan Buddhism, so too within Celtic practice. In the 350 stories that were memorized by all initiates, knowledge of otherworldly pathways, inhabitants and scenarios were encoded. Such stories helped map the otherworlds and gave a complete cross-correlation of information which had been gained by other, ancestral shamans. Knowledge of the divinatory and prophetic skills was reserved until the seventh, eighth and ninth years of training, based upon a groundwork of law, prosody, grammar, language and history, thus ensuring that candidates were well prepared for soul-journeying.

Soul-journeying was begun by a variety of means. We have seen how the silver branch acts as an agent of transferance from one reality to another in the stories. Such branches were carried by poets as their symbol of office, indicative of the fact that they journeyed under the protection of the great tree of the otherworld, of which their rod was a scion. The *riocht* was propelled by a variety of different methods, usually sound-sources, which are generally given as bird-song, harp or timpan (hammered psaltery) music, singing, incantation, darkness and silence, or the sounding of the silver branch. Given the training of the *filidh*, incantation alone often served to send the *riocht* upon its way, a weaving of words which detailed the soul-route and called upon personal allies or spiritual helpers. The incubatory sleep of the *iombas forosna* is often mentioned as a mode of journeying. Ordinary sleep is the usual and involuntary resort of the non-specialist journeyer, when the *riocht* may leave the body in order to seek out solutions or resolve difficulties.

Once the journey had begun, the *filidh* followed wherever the accompanying otherworldly ally led, guided by the handholds of imagery, sensations, smells and sounds that served as the orientation points of the Celtic otherworld, handholds that more experienced soul-travellers had noted. The duration of the journey varied according to the method used. The recumbent method of the traditional *tarbh feis* and *iombas forosna* probably lasted for several hours, but the incantatory *teinm laegda* seems to have been undertaken while in full consciousness and constituted a mini-journey, swiftly using the scaffolding of song to retrieve the necessary information. The *teinm laegda* method is analogous to a computer 'window', which sees through one program into another. *Dichetal do chennaib*, whereby touch and incantation were used together, probably worked by a similarly direct 'reaching through the worlds' method.

The nature of animal allies in Celtic tradition has already been hinted at in Chapter 3. Totemic alliances between people and creatures were largely personal, as in the cases of Diarmuid O' Duibhne and Cuchulainn, but they might also be ancestral, pertaining to a whole race or tribe, becoming a sacred animal which was widely depicted in heraldic tribal ways. A series of animal allies seems normal among trained practitioners, related to the *tuirgen* of the soul. Other allies might be revered ancestors or otherworldly beings such as the *sidhe*, the faery folk. The intimate relationship between ally and practitioner is based on trust, for allies guide the *riocht* through the worlds, leading it to its goal. Again and again, traditional stories stress this interdependence and the consequences when it is severed due to disrespect or selfish pride.

The legacy of the traditional storyteller to those who wish to reconnect with their ancestral shamanic lore is indeed great. By a judicious sampling of both the *echtraí* and *immrama* stories and by personal shamanic experience, a great body of traditional lore is recoverable today. Such a task is not undertaken out of atavistic yearning or historical curiosity, however. The sacred Celtic journey is and has always been taken in order to seek re-enchantment and revalidation of the creative, imaginative and spiritual dimensions of human life, to bring healing, to solve problems, to restore nourishment to spiritual and physical wastelands.

This tradition of wisdom through story and quest can be maintained by modern practitioners who can begin to work towards Celtic shamanic experience by utilizing these scenarios. Starting with meditative repetition enhances the stories thus used, creating distinct cosmological pathways for all spiritual explorers. In this way, traditional stories and myths can be memorized and retold, not in any pretentious folkloric way, but as living pathways of spiritual wisdom. The spiritual beings encountered in these scenarios give actual teaching and often provide otherworldly and ancestral guidance to those bereft of living teachers.

These stories and the scenarios which they contain are ancestral pathways which wait to be reactivated. By visionary, meditative and shamanic interface with these stories, the Celtic tradition is passed on. Since these stories are part of living memory, the necessity for book or 'scripture' is obviated, and the scenarios can be used anywhere from a prison cell to a barren desert.

Whatever problems we face today, we may take these pathways, seek spiritual and ancestral helpers and find solutions with their help. Whether we seek healing, wisdom or an end to conflict, the Celtic quest continues through purposeful shamanic journeying. This open secret is the key to the ongoing spiritual cohesion of the Celtic tradition: a challenge for all practitioners to seek the ancient pathways which lead into our future.

The Death of Fergus mac Leide[3]

The Celts love a wonder-tale, the more fantastic the better. It is when reading tales like that of Fergus mac Leide that we lack that essential component – a storyteller who can bring out the fun and the humour embedded in the story. For here a miniature poet is dropped into a wine-cup, the lepra King falls into the porridge and the Ultonian king and queen squabble about first use of the bath stone to heat their bath.

The story of Fergus and his encounter with the little people was composed about 1100, and is unusual in that the adventure starts in the realm of the leprechaun and travels into mortal realms. We have included it because of its wealth of detail and to demonstrate the fact that it is often otherworldly beings who instigate the journey between the worlds.

Fergus, King of Ulster, gives a feast at the exact same time as Iubdan, King of the lepra or little people is giving his. It is Iubdan's boast of the primacy of himself and his people that causes his poet, Esirt, to laugh aloud and say that Fergus is a greater king. Iubdan causes Esirt to prove his words and the adventure begins with the little poet's journey to Fergus' court where, despite his diminutive stature he proves his worth and is eventually received with honour. Fergus' own poet is the dwarf, Aed; he accompanies Esirt to the oversea home of the lepra. In these sojourns, both poets enjoy bardic immunity; but Esirt has suffered the derision of men and has been mishandled by Iubdan. He lays Iubdan under a *geas* that he view Fergus' court for himself. There the little king will receive his just come-uppance for shaming his poet.

The usual niceties of honour and guest-right subside into Iubdan's being kept hostage by Fergus, and the lepra king has first-hand experience of the foolishness and forgetfulness of human beings. Fergus

suffers the vengeance of the lepra folk, who ruin his possessions in
their attempts to gain their king's release. Finally, Iubdan is forced to
enumerate his treasures that Fergus may choose one for his own in
return for letting the lepra king go free. Fergus chooses Iubdan's
shoes, which have the ability to travel over land and sea, because he
wishes to revenge himself upon a sea-monster which blighted and
distorted his face. During this encounter, he is mortally wounded and
his adventure in the magical shoes comes to an abrupt halt.

In modern lore, leprechauns have become quaintly 'Disneyfied',
with little hint of their sharp and deadly wit; yet even so their fame as
shoe-makers is still remembered. In this story, Iubdan's magical shoes
are the way-showers to otherworldly adventure.

A righteous king, a maintainer of truth and a giver of just judgments
over the happy Clan Rudraige, or 'Children of Rury,' of Ulster, was
Fergus son of Leide son of Rury; and these are they that were his
heroes and men of war: Eirgenn, Amergin the Ravager, Conna Buie
son of Iliach, and Dubtach son of Lugaid.

This king gave a great feast in Emain Macha, the capital of Ulster,
and it was ready, fit to be consumed, and all set in order at the very
season and hour at which the king of the Lepra and Lepracan held a
banquet: whose name was Iubdan son of Abdan.

These are the names of the men of war that were Iubdan's: Conan
son of Ruiched, Gerrcu son of Cairid, and Rigbeg son of Robeg; Luigin
son of Luiged, Glunan son of Gabarn, Febal son of Feornin, and
Cinnbeg son of Gnuman; together with Buan's son Brigbeg, Liran son
of Luan, and Mether son of Mintan. To them was brought the strong
man of the region of the Lepra and Lepracan, whose prize feat that he
used to perform was the hewing down of a thistle at a single stroke;
whereas it was a twelve men's effort of the rest of them to give him
singly a wrestling-fall. To them was brought the king's presumptive
successor, Beg son of Beg ('Little son of Little'). So also was brought
the king's poet and man of art likewise: Esirt son of Beg son of
Buaidgen, and the other notables of the land of the Lepra and
Lepracan.

The guests were placed according to their qualities and to precedence: at one side Iubdan was placed, having next to him on either
hand Bebo his wife, and his chief poet; at the other side of the hall and
facing Iubdan sat Beg son of Beg, with the notables and chiefs; the
king's strong man too, Glomar son of Glomrad's son Glas, stood
beside the doorpost of the house. Now were the spigots drawn from

the vats, the color of those vats being of a dusky red like the tint of
red yew. The carvers stood up to carve and the cup-bearers to pour;
and old ale, sleep-compelling, delicious, was served out to the throng
so that on one side as on the other of the hall they were elated and
made huge noise of mirth.

At last Iubdan, who was their king and the head of all their counsel, having in his hand the *corn breac* or 'variegated horn' stood up, and
on the other side, opposite to Iubdan and to do him honor, arose Beg
son of Beg. Then the king, by this time affably inclining to converse,
inquired of them, 'Have you ever seen a king that was better than
myself?'

And they answered, 'We have not.'

'Have you ever seen a strong man better than my strong man?'

'We have not.'

'Horses or men of battle have you ever seen better than they which
to-night are in this house?'

'By our word,' they made answer, 'we never have.'

'I, too,' Iubdan went on, 'give my word that it would be a hard
task forcibly to take out of this house to-night either captives or
hostages: so surpassing are its heroes and men of battle, so many its
lusty companions and men of might, so great the number of its fierce
and haughty ones, that are stuff out of which kings might fittingly be
made.'

All which when he had heard, the king's chief poet Esirt burst out
laughing; whereupon Iubdan asked: 'Esirt, what moved thee to that
laugh?' Said the poet: 'I know of a province in Ireland, one man of
which could take hostages and captives from all four battalions of the
Lepracan.'

'Lay the poet by the heels,' cried the king, 'that vengeance be taken
of him for his bragging speech!'

So it was done; but Esirt said, 'Iubdan, this seizure of me will bear
evil fruit; for in requital of the arrest thou shalt thyself be for five years
captive in Emain Macha, whence thou shalt not escape without leaving behind thee the rarest thing of all thy wealth and treasures. By reason of this seizure Cobthach Cas also, son of Munster's king, shall fall,
and the king of Leinster's son Eochaid; whilst I myself must go to the
house of Fergus son of Leide and in his goblet be set floating till I be
all but drowned . . .'

'An evil arrest is this thou hast made on me, O king,' Esirt went
on, 'but grant me now a three-days' and three-nights' respite that I

may travel to Emain Macha and to the house of Leide's son Fergus, to the end that if there I find some evident token by which thou shalt recognize truth to be in me, I may bring the same hither; or if not, then do to me what thou wilt.'

Then Esirt, his bonds being loosed, rose and next to his white skin put on a smooth and glossy shirt of delicate silk. Over that he donned his gold-broidered tunic and his scarlet cloak, all fringed and beautiful, flowing in soft folds, the scarlet being of the land of the Finn, and the fringe of pale gold in varied pattern. Betwixt his feet and the earth he set his two dainty shoes of white bronze, overlaid with ornament of gold. Taking his white bronze poet's wand and his silken hood, he set out, choosing the shortest way and the straightest course, nor are we told how he fared until he came to Emain Macha and at the gate of the place shook his poet's rod.

When at the sound the gate-keeper came forth, he beheld there a man, comely and of a most gallant carriage, but so tiny that the close-cropped grass of the green reached to his knee, aye, and to the thick of his thigh. At sight of him wonder fell upon the gate-keeper; and he entered into the house to report the arrival to Fergus and to the company. All inquired whether he [Esirt] were smaller than Aed, this Aed being the poet of Ulster, and a dwarf that could stand on full-sized men's hands. And the gate-keeper said, 'He would have room enough upon Aed's palm, by my word.' Hereupon the guests with pealing laughter desired to see him, each one deeming the time to be all too long till he should view Esirt and, after seeing him, speak with him. Then upon all sides both men and women had free access to him, but Esirt cried, 'Huge men that you are, let not your infected breaths so closely play upon me! but let yon small man that is the least of you approach me; who, little though he be among you, would yet in the land where I dwell be accounted of great stature.' Into the great house therefore, and he standing upon his palm, the poet Aed bore him.

Fergus, when he had sought of him tidings who he might be, was answered: 'I am Esirt son of Beg son of Buaidgen: chief poet, bard and rhymer, of the Lepra and Lepracan.' The assembly were just then in actual enjoyment of the feast, and a cup-bearer came to Fergus. 'Give to the little man that is come to me,' said the king.

Esirt replied, 'Neither of your meat will I eat, nor of your liquor will I drink.'

'By our word,' said Fergus, 'seeing thou art a flippant and a mocking fellow, it were but right to drop thee into the beaker, where at all points round about thou shouldst then impartially quaff the liquor.'

The cup-bearer closed his hand on Esirt and popped him into the goblet, in which upon the surface of the liquor that it contained he floated round. 'You poets of Ulster,' he vociferated, 'much desirable knowledge and instruction there is which upon my conscience, ye sorely need to have of me, yet ye allow me to be drowned!'

With fair satin napkins of great virtue and with special silken fabrics he was plucked out and was cleaned spick and span, and Fergus inquired, 'Of what impediment spakest thou a while ago as hindering thee from sharing our meat?'

'That will I tell thee,' the little man replied: 'but let me not incur thy displeasure.'

'So be it,' promised the king; 'only explain to me the whole impediment'. Then Esirt spoke and Fergus answered him.

> *Esirt.* With poet's sharp-set words never be angered, Fergus; thy stern hard utterance restrain, nor against me take unjustifiable action.
>
> *Fergus.* O wee man of the seizure, I will not.
>
> *Esirt.* Judgments lucid and truthful, if they be those to which thou dost provoke me: then I pronounce that thou triflest with thy steward's wife, while thine own foster-son ogles thy queen. Women fair-haired and accomplished, rough kings of the ordinary kind [*i.e.*, mere chieftains]: how excellent so ever be the form of these, 'tis not on them the former let their humor dwell [*i.e.*, when a genuine king comes in their way].
>
> *Fergus.* Esirt, thou art in truth no child, but an approved man of veracity; O gentle one, devoid of reproach, no wrath of. Fergus shalt thou know!

The king went on, 'My share of the matter, by my word, is true; for the steward's wife is indeed my pastime, and all the rest as well therefore I the more readily take to be true.'

Then said Esirt, 'Now will I partake of thy meat, for thou hast confessed the evil; do it then no more.' Here the poet, waxing cheerful and of good courage, went on, 'Upon my own lord I have made a poem which, were it your pleasure, I would declaim to you.' Fergus answered, 'We would esteem it sweet to hear it,' and Esirt began:

> A king victorious, and renowned and pleasant, is Iubdan son of Abdan, king of Mag Life, king of Mag Faithlenn. His is a voice clear and sweet as copper's resonance, like the blood-colored

rowan-berry is his cheek; his eye is bland as it were a stream of mead, his color that of the swan or of the river's foam. Strong he is in his yellow-haired host, in beauty and in cattle he is rich; and to brave men he brings death when he sets himself in motion. A man that loves the chase, active, a generous feast-giver; he is head of a bridle-wearing army, he is tall, proud and imperious. His is a solid squadron of grand headlong horses, of bridled horses rushing torrent-like; heads with smooth adorn-ment of golden locks are on the warriors of the Lepra. All the men are comely, the women all light-haired; over that land's noble multitude Iubdan of truthful utterance presides. There the fingers grasp silver horns, deep notes of the timpan are heard; and however great be the love that women are reputed to bear thee, Fergus, 'tis surpassed by the desire that they feel for Iubdan.

The lay ended, the Ulstermen equipped the poet of the Lepracan with abundance of good things, until each heap of these as they lay there equalled their tall men's stature. 'This, on my conscience,' said Esirt, 'is indeed a response that is worthy of good men; nevertheless take away those treasures, for I have no need of them, since in my lord's following is no man but possesses sufficient substance.'

The Ulstermen said, however, 'We pledge our words that we never would take back anything, though we had given thee our very wives and our cows . . .'

'Then divide the gifts, bards and scholars of Ulster!' Esirt cried; 'two thirds take for yourselves, and the other bestow on Ulster's horseboys and jesters.'

So to the end of three days and three nights Esirt was in Emain, and he took his leave of Fergus and of the nobles of Ulster. 'I will go with thee,' said the Ulster poet and man of science, Aed, that dwarf who used to lie in their good warriors' bosoms, yet by Esirt's side was a giant. Esirt said, ''Tis not I that will bid thee come: for were I to invite thee, and kindness to be shown thee in consequence, thou wouldst say 'twas but what by implication had been promised thee; whereas if such be not held out to thee and thou yet receive it thou wilt be grateful.'

Out of Emain the pair of poets now went their way and, Aed's step being the longer, he said, 'Esirt thou art a poor walker.' Esirt then took such a fit of running that he was an arrow's flight in front of Aed, who said again, 'Between those two extremes lies the golden mean.'

'On my word,' retorted Esirt, 'that is the one category in which since I have been among you I have heard mention made of the golden mean!'

On they went then till they gained Traig na Trenfer, or 'Strand of the Strong Men,' in Ulster. 'And what must we do now?' Aed asked here.

'Travel the sea over her depths,' said the other.

Aed objected, 'Never shall I come safe out of that trial.'

Esirt made answer: 'Seeing that I accomplished the task, it would be strange that thou shouldst fail.' Then Aed uttered a strain and Esirt answered him:

Aed. In the vast sea what shall I do? O generous Esirt, the wind will bear me down to the merciless wave on which, though I mount upwards, yet none the less shall I perish in the end.

Esirt. To fetch thee, fair Iubdan's horse will come. Get thee upon him and cross the stammering sea: an excellent horse truly and of passing color, a king's valued treasure, good on sea as upon land. A beautiful horse that will carry thee away. Sit on him and be not troubled; go, trust thyself to him.

They had been no long time there when they marked something which, swiftly careering, came towards them over the billows' crests. 'Upon itself be the evil that it brings,' Aed cried.

'What seest thou?' Esirt asked.

'A russet-clad hare I see,' answered Aed.

But Esirt said, 'Not so — rather is it Iubdan's horse that comes to fetch thee.' Of which horse the fashion was this: two fierce flashing eyes he had, an exquisite pure crimson mane, with four green legs and a long tail that floated in wavy curls. His general color was that of prime artificers' gold-work, and a gold-encrusted bridle he bore withal. Esirt bestriding him said, 'Come up beside me, Aed.'

But again Aed objected, 'Nay, poet, to serve even thee alone as a conveyance is beyond his powers.'

'Aed, cease from fault-finding, for ponderous as may be the wisdom that is in thee, yet will he carry us both.'

They both being now mounted on the horse traversed the combing seas, the mighty main's expanse and ocean's great profound, until in the end they, undrowned and without mishap, reached Mag Faithlenn, and there the Lepracan were before them in assembly. 'Esirt approaches,' they cried, 'and a giant bears him company!'

Then Iubdan went to meet Esirt, and gave him a kiss. 'But, poet,' said he, 'wherefore bringest thou this giant to destroy us?'

'No giant is he, but Ulster's poet and man of science, and the king's dwarf. In the land whence he comes he is the least, so that in their great men's bosoms he lies down and, as it were an infant, stands on the flat of their hands. Yet he is such that before him you would do well to be careful of yourselves.'

'What is his name?' they asked.

'Poet Aed.'

'Alack, man,' they cried to Esirt, 'thy giant is huge indeed!'

Next, Esirt addressing Iubdan said, 'On thee, Iubdan, I lay taboos which true warriors may not break that in thine own person thou go to view the region out of which we come, and that of the "lord's porridge" which for the king of Ulster is made to-night thou be the first man to make trial.'

Then Iubdan, grieving and faint of spirit, proceeded to confer with Bebo his wife. He told her how that by Esirt he was laid under taboos, and bade her bear him company. 'That will I,' she said; 'but by laying Esirt in bonds thou didst unjustly.' So they mounted Iubdan's golden horse and that same night made good their way to Emain, where they entered unperceived into the place. 'Iubdan,' said Bebo, 'search the town for the porridge spoken of by Esirt, and let us depart again before the people of the place shall rise.'

They gained the inside of the palace and there found Emain's great cauldron, having in it the remnant of the 'people's porridge.' Iubdan drew near, but could by no means reach it from the ground. 'Get upon thy horse,' said Bebo, 'and from the horse upon the cauldron's rim.' This he did, but, the porridge being too far down and his arm too short, he could not touch the shank of the silver ladle that was in the cauldron; whereupon, as he made a downward effort, his foot slipped, and up to his very navel he fell into the cauldron; in which as though all existing iron gyves had been upon him he now found himself fettered and tethered both hand and foot. 'Long thou tarriest, dark man!' Bebo cried to him (for Iubdan was thus: hair he had that was jet-black and curled, his skin being whiter than foam of wave and his cheeks redder than the forest's scarlet berry: whereas – saving him only – all the Lepra people had hair that was ringleted indeed, but of a fair and yellow hue; hence then he was styled 'dark man'). Bebo spoke now, Iubdan answering her:

She. O dark man, and O dark man! dire is the strait in which
thou art: to-day it is that the white horse must be saddled,
for the sea is angry and the tide at flood.

He. O fair-haired woman, and O woman with fair hair! gyves
hold me captive in a viscous mass nor, until gold be given for
my ransom, shall I ever be dismissed. O Bebo, and O Bebo!
morn is at hand; therefore flee away; fast in the doughy remnant sticks my leg, if here thou stay thou art but foolish, O
Bebo!

She. Rash word it was, 'twas a rash word, that in thy house thou
utteredst: that but by thine own good pleasure none under
the sun might hold thee fast, O man!

He. Rash was the word, the word was rash, that in my house I
uttered: a year and a day I must be now, and neither man
nor woman of my people see!

'Bebo,' cried Iubdan, 'flee away now, and to the Lepraland take back
that horse.'

'Never say it,' she answered; 'I will surely not depart until I see
what turn things shall take for thee.'

The dwellers in Emain, when they were now risen, found Iubdan
in the porridge cauldron, out of which he could not contrive to escape;
in which plight when they saw him the people sent up a mighty roar
of laughter, then picked Iubdan out of the cauldron and carried him
off to Fergus. 'My conscience,' said the king, 'this is not the tiny man
that was here before: seeing that, whereas the former little fellow had
fair hair, this one has a black thatch. What art thou at all, mannikin,
and out of what region dost thou come?'

Iubdan made answer: 'I am of the Lepra-folk, over whom I am
king; this woman that you see by me is my wife, and queen over the
Lepra: her name is Bebo, and I have never told a lie.'

'Let him be taken out,' cried Fergus, 'and put with the common
rabble of the household — guard him well!' Iubdan was led out accordingly . . .

Said Iubdan, 'But if it may please thee to show me some favor, suffer me no longer to be among yonder loons, for the great men's
breaths do all infect me; and my word I pledge that till by Ulster and
by thee it be permitted, I will never leave you.'

Fergus said, 'Could I but believe that pledge, thou shouldst no more
be with the common varlets.'

Iubdan's reply was, 'Never have I overstepped, nor ever will transgress, my plighted word.'

Then he was conducted into a fair and private chamber that Fergus had, where a trusty servant of the king of Ulster was set apart to minister to him. 'An excellent retreat indeed is this,' he said, 'yet is my own retreat more excellent than it'; and he made a lay:

> In the land that lies away north I have a retreat, the ceiling of which is of the red gold, and the floor all of silver. Of the white bronze its lintel is, and its threshold of copper; of light-yellow bird-plumage is the thatch on it indeed. Golden are its candelabra, holding candles of rich light and gemmed over with rare stones, in the fair midst of the house. Save myself only and my queen, none that belongs to it feels sorrow now; a retinue is there that ages not, that wears wavy yellow tresses. There every man is a chess-player, good company is there that knows no stint: against man or woman that seeks to enter it the retreat is never closed.

Ferdiad, or 'man of smoke,' Fergus's fire-servant, as in Iubdan's presence he kindled a fire, threw upon it a woodbine that twined round a tree, together with somewhat of all other kinds of timber, and this led Iubdan to say, 'Burn not the king of trees, for he ought not to be burnt; and wouldst thou, Ferdiad, but act by my counsel, then neither by sea nor by land shouldst thou ever be in danger.' Here he sang a lay:

> O man that for Fergus of the feasts dost kindle fire, whether afloat or ashore never burn the king of woods. Monarch of Inis Fail's forests the woodbine is, whom none may hold captive; no feeble sovereign's effort is it to hug all tough trees in his embrace. The pliant woodbine if thou burn, wailings for misfortune will abound; dire extremity at weapons' points or drowning in great waves will come after. Burn not the precious appletree of spreading and low-sweeping bough: tree ever decked in bloom of white, against whose fair head all men put forth the hand. The surly blackthorn is a wanderer, and a wood that the artificer burns not; throughout his body, though it be scanty, birds in their flocks warble. The noble willow burn not, a tree sacred to poems; within his bloom bees are a-sucking, all love the little cage. The graceful tree with the berries, the wizards' tree, the rowan, burn; but spare the limber tree: burn not the slender hazel. Dark is the color of the ash: timber that makes

the wheels to go; rods he furnishes for horsemen's hands, and his form turns battle into flight. Tenterhook among woods the spiteful briar is, by all means burn him that is so keen and green; he cuts, he flays the foot, and him that would advance he forcibly drags backward. Fiercest heat-giver of all timber is green oak, from him none may escape unhurt; by partiality for him the head is set on aching and by his acrid embers the eye is made sore. Alder, very battle-witch of all woods, tree that is hottest in the fight – undoubtingly burn at thy discretion both the alder and the whitethorn. Holly, burn it green; holly, burn it dry; of all trees whatsoever the best is holly. Elder that hath tough bark, tree that in truth hurts sore: him that furnishes horses to the armies from the fairy-mound burn so that he be charred. The birch as well, if he be laid low, promises abiding fortune. Burn up most surely and certainly the stalks that bear the constant pods. Suffer, if it so please thee, the russet aspen to come headlong down; burn, be it late or early, the tree with the trembling branch. Patriarch of long-lasting woods is the yew, sacred to feasts as is well known: of him now build dark-red vats of goodly size. Ferdiad, thou faithful one, wouldst thou but do my behest, to thy soul as to thy body, O man, 'twould work advantage!

After this manner then, and free of all supervision, Iubdan abode in the town; while to them of Ulster it was recreation of mind and body to look at him and to listen to his words . . .

One day Iubdan went to the house of a certain soldier of the king's soldiers who chanced to fit on himself new brogues that he had: discoursing as he did so, and complaining, of their soles that were too thin. Iubdan laughed. The king asked: 'Iubdan, why laughest thou thus?'

'Yon fellow it is that provokes my laughter, complaining of his brogues while for his own life he makes no moan. Yet, thin as be those brogues, he never will wear them out.' Which was true for Iubdan, seeing that before night that man and another one of the king's people fought and killed each other . . .

Yet another day the household disputed of all manner of things, how they would do this or that, but never said: 'if it so please God.' Then Iubdan laughed and uttered a lay:

Man talks but God sheweth the outcome; to men all things are but confusion, they must leave them as God knoweth them to be. All that which Thou, Monarch of the elements, hast ordained must be right; He, the King of kings, knows all that I crave of thee, Fergus. No man's life, however bold he be, is more than the twinkling of an eye; were he a king's son he knoweth not whether it be truth that he utters of the future.

Iubdan now tarried in Emain until the Lepracan folk, being seven battalions strong, came to Emain in quest of him; and of these no single one did, whether in height or in bulk, exceed another. Then to Fergus and to Ulster's nobles that came out to confer with them they said, 'Bring us our king that we may redeem him, and we will pay for him a good ransom.'

Fergus asked, 'What ransom?'

'Every year, and that without ploughing, without sowing, we will cover this vast plain with a mass of corn.'

'I will not give up Iubdan,' said the king.

'To-night we will do thee a mischief.'

'What mischief?' asked the king.

'All Ulster's calves we will admit to their dams, so that by morning time there shall not in the whole province be found the measure of one babe's allowance of milk.'

'So much ye will have gained,' said Fergus, 'but not Iubdan.'

This damage accordingly they wrought that night; then at morn returned to the green of Emain Macha and, with promise of making good all that they had spoiled, again asked for Iubdan. Fergus refusing them, however, they said, 'This night we will do another deed of vengeance: we will defile the wells, the rapids, and the river-mouths of the whole province.'

But the king answered, 'That is but a puny mischief' (whence the old saying 'dirt in a well'), 'and ye shall not have Iubdan.'

They, having done this, came again to Emain on the third day and demanded Iubdan. Fergus said, 'I will not give him.'

'A further vengeance we will execute upon thee.'

'What vengeance is that?'

'To-night we will burn the millbeams and the kilns of the province.'

'But you will not get Iubdan,' said the king.

Away they went and did as they had threatened, then on the fourth day repaired to Emain and clamored for Iubdan. Said Fergus, 'I will not deliver him.'

'We will execute vengeance on thee.'

'What vengeance?'

'We will snip the ears off all the corn that is in the province.'

'Neither so shall you have Iubdan.'

This they did, then returned to Emain Macha on the fifth day and asked for Iubdan. Fergus said, 'I will not give him up.'

'Yet another vengeance we will take on thee.'

'What vengeance?'

'Your women's hair and your men's we will shave so that they shall for ever be covered with reproach and shame.'

Then Fergus cried, 'If you do that, by my word I will slay Iubdan!'

But here Iubdan said, 'That is not the right thing at all; rather let me be freed, that in person I may speak with them and bid them first of all to repair such mischief as they have done, and then depart.'

At sight of Iubdan they then, taking for granted that the license accorded him must needs be in order to let him depart with them, sent up a mighty shout of triumph. Iubdan said, however, 'My trusty people, depart now, for I am not permitted to go with you; all that which you have spoiled make good also, neither spoil anything more for, if you do so, I must die.' They thereupon, all gloomy and dejected, went away; a man of them making this lay:

A raid upon thee we proclaim this night, O Fergus, owner of many strong places! from thy standing corn we will snip the ears, whereby thy tables will not benefit. In this matter we have already burnt thy kilns, thy millbeams too we have all consumed; thy calves we have most accurately and universally admitted to their dams. Thy men's hair we will crop, and all locks of thy young women: to thy land it shall be a disfigurement, and such shall be our mischief's consummation. White be thy horse till time of war, thou king of Ulster and of warriors stout! but crimsoned be his trappings when he is in the battle's press. May no heat inordinate assail thee, nor inward flux e'er seize thee, nor eye-distemper reach thee during all thy life: but Fergus, not for love of thee! Were it not for Iubdan here, whom Fergus holds at his discretion, the manner of our effecting our depredations would have been such that the disgrace incurred by Fergus would have shown his refusal to be an evil one.

'And now go,' said Iubdan; 'for Esirt has prophesied of me that before I shall have left here the choicest one of all my precious things I may not retain.'

So till a year's end all but a little he dwelt in Emain, and then said to Fergus: 'Of all my treasures choose thee now a single one, for so thou mayest. My precious things are good too'; and in a lay he proceeded to enumerate them:

Take my spear, O take my spear, thou, Fergus, that hast enemies in number! in battle 'tis a match for a hundred, and a king that holds it will have fortune among hostile spear-points. Take my shield, O take my shield, a good price it is for me, Fergus! be it stripling or be it grey-beard, behind his shelter none may wounded be. My sword, and O my sword! in respect of a battle-sword there is not in a prince's hand throughout all Inis Fail a more excellent thing of price. Take my cloak, O take my cloak, the which if thou take it will be ever new! my mantle is good, Fergus, and for thy son and grandson will endure. My shirt, and O my shirt! whoe'er he be that in time to come may be within its weft — my grandsire's father's wife, her hands they were that spun it. Take my belt, O take my belt! gold and silver appertain to a knowledge of it; sickness will not lay hold on him that is encircled by it, nor on skin encompassed by my girdle. My helmet, O my helmet, no prize there is more admirable! no man that on his scalp shall assume it will ever suffer from the reproach of baldness. Take my tunic, O my tunic take, well-fitting silken garment! the which though for an hundred years it were on one, yet were its crimson none the worse. My cauldron, O my cauldron, a special rare thing for its handy use! though they were stones that should go into my cauldron, yet would it turn them out meat befitting princes. My vat, and O my vat! as compared with other vats of the best, by any that shall bathe in it life's stage is traversed thrice. Take my mace, O take my mace, no better treasure canst thou choose! in time of war, in sharp encounter, nine heads besides thine own it will protect. Take my horse-rod, O my horse-rod take — rod of the yellow horse so fair to see! let but the whole world's women look at thee with that rod in thy hand, and in thee will center all their hottest love. My timpan, O my timpan endowed with string-sweetness, from the Red Sea's borders! within its wires resides minstrelsy sufficing to delight all women of the universe. Whosoe'er should in the matter of tuning up my timpan be suddenly put to the test, if never hitherto he had been a man of art, yet would the instrument of itself perform the minstrel's function. Ah, how melodious is its martial strain, and its low cadence, ah, how sweet! all of itself too how it plays, without a finger on a single string of all its strings. My shears, and O my shears, that Barran's smith did make! of them that take it into their hands every man will secure a sweetheart. My needle, O my needle, that is made of the finest gold! . . . Of my swine two porkers take! they will last thee till thy dying day; every night they may be killed, yet within the watch will live again. My halter, O my halter! whoe'er should be on booty bent, though 'twere a black cow he put into it, incontinently she would become a white one. Take my shoes, my shoes, O take, brogues of the white bronze, of virtue marvellous! alike they travel land and sea, happy the king whose choice shall fall on these!

'Fergus,' said Iubdan, 'from among them all choose thee now one precious thing, and let me go.'

But this was now the season and the hour when from his adventure the Ulster poet Aed returned; and him the sages examined concerning Iubdan's house, his household, and the region of the Lepra. Concerning all which Aed forthwith began to tell them, inditing a lay:

A wondrous enterprise it was that took me away from you, our poets, to a populous fairy palace with a great company of princes and with little men. Twelve doors there are to that house of roomy beds and window-lighted sides; 'tis of vast marble blocks, and in every doorway doors of gold. Of red, of yellow and green, of azure and of blue its bedclothes are; its authority is of ancient date: warriors' cooking-places it includes, and baths. Smooth are its terraces of the egg-shells of Iruath; pillars there are of crystal, columns of silver and of copper too . . . Reciting of tales, of the fian-lore, was there every day; singing of poems, instrumental music, the mellow blast of horns, and concerted minstrelsy. A noble king he is: Iubdan son of Abdan, of the yellow horse; he is one whose form under-goes no change, and who needs not to strive after wisdom. Women are there, that in a pure clear lake disport themselves: satin their raiment is, and with each one of them a chain of gold. As for the king's men-at-arms, that wear long tresses, hair ringleted and glossy: men of the mould ordinary with the Lepra can stand upon those soldiers' palms. Bebo — Iubdan's blooming queen — an object of

desire — never is the white-skinned beauty without three hundred women in her train. Bebo's women — 'tis little they chat-
ter of evil or of arrogance; their bodies are pure white, and their
locks reach to their ankles. The king's chief poet, Esirt son of
Beg son of Buaidgen: his eye is blue and gentle, and less than a
doubled fist that man of poems is. The poet's wife — to all things
good she was inclined; a lovely woman and a wonderful: she
could sleep in my rounded glove. The king's cup-bearer — in the
banquet-hall a trusty man and true: well I loved Feror that could
lie within my sleeve. The king's strong man — Glomar son of
Glomrad's son Glas, stern doer of doughty deeds: he could fell
a thistle at a blow. Of those the king's confidentials, seventeen
'swans' [*i.e.*, pretty girls] lay in my bosom; four men of them in
my belt and, all unknown to me, among my beard would be
another. They (both fighting men and scholars of that fairy-
mound) would say to me, and the public acclamation ever was:
'Enormous Aed, O very giant!' Such, O Fergus mac Leide of
forests vast, such is my adventure: of a verity there is a wondrous thing befallen me.

Of all Iubdan's treasures then Fergus made choice, and his choice was
Iubdan's shoes. This latter therefore, leaving them his blessing and taking theirs, bade Fergus and the nobles of Ulster farewell, Ulster grieving for his departure, and with him the story henceforth has no more
to do.

As regards Fergus, however, this is why he picked out Iubdan's
shoes: he with a young man of his people walking one day hard by
Loch Rudraige, they entered into the loch to bathe; and the monster
that dwelt in the loch — the *sinech* ('Stormy One') of Loch Rudraige —
was aware of them. Then she, shaking herself till the whole loch was
in great and tempestuous commotion, reared herself on high as if it
had been a solid arc hideous to behold, so that in extent she equalled
a rainbow of the air. They both, marking her coming towards them,
swam for the shore, she in pursuit with mighty strokes that in bursting deluge sent the water spouting from her sides. Fergus allowed his
attendant to gain the land before himself, whereby the monster's
breath reaching the king turned him into a crooked and distorted
squint-eyed being, with his mouth twisted round to the back of his
head. But he knew not that he was so; neither dared any enquire of
him what it might be that had wrought this change in him, nor venture to leave a mirror in the same house with him.

The servant, however, told all the matter to his wife and the woman showed it to Fergus's wife, the queen. Later, therefore, when there was a falling-out between the king and queen over precedence in use of the bath-stone, the king gave her a blow with his fist which broke a tooth in her head; whereupon anger seized the queen, and she said, 'To avenge thyself on the *sinech* of Loch Rudraige that dragged thy mouth round to thy poll would become thee better than to win bloodless victories over women.' Then to Fergus she brought a mirror, and he looking upon his image said, 'The woman's words are true, and to this appearance it is indeed the *sinech* of Loch Rudraige that hath brought me.' And hence it was that before all Iubdan's other precious wares Fergus had taken his shoes.

In their ships and in their galleys the whole province of Ulster, accompanying Fergus, now gathered together to Loch Rudraige. They entering the loch gained its center; the monster rose and shook herself in such fashion that of all the vessels she made little bits and, as are the withered twigs beneath horses' feet, so were they severally crushed, and all swamped before they could reach the strand.

Fergus said to the men of Ulster: 'Bide here and sit you all down, that ye may witness how I and the monster shall deal together.' Then he, being shod with Iubdan's shoes, leaped into the loch, erect and brilliant and brave, making for the monster. At sound of the hero's approach she bared her teeth as does a wolf-dog threatened with a club; her eyes blazed like two great torches kindled, suddenly she put forth her sharp claws' jagged array, bent her neck with the curve of an arch and clenched her glittering tusks, throwing back her ears hideously, till her whole semblance was one of gloomy cruel fury. Alas, for any in this world that should be fated to do battle with that monster: huge-headed long-fanged dragon that she was! The fearsome and colossal creature's form was this: a crest and mane she had of coarse hair, a mouth that yawned, deep-sunken eyes; on either side thrice fifty flippers, each armed with as many claws recurved; a body impregnable. Thrice fifty feet her extended altitude; round as an apple she was in contraction, but in bulk equalled some great hill in its rough garb of furze.

When the king sighted her he charged, instant, impetuous, and as he went he made this rhapsody:

The evil is upon me that was presaged . . .

Then both of them came to the loch's middle part and so flogged it that the salmon of varied hue leaped and flung themselves out upon the shore because they found no resting-place in the water, for the white bottom-sand was churned up to the surface. Now was the loch whiter than new milk, at once all turned to crimson froth of blood. At last the beast, like some vast royal oak, rose on the loch and before Fergus fled. The hero-king, pressing her, plied her with blows so stalwart and so deadly that she died; and with the sword that was in his hand, with the *caladcolg,*[4] best blade that was then in Ireland, he hewed her all in pieces. To the loch's port where the Ulstermen were he brought her heart; but though he did, his own wounds were as many as hers, and than his skin no sieve could be more full of holes. To such effect truly the beast had given him the tooth, that he brought up his very heart's red blood and hardly might make utterance, but groaned aloud.

As for the Ulstermen, they took no pleasure in viewing the fight, but said that were it upon land the king and the beast had striven they would have helped him, and that right valiantly. Then Fergus made a lay:

My soul this night is full of sadness, my body mangled cruelly; red Loch Rudraige's beast has pushed sore through my heart. Iubdan's shoes have brought me through undrowned; with sheeny spear and with the famous sword I have fought a hardy fight. Upon the monster I have avenged my deformity — a signal victory this. Man! I had rather death should snatch me than to live misshapen. Great Eochaid's daughter Ailinn it is that to mortal combat's lists compelled me; and 'tis I assuredly that have good cause to sorrow for the shape imposed on me by the beast.

He went on: 'Ulstermen, I have gotten my death; but lay ye by and preserve this sword, until out of Ulster there come after me one that shall be a fitting lord; whose name also shall be Fergus; namely, Fergus mac Roig.'[5]

Then lamentably and in tears the Ulstermen stood over Fergus. The poet Aed also, the king's bard, came and standing over him mourned for Fergus with this quatrain:

By you now be dug Fergus's grave, the great monarch's, grave of Leide's son; calamity most dire it is that by a foolish petty woman's words he is done to death!

Answering whom Fergus said:

By you be laid up this sword wherewith 'the iron-death' is
wrought; here after me shall arise one with the name of Fergus.
By you be this sword treasured, that none other take it from
you; my share of the matter for all time shall be this: that men
shall rehearse the story of the sword.

So Fergus's soul parted from his body: his grave was dug, his name
written in the ogam, his lamentation-ceremony all performed; and
from the monumental stones (*ulad*) piled by the men of Ulster this
name of *Ulad* (Ulster) had its origin.

Thus far the Death of Fergus and the Lepra-people's doings.

The Adventures of Art Son of Conn[6]

In this story, as in the last, we find two simultaneous events occurring
on either side of the worlds: just as Conn is bewailing the loss of his
dear wife in the mortal realm, so the faery woman Becuma is
expelled from the regions of the Land of Promise. Calling herself
Delbchaem ('Fair Shape'), she marries Conn, although she has set her
heart on his son, Art, thus choosing honour over love.

This story revolves around the healing of the land, which has been
wounded by the King's marriage to an unworthy woman. All the ills
that innately surround her light upon Ireland, where neither grain
nor milk is available. Two quests are necessary to resolve the matter.
First, Conn must discover the son of a sinless couple, that he may be
sacrificed at Tara and his blood cure the blight. Secondly, Becuma
sets a *geas* upon Art that he find the real Delbchaem ní Morgan.
Father and son both take the faery coracle on their quests which take
them over the western seas to islands. Conn's quest is only partially
successful, since he refuses to put away Becuma. Art passes through a
complex magical landscape complete with terrors to overcome, until
he gains Delbchaem, brings her home and banishes Becuma from
Tara.

The synchronous complementary of mortal and otherworldly
lives is woven together in such a way that, whatever affects one side
also has repercussions on the other. The unity of existence, known to

shamans and indigenous peoples the world over, is only now being reluctantly acknowledged in scientific and environmental circles. What has been accepted as a mystical truth by spiritualities of all times is now shown to be so intertwined that we ignore the interrelationship of life with life to our peril. However, this acceptance is chiefly acknowledged on one side of the worlds only, where earth's habitat and inhabitants are now seen as interreliant. The greater truth, that our world and the unseen worlds of the spirit which lie around us are similarly interreliant has yet to be fully understood.

Conn's acceptance of a proscribed and ill-intentioned faery woman for a wife and his inability to give her up cause his land to suffer blight and dearth; it is Art's actions which restore the land to rights, by his courage and resolve upon his quest, and by his bringing back a well-intentioned faery woman for his wife.

Conn the Hundred-Fighter son of Fedlimid Rechtmar son of Tuathal Techtmar son of Feradach Findfechtnach son of Crimthann Nia Nair son of Lugaid Riab Derg son of the three white triplets, Bres and Nar and Lothar, the names of the sons of Eochaid Find, was once at Tara of the kings, the noble conspicuous dwelling of Ireland, for a period of nine years, and there was nothing lacking to the men of Ireland during the time of this king, for, indeed, they used to reap the corn three times in the year. And his wife was Ethne Taebfada (Long-Side) daughter of Brislinn Binn the king of Norway. He loved her dearly.

After their living a long time together Ethne died, and was buried with honor in Tailltiu; for Tailltiu was one of the three chief burial-places of Ireland, which were the Fair of Tailltiu, and the Brug beside the Boyne, and the cemetery of Cruachan. And he was dejected on account of his wife Ethne's death, and it weighed so heavily on him, that he was unable any longer to rule or govern the kingdom. And there was lacking to Ireland at that time one thing only, that the king of Ireland should find a helpmate worthy of him in her stead.

One day, however, he was all alone; and he went straight out of Tara to Benn Etair maic Etgaith. There he bewailed and lamented his wife and helpmate. It was on that very day the Tuatha De Danann happened to be gathered in council in the Land of Promise, because of a woman who had committed transgression, and whose name was Becuma Cneisgel daughter of Eogan Inbir, that is, the wife of Labraid Luathlam-ar-Claideb (Swift-Hand-on-Sword); and Gaidiar, Manannan's son, it was that had committed transgression with her. And this was the sentence passed on her: to be driven forth from the Land of

Promise, or to be burned according to the counsel of Manannan, and Fergus Findliath, and Eogan Inbir, and Lodan son of Lir, and Gaidiar, and Gaei Gormsuilech, and Ilbrec son of Manannan. And their counsel was to banish her from the Land of Promise. And Manannan said not to burn her lest her guilt should cleave to the land or to themselves.

Messengers came from Labraid to the house of Angus of the Brug, his own son-in-law; for a daughter of Labraid's was the wife of Angus of the Brug, and her name was Nuamaisi. It was for this reason messengers were despatched: in order that Becuma Cneisgel should not find a place for her head in any of the fairy-mounds of Ireland. Accordingly she was banished beyond the expanse of the sea and the great deep; and it was into Ireland in particular she was sent, for the Tuatha De Danann hated the sons of Mil after they had been driven out of Ireland by them.

The girl had a lover in Ireland, Art son of Conn the Hundred-Fighter, but Art did not know that he was her lover. As for the girl, she found a coracle (boat) which had no need of rowing, but leaving it to the harmony of the wind over sea she came to Ben Etair maic Etgaith. Thus was the girl. She had a green cloak of one color about her, with a fringe of red thread of red gold, and a red satin smock against her white skin, and sandals of white bronze on her, and soft yellow hair, and a gray eye in her head, and lovely-colored teeth, and thin red lips, black eyebrows, arms straight and fair of hue, a snowy white body, small round knees, and slender choice feet, with excellence of shape, and form, and complexion, and accomplishments. Fair was the attire of that maiden, even Eogan Inbir's daughter. One thing only, however, – a woman was not worthy of the high-king of Ireland who was banished for her own misdeed.

When she arrived, Conn was on Ben Etair, sorrowful, restless, and lamentful, bewailing his wife. The maiden recognized him as the high-king of Ireland, and she brought her coracle to land and sat down beside Conn. Conn asked tidings of her. The maiden answered, and said that she was come from the Land of Promise in quest of Art, whom she had loved from afar, because of the tales about him. And she said that she was Delbchaem daughter of Morgan. 'I would not come between thee and thy choice of courtship,' said Conn, 'though I have no wife.'

'Why hast thou no wife?' said the maiden.

'My helpmate died,' replied Conn.

'What then shall I do?' said the maiden; 'is it with thee or with Art that I shall sleep?'

'Make thine own choice,' replied Conn.

'This is my choice,' said the maiden, 'since thou dost not accept me: let me have my choice of courtship in Ireland.'

'I see no defects in thee for which it were right to refuse thee, unless they are concealed in thee.'

Then the maiden asked her own judgment of Conn, and it was granted her. And they made a union, Conn and the maiden, and she bound him to do her will. And her judgment was that Art should not come to Tara until a year was past. Conn's mind was vexed because of the banishing of his son from Ireland without cause. After that they both set out for Tara; and the maiden left her coracle in the clefts of the rocks in shelter and concealment, for she knew not when she might need that coracle again.

Art was at Tara then playing chess, and Cromdes, Conn's druid, along with him. And the druid said, 'A move of banishment of thine, my son, and because of the woman thy father marries thou art being banished.' The king and his wife arrived at the place, and his son was brought to him straightway. And Conn said to Art, 'Leave Tara and Ireland for a year, and make thy preparation at once, for I have pledged myself to this.' And the men of Ireland deemed it a great wrong that Art should be banished for the sake of a woman. Nevertheless, Art left Tara that night, and Conn and Becuma were a year together in Tara, and there was neither corn nor milk in Ireland during that time. And the men of Ireland were in the greatest difficulty about that matter; and the druids of all Ireland were sent with the help of their science and their true wisdom to show what had brought that dreadful evil into Ireland. The question was put to them, and the druids related to the king of Tara and the nobles of Ireland the cause of the evil: because of the depravity of Conn's wife and her unbelief it was sent. And it was declared, through whom their deliverance would be possible, namely, that the son of a sinless couple should be brought to Ireland and slain before Tara, and his blood mingled with the soil of Tara. This was told to Conn, but he knew not where there was such a boy. And he assembled the men of Ireland in one place, and said to them, 'I will go in quest of that sinless boy; and do you give the kingdom of Ireland to Art yonder so long as I am away, and, moreover, let him not leave Tara while I am absent until I come again.'

Then Conn proceeded straight to Ben Etair, and he found a coracle there. And he was a fortnight and a month on the sea wandering from one isle to another without knowledge or guidance save that of trusting to the course of the stars and the luminaries. And seals and leviathans, and adzeheads and porpoises, and many strange beasts of the sea rose up around the coracle, and swiftly uprose the waves, and the firmament trembled. And the hero all alone navigated the coracle until he came to a strange isle. He landed and left his coracle in a secret lonely place. And it is thus the island was: having fair fragrant apple-trees, and many wells of wine most beautiful, and a fair bright wood adorned with clustering hazel-trees surrounding those wells, with lovely golden-yellow nuts, and little bees ever beautiful humming over the fruits, which were dropping their blossoms and their leaves into the wells. Then he saw near-by a shapely hostel thatched with birds' wings, white, and yellow, and blue. And he went up to the hostel. 'Tis thus it was: with doorposts of bronze and doors of crystal, and a few generous inhabitants within. He saw the queen with her large eyes, whose name was Rigru Rosclethan daughter of Lodan from the Land of Promise, that is, the wife of Daire Degamra son of Fergus Fialbrethach from the Land of Wonders. Conn saw there in the midst of the hostel a little boy with excellence of shape and form, in a chair of crystal, and his name was Segda Saerlabraid son of Daire Degamra.

Conn sat down on the bedside of the hostel, and was attended upon, and his feet washed. And he knew not who had washed his feet. Before long he saw a flame arising from the hearth, and the hero was taken by an invisible hand which guided him to the fire, and he went towards the fire. Then food-laden boards of the house with varied meats rose up before him, and he knew not who had given them to him. After a short space he saw a drinking-horn there, and he knew not who had fetched the horn. Then the dishes were removed from him. He saw before him a vat excellent and finely wrought of blue crystal, with three golden hoops about it. And Daire Degamra bade Conn go into the vat and bathe, so that he might put his weariness from him. And Conn did so . . . A fair cloak was thrown over the king, and he awoke refreshed. Food and nourishment was set before him. He said that it was taboo for him to eat by himself. And they answered that there was no taboo at all among them, save that none of them ever ate with the other. 'Though no one has eaten,' said the little boy Segda Saerlabraid, 'I will eat along with the king of Ireland, so that he may not violate his taboo.' And they lay in the same bed that night.

Conn arose on the morrow, and laid before the household his need and his trouble. 'What is thy need?' said they.

'That Ireland is without corn and milk for a year now.'

'Why hast thou come hither?'

'In quest of your son,' replied Conn, 'if you are willing; for it has been told us that it is through him our deliverance will come; namely, that the son of a sinless couple should be invited to Tara, and afterwards bathed in the water of Ireland; and it is you that possess the same, so let this young person, even Segda Saerlabraid, be given up.'

'Alas,' said Daire son of Fergus Fialbrethach, 'we would not lend our son for the kingship of the world; for never did his father and mother come together except when yonder little boy was made; and moreover our own fathers and mothers never came together save at our making.'

'Evil is the thing you say,' said the boy, 'not to respond to the king of Ireland; I will go myself with him.'

'Do not say that, son,' said the household.

'I say that the king of Ireland should not be refused.'

'If that is so,' said the household, 'it is thus we shall let thee go from us, under protection of the kings of all Ireland, and Art son of Conn, and Finn son of Cumall, and the men of art, so that thou shalt come back safe to us again.'

'All that shall be given,' said Conn, 'if I can.'

As for Conn and his coracle, after having had this adventure, it was only a sail of three days and three nights for them to Ireland. The men of all Ireland were then gathered in assembly awaiting Conn at Tara. And when the druids saw the boy with Conn, this is the counsel they gave: to slay him and mingle his blood with the blighted earth and the withered trees, so that its due mast and fruit, its fish, and its produce might be in them. And Conn placed the boy he had brought with him under the protection of Art and Finn, and the men of art, and the men of Ireland. The latter, however, did not accept that responsibility, but the kings accepted it at once, that is Conn, and Finn, and Art Oenfer, and they were all outraged as regards the boy.

As soon as they had finished this council, the boy cried out with a loud voice: 'O men of Ireland, leave me alone in peace, since you have agreed to slay me. Let me be put to death, as I shall say myself,' said the boy. Just then they heard the lowing of a cow, and a woman wailing continually behind it. And they saw the cow and the woman making towards the assembly. The woman sat down between Finn and

Conn the Hundred-Fighter. She asked tidings of the attempt of the men of Ireland, that the innocent boy should be put to death in despite of Finn, and Art, and Conn. 'Where are those druids?'

'Here,' said they.

'Find out for me what those two bags are at the cow's sides, that is, the bag at each side of her.'

'By our conscience,' said they, 'we know not indeed.'

'I know,' said she; 'a single cow that has come here to save that innocent youth. And it is thus it will be done to her: let the cow be slaughtered, and her blood mixed with the soil of Ireland, and save the boy. And moreover, there is something which it were more fitting for you to take heed to, that is, when the cow is cut up, let the two bags be opened, and there are two birds inside, a bird with one leg, and a bird with twelve legs.'

And the cow was slaughtered and the birds taken out of her. And as they were beating their wings in the presence of the host, the woman said, 'It is thus we shall discover which is the stronger if they encounter.' Then the one-legged bird prevailed over the bird with twelve legs. The men of Ireland marvelled at that. Said the woman, 'You are the bird with the twelve legs, and the little boy the bird with one leg, for it is he who is in the right. Take those druids there,' said the woman, 'for it were better for them to die, and let them be hanged.' And the young man was not put to death. Then the woman rose up and called Conn aside, and spoke as follows: 'Put this sinful woman away, this Becuma Cneisgel, daughter of Eogan Inbir, and wife of Labraid Luathlam-ar-Claideb, for it is through transgression she has been driven out of the Land of Promise.'

'That is good counsel,' said Conn, 'if I could put her away; but since I cannot, give us good advice.'

'I will,' said the woman, 'for it is worse it will be; a third of its corn, and its milk, and its mast will be lacking to Ireland so long as she is with you.' And she took leave of them then and went off with her son, Segda. Jewels and treasures were offered to them, but they refused them.

Becuma chanced to be out on the green then, and she saw Conn's son Art playing chess there. It was not pleasant for Art to see his enemy. 'Is that Conn's son Art?' said she.

'It is indeed,' said they.

'I lay a taboo upon him,' said she, 'unless he play chess with me for stakes.'

This was told to Art son of Conn. A chess-board was brought to them then, and they played, and Art won the first game. 'This is a game on thee, girl,' said Art.

'That is so,' said she.

'And I lay a taboo on thee,' said he, 'if thou eat food in Ireland until thou procure the warrior's wand which Cu Roi mac Dairi had in his hand when taking possession of Ireland and the great world, and fetch it to me here.'

Then the girl proceeded to the dewy light-flecked brug, wherein was Angus, with his dear wife at his side, even Nuamaisi daughter of Labraid. However, she searched most of the fairy-mounds of Ireland, and found no tidings of the wand until she came to the fairy-mound of Eogabal, and a welcome was given her here by Aine daughter of Eogabal, for they were two foster-sisters. 'Thou wilt get thy quest here,' said she; 'and take yonder thrice fifty youths with thee until thou come to the stronghold of Cu Roi on the top of Sliab Mis.' And they found it there, and she rejoiced.

Thereupon she set out for Tara, and she brought the wand to Art, and laid it upon his knees. The chess-board was brought to them, and they played. And the men of the fairy-mound began to steal the pieces. Art saw that, and said, 'The men of the fairy-mound are stealing the pieces from us, girl; and it is not thou that art winning the game, but they.'

'This is a game on thee,' said the girl.

'It is so indeed,' said the young man; 'and give thy judgment.'

'I will this,' said she; 'thou shalt not eat food in Ireland until thou bring with thee Delbchaem the daughter of Morgan.'

'Where is she?' said Art.

'In an isle amid the sea, and that is all the information thou wilt get.'

Art set out for Inber Colptha; and he found a coracle with choice equipment on the shore before him. And he put forth the coracle, and travelled the sea from one isle to another until he came to a fair, strange island; and lovely was the character of that island, full of wild apples and lovely birds, with little bees ever beautiful on the tops of the flowers. A house, hospitable and noble, in the midst of the island, thatched with birds' wings, white and purple, and within it a company of blooming women, ever beautiful, among them Creide Firalainn daughter of Fidech Foltlebor.

A hearty welcome was then given to him, and food set before him, and tidings are asked of him. And he said that he was come from Ireland, and that he was the King of Ireland's son, and his name was Art. 'That is true,' said Creide. After that she put out her hand, and gave him a variegated mantle with adornments of burnished gold from Arabia, and he put it on him, and it was right for him. ''Tis true,' said she, 'that thou art Conn's son Art, and it is long since thy coming here has been decreed.' And she gave him three kisses, dearly and fervently. And she said, 'Look at the crystal bower.' And fair was the site of that bower, with its doors of crystal and its inexhaustible vats, for, though everything be emptied out of them, they were ever full again.

He remained a fortnight and a month in that island, after which he took leave of the girl, and related his errand. ''Tis true,' said she, 'that is thine errand; and it will be no little time until the maiden will be found, for the way is bad thither, and there is sea and land between thee and her, and, even if thou dost reach it, thou wilt not go past it. There is a great ocean and dark between; and deadly and hostile is the way there, for there is a wood that is traversed as though there were spear-points of battle under one's feet, like leaves of the forest under the feet of men. There is a luckless gulf of the sea full of dumb-mouthed beasts on this side of that wood, even an immense oak forest, dense and thorny before a mountain, and a narrow path through it, and a dark house in the mysterious wood at the head of the same path, with seven hags and a bath of molten lead awaiting thee, for thy coming there has been fated. And there is somewhat more grievous still, even Ailill Black-tooth son of Mongan Minscothach. And weapon cannot harm him. And there are two sisters of mine there, daughters of Fidech Foltlebor, Finscoth and Aeb their names. There are two cups in their hands – a cup filled with poison, and one filled with wine. And the cup which is on thy right hand, drink therefrom when thou hast need. And near at hand is the stronghold of the maiden. Thus it is, with a palisade of bronze round about it, and a man's head on every stake of it, after being slain by Coinchenn Cennfada (Dog-Head Long-Head), save on one stake alone. And Coinchenn daughter of the king of the Coinchinn the mother of the girl, even Delbchaem daughter of Morgan.'

Art then set out after he had been instructed by the girl, until he came to the crest of that hapless sea full of strange beasts. And on all sides the beasts and great sea-monsters rose up around the coracle. And Art son of Conn donned his battle attire, and engaged them warily and circumspectly. And he began to slaughter them and maim them until they fell by him.

After that he came to the forest wild where the Coinchenn and the wicked, perverse hags were, and Art and the hags encountered. It was not a fair encounter for him, the hags piercing and hacking at him until morning. Nevertheless the armed youth prevailed over that hapless folk. And Art went on his way using his own judgment until he came to the venomous icy mountain; and the forked glen was there full of poisonous toads, which were lying in wait for whoever came there. And he passed thence to Saeb Mountain beyond, wherein were full many lions with long manes lying in wait for the beasts of the whole world.

After that he came to the icy river, with its slender narrow bridge, and a warrior giant with a pillar-stone, and he grinding his teeth on it, namely, Curnan Cliabsalach. Nevertheless they encountered, and Art overcame the giant, so that Curnan Cliabsalach fell by him. And he went thence to where Ailill Dubdedach son of Mongan was. And 'tis thus that man was: a fierce champion was he; no weapon could harm him, or fire burn him, or water drown him. Then Art and he took to wrestling, and they made a manly combat, a stern, heroic, equally-sharp fight. And Ailill Dubdedach began abusing Art, and they were haranguing one another. But Art overcame the giant, so that his head came off the back of his neck. After that Art wrecked the stronghold; and he seized Ailill's wife, and he threatened to do her injury until she told him the way to Morgan's stronghold, and the Land of Wonders.

It was there Coinchenn Cennfada, Morgan's wife, was; and she had the strength of a hundred in battle or conflict. She was the daughter of Conchruth king of the Coinchinn. And the druids had foretold her that if ever her daughter should be wooed, in that same hour she would die. Therefore, she put to death everyone that came to woo her daughter. And it was she that had organized the hags with the bath of lead to meet him, and Curnan Cliabsalach son of Duscad, the door-keeper of Morgan's house. And it was she that had put Ailill Dubdedach in the way of Art son of Conn, because Art would come on that expedition to woo her daughter, as it had been foretold her. And it was she that had contrived the venomous toads, and the icy bridge, and the dark forest, and the mountain full of lions, and the hapless sea-gulf.

Thus came Art to the stronghold which he was in quest of, that is, Morgan's stronghold, and pleasant it was. A fair palisade of bronze was round about it, and houses hospitable and extensive, and a stately palace . . . in the midst of the enclosure. An ingenious, bright, shining bower set on one pillar over the enclosure, on the very top, where that maiden was. She had a green cloak of one hue about her, with a gold pin in it over her breast, and long, fair, very golden hair. She had dark-black eyebrows, and flashing grey eyes in her head, and a snowy-white body. Fair was the maiden both in shape and intelligence, in wisdom and embroidery, in chastity and nobility. And the maiden said: 'A warrior has come to this place to-day, and there is not in the world a warrior fairer in form, or of better repute. It is true,' said she, 'he is Art; and it is long since we have been preparing for him. And I will go into a house apart,' said she, 'and do thou bring Art into the bower; for I fear lest the Coinchenn may put him to death, and have his head placed on the vacant stake before the stronghold.'

With that Art went into the bower, and when the women-folk saw him they made him welcome, and his feet were bathed. After that came the Coinchenn, and the two daughters of Fidech along with her, Aeb and Finscoth, to pour out the poison and the wine for Art.

Then the Coinchenn arose and put on her fighting apparel, and challenged Art to combat. And it was not Art who refused a fight ever. So he donned his fighting gear, and before long the armed youth prevailed over the Coinchenn; and her head came off from the back of her neck, and he placed it on the vacant stake in front of the fortress.

Now concerning Art son of Conn and Delbchaem daughter of Morgan. That night they lay down merry, and in good spirits, the whole stronghold in their power, from small to great, until Morgan king of the Land of Wonders arrived; for indeed he was not there at the time. Then, however, Morgan arrived, full of wrath, to avenge his fortress and his good wife on Art son of Conn. He challenged Art to combat. And the young man arose, and put on his battle-harness, his pleasant, satin mantle, and the white light-speckled apron of burnished gold about his middle. And he put his fine dark helmet of red gold on his head. And he took his fair, purple, embossed shield on the arched expanse of his back. And he took his wide-grooved sword with its blue hilt, and his two thick-shafted, red-yellow spears, and they attacked each other, Art and Morgan, like two enormous stags, or two lions, or two waves of destruction. And Art overcame Morgan, and he did not part from him until his head had come off his neck. After which Art took hostages of Morgan's people, and also possession of the Land of Wonders. And he collected the gold and silver of the land also, and gave it all to the maiden, even Delbchaem daughter of Morgan.

The stewards and overseers followed him from the land, and he brought the maiden with him to Ireland. And they landed at Benn Etair. When they came into port, the maiden said: 'Hasten to Tara, and tell to Becuma daughter of Eogan that she abide not there, but to depart at once, for it is a bad hap if she be not commanded to leave Tara.'

And Art went forward to Tara, and was made welcome. And there was none to whom his coming was not pleasing, but the wanton and sorrowful Becuma. But Art ordered the sinful woman to leave Tara. And she rose up straightway lamenting in the presence of the men of Ireland, without a word of leave-taking, until she came to Benn Etair.

As for the maiden Delbchaem, the seers, and the wise men, and the chiefs were sent to welcome her, and she and Art came to Tara luckily and auspiciously. And the nobles of Ireland asked tidings of his adventures from Art; and he answered them, and made a lay.

Thus far the Adventures of Art son of Conn, and the Courtship of Delbchaem daughter of Morgan.

CHAPTER 12

In the House of the Sidhe

Finally, we come to the heart of the Celtic otherworld itself and its inhabitants. Throughout this book it has become clear that there is no part of this world which does not impinge upon or act as a gateway to the otherworld. The Celtic otherworld is contiguous to ours, overlapping it, its waters forever seeping through the barely perceptible cracks which mark the unseen borders. To focus our intention upon it is tantamount to travelling thither.

The inhabitants of the otherworld are the people of the *sidhe*, or mounds, those whom we call the faery-kind. The name 'faery' has acquired unfortunate connotations, evoking images of butterfly-winged and saccharine creatures slightly bigger than insects. If we are to have any understanding of the people of the *sidhe* in Celtic tradition, we must erase such connotations and understand that they have a far greater stature and power than we can conceive. Immortal, able to pass between the worlds at will, with resources that seem magical to humans, they appear as major protagonists in Celtic tradition, both then and now.

Awareness of the faeries is still strong in Celtic countries. They are considered as neighbours, a race who requires a great deal of respect, who can help or harm according to the nature of the alliance that mortals have with them. Among people with little or no esoteric framework, there is a healthy and exaggerated care not to become too involved with the faeries, lest they fall unawares into their realms and cannot find their way out again. It is only the foolhardy or the intrepid otherworldly explorers who actively seek out the faery and walk the pathways to their realms.

The faery have ever been a race apart. They are not, nor have they

ever been, human. In Irish tradition it is possible to see them as primal deities, as we see in 'The Fosterage in the House of the Two Pails',
where the Tuatha de Danann retire into the *sidhe* mounds of the
hollow hills, leaving the land to the Milesians. Yet their separate existence still impinges upon mortal existence, throwing light upon the
nature of our spiritual intentions towards the environment, of which
they are the natural guardians. In the newly translated text, 'The Yew
Tree of the Disputing Sons', we see how careful we must be when we
invade faery territory without making restitution or alliance.

W.Y. Evans-Wentz's admirable book *The Fairy Faith in Celtic
Countries* reveals the extent of our continued alliance with the faeries
and remarks upon the urban-dweller's dislocation from such
alliances. He stresses the importance of our study of the faeries as 'a
key to unlock the mysteries of Celtic mythology', and points out that

> In truth the Celtic empire is greater than it ever was before
> Caesar destroyed its political unity; and its citizens have not for-
> gotten the ancient faith of their ancestors in a world invisible.

The Wooing of Etain

It is rare that we read of the internal affairs of Faery, but this story is
related from that viewpoint. In the first half, we discover how the
Brugh (Newgrange) comes into the keeping of Aengus mac Og.
Eochaid Ollathair (the Dagda) lies with Eithne (Boand), the Dagda
having sent Elcmar, Boand's husband away. We discover from other
versions that in Elcmar's absence, the Dagda causes a year to seem
like a day; in this 'day' Aengus is conceived and born. Raised by
Midir, Aengus suffers the mockery of his foster-siblings until he is
informed of his parentage, whereupon he decides to claim their
acknowledgement. The Dagda wishes to gift his son with the Brugh,
but this is occupied by Elcmar. Aengus is instructed to ask Elcmar for
the kingship of the Brugh for a night and a day only on the feast of
Samhain, when no reprisals can be exacted. When Elcmar comes to
take up his kingship again, Aengus refuses to yield it. Elcmar is rec-
ompensed by being given the land of Cleitach in place of the Brugh.

Midir visits the Brugh and accidentally loses one eye in trying to
resolve a conflict between some youths. Thus blemished, he may not
remain a ruler but Diancecht heals him. Midir then requests the
fairest maiden of Ireland, Etain Echraide, King Ailill's daughter, for
his own. Aengus goes to ask for her hand on Midir's behalf; Ailill will

not part with her unless Aengus performs many onerous tasks in fulfilment of the bride-price – to clear twelve plains for agriculture, to create twelve rivers, and to provide the weight of Etain in gold and silver. Midir takes her home, but is warned about the jealousy of his other wife, Fuamach, who enchants Etain into a pool of water. The elemental mixture of the heat of the fire, the air, the water and the earth spawns a worm which becomes a purple fly. Etain subsequently wanders for seven years on a druidic wind evoked by Fuamnach until rescued by Aengus and restored by him in his *grianan*. But Fuamnach finds a way of gaining entrance and evokes the same wind to blow Etain away. As a fly she wanders until she falls into the goblet of Etar and is drunk by her, becoming her child Etain ni Etar.

In Part 2 of the story, from a different and later source, we hear of the subsequent career of Etain ni Etar, her wooing by Eochaid Airem and her rescue by Midir, after many generations. The style of this part is more detailed and approachable than that of Part 1. Midir triumphs because of his skill with the gaming board, which is a frequent feature of wooing stories.

It is worth noting that the chief protagonists have both titles as well as names. Eochaid Ollathair is the Dagda, the Good God; Eithne is Boann, Cow-Wealth; and Elcmar is elsewhere also called Nechtan, the Pure One. This primary faery love triangle is subsequently replaced by that of Aengus, Midir and Etain.

The example of Etain is frequently given in support of a Celtic belief in reincarnation, but Etain's *tuirgen* is more complex than this; that her soul-life is continuous is shown by the fact that Midir and Aengus both regard her as the same being, who is worthy of their love and care. Both this story and the one which follows it demonstrates the central importance of Brugh na Boyne (Newgrange) as a house of the soul.

Part 1[1]

There was a famous king of Ireland of the race of the Tuatha Dé, Eochaid Ollathair his name. He was also named the Dagda [i.e. good god], for it was he that used to work wonders for them and control the weather and the crops. Wherefore men said he was called the Dagda. Elcmar of the Brug had a wife whose name was Eithne, and another name for her was Boand. The Dagda desired her in carnal union. The woman would have yielded to the Dagda had it not been for fear of Elcmar, so great was his power. Thereupon the Dagda sent Elcmar away on a journey to Bres son of Elatha in Mag nInis, and the

Dagda worked great spells upon Elcmar as he set out, that he might not return betimes [that is, early] and he dispelled the darkness of night for him, and he kept hunger and thirst from him. He sent him on long errands, so that nine months went by as one day, for he had said that he would return home again between day and night. Meanwhile the Dagda went in unto Elcmar's wife, and she bore him a son, even Aengus, and the woman was whole of her sickness when Elcmar returned, and he perceived not her offence, that is, that she had lain with the Dagda.

The Dagda meanwhile brought his son to Midir's house in Brí Léith in Tethba, to be fostered. There Aengus was reared for the space of nine years. Midir had a great playing-field in Brí Léith. Thrice fifty lads of the young nobles of Ireland were there and thrice fifty maidens of the land of Ireland. Aengus was the leader of them all, because of Midir's great love for him, and the beauty of his form and the nobility of his race. He was also called in Mac Óc (the Young Son), for his mother said: 'Young is the son who was begotten at the break of day and born betwixt it and evening.'

Now Aengus quarrelled with Triath son of Febal [or Gobor] of the Fir Bolg, who was one of the two leaders in the game, and a fosterling of Midir. It was no matter of pride with Aengus that Triath should speak to him, and he said: 'It irks me that the son of a serf should hold speech with me,' for Aengus had believed until then that Midir was his father, and the kingship of Brí Léith his heritage, and he knew not then of his kinship with the Dagda.

Triath made answer and said: 'I take it no less ill that a hireling whose mother and father are unknown should hold speech with me.' Thereupon Aengus went to Midir weeping and sorrowful at having been put to shame by Triath. 'What is this?' said Midir. 'Triath has defamed me and cast in my face that I have neither mother nor father.' ''Tis false,' said Midir. 'Who is my mother, from whence is my father?' 'No hard matter. Thy father is Eochaid Ollathair,' said Midir, 'and Eithne, wife of Elcmar of the Brug, is thy mother. It is I that have reared thee unknown to Elcmar, lest it should cause him pain that thou wast begotten in his despite.' 'Come thou with me,' said Aengus, 'that my father may acknowledge me, and that I may no longer be kept hidden away under the insults of the Fir Bolg.'

Then Midir set out with his fosterling to have speech with Eochaid, and they came to Uisnech of Meath in the centre of Ireland, for 'tis there was Eochaid's house, Ireland stretching equally far from it on

every side, to south and north, to east and west. Before them in the
assembly they found Eochaid. Midir called the king aside to have
speech with the lad. 'What does he desire, this youth who has not
come until now?' 'His desire is to be acknowledged by his father, and
for land to be given him,' said Midir, 'for it is not meet that thy son
should be landless while thou art king of Ireland.' 'He is welcome,'
said Eochaid, 'he is my son. But the land I wish him to have is not yet
vacant.' 'What land is that?' said Midir. 'The Brug, to the north of the
Boyne,' said Eochaid. 'Who is there?' said Midir. 'Elcmar,' said
Eochaid, 'is the man who is there. I have no wish to annoy him further.'

'Pray, what counsel dost thou give this lad?' said Midir. 'I have this
for him,' said Eochaid. 'On the day of Samain let him go into the Brug,
and let him go armed. That is a day of peace and amity among the
men of Ireland, on which none is at enmity with his fellow. And
Elcmar will be in Cnoc Síde in Broga unarmed save for a fork of white
hazel in his hand, his cloak folded about him, and a gold brooch in his
cloak, and three fifties playing before him in the playing-field; and let
Aengus go to him and threaten to kill him. But it is meet that he slay
him not, provided he promise him his will. And let this be the will of
Aengus, that he be king a day and a night in the Brug; and see that
thou yield not the land to Elcmar till he submit himself [?] to my decision; and when he comes let Aengus' plea be that the land has fallen
to him in fee simple for sparing Elcmar and not slaying him, and that
what he had asked for is kingship of day and night, and' said he, 'it is
in days and nights that the world is spent.'

Then Midir sets out for his land, and his foster-son along with him,
and on Samain following, Aengus having armed himself came into the
Brug and made a feint at Elcmar, so that he promised him in return
for his life kingship of day and night in his land. The Mac Óc straightway abode there that day and the following night as king of the land,
Elcmar's household being subject to him. On the morrow Elcmar
came to claim his land from the Mac Óc, and therewith threatened
him mightily. The Mac Óc said that he would not yield up his land
until he should put it to the decision of the Dagda in presence of the
men of Ireland.

Then they appeal to the Dagda, who adjudged each man's contract
in accordance with his undertaking. 'So then this land accordingly
belongs henceforth to this youth,' said Elcmar. 'It is fitting,' said the
Dagda. 'Thou wast taken unawares on a day of peace and amity. Thou

gavest thy land for mercy shown thee, for thy life was dearer to thee than thy land, yet thou shalt have land from me that will be no less profitable to thee than the Brug.' 'Where is that?' said Elcmar. 'Cleitech,' said the Dagda, 'with the three lands that are round about it, thy youths playing before thee every day in the Brug, and thou shalt enjoy the fruits of the Boyne from this land.' 'It is well,' said Elcmar; 'so shall it be accomplished.' And he made a flitting to Cleitech, and built a stronghold there, and the Mac Óc abode in the Brug in his land.

Then Midir came on that day year to the Brug on a visit to his fosterling, and he found the Mac Óc on the mound of Síd in Broga on the day of Samain, with two companies of youths at play before him in the Brug, and Elcmar on the mound of Cleitech to the south, watching them. A quarrel broke out among the youths in the Brug. 'Do not stir,' said Midir to the Mac Óc, 'because of Elcmar, lest he come down to the plain. I will go myself to make peace between them.' Thereupon Midir went, and it was not easy for him to part them. A spit of holly was thrown at Midir as he was intervening, and it knocked one of his eyes out. Midir came to the Mac Óc with his eye in his hand and said to him: 'Would that I had not come on a visit to thee, to be put to shame, for with this blemish I cannot behold the land I have come to, and the land I have left, I cannot return to it now.'

'It shall in no wise be so,' said the Mac Óc. 'I will go to Dian Cécht that he may come and heal thee, and thine own land shall be thine and this land shall be thine, and thine eye shall be whole again without shame or blemish because of it.' The Mac Óc went to Dian Cécht. '[. . .] that thou mayest go with me,' said he, 'to save my foster-father who has been hurt in the Brug on the day of Samain.' Dian Cécht came and healed Midir, so that he was whole again. 'Good is my journeying now,' said Midir, 'since I am healed.' 'It shall surely be so,' said the Mac Óc. 'Do thou abide here for a year that thou mayest see my host and my folk, my household and my land.'

'I will not stay,' said Midir, 'unless I have a reward therefore.' 'What reward?' said the Mac Óc. 'Easy to say. A chariot worth seven cumals,' said Midir, 'and a mantle befitting me, and the fairest maiden in Ireland.' 'I have,' said the Mac Óc, 'the chariot and the mantle befitting thee.' 'There is moreover,' said Midir, 'the maiden that surpasses all the maidens in Ireland in form.' 'Where is she?' said the Mac Óc. 'She is in Ulster,' said Midir, 'Ailill's daughter Étaín Echraide, daughter of the king of the north-eastern part of Ireland. She is the dearest and gentlest and loveliest in Ireland.'

The Mac Óc went to seek her until he came to Ailill's house in Mag nInis. He was made welcome, and he abode three nights there. He told his mission and announced his name and race. He said that it was in quest of Étaín that he had come. 'I will not give her to thee,' said Ailill, 'for I can in no way profit by thee, because of the nobility of thy family, and the greatness of thy power² and that of thy father. If thou put any shame on my daughter, no redress whatsoever can be had of thee.' 'It shall not be so,' said the Mac Óc. 'I will buy her from thee straightway.' 'Thou shalt have that,' said Ailill. 'State thy demand,' said the Mac Óc. 'No hard matter,' said Ailill. 'Thou shalt clear for me twelve plains in my land that are under waste and wood, so that they may be at all times for grazing for cattle and for habitation to men, for games and assemblies, gatherings, and strongholds.'

'It shall be done,' said the Mac Óc. He returns home and bewailed to the Dagda the strait he was in. The latter caused twelve plains to be cleared in a single night in Ailill's land. These are the names of the plains: Mag Macha, Mag Lemna, Mag nítha, Mag Tochair, Mag nDula, Mag Techt, Mag Lí, Mag Line, Mag Murthemne.³ Now when that work had been accomplished by the Mac Óc he went to Ailill to demand Étaín. 'Thou shalt not obtain her,' said Ailill, 'until thou draw out of this land to the sea twelve great rivers that are in wells and bogs and moors, so that they may bring produce from the sea to peoples and kindreds, and drain the earth and the land.'

He came again to the Dagda to bewail the strait he was in. Thereupon the latter caused twelve great waters to course towards the sea in a single night. They had not been seen there until then. These are the names of the waters: Find and Modornn and Slena and Nas and Amnas and Oichén and Or and Banda and Samaír and Lóche.⁴ Now when these works were accomplished the Mac Óc came to have speech with Ailill in order to claim Étaín. 'Thou shalt not get her till thou purchase her, for after thou hast taken her, I shall have no profit of the maiden beyond what I shall obtain forthwith.' 'What dost thou require of me now?' said the Mac Óc. 'I require,' said Ailill, 'the maiden's weight in gold and silver, for that is my portion of her price; all thou hast done up to now, the profit of it goes to her folk and her kindred.' 'It shall be done,' said the Mac Óc. She was placed on the floor of Ailill's house, and her weight of gold and silver was given for her. That wealth was left with Ailill, and the Mac Óc brought Étaín home with him.

Midir made that company welcome. That night Étaín sleeps with

Midir, and on the morrow a mantle befitting him and a chariot were given to him, and he was pleased with his foster-son. After that he abode a full year in the Brug with Aengus. On that day year Midir went to his own land, to Brí Léith, and he brought Étaín with him. On the day he went from him the Mac Óc said to Midir 'Give heed to the woman thou takest with thee, because of the dreadful cunning woman that awaits thee, with all the knowledge and skill and craft that belongs to her race,' said Aengus, 'also she has my word and my safe-guard before the Tuatha Dé Danann,' that is, Fuamnach wife of Midir, of the progeny of Beothach son of Iardanél. She was wise and prudent and skilled in the knowledge and magic power of the Tuatha Dé Danann, for the wizard Bresal had reared her until she was betrothed to Midir.

She made her husband welcome, that is Midir, and the woman spoke much of . . . to them. 'Come, O Midir,' said Fuamnach, 'that I may show thee thy house and thy meed of land' . . . Midir went round all his land with Fuamnach, and she showed his seizin to him and . . . to Étaín. And after that he brought Étaín again to Fuamnach. Fuamnach went before them into the sleeping chamber wherein she slept, and she said to Étaín: 'The seat of a good woman hast thou come into.' When Étaín sat down on the chair in the middle of the house, Fuamnach struck her with a rod of scarlet quickentree, and she turned into a pool of water in the middle of the house; and Fuamnach comes to her fosterfather Bresal, and Midir left the house to the water into which Étaín had turned. After that Midir was without a wife.

The heat of the fire and the air and the seething of the ground aided the water so that the pool that was in the middle of the house turned into a worm, and after that the worm became a purple fly. It was as big as a man's head, the comeliest in the land. Sweeter than pipes and harps and horns was the sound of her voice and the hum of her wings. Her eyes would shine like precious stones in the dark. The fragrance and the bloom of her would turn away hunger and thirst from any one around whom she would go. The spray of the drops she shed from her wings would cure all sickness and disease and plague in any one round whom she would go. She used to attend Midir and go round about his land with him, as he went. To listen to her and gaze upon her would nourish hosts in gatherings and assemblies in camps. Midir knew that it was Étaín that was in that shape, and so long as that fly was attend-ing upon him, he never took to himself a wife, and the sight of her would nourish him. He would fall asleep with her humming, and whenever any one approached who did not love him, she would awaken him.

After a time Fuamnach came on a visit to Midir, and along with her as sureties came the three gods of Dana, namely Lug and the Dagda, and Ogma. Midir reproached Fuamnach exceedingly and said to her that she should not go from him were it not for the power of the sureties that had brought her. Fuamnach said that she did not repent of the deed she had done, for that she would rather do good to herself than to another, and that in whatsoever part of Ireland she might be she would do naught but harm to Étaín so long as she lived, and in whatsoever shape she might be. She brought powerful incantations and . . . spells from Bresal Etarlam the wizard to banish and warn off Étaín from Midir, for she knew that the purple fly that was delighting Midir was Étaín herself, for whenever he saw the scarlet fly, Midir loved no other woman, and he found no pleasure in music or in drinking or eating when he did not see her and hear the music of her and her voice. Fuamnach stirred up a wind of assault and magic so that Étaín was wafted [?] from Brí Léith, and for seven years she could not find a summit or a tree or a hill or a height in Ireland on which she could settle, but only rocks of the sea and the ocean waves, and [she was] floating through the air until seven years from that day when she lighted on a fringe [?] on the breast of the Mac Óc as he was on the mound of the Brug.

There it was that the Mac Óc said, 'Welcome, Étaín, wanderer careworn, thou that hast encountered great dangers through the cunning of Fuamnach.'

The Mac Óc made the girl welcome, that is, the purple fly, and gathered her to his bosom in the fleece of his cloak. He brought her to his house and his sun-bower with its bright windows for passing out and in, and purple raiment was put on her; and wheresoever he went that sun-bower was carried by the Mac Óc, and there he used to sleep every night by her side, comforting her, until her gladness and colour came to her again. And that sun-bower was filled with fragrant and wondrous herbs, and she throve on the fragrance and bloom of those goodly precious herbs.

Fuamnach was told of the love and honour that was bestowed by the Mac Óc on Étaín. Said Fuamnach to Midir, 'Let thy fosterling be summoned that I may make peace between you both, while I myself go in quest of Étaín.' A messenger comes to the Mac Óc from Midir, and he went to speak to him. Meanwhile Fuamnach came by a cir-

cuitous way until she was in the Brug, and she sent the same blast on
Étaín, which carried her out of her sun-bower on the very flight she
had been on before for the space of seven years throughout Ireland.
The blast of wind drove her along in misery and weakness until she
alit on the rooftree of a house in Ulster where folk were drinking, and
she fell into the golden beaker that was before the wife of Étar the
champion from Inber Cíchmaine, in the province of Conchobar, so that
she swallowed her with the liquid that was in the beaker, and in this
wise she was conceived in her womb and became afterwards her
daughter. She was called Étaín daughter of Étar. Now it was a thousand and twelve years from the first begetting of Étaín by Ailill until
her last begetting by Étar.

After that Étaín was brought up at Inber Cíchmaine by Étar, and
fifty daughters of chieftains along with her, and he it was that fed and
clothed them to be in attendance on Étaín always. On a day it befel
that all the maidens were bathing in the estuary when they saw from
the water a horseman entering the plain towards them. He was mounted on a broad brown steed, curvetting and prancing, with curly mane
and curly tail. Around him a . . . green mantle in folds, and a red-
embroidered tunic, and in his mantle a golden brooch which reached
to his shoulder on either side. A silvern shield with rim of gold slung
over his back, and a silver strap to it and boss of gold thereon. In his
hand a five-pronged spear with bands of gold round about it from haft
to socket. Bright yellow hair he had reaching to his forehead. A fillet
of gold against his forehead so that his hair should not fall over his face.
He halted a while on the bank gazing at the maiden, and all the maidens loved him. Thereupon he uttered this lay:

This is Étaín here to-day
at Síd Ban Find west of Ailbe,
among little boys is she
on the brink of Inber Cíchmaine.

She it is who healed the King's eye
from the well of Loch Dá Líg;
she it is that was swallowed in a drink
from a beaker by Étar's wife.

Because of her the King shall chase
the birds from Tethba,
and drown his two steeds
in the pool of Loch Dá Airbrech.

> Full many a war shall be
> on Eochaid of Meath because of thee;
> there shall be destruction of elfmounds,
> and battle against many thousands.
>
> 'Tis she that was sung of [?] in the land;
> 'tis she that strives to win the King;
> 'tis she . . . Bé Find,
> She is our Étaín afterwards.

The warrior departed from them after that, and they knew not whence he had come or whither he had gone.

When the Mac Óc came to confer with Midir, he did not find Fuamnach there, and he [Midir] said to him: 'The woman has played us false, and if she be told that Étaín is in Ireland and she will go to do her ill.' ['Methinks 'tis likely so,' said the Mac Óc.] 'Étaín has been at my house in the Brug since a little while in the shape in which she was wafted [?] from thee, and perhaps it is she that the woman is making for.'

The Mac Óc returns home and finds the crystal sun-bower without Étaín in it. The Mac Óc turns upon Fuamnach's traces and came up on her at Aenach Bodbgna at the house of the druid Bresal Etarlám. The Mac Óc attacked her and shore off her head, and he brought that head with him until he was on the brink of the Brug.

Howbeit, this is the version elsewhere, that they were both slain by Manannán, namely Fuamnach and Midir, in Brí Léith, whereof was said:

> Fuamnach the foolish one was Midir's wife,
> Sigmall, a hill with ancient trees,
> in Brí Léith, 'twas a faultless arrangement,
> they were burned by Manannán.

Part 2 [5]

There was an admirable, noble king in the high-kingship over Ireland, namely, Eochaid Airem . . . The first year after he ascended the throne, a proclamation was made throughout Ireland that the feast of Tara was to be celebrated, and that all the men of Ireland should attend it, that their taxes and their levies might be known. And the one answer made by all the men of Ireland to Eochaid's summons was: That they would not attend the feast of Tara during such time, whether it be long or short, as the king of Ireland was without a wife that was suitable for him; for there was not a noble of the men of Ireland who was without a wife suitable for him, and there was not a king without a queen, and there would not come a man without his wife to the feast of Tara, nor would there come a woman without a husband.

Thereupon Eochaid sent out from him his horsemen, and his entertainers, and his spies, and his messengers of the border throughout Ireland, and they searched all Ireland for a woman who should be suitable for the king in respect to form, and grace, and countenance, and birth. And besides all this, there was one more condition regarding her: the king would never take a wife who had been given to any one else before him. And the king's officers sought all Ireland, both south and north, and they found at Inber Cichmany a woman suitable for him; that is, Etain the daughter of Etar, who was king of Echrad. Then his messengers returned to Eochaid and gave him a description of the maiden in regard to form and grace and countenance.

And Eochaid set forth to take the maiden, and the way that he went was across the fair-green of Bri Leith. And there he saw a maiden upon the brink of a spring. She held in her hand a comb of silver decorated with gold. Beside her, as for washing, was a basin of silver whereon were chased four golden birds, and there were little bright gems of carbuncle set in the rim of the basin. A cloak pure-purple, hanging in folds about her, and beneath it a mantle with silver borders, and a brooch of gold in the garment over her bosom. A tunic with a long hood about her, and as for it, smooth and glossy. It was made of greenish silk beneath red embroidery of gold, and marvellous bow-pins of silver and gold upon her breasts in the tunic, so that the redness of the gold against the sun in the green silk was clearly visible to the men. Two tresses of golden hair upon her head, and a plaiting of four strands in each tress, and a ball of gold upon the end of each plait.

And the maiden was there loosening her hair to wash it, and her two arms out through the armholes of her smock. As white as the snow of one night was each of her two arms, and as red as the foxglove of the mountain was each of her two cheeks. As blue as the hyacinth was each of her two eyes; delicately red her lips; very high, soft, and white her two shoulders. Tender, smooth, and white were her two wrists; her fingers long and very white; her nails pink and beautiful. As white as snow or as the foam of the wave was her side, slender, long, and as soft as silk. Soft, smooth, and white were her thighs; round and small, firm and white were her two knees; as straight as a rule were her two ankles; slim and foam-white were her two feet. Fair and very beautiful were her two eyes; her eyebrows blackish blue like the shell of a beetle. It was she the maiden who was the fairest and the most beautiful that the eyes of men had ever seen; and it seemed probable to the king and his companions that she was out of a fairy-mound. This is the maiden concerning whom is spoken the proverb: 'Every lovely form must be tested by Etain, every beauty by the standard of Etain.'

A desire for her seized the king immediately, and he sent a man of his company to hold her before him. Then Eochaid approached the maiden and questioned her. 'Whence art thou, O maiden?' said the king, 'and whence hast thou come?'

'Not hard to answer,' replied the maiden. 'Etain the daughter of the king of Echrad out of the fairy-mounds I am called.'

'Shall I have an hour of dalliance with thee?' said Eochaid.

'It is for that I have come hither under thy protection,' said she. 'I have been here for twenty years since I was born in the fairy-mound, and the men of the fairy-mound, both kings and nobles, have been wooing me, and naught was got by any of them from me, because I have loved thee and given love and affection to thee since I was a little child and since I was capable of speaking. It was for the noble tales about thee and for thy splendor that I have loved thee, and, although I have never seen thee before, I recognized thee at once by thy description. It is thou, I know, to whom I have attained,' said she.

'That is by no means the invitation of a bad friend,' replied Eochaid; 'thou shalt be welcomed by me, and all other women shall be left for thy sake, and with thee alone will I live as long as it is pleasing to thee.'

'Give me my fitting bride-price,' said the maiden, 'and thereafter let my desire be fulfilled.'

'That shall be to thee,' said the king.

The value of seven bond-slaves was given to her for a bride-price; and after that he took her with him to Tara, and a truly hearty welcome was given to her.

Now there were three brothers of one blood who were the sons of Finn: Eochaid Airem and Eochaid Fedlech and Ailill Anglonnach, or Ailill of the One Stain, because the only stain that was upon him was that he loved his brother's wife. At that time came the men of Ireland to hold the feast of Tara, and they were there fourteen days before Samain [Hallowe'en] and fourteen days after Samain. It was at the feast

of Tara that Ailill Anglonnach fell in love with Etain the daughter of
Etar. Ailill gazed at the woman as long as he was at the feast of Tara.
Then Ailill's wife, the daughter of Luchta Red-Hand from the borders
of Leinster, said to her husband: 'Ailill,' said she, 'why doest thou
keep gazing far off from thee? for such long-looking is a sign of love.'
Thereupon Ailill became ashamed and blamed himself for that thing,
and he did not look at Etain after that.

After the feast of Tara the men of Ireland separated from one another, and then it was that the pains of jealousy and great envy filled Ailill,
and a heavy illness came upon him. As a result he was carried to Dun
Fremain in Tethba, the favorite stronghold of his brother, the king.
Ailill remained there to the end of a year in long-sickness and in long-
pining, but he did not confess the cause of his sickness to any one. And
thither came Eochaid to enquire after Ailill. He put his hand upon
Ailill's breast, whereupon Ailill heaved a sigh.

'Now,' said Eochaid, 'the sickness in which thou art does not
appear to be serious. How is everything with thee?'

'By my word,' replied Ailill, 'not easier is it with me, but worse
in all respects every day and every night.'

'What ails thee?' asked Eochaid.

'By my true word,' said Ailill, 'I do not know.'

'Let there be brought to me some one who shall make known the
cause of this illness,' said Eochaid.

Then was brought to them Fachtna, the physician of Eochaid. And
Fachtna put his hand upon Ailill's breast, and Ailill sighed.

'Now,' said Fachtna, 'the matter is not serious. There is nothing
the matter with thee but one of two things; that is, either the pains of
jealousy or love which thou hast given, and thou hast found no help
till now.' Thereupon Ailill was ashamed. He did not confess the cause
of his illness to the physician, and the physician went from him.

Now, as regards Eochaid, he went out to make his royal circuit
throughout Ireland, and he left Etain in the stronghold of Fremain, and
he said to her: 'Deal gently with Ailill as long as he is alive, and should
he die,' said he, 'have his grave of sod dug, and let his pillar-stone be
raised, and let his name be written on it in ogam.' The king then
departed on his royal circuit of Ireland, leaving Ailill there in Dun
Fremain in expectation of death and dissolution for the space of that
year.

Into the house in which Ailill was, Etain used to go each day to consult with and minister to him. One day she asked him: 'What is the

matter with thee? Thy sickness is indeed great, and if we knew anything that would satisfy thee, thou shouldst get it from us.' It was thus
that she spoke, and she sang a little lay and Ailill answered her . . .

[As the result of their dialogue Etain finally understands that her
brother-in-law is suffering from love of herself.]

Etain continued to come every day to Ailill to bathe him and to
divide his food for him, and she helped him greatly, for she was sad
at seeing him perish because of her. One day she said to Ailill, 'Come
to-morrow at daybreak to tryst with me in the house that stands outside the stronghold, and there shalt thou have granted thy request and
thy desire.' On that night Ailill lay without sleep until the coming of
the morning; and when the time had come that was appointed for his
tryst, his sleep lay heavily upon him; so that till the hour of his rising
he lay deep in his sleep. And Etain went to the tryst, nor had she long
to wait ere she saw a man coming towards her in the likeness of Ailill,
weary and feeble; but she knew that he was not Ailill, and continued
there waiting for Ailill. And the lady came back from her tryst, and
Ailill awoke, and thought that he would rather die than live; and he
was in great sadness and grief. And the lady came to speak with him,
and when he told her what had befallen him: 'Come,' said she, 'to the
same place to meet with me to-morrow.' And upon the morrow it
was the same as upon the first day; each day came the same man to
her tryst. And she came again upon the last day that was appointed for
the tryst, and the same man met her. ''Tis not with thee that I tryst-
ed,' said she, 'why dost thou come to meet me? and for him whom I
would have met here, neither from desire of his love nor for fear of
harm from him had I appointed to meet him, but only to heal him,
and to cure him from the sickness which had come upon him for his
love of me.' 'It were more fitting for thee to come to tryst with me,'
said the man, 'for when thou wast Etain, daughter of the king of
Echrad, and when thou wast the daughter of Ailill, I myself was thy
first husband.' 'Why,' said she, 'what is thy name at all, if it were to
be demanded of thee?' 'It is not hard to answer thee,' he said, 'Mider
of Bri Leith is my name.' 'And what made thee to part from me, if
we were as thou sayest?' said Etain. 'Easy again is the answer,' said
Mider; 'it was the sorcery of Fuamnach and the spells of Bressal
Etarlam that put us apart.' And Mider said to Etain: 'Wilt thou come
with me?'

'Nay,' answered Etain, 'I will not exchange the king of all Ireland
for thee; for a man whose kindred and whose lineage is unknown.' 'It

was I myself indeed,' said Mider, 'who filled all the mind of Ailill with love for thee; it was I also who prevented his coming to the tryst with thee, and allowed him not to spoil thy honor.'

After all this the lady went back to her house, and she came to speech with Ailill, and she greeted him. 'It hath happened well for us both,' said Ailill, 'that the man met thee there: for I am cured forever from my illness, thou also art unhurt in thine honor, and may a blessing rest upon thee!' 'Thanks be to our gods,' said Etain, 'that both of us do indeed deem that all this hath chanced so well.' And after that, Eochaid came back from his royal progress, and he asked at once for his brother; and the tale was told to him from the beginning to the end, and the king was grateful to Etain, in that she had been gracious to Ailill; and 'What hath been related in this tale,' said Eochaid, 'is well-pleasing to ourselves.'

.   .   .   .

Now upon another time it chanced that Eochaid Airem, the king of Tara, arose upon a certain fair day in the time of summer and he ascended the high ground of Tara to behold the plain of Breg; beautiful was the color of that plain, and there was upon it excellent blossom, glowing with all hues that are known. And, as the aforesaid Eochaid looked about and around him, he saw a young strange warrior upon the high ground at his side. The tunic that the warrior wore was purple in color, his hair was of golden yellow, and of such length that it reached to the edge of his shoulders. The eyes of the young warrior were lustrous and grey; in the one hand he held a five-pointed spear, in the other a shield with a white central boss, and with gems of gold upon it. And Eochaid held his peace, for he knew that none such had been in Tara on the night before, and the gate that led into the enclosure had not at that hour been thrown open.

The warrior came, and placed himself under the protection of Eochaid; and 'Welcome do I give,' said Eochaid, 'to the hero who is yet unknown.'

'Thy reception is such as I expected when I came,' said the warrior.

'We know thee not,' answered Eochaid.

'Yet thee in truth I know well!' he replied.

'What is the name by which thou art called?' said Eochaid.

'My name is not known to renown,' said the warrior; 'I am Mider of Bri Leith.'

'And for what purpose art thou come?' said Eochaid.

'I have come that I may play a game of chess with thee,' answered Mider. 'Truly,' said Eochaid, 'I myself am skilful at chess-play.'

'Let us test that skill!' said Mider.

'Nay,' said Eochaid, 'the queen is even now in her sleep; and hers is the apartment in which the chessboard lies.'

'I have here with me,' said Mider, 'a chessboard which is not inferior to thine.' It was even as he said, for that chessboard was silver, and the men to play with were gold; and upon that board were costly stones, casting their light on every side, and the bag that held the men was of woven chains of brass.

Mider then set out the chessboard, and he called upon Eochaid to play. 'I will not play,' said Eochaid, 'unless we play for a stake.'

'What stake shall we have upon the game then?' said Mider.

'It is indifferent to me,' said Eochaid.

'Then,' said Mider, 'if thou dost obtain the forfeit of my stake, I will bestow on thee fifty steeds of a dark grey, their heads of a blood-red color, but dappled; their ears pricked high, and their chests broad; their nostrils wide, and their hoofs slender; great is their strength, and they are keen like a whetted edge; eager are they, high-standing and spirited, yet easily stopped in their course.'

Several games were played between Eochaid and Mider; and since Mider did not put forth his whole strength, the victory on all occasions rested with Eochaid. But instead of the gifts which Mider had offered, Eochaid demanded that Mider and his folk should perform for him services which should be of benefit to his realm; that he should clear away the rocks and stones from the plains of Meath, should remove the rushes which made the land barren around his favorite fort of Tethba, should cut down the forest of Breg, and finally should build a causeway across the moor or bog of Lamrach that men might pass freely across it. All these things Mider agreed to do, and Eochaid sent his steward to see how that work was done. And when it came to the time after sunset, the steward looked, and he saw that Mider and his fairy host, together with fairy oxen, were laboring at the causeway over the bog; and thereupon much of earth and of gravel and of stones was poured into it. Now it had, before that time, always been the custom of the men of Ireland to harness their oxen with a strap over their foreheads, so that the pull might be against the foreheads of the oxen; and this custom lasted up to that very night, when it was seen that the fairy folk had placed the yoke upon the shoulders of the oxen, so that the pull might be there; and in this way were the yokes of the oxen

afterwards placed by Eochaid, and thence comes the name by which
he is known; even Eochaid Airem, or Eochaid the Ploughman, for he
was the first of all the men of Ireland to put the yokes on the necks
of the oxen, and thus it became the custom for all the land of Ireland.
And this is the song that the host of the fairies sang, as they labored
at the making of the road:

> Thrust it in hand! force it in hand!
> Noble this night, the troop of oxen:
> Hard is the task that is asked, and who
> From the bridging of Lamrach shall receive gain or harm?

Not in all the world could a road have been found that should be better than the road that they made, had it not been that the fairy folk
were observed as they worked upon it; but for that cause a breach has
been made in that causeway. And the steward of Eochaid thereafter
came to him; and he described to him that great laboring band that
had come before his eyes, and he said that there was not over the char-
iot-pole of life a power that could withstand its might. And, as they
spoke thus with each other, they saw Mider standing before them; high
was he girt, and ill-favored was the face that he showed; and Eochaid
arose, and he gave welcome to him. 'Thy welcome is such as I expected when I came,' said Mider. 'Cruel and senseless hast thou been in
thy treatment of me, and much of hardship and suffering hast thou
given me. All things that seemed good in thy sight have I got for thee,
but now anger against thee hath filled my mind!' 'I return not anger
for anger,' answered Eochaid; 'what thou wishest shall be done.' 'Let
it be as thou wishest,' said Mider; 'shall we play at the chess?' said he.
'What stake shall we set upon the game?' said Eochaid. 'Even such
stake as the winner of it shall demand,' said Mider. And in that very
place Eochaid was defeated, and he forfeited his stake.

'My stake is forfeited to thee,' said Eochaid.

'Had I wished it, it had been forfeited long ago,' said Mider.

'What is it that thou desirest me to grant?' said Eochaid.

'That I may hold Etain in my arms and obtain a kiss from her!'
answered Mider.

Eochaid was silent for a while, and then he said: 'One month from
this day thou shalt come, and that very thing that thou hast asked for
shall be given to thee.' Now for a year before that Mider first came
to Eochaid for the chess-play, had he been at the wooing of Etain, and
he obtained her not; and the name which he gave to Etain was Befind,

or Fair-haired Woman, so it was that he said:

Wilt thou come with me, fair-haired woman?

as has before been recited. And it was at that time that Etain said: 'If thou obtainest me from him who is the master of my house, I will go; but if thou art not able to obtain me from him, then I will not go.' And thereupon Mider came to Eochaid, and allowed him at the first to win the victory over him, in order that Eochaid should stand in his debt; and therefore it was that he paid the great stakes to which he had agreed, and therefore also was it that he had demanded of him that he should play that game in ignorance of what was staked. And when Mider and his folk were paying those agreed-on stakes, which were paid upon that night; to wit, the making of the road, and the clearing of the stones from Meath, the rushes from around Tethba, and the forest that is over Breg, it is thus that he spoke, as it is written in the Book of Drum Snechta:

> Pile on the soil; thrust on the soil;
> Red are the oxen who labor;
> Heavy the troops that obey my words.
> Heavy they seem, and yet men are they.
> Strongly, as piles, are the tree-trunks placed:
> Red are the wattles bound above them:
> Tired are your hands, and your glances slant;
> One woman's winning this toil may yield!
> Oxen ye are, but revenge shall see;
> Men who are white shall be your servants:
> Rushes from Tethba are cleared:
> Grief is the price that the man shall pay:
> Stones have been cleared from the rough Meath ground;
> Whose shall the gain or the harm be?

Now Mider appointed a day at the end of the month when he was to meet Eochaid, and Eochaid called the armies of the heroes of Ireland together, so that they came to Tara; and all the best of the champions of Ireland, ring within ring, were about Tara, and they were in the midst of Tara itself, and they guarded it, both without and within; and the king and the queen were in the midst of the palace, and the outer court thereof was shut and locked, for they knew that the great night of men would come upon them. And upon the appointed night Etain was dispensing the banquet to the kings, for it was her duty to pour out the wine, when in the midst of their talk they saw Mider standing before them in the center of the palace. He was always fair, yet fairer than he ever was seemed Mider to be upon that night. And he brought to amazement all the hosts on which he gazed, and all thereupon were silent, and the king gave a welcome to him.

'Thy reception is such as I expected when I came,' said Mider; 'let that now be given to me that has been promised. 'Tis a debt that is due when a promise hath been made; and I for my part have given to thee all that was promised by me.'

'I have not yet considered the matter,' said Eochaid.

'Thou hast promised Etain's very self to me,' said Mider; 'that is what has come from thee.' Etain blushed for shame when she heard that word.

'Blush not,' said Mider to Etain, 'for in no wise has thy wedding-feast been disgraced. I have been seeking thee for a year with the fairest jewels and treasures that can be found in Ireland, and I have not taken thee until the time came when Eochaid might permit it. 'Tis not through any will of thine that I have won thee.' 'I myself told thee,' said Etain, 'that until Eochaid should resign me to thee I would grant thee nothing. Take me then for my part, if Eochaid is willing to resign me to thee.'

'But I will not resign thee!' said Eochaid; 'nevertheless he shall take thee in his arms upon the floor of this house as thou art.'

'It shall be done!' said Mider.

He took his weapons in his left hand and the woman beneath his right shoulder; and he carried her off through the smoke-hole of the house. And the hosts rose up around the king, for they felt that they had been disgraced, and they saw two swans circling round Tara, and the way that they took was the way to the elf-mound of Femen. And Eochaid with an army of the men of Ireland went to the elf-mound of Femen, which men call the mound of the Fair-haired Women. And he followed the counsel of the men of Ireland, and he dug up each of the elf-mounds that he might take his wife from thence. And Mider and his host opposed them and the war between them was long: again and again the trenches made by Eochaid were destroyed; for nine years, as some say, lasted the strife of the men of Ireland to enter into the fairy palace. And when at last the armies of Eochaid came by digging to the borders of the fairy-mound of Bri Leith, Mider sent to the side of the palace sixty women all in the shape of Etain, and so like to her that none could tell which was the Queen, and Eochaid himself was deceived, and he chose instead of Etain her daughter Mess Buachalla (or, as some say, Esa). But when he found that he had been deceived, he returned again to sack Bri Leith, and this time Etain made herself known to Eochaid by proofs that he could not mistake, and he bore her away in triumph to Tara, and there she abode with the king.

[Another version of the story adds: It was on this account that the fairy folk of Mag Breg and Mider of Bri Leith broke the taboos of Conaire and ended his life and brought about the laying waste of Mag Breg — because of the destruction of Bri Leith and Eochaid Airem's taking away Etain by force.]

The Fosterage in the House of the Two Pails[6]

This story from *The Book of Fermoy* is usually entitled 'The Fosterage in the House of the Two Goblets'; however, from the context of the story it is obvious that 'milking-pails' (*meadar*) is a nearer translation. It was transcribed in the fourteenth to fifteenth centuries from an earlier text, since this version omits poems from the original. It looks as if it has also gone through a few retellings, since many of the mythological references are adrift from earlier received tradition.

The story juxtaposes the Pagan and Christian worlds, with Eithne (Enya) acting as an unfortunate heroine. It tells of the withdrawal of the Tuatha de Danann into the otherworlds, leaving the Milesian race in possession of Ireland. Here we encounter the joint theme of 'the leaving of Middle Earth' and 'the coming of Christianity'.

This story might seem of little account to those who prefer their Celtic tales to be informed solely by the high classical pre-Christian traditions, but it is nonetheless an important one for an understanding of how the ancient traditions mesh with the later ones. The story of Eithne is primarily one about family relationship, fosterage and ancestral belonging. When Aengus mac Og, her foster-father, comes to beg her return to Faery, Patrick counters with, 'The maid is not thy ward, but the ward of the God of Creation, though she was lent by her father to thee.'

Here we find the fundamental disagreement between ancient Celtic tradition and its Christian counterpart: the faery world lives in the moment, in the joys of everyday life, in the pursuits of immortality; the Christian world lives for a future state, sees daily life as transitory and looks for immortality in heaven. There can be no understanding between Aengus and Patrick.

The title of this story is significant to our understanding of how Christianity and Celtic belief come together. The two milking pails seem to represent both spiritual and physical nurture. We may also see them as the containers of the essential stream of tradition which pours from age to age and which is passed down in its full strength to those who have pure hearts.

Eithne's lot strikes hard at the heart of the lover of Faery, for she relinquishes the bliss of the earthly paradise for a short mortality and a perpetuity of heavenly life. Although the Children of Lir and Liban also find release from their long lives through baptism, it is Eithne, alone among the Faery, who was fostered in the two otherworldly houses of the Brugh and Emain Abhlach, who has also seen heaven!

1. A valiant victorious king of the numerous active rude and spirited race . . . three sons of Cearmad Midbeoil son of the Dagda . . . the first great king of Eire, Erimon . . . held Banba for his brothers. It was he inflicted [defeats?] and great losses on the Tuatha De Danann at Druim Lighean and at Loch Foyle so that he held Eire firmly for his brother, Emer Find, and for himself, so that he and his brother were rulers of Eire for a year till there arose war-madness and fierce anger and rupture of brotherliness . . . for it was Emer who was responsible for that revolt for he acted on the envy and evil council of his own wife. It was he who haughtily challenged Erimon to battle and prepared difficulty and tyranny for his own descendants, for the fierce battle of Geashill was fought between those kings till Emer fell by Erimon in that contest. But there is one thing: it was wrong of Emer to revolt because it was Erimon who held the kingdom of Eire for himself and his brother and it was he won the battle of Tailltiu at the start over the Tuatha De Danann in which fell three kings of Eirc, viz. Mac Cuill, Mac Cecht and Mac Greine. He also won the battle of Druim Lighean over the Tuatha De Danann and, not only over them, but over the warriors of Scandinavia also. [Though the aforesaid prophecy occurs here as well as the matter of Emer and Erimon, the end of this story is not written about them: so far concerning the Sons of Mil.)

2. Here we give the adventures of the Tuatha de Danann aloud: the victories of Tailltiu and Druim Lighean gave Erimon's heroes and soldiers a military grip of the divisions of Eire's territory. The noble monarch, almighty Manannan, was brought to settle their [Tuatha D. D.] problems and councils and his advice to the warriors was to scatter and quarter themselves on the hills and plains of Eire. The men made Bodb Derg and Manannan their rulers and Manannan ordained the settlement of the nobles in their magic dwellings: Bodb Derg at Sith Buidb on Lake Derggert, haughty Midir at fair-sided Sith Truim, aimiable Sithmall at Sith Neannta of the shining form, Finnbarr Meadha at bare-topped Sith Meadha, Thadg Mor son of Nuadu at the Sith of Druim Dean, Abhartach son of Illathar at Sidh Buidhe of the fair summit, and Fagartach at most lovely Sith Finnabrach, Ilbreac at Sith Aeda of Assaroe, Lir son of Lugaid at verdant Sith Finnachadh, Derg Diansgothach at Sith Cleitidh, and every single . . . house and place of residence left to the Tuatha De D. Manannan assigned a special dwelling to each noble and made for the warriors the Feth Fiadha, the Feast of Goibniu and Manannan's Swine: that is, the princes could not be seen through the Feth Fiadha, the monarchs escaped age and decay by the Feast of Goibniu and Manannan's Swine could be killed by the warriors but come alive again. Manannan taught the nobles their array at Sidh Brugh and to carry on their mansions in the manner of the peoples of the fair-sided Land of Promise and fair Emain Ablach. The nobles conceded to Manannan that when they had possession of their dwellings he should be over the wedding of every house and the feast of every lord so that his statute and due and law were over every mansion.

3. There was another ruler in Eire at that time who was not haughty, and Ealcmar was that warrior's name. With him was Cairbre Cromm son of Sigmall son of Cairbre Cromm another ruler and also Aengus Og son of the Dagda. His home was in Brugh over the Boyne . . . the nobles of the Tuatha De D. to that noble and he undertook . . . charge of a feast in his house by Bodb Derg son of the Dagda to send word to fetch Manannan and to the nobles of his people to eat that feast of report and fame . . . 'But we knew there was no scarcity of good things' said the people.

But one thing now: Manannan made a round of visits to every Sidh he owned and when Ealcmar heard he was on that round . . . he sent his foster-son to meet him and invite him [that is Aengus Og son of the Dagda] and Manannan went . . . on to the dewy-green bank of the Boyne . . . Assaroe and to Irluachair . . . the light of the mansion opposite Manannan . . . and Manannan came at the head of the hosts . . . [to the] fortress and this was the description of the mansion: a beautiful bronze floor from each door . . . [to that] opposite in the mansion, and structures . . . of findruine on the floors, and wellshaped silver couches on the structures with beautiful posts with shapely edges to them and corners, with crimson[?] birds sweetly musical on top of those corners . . . and it was not . . . the monarch making merry . . . listening to the . . . and jollity of the youths and the merriment of the maidens at their slow embroidery and the noise of chess being played. Howbeit it were almost carelessly done to report . . . of that house though . . . But one thing: the rulers of the Tuatha and the nobles of the Land of Promise were all there and there was not one of them prince or lord who was not envious and jealous of that house.

4. Ealcmar took thought and counsel and called his servants and his head-steward to come to him (Dicu was his honourable name) and this is what he said: 'go for me, my good people' said he 'to the ravines and cataracts and river-mouths of Eire to seek fish, fowl and venison for the sovereign.' Dichu went along with his good son, Roc, and the princes sat down to the feast. Manannan sat with the warriors. Bodb Derg sat at his right hand, Ealcmar at the hand that holds the shield in every fray, Eachdond Mor, Manannan's son, sat at the side of the palace and Abartach to that noble's right and Sidhmall Siteach to his left, and every man of the warriors from that on in his place of safety among contemporaries. Aengus was with the attendants arranging and giving orders, and every kind of drink and delicacy was given out correctly so that the company were cheerful and gay.

But one thing: the heroes spent three days and three nights in that manner, and at the end of the fourth day Manannan was obliged to clear the house, for not a mother's son was left in the mansion with a spark of consciousness except Manannan and Aengus. He began to argue with Aengus and spoke as follows: 'this is a pleasant house, Aengus, and I never saw its like save Cruitin na Cuan or Emain Ablach and the situation on the bank of the Boyne at the border of the five provinces is good. If I were you, Aengus, this house would be mine and I would summon Ealcmar to quit it. You would get ''luck and prosperity'' from your powerful friends to do it.' He recited the poem. After that poem Manannan addressed Aengus again and said:

'Do you know, Aengus, that of all you of the Tuatha De Danann who are alive that I am chief of your kings, senior of your hosts, shining light of your battalions and lord of your champions, and though Ealcmar be your tutor yet it is I am your tutor in valour, in feats of arms, in magic, and I am foster-son of your good father, the Daghda, and to any child of your father who has wealth I have somewhat also to give him.' 'I am glad you admit that', said Aengus. 'What is the reason this cairn of worship is so called?' 'I will inform you' said Manannan, 'and pledge your word, your crimson shield, your sword and the fair adorable gods that you will act on my advice this time.' He convinced Aengus by his urgency for he almost understood . . . 'do you know, Aengus, that it is not fitting that Ealcmar . . . and that it is not for him to defend the fort or establish the mansion and the lordship. We shall sit in the house which he made before Ealcmar and do you summon him to depart, for that will bring to you good luck and prosperity and to him misfortune and adversity and exile. (That is; the luck that angels came from the king of the palace and the Creator of the universe, the luck that we took the kingship of Fodla from the Fir Bolg, the luck that the Milesians took the throne of Eire themselves again.) Warn him that he may not come to the house he leaves till ogham and pillar be blent together, till heaven and earth, till sun and moon be blent together.' 'God is not above our gods' said Aengus. 'There is one thing', said Manannan. 'The one almighty God is able to subdue our idol gods and they are not able to despoil Him who is the powerful Lord made heaven and earth and the sea with wonders, and made the universe complete.'

'Do you know, Aengus' said Manannan, 'why mankind were first created?' 'I know not' said Aengus. 'This is the cause' said Manannan. 'The one God of whom we spoke fashioned ten orders of angels round Him. The lord of the tenth order grew scornful and envious in his mind and they left the heavenly plain without cause and God . . . the tenth order of his land . . . and fashioned mankind . . . and those who left His land with scorn He turned into demons and made a dungeon and prison for their torments. Everyone who does His will is brought to the palace and everyone who goes against it is put in that dungeon for torments and that is the urgent cause of creation' said Manannan. 'We are not of that origin' he said: 'but act on my advice this time.' 'It moves me to pity' said Aengus, 'for the pleasure and honour of the house are under my control and its profit and substance are mine, and foster-sons will not be honoured after me if I do this thing.' 'Stop that', said Manannan; 'for a king is nobler than a kingdom, and a lord than the heir, and control is better than assisting and assured means better than doles. Your own will is better than your father's or mother's, or a request to either of them from behind their yoke.' That convinced Aengus completely, and he said: 'your advice shall be acted on this time, oh wizard.'

5. As to Ealcmar: he was consulting his friends as to whether the king's dinner should be cooked by those messengers who went to seek fish and fowl and venison. It was the general opinion that the king should not be kept waiting for them and that there was no shortage of liquor. Manannan came forth bringing goblin treachery, and the mansion was prepared by Ealcmar for Manannan, and he came into the Sidh with his people and sat with the warriors and each one of them sat in his right and natural place from that time on. They were eating their dinner and consuming their food till all the company were merry and cheerful save Aengus only, for he was sick with fright at challenging his tutor, yet nevertheless he came before Ealcmar at the moment Manannan had arranged for the challenge to be made and wrought a horrible incantation to challenge his tutor. He summoned Ealcmar to leave the mansion without halt or delay. After that speech he recited to his tutor:

> Ealcmar arose quickly, wondrously, lightly, as rises
> the timid flitting deer when chased to the hill;
> or as rises the bird-flock before a hawk.

Ealcmar went out of the mansion with all his people both men and women. (And since that summons no foster-father but has power from the devil; for if all the people in Eire were trying to hinder one of them they could not do it by reason of the strength of that 'luck and prosperity'.) When Ealcmar came out on the dewy-sloped lawn of the mansion he looked upon his wife and on his household. 'It is pitiful and wretched ye are now, dear people' he said, 'ye are reluctant to leave the Boyne and the mansion and hence-forward ye will find great woe and final madness. It is treacherous Manannan who taught "luck and prosperity" to my fosterling by magic and devilry so as to banish me, and woe to him, but it is well for my fosterling after me. I swear by my doom', said Ealcmar, 'that had Aengus begged the rule of the mansion of me I would certainly have given it to him without being challenged.' After that Ealcmar left them and Aengus came out on the lawn and began to talk to him earnestly. He came to delay and stop him for shame and repentance had seized him. But he could not be delayed by reason of the power of the 'luck and prosperity' which Aengus had laid on him. After that Ealcmar went forward and, before he was out of sight, the company had gone. At that moment Aengus saw the steward of the mansion, his wife and his fair son approaching. They told each other their news and the steward accepted Aengus' protection, and Aengus said to him; 'remain in office as you did not arrive before the summons'; and the whole superintendance of the mansion was put in his charge.

6. It so happened that the wife of the steward was pregnant at that time. When Aengus perceived it he asked to be foster-father and they came together into the mansion and the chief steward asked for Manannan's friendship. The nobles inquired of Manannan where Ealcmar would find rest. 'I know not', said Manannan, 'and no prophet or sage in the whole world knows, but the one God almighty knows.' Then Aengus held the feast of the mansion in honour of Manannan and the nobles of the Tuatha De Danann. When the time came at the end of the feast for the nobles . . . to listen to singing . . . Aengus said to him . . . 'your wife is pregnant and whatever child is born I receive to bring up and educate.' 'The child of every other member of the Tuatha De Danann shall get the same' said Manannan, and so said all in general. Aengus enjoined noble marriage on all in general. Manannan went away to his fort and the time came and his wife bore the fruit of her womb, a shapely lovely daughter with a tip[?] of curly yellow-coloured hair on her head, for which reason she was baptized and called by the name of Curcog (= bushy tuft). She was given to Aengus to bring up and educate and daughters of other rulers of her own age along with her.

As to the steward's wife; she bore a daughter at that time and she was named Eithne and Aengus took her like every other foster-child to educate. A beautiful sunny house of varied design was made for the maidens and they were there for a good while being educated. There was never before or after them a band of women so severe and so chaste as that band of Curcog's and one of them excelled all the others in appearance in severity and in chastity viz., Eithne the daughter of Dicu. There was no one who saw her who did not fall in love with her. It is she was most pleasing to Aengus of the maidens and the fame of that company spread to the four corners of Eire. The daughter of the steward was more famous than all the womenfolk or than Curcog, and the nobles of the Tuatha De Danann came by reason of the repute of those women. Finnbarr Meadha came from the Sidh of the bare hill of Meadha to the mansion on the Boyne to behold those women. He was warmly welcomed, his horses and chariot were unyoked, and he entered the mansion with Aengus and they were drinking and making merry. Finnbarr said he came in order to see the women. Aengus said, 'which do you choose: to go to the apartment where they are, or for them to be brought to you?' Finnbarr chose that the women should come before him, and Aengus sent word to Curcog and her ladies, and Curcog came with them before Aengus and Finnbarr. Finnbarr gazed at Curcog and all her ladies. He looked keenly at Eithne daughter of Dicu and he asked who was she who made[?] a dirty mess and, though he asked, he said: 'it is the daughter of the worthless steward and I had almost christened her "dirty mess."' He quoted the verse:

> The royal daughter of the Munster steward,
> the delicate stately swan,
> is a woman of the race abhorrent to us
> who made the dirty mess.

And after that the maiden's lovely face grew white, then livid, then red; she went away sorrowful and troubled with wet cheeks and flushed face to her accustomed dwelling, the sunny house. When Aengus saw that he became terribly [angry] and nearly killed Finnbarr and his people. But one thing: he remembered their friendship and repented in his heart and changed his mind. And after that Finnbarr set forth to depart from his joyance while at variance with Aengus, and his people counselled him not to separate from his brother at variance. Finnbarr went back again to the mansion and went into Aengus' presence and bent low on his two active white knees before his brother. 'Why is this done, oh Finnbarr?' said Aengus. 'Because thou art the eldest and noblest and I am the youngest of the Daghda's fair children, because it behoves every criminal to make his own amends.' 'It is accepted' said Aengus, and they put their two fair red mouths together and kissed each other warmly. The mansion was got ready for Finnbarr and Aengus, and Curcog and her ladies were fetched to the hall and Aengus and Finnbarr sat with the princes and they put Curcog between them to do her honour, and Aengus put his loved ward at his side, that is, Eithne daughter of Dicu.

Howbeit, there was no lack of food in the hall or of the best of

drink and there was not one of them who was not cheerful and satis-
fied save Eithne only, and there was not one of Finnbarr's or Aengus'
or Curcog's people who did not kneel before her to oblige her to eat
and she consented not. One thing however: Finnbarr feasted for three
days and three nights in the fort. They said farewell on the third day
and Finnbarr went away to Cnoc Medha of delicate beauty.

7. As regards Eithne: she was seven days and nights without touching
food or drink, and if all the men of Ireland were ordering her to eat
or drink she would not, and there was no sort of food or drink in the
world they did not ask the maiden if she could eat it, and when they
persisted she would say she would not. And Aengus bethought him
would she drink the milk of the Dun Cow, milked into a beautiful gold
goblet; that is, a dun cow belonging to Aengus then and so unique and
remarkable that its like was not in Eire or in the whole world save one
other. 'Who will milk her for me, Aengus?' said the maiden. 'Take
your choice of any woman in the house including Curcog or yourself,
my maid', said Aengus. 'I will milk her myself' said the maiden. 'You
shall get your wish' said Aengus, and the cow was brought to Eithne
to be milked with its spancel of special silk and with the beautiful gold
goblet. The maiden washed her sharp white-fingered fair-hued brown-
nailed hands, and she milked the cow after that without delay, and she
and Aengus drank the milk of the Dun Cow thereupon. At every hour
of the common meals the cow was brought to the maiden to be milked
and that milk was her food and drink. If all the food in the world had
been brought to the maiden she would have had none of it save the
milking of the Dun Cow only. One day that she was milking the Dun
Cow she asked Aengus: 'how did you find the Dun or was she
[brought(?)] to the mansion by Ealcmar?' 'You shall know that', said
Aengus. 'I went a journey with Manannán eastward over-seas till we
reached the Golden Pillars in the East and we went from that to India
and we found there a wonderful acquisition whose like we never found
before, that is: two cows with twisted horns always in milk, a speckled cow and a dun cow, and two beautiful gold goblets and two
spancels of rare silk along with them. We took them with us to Eire
and we divided our gains and Manannan gave half of them to me' said
Aengus, 'namely; a goblet, a cow and a spancel and I brought with me
the share you see, the Dun of Aengus. It is in full milk every season
of the year and its milk tastes of honey and intoxicating wine and the
satisfaction of good food. That is how I got the Dun Cow', said Aengus.

8. After that Aengus inquired of every druid and seer and sage and ruler in Eire for what cause the maiden would eat no earthly food save the milking of the Dun Cow only and he learnt nothing from anyone. The story reached Cruitin na Cuan and Emain Ablach and the Nobles of the Land of Promise, and they were astonished at the story they heard of Eithne in Eire. Manannan sent envoys to Curcog and her ladies, and to Ethne also in particular, to find out what caused her to go without food and those envoys came to Brugh na Boinne. Aengus sent his loved ones and his servants to Emain Ablach and they came to the lawn of Cruitin na Cuan and all the youths rose up to meet them, and Manannan [with his nobles] and his wife with her ladies, and they heartily welcomed the women . . . making much of the maidens. And Manannan called Curcog and Eithne into a lonely spot and said to Eithne; 'Is it true you eat no food?' 'It is quite true' said the maiden. 'How comes it thus with you, oh maid?' said Manannan. 'I know not' said Eithne 'save one thing. After the insult I received from Finnbarr I could not eat earthly food save the milking of the Dun of Aengus milked by myself into a golden goblet'. 'I myself will prepare your helping to night,' said Manannan. (But there is one thing. It is thus it was with the man who made that speech: there was never a man sick or ill he did not discern and diagnose the damage and he was healed by his aid, and there was never a man loathed food or drink to whom he did not restore his liking with diligence.) Manannan went to where was his head-steward, and piquant flavours must be put in every dish prepared for Eithne, and Manannan practised all his powers on them, and he came with the ladies of the mansion into the hall and . . . of every food and flavour was brought to them. Nothing was gained by that plot . . . to make Eithne taste it and all who were there wondered that Manannan could not get the maiden to taste food or drink. Manannan wondered that his power was brought to nought, and he felt it a shame that anyone[?] should be fasting in his house, and he asked the maiden would she drink the milking of the Speckled Cow and she herself or some other woman to milk it . . . a golden goblet as in Asia . . . whence they were brought; that is, the Dun [and the Speckled] . . . goblets and spancels which are for the milking, and the cow's buttock was given to Eithne (that is the Speckled Cow of Manannan) and the golden goblet and the silken spancel and the maiden milked her after that and her milking was her food and drink that night and she was not weak in that house.

'Do you know', said Manannan to his people, 'wherefore you maiden eats no food?' 'We know not' said they. 'I will inform you' said Manannan. 'She belongs neither to the people of Aengus nor yet to our people. For when Finnbarr insulted yon maiden her guardian demon left her heart and an angel came in his place, and that prevents us searching her heart and she worships neither wizardry nor devilry, and that is why she drinks the milk of yonder cow because it was brought from a righteous land, from India, and . . . nourishing and fosterage of yon maiden watching over her . . . that is: the nourishing of the house of two goblets. It is the Trinity . . . are the gods whom that maiden adores' said he.

But one thing also: Curcog and her ladies and Eithne were a month and a fortnight at Emain Ablach and she tasted no food in the house save the milking of the Speckled Cow; and then they travelled to their own home for, though great was the mirth and frisking and the pleasure and gaiety of Emain Ablach, . . . to Curcog [it fell] short of being in the mansion on the Boyne at that time. Manannan was trying to delay Curcog, and repeated the poem:

> Oh Curcog, of pure beauty,
> be not reluctant to remain.
> Thy nourishment every evening
> the songs of the Land of Promise.
>
> . . . .
>
> the vast appeasement of every trouble.
> . . . of its rough clean wave-loud strand.
>
> . . . .

9. After that Curcog went on with her ladies and she bade farewell to Manannan and to his wife and household and travelled to Brugh na Boinne. Aengus came to meet them and welcomed the company and asked news of them. He inquired of Curcog what food or drink had Eithne taken or did Manannan not know the cause why she did not eat. 'She tasted no food or drink during the visit', said Curcog, 'save the milking of Manannan's Speckle . . . the stoppage of Manannan's great power, food or drink . . . Nevertheless he recognized the cause why she would not taste food on the Isle of Man.' '. . . the cause' said Aengus. 'He said it soon,' said Curcog 'and this is what he said: that it is the one almighty God is the cause why she eats no food of the Tuatha De Danann, and he said when Finnbarr insulted the maiden that she parted from her magic and an angelic spirit came in her heart's place, and he said that was the cause of her desertion and that she belonged to no other people but the true people of the Almighty Monarch.' Howbeit from the time of Eremon son of Mil the maiden abode in that manner to the time of Laegaire son of Niall Noigiallach (that is; the time when the Tailginn came to Ireland). This was the maiden's manner of life in that age: a while in the house of her guardian Aengus at Brugh na Boinne and a while in Manannan's house at Emain Ablach and she tasted no food or drink in the house of Manannan save the milking of the Speckled Cow nor in the Brugh save the milking of Aengus' Dun Cow and she herself milking each cow into a golden goblet as we said before. But one thing: the nourishing of the house of two goblets was magnified throughout Eire by the Tuatha De Danann and by the Milesians, and it was also called 'the fosterage of the house of the two goblets', and that nourishing is proverbial still and shall be for ever.

10. When the Tailginn came, and when druids and demons were expelled by him from Eire, and when every one in the community had submitted to religion and piety, Curcog and her ladies were on the lawn of Brugh na Boinne in summer weather. Heat and sultriness overcame the ladies and they went to swim in the Boyne. When the maidens had had enough of swimming and diving each one of them went to her garments and left the river. Eithne did not notice the maidens' departure and it so happened to them that the 'Fed Fiar' and the magic left that lovely maiden, that is Eithne. (For it is through that the company could not be seen at the beginning and that Eithne was not seen till that hour.) Eithne did not see the company then (and every one could see her) and she came ashore and put on her clothes and began to search for them on the banks of the Boyne and found them not. And before long she saw a branchy blue-boughed garden and the bare wall of a cemetery built round it and the maiden went towards that cemetery and saw a greyhaired joyous cleric in the door of the church, and a Testament, and he was earnestly praising the Creator. The maiden at once saluted the cleric and he answered; 'What brings thee here alone oh maiden?' said he. She told him her adventures. 'Who art thou, oh cleric?' said the maiden 'and to what household dost thou belong?' 'I am of the household of God', said the cleric, 'and Patrick son of Calpurnius is my lord and viceroy. Who are thy people, oh maiden?' said the cleric. 'I am of the Tuatha De Danann' said she 'till now, and my people and thine are the same.' 'Thy coming to us is welcome' said the cleric 'and not to thee . . .' '. . . . if of God's faithful people, that faith of thine?' said the maiden. 'Praising the Lord and reading aloud from this book, and if thou art of God's faithful people it were strange thou didst not know it.' 'Teach me to know it' said the maiden 'for I never saw its like. Moreover I would like thee to teach me henceforward and give me a lesson on every poem.' She said:

> Give me its own profit,
> oh warrior, to whom I vow my service.
> Its like for sweetness
> I heard not in the Land of Promise.

> If sweet to thee to hear it,
> oh fair yellow-haired maiden,
> you will listen indeed this time
> to what is in this book.

> Take the little psalter steadfastly,
> oh pregnant cleric of the Tailginn.
> Put in memory all the learning
> that is in it. Give.

11. After that poem Eithne bent her head over the book and read it without delay as if she had learnt it from the night she was born. The cleric was amazed at the maiden's recitation and how she read the book for if she had had all the books Patrick brought to Ireland she would have read them without delay and the cleric loved and respected her the more. They were at this till the cleric's dinner hour. He then rose and took his fishing-rod and went to the river and Eithne had not long to wait till he came to the house with a beautiful salmon. 'What hast thou got?' said the maiden. 'My share of provisions from the Lord' said the cleric 'and I have need of it tonight that I never had before.' 'What wilt thou eat?' said the maiden. 'I am pledged to an individual inordinate appetite.' 'If I knew how thou didst it, noble sir' said the maiden 'I would not take from thy share but take thou the rod and seek my share from the Lord as thou didst get for thyself.' 'I will go myself, oh maiden', said he. The cleric went to the river and let down the rod and he had not long to wait till he caught a most splendid salmon. Its like was never seen and he took it to the maiden and it was an exploit to carry it from the river to the church. He laid the salmon down and did reverence to the maiden after that, and said: 'thou art indeed one of God's people, oh maiden', said he, 'and may my soul be under thy soul's protection.' Then the cleric sat down and began to pound the fish till it was ready and they ate the roe of it, that is half and half . . . every morsel of it tasted like honey. Then he made a bed for the maiden and another bed for himself, and they were sharing everything fairly with harmony and unanimity for a long time.

But as to the company of ladies: they had left Eithne and could not find her and they approached Aengus sadly and told him timidly of the loss of the maiden. Aengus at once transformed Curcog, and his steed was brought him, and Curcog went with him on the search. Aenghus went forward to Ros Dighair and he searched every fort in Eire for the maiden and he found her not, and he came to the banks of the Boyne and searched for her. While they were there they saw the oratory and the dwelling and came just opposite on the far side of the river. Eithne looked forth on the riders and recognized Aengus and Curcog and their companions. The cleric brought her food, also for himself, on the side near the maiden's fishing-weir and, though he looked, he did not see them because the 'Feth Fiar' was over them. The cleric asked the maiden: 'What see'st thou, oh maiden?' said he. 'I see Aengus my guardian searching for me, and my comrade, Curcog, and the household of the Brugh, and her ladies. It will be a vain search for them' said the maiden. '. . . indeed if it be the will of God' said the cleric.

> Dear to me is yon host of riders
> whom I see along the blue-banked Boyne,
> a royal haughty company.
> There was no strife or calamity.
> The joy of the company
> Aengus Og, son of the Dagda,
> is a horseman, is a sailor.
> The pleasant household of the fair Brugh
> are warlike, wound-dealing, valiant.
> The sad and sorrowful lad
> shall be Aengus' name to night.
> The women of the fair-shielded Brugh
> find no rest from searching,
> and my comrade Curcog
> ceases not from lamenting me.
> It was the duty of all to guard her.
> From the day I was taunted
> by Finnbarr, by my guardian's brother,
> I will not wait for Manannan

for noble Ilbrec or Sigmall.
I bless that Finnbarr
through whom came my love of God,
the speech of the long haired one
which put me to shame that day.
I will not wait for Abhartach who withstood Bodhb of arma-
    ments
His religion is a shield which shall be praised

. . . .

The escort on this journey
is for none of the Tuatha De Danann.
My body to Jesus and my soul.
Welcome is the arrival of the Tailgenn
who came to Eire of the yew-wood.
Without this suffering
death with him would yet be sweet.

12. After that poem the cleric prayed to the Lord for Patrick to come
to comfort and succour him for fear the maiden should be taken from
them against her will. The Lord granted to the cleric to get his righteous prayer so that at the same moment Patrick came with his clerics
to the door of the oratory and Aengus to the other side of the river.
Then Patrick asked the cleric for the maiden's story and an argument
began between him and Aengus concerning her so that Aengus asked:
'Will you let my ward come to me, oh cleric?' 'The maid is not thy
ward' said Patrick 'but the ward of the God of creation though she
was lent by her father to thee.' 'I impute capability . . . to the maid-
en' said Aengus 'if she thinks it to her advantage to come to . . . and
I lacking the power of the Lord.' 'I am afraid' said Patrick. 'If you
took my advice Aengus' said he 'I fear not your interference in any
righteous affair.' 'What is it?' said Aengus. 'Worship the true Almighty
God and shun vain gods and arise in the name of the Trinity and change
thy name and depart from torments.' 'That is not the cause for which
we came from our home' said Aengus. He then spurred his horse from
the river and retired sadly and sorrowfully, and his ward perceived his
reluctance. He recited the poem:

Let us return in sorrow. Oh Eithne of the bright shapely head,
the fair white ungrateful swan [whom I shall] cherish no more.
[Since] they took away her comrade it is useless guarding
    Curcog.

. . . of the treachery since parting I will put away most of
  them.
There is an edge of three loud cries lamenting as a wounded
  man
the departure from the mansion on the right of the brown
  river-side pasture.
Eithne is no more my child from this out . . .
oh host of the Land of Promise, but though grievous for us let
  us do it.
The coming of the Tailgenn to this land is my misfortune (I do
  not conceal it)
departing from her I leave. But though hard and harsh let us
  do it.

After that Aengus and his household uttered a terrible wailing cry
lamenting Eithne. When Eithne heard Aengus' people weeping her
heart leapt in her bosom and from that start came grief from one breast
into the other. She asked Patrick for baptism and remission of sins and
received it from him and was named after him. But one thing: for a
whole fortnight the maiden grew steadily worse and was praying to
God and to Patrick who with his clerics was much grieved. When
Eithne felt her death was near she commended her soul to God and
to Patrick and recited the poem:

Call me, ye people of heaven, call my soul by your prayers.
I will not forsake God's heaven for the mansion of my
  guardian Aengus.
Pleasant is the house where are the people of the Holy Lord.
His grace shall be sung and his changeless felicity.

Though the women of the Brugh weep and wail greatly
I prefer the cry of clerics at my head defending my soul from
  hell.
I thank Christ of the children for my parting from the Tuatha
  De Danann.
Though I am of their race I am not one of them. I believe in
  Jesus, the great king.

The story of the Fosterage of the House of Two Goblets is not
  an unknown story.
All the nobles of grassy Fodla will ask for it.

> Oh Patrick son of noble Calpurnius, defend my soul from
>   anguish,
> Absolve me of my sins and faults if you hear my appeal.

After that poem Patrick took the maiden's head on his breast and sent
her spirit to heaven and they gave her honourable burial. So that Ceall
Eithne (= Eithne's Church) at Brugh of the Boyne is called after her.
The name of the cleric to whom the maiden came was Ceasan, a
Scotch prince and chaplain to Patrick. He could not bear the hermitage
because Eithne had died there and left it and went to Fid Gaible and
there led a holy life so that the church named after him is there, Cluain
Cesain at Ros Mic Treoin in Fid Gaible. It was a pleasant camp of the
Fianna before that. That is 'the Fosterage of the House of Two
Goblets' so far.

And Patrick commanded that no one should sleep or talk during
this story and that it should not be told save at the prayer of good
people who were worthiest to hear it and he ordained many other
distinctions concerning it as is told in this elegy:

> Dig ye the grave of generous Eithne
> in the church above the dewy-green Boyne:
> a fair scion of bright knowledge.
> The host of Aengus were distressed.
> I and Aengus, expert in arms,
> a pair whose hidden mystery had not its like,
> there was never in the wide world
> one we loved like Eithne.
> I will attach these blessings
> to the story of Eithne of Finn-magh:
> the best of children, the best of companions,
> shalt thou see when sleeping with fair women.
> If thou repeatest the 'Nourishing'
> going on a ship or vessel
> thou shalt go safe and sound.
> . . . wave or billow.
> If thou repeatest the 'Nourishing'
>
> .   .   .   .
>
> If thou repeatest the story of Eithne
> when taking a stately wife
> good is the step thou takest
> thou shalt have the best of wives and children.

Repeat the story of noble Eithne
when going into a new ale-house;
there will be no squabbling or foolishness
no drawing of curved valiant weapons.
Repeat to a wealthy king
the story of Eithne during destruction
he will not lose his throne
if he listens in silence.
If you repeat this wondrous story
to the prisoners of Ireland.
. . . they will be freed of their fetters and prisons.
Blessed be the soul was in Eithne's fair body.
Who ever knows this elegy
shall carry off the victory.
Beloved was the smooth golden hair
and the fair rosy countenance
the fair foam-like body
and the sweet-spoken mouth.
Beloved was the noble attractive body
and the fair face,
the lovely modest mouth and white thighs.

Let her festival be written in our songs
and seen and ordered in our world.
Let her body be buried in this church.

The following commentary uses the numeration of the text.

1. The overthrow of the Tuatha de Danann and their representatives by the Milesians may be seen from this family tree (female names in italics).

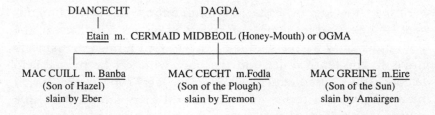

Fig. 9. Family tree showing the overthrow of the Tuatha de Danann

2. The Dananns consult Manannan, who is a more ancient being than they, already an established inhabitant of the otherworld of Faery. He assigns each of them to a different faery house and institutes three practices which will sustain them: the *feth fiadha* ('deer's appearance' or *ceo-druidechta*, 'druid's fog'), which confers invisibility; the feast of Goibniu, conferring immortality and health; and Manannan's swine, conferring everlasting supplies of pork for feasting.

The *feth fiadha* we encountered in Chapter 6, as a method of gaining invisibility or conferring the ability to shapeshift. At Goibniu's feast a special ale is dispensed, conferring immortality and health. Manannan's swine are encountered by Cormac mac Airt when he enters the otherworld; in this tale we learn that its four quarters can only be cooked if four truths are told over it. Usually there is also a stricture that no bone shall be broken. In any case, the pig is alive again the next day and ready to be slaughtered and cooked anew. This theme of everlasting or renewing feasts is one that permeates Celtic story, and returns in the medieval Grail legends. Manannan initiates them into the ways of the inhabitants of Tir Tairngire (the Land of Promise) and of Emain Abhlach (the Island of Apples, identified as Arran in Scotland).

3. Manannan begins a round of visitations, visiting each *sidhe* hill in turn. In this version, Elcmar owns Brugh na Boinne and Aengus is his foster-son. As in the story above, there is a great deal of rivalry and jealousy surrounding the Brugh.

4. Elcmar and Aengus provide overwhelming hospitality, together with diplomatic table-placement. At the end of four days of carousal, only Aengus and Manannan are conscious, and it is Manannan who urges Aengus to tell Elcmar to leave his house and not to return to it until 'ogham and pillar, heaven and earth or sun and moon come together', in the hope that they might regain the luck that they had before the Milesians came.

In their theological discussion, Manannan relates why humans were created. God fashioned ten orders of angels. The chief of the tenth order grew jealous and left heaven. God formed mankind to make up the tenth order and the ones who left he turned into demons. This Christian interpolation in the faery conversation is very interesting since it recurs throughout oral faery lore in the Celtic countries, and does validate the general belief that the faeries are a separate race, as Manannan says here – that they are not of that origin.

5. The expulsion of Elcmar and his family from the Brugh is given another rationale in this story. Elcmar's steward, Dichu, returned from finding provisions, is kept on at the Brugh. His retention in the Brugh is significantly paralleled by the medieval Gaelic story of the expulsion of the faery from heaven and hell; Eithne thus becomes a child of human parentage but of faery foster-parentage.

6. Elcmar fades from the narrative here. Aengus now takes over his role as foster-father, taking Manannan's daughter, Curcog and the steward's daughter, Eithne, into his fostership. The transcriber would have us believe that these girls lived a semi-monastic life within the *sidhe* 'in severity and chastity', but the simple beauty and harmony of faery existence within Aengus' *grianan* has its own integrity. When Finnbarr comes courting one of the foster-sisters, his faery blood instinctively realizes something different about Eithne: despite her beauty, she is of the race who made 'the dirty mess' – his view of Christianity. His offensive behaviour causes her a very real soul-loss which manifests in her inability to eat.

7. Eithne's inability to eat faery food emphasizes her dislocation from faery society, from which she feels more and more alienated. Her ability to imbibe only the milk of the dun cow is paralleled in the Life of St Brigit, who is raised in a druid's household and becomes unable to eat his food, which she vomits up, until the druid gives a red-eared cow to a Christian woman to milk. The otherworldly abundant cow is a cosmic motif which Ireland shares with India; interestingly, the text validates this shared symbolism.

8. The great love and care of the Faery for Eithne is apparent here. Aengus allows the girls to visit Manannan whose wisdom is greater than his. It is a great slight on Celtic hospitality for Eithne to be fasting while others eat. Manannan divines that Eithne is not of their race and that when Finnbarr insulted her, her guardian spirit (*deman comuidachta*) and was replaced by an angelic spirit. This concept of guardian spirit seems related to Rev. Robert Kirk's understanding of the 'co-walker' or *coimimeadh* (literally, the one who accompanies). Eithne does not believe in sorcery (*idhera*) nor druidism (*draoideacht*). She can only be nourished by the milk of the two pails because India is a righteous land. Manannan construes that she is governed by the Trinity.

9. Eithne lives for several hundred years on the milk of the two cows alone, until the coming of Tailginn (Taillcenn, 'Adzehead', the name given to St Patrick).

10. Eithne finds herself outside the *feth fiadh*, and can no longer return to Faery.

11. With the ability of one raised in Aengus' house, she takes Cesarn's testament and is able to read it. He catches a salmon from the Boyne for her and she takes her first meal for many centuries. Eithne's ability to see Aengus and Curcog within the *feth fiadh* is interesting, although she chooses to remain in the service of God.

12. The contention for Eithne between Patrick and Aengus is both a legal and a spiritual one. Aengus has the legal right, since she is his foster-daughter and under his protection. Patrick contends that this fostership is supplanted by a higher spiritual fosterage, for Eithne has chosen the Father of Creation in his stead. Aengus politely refuses Patrick's offer of baptism and departs, grieving his loss and the arrival of Taillcenn. After receiving baptism and confession at Patrick's hands, being renamed Patricia, Eithne falls into her inevitable decline as mortality strikes home.

Patrick's command that during this story no one was to sleep or talk, and that it should be told only in the company of worthy folk, is consistent with a long tradition that each story carries with it its own blessing. This one has the ability to protect travellers from harm, to confer happy family life, to promote harmony to new enterprises, to confirm secure reigns for kings and to convey freedom to prisoners.

The Yew Tree of the Disputing Sons
translated by Caitlín Matthews

This story tells of the cause of the Battle of Mag Mucrama which was fought between Eogan mac Ailill Olom and Lugaid mac Con. It reveals the close interrelation between the middleworld and the world of the *sidhe*, the faery-folk, and the necessity for care in our dealings with them.

Initially, it is Ailill who causes an imbalance between the worlds by his action of pasturing horses in the domain of the *sidhe*. In return they trample his pasture, so Ailill and his companions go to investigate and catch the culprits. They kill the faery Eogabul, also raping and killing Aine, the faery woman. Fer Fí's revenge for the killing of his father and sister is very subtle. He fashions a yew tree of such unparalled growth and beauty that Ailill's son, Eogan, and his foster-sons, (Lugaid) Mac Con and Cian, all claim it for themselves. In another version of this tale, the reason why the three claimants are drawn to the yew is that Fer Fí, the faery harper, makes music therein. The dispute turns about the possession of the musician. In this version, Ailill awards the tree to his own son, and one battle leads to another. In the terrible slaughter that follows, the *sidhe* are fully avenged.

It may be thought strange for princely warriors to fight over a tree, but the ancient trees of Ireland were focal points of tribal meeting and were thought to possess memory and have the power of witness. Trees were central emblems of tribal continuity. The yew tree of this tale is fashioned by the skills of the *sidhe* and can only be discovered by those whom the faery wish to punish. This text is ascribed to Cormac mac Culennáin, the king-bishop of Cashel (d. 908) and is found in the twelfth-century compilation, the *Leabhar Laignech*.

1. Let one of you ask me the history of the wonderful yew: why is it alone called the Yew of the Disputing Sons?
2. Of what wood is the poisonous, handsome tree – subject of such treachery? What nature of friendship originally existed before the disputing sons gave their name to it?
3. From his territory Ailill chose this meadow for the pasture of his horses: from Dún Cláre to Dún Gair, from Ane to Dún Ochair.
4. The slender *sidhe*-folk disliked this invasion of their land; they used to destroy the grass every Samhain – no story to equal this!
5. Ailill went with Ferchess mac Commán to view the fine grass; they saw on the plain three cows and three people herding them.
6. 'These are the thieves!' said Ailill, haughtily. 'A woman and two men, without doubt, and their three hornless cows.'
7. 'It is they who have trampled the grass and consumed our property to rob us, singing the sweet music of the *sidhe* to put the race of Adam to sleep.'
8. 'If they are singing the music of the *sidhe*,' said Ferchess mac Commán, 'let us go no nearer until we melt some wax for our ears!'
9. They could not hear the sweet music after they had thrust wax into their ears. Suddenly, each party saw the other: a surprising encounter!
10. Furiously, Eogabul (of the *sidhe*) and Ailill grappled point to point; Eogabul was stricken down, and Aine (of the *sidhe*) was overthrown.

11. Ailill came to Aine, overpowered her and lay upon her; he had knowledge of her then, not by consent but by force.

12. Aine took her knife to Ailill, no lying testimony mine! She sliced off his right ear from the head bent over her, so that afterwards he was called Ailill Bare-ear.

13. This enraged Ailill then; he thrust his spear into Aine; he did her no honour, he left her dead.

14. As for Ferchess, no one ever escaped him when he had unsheathed his weapon without receiving wounds and bruises, even though it were a friendly demonstration of his battle-skills.

15. Fer Fí retired to the *sidhe*-mound where his kinfolk lived; many were the lamentations on account of Aine and Eogabul's deaths.

16. The next day, at dawn, the mounted hosts of the *sidhe* came out; they burned Dún Cláre and Dún Crott, they caused a scouring blaze.

17. 'Let us go to Dún Ochair Mág,' they said among them themselves. 'Let us kill Ailill in his house and the daughter of Conn of the Hundred Battles.'

18. 'We have no claim upon fair Conn's daughter,' said Fer Fí, son of Eogabul. 'Not without danger, but by valour will I avenge my father.'

19. Fer Fí travelled westwards with Aebléan, his brother; they devised a strategy that was honourable to them, they shaped the Yew of the Disputing Sons.

20. The place that they created the tree was at Ess Máge of the great clans; three came to the tree who desired it for their own: Mac Con, Cían and Eogan.

21. Mac Con claimed the tree forthrightly, both the old wood and the green growth; Cían here claimed it from the seed, both the straight and crooked growth.

22. No less comprehensively was it claimed by Eogan, who claimed all that grew above ground and all that grew beneath.

23. Such were the disputes of the men, the sons of one mother; each stalwart fellow claimed the whole tree for himself.

24. 'I shall accept your father's judgement,' said Mac Con of the Red Sword. 'Wherever he awards it to you or to me, I shall not appeal if I lose.'

25. Then Ailill gave harsh judgement; Mac Con was greatly annoyed thereby. Ailill awarded the yew to Eogan, and slighted Mac Con.

26. Mac Con then challenged Ailill to a battle to avenge it; so it was, without delay, that the Battle of Cenn Febrat was fought.

27. Mac Con was wounded there and limped thereafter, a sad affair;

Da Dera, the fool of the Dárine, fell at the hand of Cairpre.

28. This conflict caused the furious battle of Mag Mucrama of the red grasses; on Tuesday it was fought, where the heads of Ireland fell.

29. So fell Art mac Conn, high king of Ireland the unconquered; there fell dreadfully the seven fine sons of Ailill.

30. There was wounded Lug Lága, who performed the daring feat: he slew Art mac Conn the Fair, and Bénne Britt of the Britons.

31. There fell the vengeful Mac Con and Ferchess mac Commán, and Sadb, daughter of Conn, from the venom of the beautiful yew.

32. It is no tree but an apparition of the *sidhe*, its nature is not of this world; not of wood is its trunk, but of an horrific gloom.

33. The tree gave shelter from the cutting winds, enough for three hundred warriors; its seasoned wood would have been sufficient for a house, it was a protection against all dangers.

34. It is mysteriously hidden by the *sidhe* with artful skill. Only one in a hundred is unlucky enough to find it; then it is everlasting discovery of misfortune.

35. From north and south fell warriors, from the venom of the russet-boughed yew; from east and west they fell – do not seek further to ask me why.

The Sacred Celtic Heritage

We hope that your reading of this wide-ranging source-book has given you a greater understanding of the Celtic interrelationship with the otherworlds. We have tried to cover as much ground as possible, although inevitably some texts have had to be omitted.

As we write, negotiations are under way between British and Irish governments to obtain a lasting peace in Northern Ireland. During these last months, we have once more been reminded how the radical cultural differences between Britain and Ireland are maintained by an ignorance of Celtic history in general, which is not taught in British schools. The high Celtic ages, from just before the inception of Christianity until the Middle Ages, warrant but a few sentences in most school history books. A general ignorance of the steady colonization of Celtic nations over the centuries is widespread.

International organizations, such as the United Nations and Survival International, alert us to the dangers facing indigenous peoples who are threatened by overwhelming Westernization. It is necessary to view Celtic colonization in these terms, not in order to promote blinkered nationalism or condone terrorist activity, but in order to value the loss of sacred heritage which is truly a loss to the whole world.

The sacred heritage of Native American and Tibetan cultures, still threatened by invasive colonization, have found new spiritual seedbeds around the world, while less familiar peoples and their heritage are daily becoming extinct worldwide through an inability to adapt.

It is time to view the Celtic spiritual tradition as an *international* sacred heritage not bounded by territory or genetics.

The Celtic peoples have already had to face the test of whether a spiritual tradition can exist outside its original social framework. Our sacred heritage is now fragmented but it is by no means wholly lost. A great number of indigenous peoples worldwide have become fully integrated into Western society yet have rediscovered the spiritual path of their ancestors and have returned to simpler ways of life. Many such people have become teachers, bridge-builders between disparate traditions, able to interpret one culture to the other and so defuse conflict. We need such interpreters in the Celtic tradition, people who honour our sacred heritage and yet who can interface with the predominant culture without loss of respect. The task of the *filidh*, the *awenydd* or the *drui* descends to such interpreters as these.

The rediscovery of our sacred Celtic heritage is not an easy one. It entails patience, perseverence and an endlessly receptive spirit with which to quest; it requires real practice, for without modern application no tradition can endure; it necessitates our listening to the ancestors and spirits where no elders survive to teach us. We have discovered that the spiritual kinship of this path is of paramount importance, for where seeker meets seeker, there the tribe reassembles and the teachings flow once more. The Celtic diaspora is vast, yet still the clans gather and the inspirational fires are rekindled to warm the children waiting to be born.

May the guardians of our sacred Celtic heritage guide us well!

Notes

Chapter 2

1. Originally published in *Hermathena*, vol. 3, n.d.
2. Originally published in *Auraicept na N-Éces* (*The Scholar's Primer*), ed. & trans. by George Calder, Edinburgh, John Grant, 1917.
3. See p. 251 for a diagram of how these fivefold sets of correspondence may have been remembered.
4. Originally published in *The Metrical Dindsenchas*, ed. & trans. by Edward Gwynn, Dubin, Hodges, Figgis & Co., 1903.

Chapter 3

1. Originally published in *Folk-Lore*, 1932.
2. Literally 'Rough was its strength'.
3. Literally 'nature'.
4. 'The Settling of the Manor of Tara' see below pp. 98–114.
5. i.e. along all its shores.
6. i.e. the strand at Dundalk, Cuchulain's home.
7. i.e. The Táin bó Cualnge or Cattle-raid of Cualnge.
8. i.e. the Commor Cinn con, or Pillar-stone of the Meeting (of rivers) of Cuchulain's Head.
9. Inis Géidh, i.e. Iniskea in the barony of Erris, County Mayo.
10. Or 'the blackbird of Druim Brice'. There are several places called Drumbrick, one in Leitrim and one in Donegal.
11. Originally published in *The Mabinogion,* Medieval Welsh *Romances*; trans. Lady Charlotte Guest. London, David Nutt, 1910.

Chapter 4

1. Originally published in 'The Voyage of Bran mac Febel to the Land of Promise', ed. and trans. by Kuno Meyer.
2. Originally published in *Eriu*, vol. 4, 1910.
3. J.L. Brunnaux, *The Celtic Gauls*.
4. E.R. Henken, *Traditions of the Welsh Saints*.
5. W.G. Wood-Martin, *Traces of the Elder Faiths of Ireland*.
6. St Adamnan, *The Life of St Columba*.

Chapter 5

1. Originally published in *Eriu*, vol. 1, 1904 translated by Kuno Meyer.
2. Originally published in *Duanaire Fionn* (The Book of the Lays of Fionn), ed. & trans. by Eoin Macneill. David Nutt, London, 1908.
3. Originally published in 'Two Tales About Find', ed. & trans. by Vernam Hull, in *Speculum*, vol. 16, 1941.
4. Originally published in *Revue Celtique*, vol. xxv, 1904.

Chapter 6

1. J. and C. Matthews, *A Fairy Tale Reader*.
2. C.J. Guyonvarc'h, *Textes Mythologiques Irlandais*.
3. C. Matthews, *Mabon and the Mysteries of Britain*.
4. J. Layard, *The Lady of the Hare*.
5. F.J. Child, *The English and Scottish Popular Ballads*.
6. E. Hull, *The Cuchullin Saga in Irish Literature*.
7. C. Matthews, *Arthur and the Sovereignty of Britain*.
8. C. and J. Matthews, *The Ladies of the Lake*.
9. D.A. Mackenzie, *Scottish Folk-Lore and Folk Life*.
10. Ibid.
11. K. Meyer, *Fianaigecht*.
12. A. Carmichael, *Carmina Gadelica*.
13. Lady Gregory, *A Book of Saints and Wonders*.
14. J. Matthews, *Taliesin*.
15. J. Gantz, *Mabinogion*.
16. P. Harbison, *Pre-Christian Ireland*.
17. T.P. Cross and C.H. Slover, *Ancient Irish Tales*.
18. R. Hayward, *Border Foray*.
19. L. and J. Laing, *The Picts and the Scots*.
20. Originally published in *Cuchulain of Muirthemne* by Lady Gregory, John Murray, London, 1902.

21. Originally published in *Ancient Irish Tales* by T.P. Cross and C.H. Slover, Figgis, Dublin 1936 and in *The Adventures of Suibhne Geilt* ed, and trans. by J.G. O'Keefe, D. Nutt, London, 1913
22. A territory south of Dál Riada, bordering on Loch Neagh. It included parts of south County Antrim and of County Down.
23. The text records only two occasions below. This first attempt fails, but it is included in the reckoning.

Chapter 7

1. F. Le Roux and C-J. Guyonvarc'h, *Les Druides*.
2. C. Matthews, *Sophia: Goddess of Wisdom*, 1991.
3. K. Müller-Lisowski, 'La Légende de St Jean dans la Tradition Irlandaise et le Druide Mog Roith'.
4. R.J. Stewart, *The Waters of the Gap*.
5. Geoffrey of Monmouth, *Life of Merlin*.
6. A. and B. Rees, *Celtic Heritage*.
7. G. Keating, *Forus Feasa ar Eirini*.
8. C. Matthews, *Sophia, Goddess of Wisdom*.
9. J. Matthews, *Household of the Grail*.
10. T.P. Cross and C.H. Slover, *Ancient Irish Tales*.
11. N. Ozaniec, *The Elements of the Chakcras*.
12. L. Spence, *Magic Arts in Celtic Britain*.
13. C. and J. Matthews, *Ladies of the Lake*.

Chapter 8

1. M. Martin, *Description of the Western Islands of Scotland*.
2. H.E. Davidson (ed.), *The Seer in Celtic and Other Traditions*.
3. R.J. Stewart, *Robert Kirk*.
4. Davidson, *The Seer in Celtic and Other Traditions*.
5. G. Keating, *Forus Feasa ar Eirini*.
6. A. Carmichael, *Carmina Gadelica*, author's translation.
7. Ibid.
8. Ibid, author's translation.
9. The definitions of *teinm laegda, dichetal do chennaib* and *imbas forosna* given in this section differ somewhat from John Matthews' findings as described in *Taliesin*. We are, however, inclined to believe the former to be the most accurate.
10. Translation by Myles Dillon, from *The Cycles of the Kings*, London, Oxford University Press, 1946.
11. H.E. Davidson, *Myths and Symbols in Pagan Europe*.
12. Translation by Myles Dillon, from *The Cycles of the Kings*.
13. T.P. Cross and C.H. Slover, *Ancient Irish Tales*.

14. Originally published in St Adamnan's *Life of St Columba,* trans. Wentworth Huyshe, London, George Routledge & Sons, n.d.
15. Originally published in: *Irische Texte* (3rd series) ed. by W.H. Stokes and E. Windisch, Leipzig, Verlag von Hirzel, 1891.
16. A bardic name for Ireland.
17. A fairy-mound in Munster, near the river Suir.

Chapter 9

1. E. Hull, *The Cuchullin Saga in Irish Literature.*
2. P.W. Joyce, *A Social History of Ancient Ireland,* 1903.
3. G. Henderson, *Survival in Belief Among the Celts.*
4. T.P. Cross and C.H. Slover, *Ancient Irish Tales.*
5. E. Hull, The Cuchullin Saga in Irish Literature.
6. W. Stokes, 1868.
7. Lady C. Guest (ed.), *The Mabinogion.*
8. E. Hull, *The Cuchullin Saga in Irish Literature.*
9. D. MacManus, *Irish Earth Folk.*
10. W.G. Wood-Martin, *Traces of the Elder Faiths of Ireland.*
11. Ibid.
12. J. and C. Bord, *Sacred Waters.*
13. T.P. Cross and C.H. Slover, *Ancient Irish Tales.*
14. W.G. Wood-Martin, *Traces of the Elder Faiths of Ireland.*
15. W. MacKenzie, *'Gaelic Invocations'.*
16. D. O'Hogain, *Myth, Legend and Romance.*
17. D. MacManus, *Irish Earth Folk.*
18. N.K. Chadwick, *The Druids.*
19. J. Curtin, 1894.
20. C. Matthews, *Arthur & the Sovereignty of Britain.*
21. H.E. Davidson, 1988.
22. M. Martin, *Description of the Western Isles of Scotland.*
23. G. Henderson, *Survival in Belief Among the Celts.*
24. A. Carmichael, *Carmina Gadelica.*
25. D. MacManus, *Irish Earth Folk.*
26. E. Hull, *The Cuchullin Saga in Irish Legend.*
27. G. Henderson, *Survival in Belief Among the Celts.*
28. W. MacKenzie, *'Gaelic Invocations',* author's translation.
29. A. Carmichael, *Carmina Gadelica.*
30. F. Delaney, *The Celts.*
31. P.W. Joyce, *A Social History of Ancient Ireland,* 1903.
32. T.P. Cross and C.H. Slover, *Ancient Irish Tales.*
33. A. and B. Rees, *Celtic Heritage.*
34. C. Matthews, *The Celtic Book of the Dead.*

35. G.S. Olmstead, *The Gundesstrup Cauldron.*
36. J. Simpson, *The Folklore of the Welsh Border.*
37. Ibid.
38. A.G. Murray (ed.), *The Romance and Prophecies of Thomas of Ercledoune.*
39. J. and C. Matthews, *A Fairy Tale Reader.*
40. R.J. Stewart, *Robert Kirk.*
41. H.E. Davidson (ed.), *The Seer in Celtic and Other Traditions.*
42. J. Curtin, *Irish Folk Tales,* 1944.
43. J. Curtin, *Myths and Folk Tales of Ireland.*
44. J.F. Campbell, *Tales of the West Highlands.*
45. G. Henderson, *Survival in Belief Among the Celts.*
46. T.P. Cross and C.H. Slover, *Ancient Irish Tales.*
47. M.J. Plotkin, 'Blood of the Moon, Semen of the Sun'.
48. P.W. Joyce, *Old Celtic Romances.*
49. P.W. Joyce, *A Social History of Ancient Ireland,* 1903.
50. D. MacManus, *Irish Earth Folk.*
51. F.J. Child, *The English and Scottish Popular Ballads.*
52. A. Carmichael, *Carmina Gadelica.*
53. F.J. Child, *The English and Scottish Popular Ballads.*
54. Ibid.
55. R.J. Stewart, *Earth Light.*
56. See C. Matthews, *The Celtic Book of the Dead.*
57. G. Keating, *Forus Feasa ar Eirini.*
58. G. Henderson, *Survival in Belief Among the Celts.*
59. J.L. Bruneux, *The Celtic Gauls.*
60. Ibid.
61. W. MacKenzie, *'Gaelic Invocations'.*
62. T.P. Cross and C.H. Slover, *Ancient Irish Tales.*
63. J. Gantz (ed. and trans.), *The Mabinogion.*
64. T.P. Cross and C.H. Slover, *Ancient Irish Tales.*
65. E. Hull, *The Cuchullin Saga in Irish Literature.*
66. F. Le Roux and C.J. Guyonvarc'h, *Les Druides.*
67. R.J. Stewart, *The Mystic Life of Merlin,* 1988.

Chapter 10

1. E. Ettlinger, 'Omens and Celtic Warfare'.
2. J. Fraser, 'The First Battle of Moytura'.
3. R.I. Best, 'Prognostications from the Raven and the Wren'.
4. F. Ettlinger, 'Omens and Celtic Warfare'.
5. Ibid.
6. C. Plummer, *Vitae Sanctorum Hiberniae.*

7. G. Keating, *Forus Feasa ar Eirini.*
8. J. Gantz (ed. and trans.), *The Mabinogion.*
9. S. Krippner, 'Dreams and Shamanism'.
10. M. Martin, *Description of the Western Isles of Scotland.*
11. E. Ettlinger, 'Omens and Celtic Warfare'.
12. C.A. Meier, 'Ancient Incubation and Modern Psychotherapy'.
13. Ibid.
14. C. Kerenyi, *Asklepios.*
15. N.K. Chadwick, 'Dreams in Early European Literature'.
16. Pausanias, *Guide to Greece.*
17. P.K. Ford, 'The Well of Nechtan and "La Gloire Luminesse" '
18. W. Stokes, 'The Siege of Howth'.
19. R.E.M. Wheeler, *Report on the Excavations of the Prehistoric, Roman and Post-Roman Site in Lydney Park, Gloucestershire.*
20. J. Rhys, *Celtic Folk-Lore.*
21. W. Bathurst, Roman Antiquities at Lydney Park, Gloucestershire.
22. Originally published in *Revue Celtique,* vol. X.

Chapter 11

1. A. and B. Rees, *Celtic Heritage.*
2. J. Matthews, *The Grail: Quest for the Eternal.*
3. Originally published in *Ancient Irish Tales,* translated by T.P. Cross and C. Slover, Figgis, Dublin, 1936.
4. The original of King Arthur's famous sword Excalibur.
5. The famous Fergus mac Roig of the Ulster cycle.
6. Originally published in *Ancient Irish Tales,* translated by T.P. Cross and C.H. Slover, Figgis, Dublin, 1936.

Chapter 12

1. Originally published in *Eriu,* vol 12, 1938 edited by O. Bergin and R.I. Best.
2. 'Power' here means, perhaps, as often, 'magic power'.
3. Nine only are named.
4. Ten only are named.
5. Originally published in *Ancient Irish Tales,* Edited and translated by T.P. Cross and C.H. Slover, Figgis, Dublin, 1936.
6. Originally published in *Zeitschrift für Celtische Philologie* vol. 18 (1929–30), edited and translated by Maighréad ni C. Dobs.

Bibliography

Source Texts

The following books include sources in translation as well as Gaelic diplomatic transcriptions from which we have made our translations.

Adamnan, St. *Life of St Columba*, edited by W. Huyshe, London, George Routledge & Sons, n.d.

Best, R.L. 'The Settling of the Manor of Tara', in *Eriu* vol. 4, 1910

Breatnach, Liam. 'The Cauldron of Poesy', in *Eriu* vol. 32, 1981

Calder, G. *Auraicept na N'Eces*, Edinburgh, John Grant, 1917

Cross, T.P. and C.H. Slover. *Ancient Irish Tales*, Dublin, Figgis, 1936

Dillon, Myles. *The Cycles of the Kings*, London, Geoffrey Cumberledge & Oxford University Press, 1946

Dillon, Myles (ed). 'The Yew of the Disputing Sons', in *Eriu* vol. 14, 1946

Guest, Lady C. (ed.). *The Mabinogion* London, J.M. Dent, 1906

Gwynn, Edward. *Metrical Dindsenchas* (5 vols), Dublin, Hodges, Figgis & Co., 1903–25

Henry, P.L. 'The Caldron of Poesy', in *Studia Celtica* vols 14–15, n.d.

Hull, Eleanor. *The Cuchullin Saga in Irish Legend*, David Nutt, 1898

Hull, Eleanor. 'The Hawk of Achill or the Legend of the Oldest Animals', in *Folklore* no. 43, 1932

Hyde, Douglas. *Legends of Saints and Sinners*, T. Fisher Unwin, n.d.

Keating, Geoffrey. *Foras Feasa ar Eirinn* vol. 2, London, Irish Texts Society, 1908

Lisowski, K.M. 'Texte Zur Mog Roith Sage', in *Zeitschrift für Celtische Philologie* vol. 14, 1922–3

Martin, M. *Description of the Western Islands of Scotland*, 1716

Meyer, K. 'Immacallam Colium Chille', in *Zeitschrift für Celtische Philologie*, vol. 2, 1909–10

Meyer, Kuno. *The Voyage of Bran, Son of Febal*, London, David Nutt, 1895

Müller-Lisowski, Kate. 'La Legende de St Jean dans la Tradition Irlandaise et le Druide Mog Roith', in *Études Celtiques* vol. 3, 1938

O'Curry, E. *Manners and Customs of the Ancient Irish* (3 vols) London, Williams & Norgate, 1873

Sjoestedt, M.L. 'Forbuis Droma Damhghaire' in *Révue Celtique* vol. 18, 1897, n.d.

Stewart MacAlister, R.A. (ed.). *Lebor Gabala Erenn* vol. 5, Dublin, Irish Texts Society, 1956

Stokes, Whitley. *Cormac's Glossary*, Calcutta, Irish Archaeological and Celtic Society, 1868

Stokes, Whitley and E. Windisch. *Irische Texte: The Irish Ordeals and the Fitness of Names*, Leipzig, Verlag von S. Hirzel, 1891

Stokes, Whitley. *The Rennes Dindsenchas, Révue Celtique*, vol. 15, 1894.

Supporting Bibliography

The following books have been used in the compilation of this volume.

Bathurst, W. *Roman Antiquities at Lydney Park, Gloucestershire*, London, Spottiswoode & Co, 1897

Best, R.I. 'Prognostications from the Raven and the Wren', in *Eriu* vol. 8, 1916.

Bord, Janet and Colin. *Sacred Waters*, London, Granada, 1985

Boyd, Douglas. *Rolling Thunder*, New York, Delta, 1974

Brennan, M. *The Boyne Valley Vision*, Portlaoise, The Dolmen Press, 1980

Brunaux, Jean Louis. *The Celtic Gauls*, London, Seaby, 1988

Campbell, J.F. *Popular Tales of the West Highlands* (4 vols), London, Wildwood House, 1984

Carmichael, A. *Carmina Gadelica* (5 vols) Edinburgh, Scottish Academic Press, 1928–72. English text, Edinburgh, Floris Books, 1992

Chadwick, Nora K. *The Druids*, Cardiff, University of Wales Press, 1966

Chadwick, N.K. 'Dreams in Early European Literature' in *Celtic Studies*, edited by J. Carney and D. Greene, London, Routledge & Kegan Paul, 1968

Child, F.J. *The English and Scottish Popular Ballads* (5 vols), New York, Dover Publications, 1965

Corkery, Daniel. *The Hidden Ireland*, Dublin, Gill & Macmillan, 1967

Curtin, Jeremiah. *Hero Tales of Ireland*, London, Macmillan, 1894

Curtin, J. *Irish Folk-Tales*, Dublin, The Talbot Press, 1944

Curtin, Jeremiah. *Myths and Folk Tales of Ireland*, New York, Dover Books, 1975

Davidson, H.E. *Myths and Symbols in Pagan Europe*, Manchester, Manchester University Press, 1988

Davidson, H.E. (ed.). *The Seer in Celtic and Other Traditions*, Edinburgh, John Donald, 1989

Delaney, Frank. *The Celts*, BBC Publications, 1986

Dumézil, Georges. *The Destiny of the Warrior*, Chicago, University of Chicago Press, 1970

Ellis, P.B. *A Dictionary of Irish Mythology*, London, Constable, 1987

Ettlinger, Ellen. 'Omens and Celtic Warfare' in *Man*, vol. 43, no. 4, 1943

Ettlinger, Ellen. 'Precognitive Dreams in Celtic Legend' in *Folklore* vol. 59, 1948

Evans-Wentz, W.Y. *The Fairy Faith in Celtic Countries*, New York, Lemma Publishing Co., 1973

Folklore, Myths and Legends of Britain, London, Reader's Digest, 1973

Ford, Patrick K. 'The Well of Nechtan and "La Gloire Luminesse"', in *Myth in Indo-European Antiquity* edited by G.J. Larson, Berkeley, University of California Press, 1974

Fraser, J. 'The First Battle of Moytura', in *Eriu* vol. 8, 1915

Gantz, J. (ed. & trans.) *Mabinogion*, Harmondsworth, Penguin Books, 1965

Gerald of Wales. *Journey Through Wales*, London, Penguin, 1978

Graves, R. *The White Goddess*, London, Faber & Faber, 1952

Green, Miranda. *Animals in Celtic Life and Myth*, London, Routledge, 1992

Green, Miranda. *Dictionary of Celtic Myth and Lore*, London, Thames & Hudson, 1992

Gregory, Lady. *A Book of Saints and Wonders*, Gerrards Cross, Colin Smythe, 1973

Guyonvarc'h, Christian-J. *Textes Mythologiques Irlandais*, vol. 1, Rennes, Ogam-Celticum, 1980

Harbison, Peter. *Pre-Christian Ireland*, London, Thames & Hudson, 1988

Hayward, Richard. *Border Foray*, London, Arthur Barker Ltd, 1957

Henderson, George. *Survival in Belief Among the Celts*, Glasgow, James Maclehose & Sons, 1911

Henken, Elissa R. *Traditions of the Welsh Saints*, Cambridge, D.S. Brewer, 1987

Hersh, J. 'Ancient Celtic Incubation' in *Sundance Community Dream Journal*, 3, Winter 1979

Hull, Eleanor *The Cuchullin Saga in Irish Literature*, London, David Nutt, 1898

Hutton, Ronald. *The Pagan Religions of the Ancient British Isles*, Oxford, Blackwell, 1993

Joyce, P.W. *Old Celtic Romances*, London, C. Kegan Paul & Co., 1879

Joyce, P.W. *A Social History of Ancient Ireland*, London, Longmans, Green & Co., 1903

Kerenyi, C. *Asklepios*, translated by R. Manheim, New York, Pantheon Books, 1959

Krippner, S. 'Dreams and Shamanism' in *Shamanism*, compiled by S. Nicholson, London, The Theosophical Publishing House, 1987

Laing, Lloyd and Jenny. *The Picts and the Scots*, Stroud, Alan Sutton, 1993

Layard, John. *The Lady of the Hare*, London, Faber & Faber, 1954

Leach Maria (ed.). *Dictionary of Folklore, Mythology and Legend*, London, New English Library, 1972

Le Roux, Françoise & Guyonvarc'h, Christian-J. *Les Druides*, Rennes, Ouest France, 1986

Liechti, Elaine. *Shiatsu*, Shaftesbury, Element Books, 1992

McBain, Alexander. 'Gaelic Invocations' in *Transactions of the Gaelic Society of Inverness* vol. 17, 1890–1

MacKenzie, William. 'Gaelic Invocations' in *Transactions of the Gaelic Society of Inverness* vol. 18, 1891–2

MacManus, Diarmiud. *Irish Earth Folk*, New York, Devin–Adair Co., 1959

MacQueen, John. *St Nynia*, Edinburgh, Polygon, 1990

Matthews, Caitlín. *Mabon and the Mysteries of Britain: An Exploration of the Mabinogion*, London, Arkana, 1987

Matthews, Caitlín. *Arthur and the Sovereignty of Britain: King and Goddess in the Mabinogion*, London, Arkana, 1989

Matthews, Caitlín. *The Elements of Celtic Tradition*, Shaftesbury, Element Books, 1989

Matthews, Caitlín. *The Celtic Book of the Dead*, New York, St Martins Press, 1991

Matthews, Caitlín. *Sophia, Goddess of Wisdom*, London, Aquarian, 1991

Matthews, Caitlín and John. *Ladies of the Lake*, London, Aquarian, 1992

Matthews, John. *Gawain, Knight of the Goddess*, London, Aquarian, 1990

Matthews, John. (ed.). *Household of the Grail*, London, Aquarian, 1990

Matthews, John. *Taliesin: Shamanism and the Bardic Mysteries in Britain and Ireland*, London, Aquarian, 1991

Matthews, John. *The Celtic Shaman*, Shaftesbury, Element Books, 1992

Matthews, John and Caitlín. *A Fairy Tale Reader*, London, Aquarian, 1993

Matthews, John and Chesca Potter, *The Celtic Shaman's Pack*, Shaftesbury, Element Books, 1994

Meier, C.A. 'Ancient Incubation and Modern Psychotherapy' in *Betwixt and Between*, edited by L.C. Mahdi, S. Foster and M. Little, Le Salle, Open Court, 1987

Meyer, Kuno. *Ancient Irish Poetry*, London, Constable, 1913

Murray, A.G. (ed.). *The Romance and Prophecies of Thomas of Ercledoune*, Felinfach, Llanerch Publishing, 1991

O Hogain, Dr Daithi. *Myth, Legend and Romance: An Encyclopedia of the Irish Folk Tradition*, London, Ryan Publishing, 1990

O'Rahilly, T.F. *Early Irish History and Mythology*, Dublin, Dublin Institute for Advanced Studies, 1976

Olmstead, Garret S. *The Gundesstrup Cauldron*, Brussels, Collection Latomus, vol. 162, 1979

Ozaniec, Naomi. *The Elements of the Chakras*, Element Books, 1990.

Pausanias. *Guide to Greece,* vol. 1, translated by P. Levi, Harmondsworth, Penguin Books, 1971.

Plotkin, Mark J. 'Blood of the Moon. Semen of the Sun', in *Shaman's Drum* no. 32, Summer 1993.

Plummer, C. *Vitae Sanctorum Hiberniae* vol. 1, Oxford, 1910

Rawson, Philip. *Sacred Tibet*, London, Thames & Hudson, 1991

Rees, Alwyn and Brinley. *Celtic Heritage*, London, Thames & Hudson, 1961

Rhys, John. *Celtic Folk-Lore, Welsh and Manx*, London, Wildwood House, 1980

Shaw-Smith, David. *Ireland's Traditional Crafts*, London, Thames & Hudson, 1986

Simpson, Jacqueline. *The Folklore of the Welsh Border*, London, Batsford, 1976

Smyth, Daragh. *Places of Mythology in Ireland*, Killala, Morrigan Book Co., 1989

Spence, Lewis. *Magic Arts in Celtic Britain*, London, Aquarian, 1970

Stewart, Bob. *The Waters of the Gap*, Bath, Bath City Council, 1981

Stewart, R.J. *Earth Light*, Element Books, 1992.

Stewart, R.J. *The Prophetic Vision of Merlin*, London, Arkana, 1986

Stewart, R.J. *The Mystic Life of Merlin*, London, Arkana, 1988

Stewart, R.J. *The Power Within the Land*, Shaftesbury, Element Books, 1991

Stewart, R.J. *Robert Kirk: Walker Between Worlds*, Shaftesbury, Element Books, 1990

Stokes, W. 'The Siege of Howth', in *Révue Celtique* 8, 1887

Sutherland, Elizabeth. *Ravens and Black Rain*, London, Constable, 1985

Wheeler, R.E.M. *Report on the Excavations of the Prehistoric Roman and Post-Roman Site in Lydney Park, Gloucestershire*, Oxford, Society of Antiquaries, 1932

Wood-Martin, W.G. *Traces of the Elder Faiths of Ireland*, London, Longmans, Green & Co, 1902

Further Reading

The following is a list of works which provide a background spanning the whole of the Celtic tradition. We include it here in the hope that it will provide those students who wish to delve deeper with sufficient material to get them started.

Aneirin. *Y Gododdin: Britain's Oldest Heroic Poem*, ed. and trans. by A.O.H. Jarman, Dyfed, The Welsh Classics, 1988

Bartrum, P.C. *Early Welsh Genealogical Tracts*, Cardiff, University of Wales Press, 1966

Bergin, O. *Irish Bardic Poetry*, Dublin, Dublin Institute for Advanced Studies, 1970

Bloomfield, M.W. and C.W. Dunn. *The Role of the Poet in Early Societies*, Cambridge, D.S. Brewer, 1989

Bonwick, J. *Irish Druids and Irish Religions*, Marlboro, Dorset Press, 1986

Bromwich, R. *Trioedd Ynys Prydein (The Welsh Triads)*, 2nd ed., Cardiff, University of Wales Press, 1978

Burland, C.A. *Echoes of Magic*, New Jersey, Rowman & Littlefield, 1972

Caldecott, M. *Taliesin and Avagddu,* Frome, Bran's Head, 1983

Caldecott, M. *Women in Celtic Myth,* London, Arrow Books, 1988

Caesar. *De Bello Gallico,* trans.by S.A. Handford, Harmondsworth, Penguin Books, 1951

Campbell, J.F. and G. Henderson. *The Celtic Dragon Myth,* North Hollywood, Newcastle Publishing Co., 1981

Carney, J. *Medieval Irish Lyrics* with *The Irish Bardic Poet,* Portlaoise, The Dolmen Press, 1985

Chadwick, H.M. *The Heroic Age,* Cambridge, Cambridge University Press, 1967

Chadwick, H.M. and N.K. *The Growth of Literature* (3 vols), Cambridge, Cambridge University Press, 1932–40

Geoffrey of Monmouth, *Life of Merlin,* ed. and trans. by B. Clarke, Cardiff, University of Wales Press, 1973

Evans, J.G. *Poems from the Book of Taliesin,* Tremvan, Llanbedrog, 1915

Flower, R. *The Irish Tradition,* Oxford, Clarendon Press, 1953

Ford, P.K. (ed. & trans.). *The Mabinogion and Other Medieval Welsh Tales,* Berkeley, University of California Press, 1977

Gantz, J. *Early Irish Myths and Sagas,* Harmondsworth, Penguin Books, 1981

Gose, E.B. Jr. *The World of the Irish Wonder Tale,* Toronto, University of Toronto Press, 1985

Green, M. *The Gods of the Celts,* Gloucester, Alan Sutton, 1986

Green, M. *Symbol and Image in Celtic Religious Art,* London, Routledge, 1989

Greene, D. and F. O'Connor (eds. & trans.). *A Golden Treasure of Irish Poetry,* London, Macmillan, 1967

Harrison, A. *The Irish Trickster,* Sheffield, Sheffield Academic Press, 1989

Hatt, J-J. *Celts and Gallo-Romans,* London, Barrie & Jenkins, 1970

Henry, P.L. *The Early English and Celtic Lyric,* London, George Allen & Unwin, 1966

Hull, E. *The Poem-Book of the Gael,* London, Chatto & Windus, 1912

Hull, E. *Folklore of the British Isles,* London, Methuen, 1928

Humphreys, E. *The Taliesin Tradition,* London, Black Raven Press, 1983

Jackson, A. *The Symbol Stones of Scotland,* Stromness, The Orkney Press, 1984

Jones, G. and T. Jones (trans.) *The Mabinogion,* London, J.M. Dent, 1974

Jones, O., Edward Williams and William Owen Pughe (eds). *The Myvyrian Archaiology of Wales,* Denbigh, Thomas Gere, 1870

Jones, Prudence and Matthews, Caitlín (eds). *Voices from the Circle,* Wellingborough, Aquarian Press, 1989

Jones, T.G. *Welsh Folk-Lore and Folk-Custom*, London, Methuen, 1930

Jubainville, H.D. *The Irish Mythological Cycle*, Dublin, O'Donoghue & Co., 1903

Kendrick, T.D. *The Druids*, London, Frank Cass, 1966

Kinsella, T. (trans.) *The Tain*, Oxford, Oxford University Press, 1970

Knott, E. and G. Murphy. *Early Irish Literature*, London, Routledge & Kegan Paul, 1966

Lloyd, J.E. *A History of Wales* (2 vols), London, Longmans, Green & Co., 1911

Lofmark, C. *Bards and Heroes*, Llanerch, Llanerch Enterprises, 1989

Loomis, R.S. *Wales and the Arthurian Legend*, Cardiff, University of Wales Press, 1956

Mackenzie, D.A. *Scottish Folk-Lore and Folk Life*, London, Blackie & Son, 1935

McNeill, F.M. *The Silver Bough* vol. 1, Edinburgh, Canongate, 1989

Mallory, J.P. *In Search of the Indo-Europeans*, London, Thames & Hudson, 1989

Mann, N.R. *The Celtic Power Symbols*, Glastonbury, Triskele, 1987

Matthews, C. and J. *The Western Way* (2 vols), London, Arkana, 1987–8 (Reprinted in 1 vol., 1994)

Matthews, C. and J. *The Aquarian Guide to British and Irish Mythology*, Wellingborough, Aquarian Press, 1988

Matthews, J. *Fionn MacCumhail*, Poole, Firebird Books, 1988

Matthews, J. *A Celtic Reader*, Wellingborough, Aquarian Press, 1991

Matthews, J. *The Song of Taliesin*, London, Unwin Hyman, 1991

Matthews, J. *King Arthur and the Grail Quest*, London, Cassell, 1994

Matthews, J. and C. *The Little Book of Celtic Wisdom*, Shaftesbury, Element Books, 1993

Megaw, R. and V. *Celtic Art*, London, Thames & Hudson, 1989

Merry, E. *The Flaming Door*, Edinburgh, Floris Books, 1983

Meyer, K. *Fianaigecht*, Dublin, Hodges & Figgis, 1910

Miles, D. *The Royal National Eisteddfod of Wales*, Swansea, Christopher Davies, 1977

Morgan, P. *Iolo Morganwg*, Cardiff, University of Wales Press, 1975

Morganwg, Iolo. *The Triads of Britain*, London, Wildwood House, 1977

Morris, J. *The Age of Arthur*, Weidenfeld & Nicholson, 1973

Morris, J. *the Matter of Wales*, Oxford, Oxford University Press, 1984

Morris, W.B. *The Prehistoric Rock-Art of Argyll*, Poole, The Dolphin Press, 1977

Murphy, G. *Early Irish Lyrics*, Oxford, Oxford University Press, 1956

Murray, L. & C. *The Celtic Tree Oracle*, London, Rider, 1988

Naddair, K. *Keltic Folk & Faerie Tales*, London, Century, 1987

Naddair, K. *Ogham, Koelbren and Runic* (2 vols), Edinburgh, Keltia Publications, 1986–7

Nennius. *British History and the Welsh Annals*, ed. and trans. by J. Morris, Chichester, Phillimore, 1980

Nichols, R. *The Book of Druidry*, Wellingborough, Aquarian Press, 1990

O'Boyle, S. *Ogam, the Poet's Secret*, Dublin, Gilbert Dalton, 1980

O'Driscoll, R. (Ed.). *The Celtic Consciousness*, Edinburgh, Canongate Publishing Portloise, The Dolmen Press, 1982

O'Grady, S. (ed. & trans.). *Silva Gadelica* (2 vols), London, Williams & Norgate, 1892.

O Hogain, D. *The Hero in Irish Folk History*, Dublin, Gill & Macmillan, 1985

O Hogain, D. *Fionn mac Cumhail: Images of the Gaelic Hero*, Dublin, Gill and Macmillan, 1988

Parry, T. *A History of Welsh Literature*, Oxford, The Clarendon Press, 1955

Parry-Jones, D. *Welsh Legends and Fairy Lore*, London, Batsford, 1953

Pennar, M (trans.). *The Black Book of Carmarthen*, Llanerch, Llanerch Enterprises, 1989

Pennar, M (trans.). *Taliesin Poems*, Llanerch, Llanerch Enterprises, 1989

Piggott, S. *Ancient Britons and the Antiquarian Imagination*, London, Thames & Hudson, 1989

Rhys, J. *Lectures on the Origin and Growth of Religion as Illustrated by Celtic Heathendom*, London, Williams & Norgate, 1888

Roberts, B.F. (ed.) *Early Welsh Poetry: Studies in the Book of Aneurin*, Aberystwyth, National Library of Wales, 1988

Ross, A *Pagan Celtic Britain*, London, Cardinal, 1974

Ross, A. and D. Robins. *The Life and Death of a Druid Prince*, London, Rider, 1989

Rowland, J. *Early Welsh Saga Poetry*, Cambridge, D.S. Brewer, 1990

Schofield, W.H. *Mythic Bards*, Cambridge, Harvard University Press, 1920

Sjoestedt, M.L. *Gods and Heroes of the Celts*, Berkeley, Turtle Island Foundation, 1982

Skene, W.F. (ed. & trans.). *The Four Ancient Books of Wales* (2 vols), New York, AMS Press, 1984–5

Stephens, M. (ed.) *The Oxford Companion to the Literature of Wales*, Oxford, Oxford University Press, 1986

Stewart, R.J. *The Underworld Initiation*, Wellingborough, Aquarian Press, 1985

Stewart, R.J. and Matthews, J. (eds). *Merlin Through the Ages,* Cassell, 1994

Tacitus. *Germania*, translated by H. Mattingly, Harmondsworth, Penguin Books, 1948

Tatlock, J.S.P. *The Legendary History of Britain*, New York, Gordian Press, 1979

Tolstoy, N. *The Quest for Merlin*, London, Hamish Hamilton, 1985

Trevelyan, M. *Folk-Lore and Folk-Stories of Wales*, London, Eliot Stock, 1909

Van Hamel, A.G. *Aspects of Celtic Mythology*, London, British Academy, 1935

Watson, W.J. *The History of the Celtic Place Names of Scotland*, Dublin, Irish Academic Press, 1986

Williams, G. *An Introduction to Welsh Poetry*, London, Faber & Faber, 1953

Williams, I. *Lectures on Early Welsh Poetry*, Dublin, Institute for Advanced Studies, 1970

Williams, I. *The Beginnings of Welsh Poetry*, ed. by R. Bromwich, Cardiff, University of Wales Press, 1980

Williamson, R. *The Craneskin Bag: Celtic Stories and Poems,* Edinburgh, Canongate, 1979

Fiction

This is a brief selection of Celtic fiction, for those who like to mingle pleasure with scholarship and practice.

Bradley, M.Z. *Mists of Avalon,* London, Michael Joseph, 1988

Chapman, V. *The Three Damosels*, London, Methuen, 1978

De Lint, C. *Moonheart*, London, Pan, 1990

Dunnett, Dorothy, *King Hereafter*, London, Michael Joseph, 1982

Gedge, P. *The Eagle and the Raven,* London, Penguin, 1986

Gordon, S. *Suibne and the Crow God*, London, New English Library, 1972

Hayton, Sian. *Cells of Knowledge*, Edinburgh, Polygon, 1991

Hayton, Sian. *Hidden Daughters*, Edinburgh, Polygon, 1992

Hayton, Sian. *The Last Flight*, Edinburgh, Polygon, 1993

Herbert, K. *Bride of the Spear*, London, Bodley Head, 1987

Herbert, K. *Ghost in the Sunlight*, London, Bodley Head, 1986

Herbert, K. *Queen of the Lightnings*, London, Bodley Head, 1988

James, J. *Not For All the Gold In Ireland*, London, Bantam, 1988

James, J. *Men Went to Catraeth*, London, Bantam, 1988

Jones, D. *The Sleeping Lord*, London, Faber, 1974

Kay, G.G. *The Finnovar Tapestry* (3 vols), London, Unwin Hyman, 1987–9

Kennealy, P. *The Copper Crown*, London, Grafton, 1984

Kennealy, P. *Throne of Scone*, London, Signet, 1986

Kenneally, P. *The Silver Branch*, London, Signet, 1990

Kennealy, P. *The Hawk's Grey Feather*, London, Roc, 1990

Lawhead, S. *Taliesin*, London, Lion Books, 1987

Lawhead, S. *Merlin*, London, Lion Books, 1988

Lawhead, S. *Arthur*, London, Lion Books, 1989

Llewellyn, M. *Bard*, London, Century, 1984

Llewellyn, M. *On Raven's Wing*, London, Heinemann, 1990

O'Neill, D. *Crucible*, London, Macdonald, 1986

O'Neill, D. *Of Gods and Men*, London, Macdonald, 1987

O'Neill, D. *Sons of Death*, London, Macdonald, 1988

Paxson, D. *The White Raven*, London, New English Library, 1989

Paxson, D. *The Serpent's Tooth*, New York, William Morrow, 1992

Paxson, D. and A. Martine-Barnes. *Master of Earth and Water*, New York, William Morrow, 1993

Powys, J.C. *Porius*, London, Village Books, 1978

Sutcliffe, R. *Sword at Sunset*, London, Hodder, 1968

Sutcliffe, R. *Sun Horse, Moon Horse*, London, Bodley Head, 1985

Sutcliffe, R. *The Shining Company*, London, Bodley Head, 1990

Taylor, K. *Bard* (4 vols), London Ace, 1981–7

Tolstoy, N. *The Coming of the King*, London, Bantam, 1988

Tremayne, P. *Raven of Destiny*, London, Methuen, 1984

Whyte, J. *A Dream of Eagles* (2 vols.), Toronto, Penguin Books, 1993–4

Resources

Hallowquest Newsletter

For details of forthcoming books, courses and events with Caitlín and John Matthews, send for their quarterly newsletter: current subscription £3.50 (UK), £7/$15(US) or 16 IRCs (worldwide). Sterling cheques only, payable to Graal Publications, BCM HALLOWQUEST, London WC1N 3XX.

Order of Bards, Ovates & Druids (OBOD)

Rooted in the teachings of the Celtic world, the OBOD aims to help individuals to develop their whole potential, integrating this with close co-operation with the natural world. A full, three-grade correspondence course is available, with groves worldwide. Send SAE or 2 IRCs to PO Box 1333, Lewes, East Sussex for current details.

R.J. Stewart

For information about courses and publications by R.J. Stewart in UnderWorld, Celtic, Faery and visionary traditions send a large SAE or 2 IRCs to Sulis Music, BCM 3721, London WC1N 3XX.

Walkers Between the Worlds

Caitlín and John Matthews teach courses which explore the practice and background of Celtic shamanism, giving practical tuition and applications of the material which appears in this book. For more details, send large SAE or 2 IRCs to BCM HALLOWQUEST, London WC1N 3XX.

Index